More En

Rick —
keep cookin' !
— Gary Henry

Also by Gary Henry

Enthusiastic Ideas
Diligently Seeking God
Reaching Forward

More Enthusiastic Ideas

*Another Good Word for Each Day
of the Year*

Gary Henry

WordPoints
Frankfort, Kentucky
WordPoints.com

WordPoints Daybook Series - Volume 2
More Enthusiastic Ideas
Another Good Word for Each Day of the Year

First Edition. Copyright © 2016 by Gary Henry
All rights reserved. Printed in the United States of America

ISBN 978-0-9713710-3-3 – Print Edition

WordPoints
238 West Main Street, Suite 200
Frankfort, KY 40601

502-682-2603

Web: *wordpoints.com*
E-mail: *garyhenry@wordpoints.com*

For

Curtis & Terri Byers

whose lifelong support has been extraordinary

CONTENTS

PREFACE

HERE IS A FRESH, NEW BOOK OF DAILY READINGS FOCUSED ON WORDS THAT ARE GOOD FOR US TO THINK ABOUT. In a previous book, *Enthusiastic Ideas*, I tried to show how words can give us hope and courage, one day at a time. In this book, *More Enthusiastic Ideas*, I am offering a new year's worth of similar readings.

Like its predecessor, this book is what the older writers used to call a "daybook." It consists of a single reading for each day of the year. The idea is to use each day's reading as the starting point for a brief, but profitable, meditation. The readings are short enough that they can be read by busy people (as most of us are these days), but don't let their brevity fool you. The readings are highly concentrated, and I hope you'll find them "provocative" and "suggestive" in the highest sense. If this book sends you off down a lot of good trails in your own thinking, then I'll be pleased. That's what a daybook is intended to do.

These two books would be placed in the "positive thinking" section of the library, I suppose. I don't mind that, although I fear that being put in that category means the books will not be taken seriously by some people. Unfortunately, books about "positive mental attitude" have a reputation for being fluffy: nothing more than cotton candy for the mind. Whatever the reasons for that reputation might be, I don't believe the situation has to be the way it is. A writer should be allowed to address the issue of positive thinking at a deeper level.

If we happen to be living our lives in a less than wonderful way, the last thing we need is for someone to make the situation more palatable by pouring "positive mental attitude" syrup over the facts. The positive thinking we need won't come from dreaming or ignoring reality; it will come from the (sometimes painful) alignment of ourselves with principles of proven validity in human character and conduct. So as a speaker and writer, I get in people's faces and challenge them to change in significant ways. There's nothing fluffy about it, believe me.

If you look over the Index for these two books, you'll see a number of words that are related to one another, sometimes very closely. For instance, *remembering, remembrances, memories,* and *mementos* each get a page of their own. This is no accident. Nuances can be very important, and it's helpful to think about shades of meaning. As Mark Twain said, "The difference between the right word and the almost right word is the difference between lightning and the lightning bug."

Together, these books include 732 different words to think about. That's a lot, but there are still others that could have been included. Perhaps I left out a word you would like to hear discussed. If so, write and tell me. There aren't any plans for a third volume of these readings, but you might convince me to take out one of my words and include yours in a future revision of the existing books.

As I explained in the Preface to *Enthusiastic Ideas,* this project began as a short list of "gifts" that one person might give another. I called them "gift words" back in the beginning. Eventually, however, the list widened out and came to include many good words of a more general nature, which I decided simply to call "positive words."

Even if you don't usually think in terms of "giving yourself to others," *Enthusiastic Ideas* and *More Enthusiastic Ideas* are books that will challenge you to improve your "self" anyway. These good words would be worth contemplating even if you lived in a hermit's cabin way out in the woods somewhere. Being all that we can be is the right thing to do — even if no one else knows or cares or thanks you for it.

But now that the project has come full circle, I'd like you to come back with me to the idea of "gift words." We do need to see character improvement as a process that builds a better connection to others. It's not only important to be people of strength and honor, but also to give ourselves to others as people who have that kind of character.

As you think about the words in these books, see them as qualities in which you can grow. Those who deal with you each day would be delighted to discover that you've grown in qualities like hope, courage, and joy. I believe that if you'll think of your personal character growth as a gift you can give to those around you, you'll be more highly motivated to grow. So what kind of new "you" would you like to give to your friends and family? I have a few suggestions . . .

GPH

More Enthusiastic Ideas

Words can sometimes, in moments of grace,
attain the quality of deeds.

— *Elie Wiesel*

FOUNDATIONS

Be sure of the foundation of your life. Know why you live as you do.
Be ready to give a reason for it. Do not, in such a matter as life,
build an opinion or custom on what you guess is true.

THOMAS STARR KING

I F WE'RE SERIOUS ABOUT IMPROVING OUR LIVES AND MAKING
PROGRESS, WE NEED TO PAY PRIMARY ATTENTION TO THE
FOUNDATIONS UPON WHICH WE LIVE. Whatever we try to build in
the year ahead, it can be no better than the quality of our most basic
principles. And if we tolerate flaws in our foundations, we doom ourselves to an inevitable collapse, in the long run if not in the short.

Solid foundations require hard work. Foundational work often
seems unexciting, and so we're tempted to spend as little time on it as
possible. The result is a life built on principles haphazardly cobbled
together from whatever materials lay at hand. Too often, the concepts
that guide our conduct are little more than those we've picked up
from entertainers and advertisers. But lasting foundations require a bit
more effort. It takes real work to think things through carefully.

The dangers of a weak foundation may not be outwardly obvious.
Even the most serious defects in a person's principles may not show
up until the structure of that person's life is seriously tested. Indeed, it
may not be until the very end that it becomes apparent that a human
being's life has been founded on a faulty basis. So it's important to
look beyond the present circumstances of our lifestyle. Our house of
cards may not have collapsed yet, but that doesn't mean it won't.

*Trends and fads can't be counted on to tell us what our principles
should be.* What is "in" today will be "out" this time next year. When
we're laying the foundations of our lives, it is much better to consult
the time-tested wisdom of many generations. This wisdom may be
counterintuitive. What our great-great-grandparents learned through
long experience may be scorned by today's common sense, and the
best strength in the world may be mocked as weakness by the popular
culture. Yet as J. R. R. Tolkien reminded us, "All that is gold does not
glitter, and all who wander are not lost." It is often true with principles as well as with people: the first shall be last, and the last first.

Do you wish to rise? Begin by descending.
You plan a tower that shall pierce the clouds?
Lay first the foundation of humility.

AUGUSTINE OF HIPPO

January 2
REBIRTH

Where, unwilling, dies the rose,
Buds the new, another year.

DOROTHY PARKER

THERE ARE NONE WHO LIVE IN THIS WORLD WHO DO NOT
FEEL FROM TIME TO TIME THAT THEIR ENTHUSIASM HAS
DIED. Life is demanding. It is exhausting. Even if we face no more
than the ordinary challenges of "homesteading" — providing food,
clothing, and shelter — we can get to the point where we feel every
drop of vitality has been drained from us, and we let go of our hopes.

A new year can bring new life to us. There is something very
special about the first few days of a brand-new year, and we ought to
seize this opportunity to get a fresh grip on everything we deal with.
The sun is coming up earlier each morning. Spring, while still some
distance away, is at least imaginable. New life is calling our names.

A new love can also bring new life to us. By "new love," we don't
necessarily mean someone or something we've never loved before,
although new loves of that sort are powerful givers of new life. A
"new love" may mean persons or things we have loved before, but
we've newly discovered how to love them in a better, or deeper, way.
Whichever kind of new love is ours, we need to be careful not to let
it go to waste. Love, especially when new, is the most potent force we
will ever know. It should be appreciated. We should feel its fire and
welcome the new world it opens up to us. Sometimes a new love can
be so strongly invigorating that we feel as did Christina Georgina
Rossetti: "The birthday of my life / Is come, my love is come to me."

Have your dreams been dead for a while now? How long has it
been since hope was yours? Does your phoenix need to rise from its
ashes? If so, don't discount the possibility that it can happen, and don't
dismiss the likelihood that it can happen right now, on the threshold
of a new year. As the snows of more than a few winters accumulate
on the head of this writer, I feel in many important ways that I'm
only just beginning to live. I am thankful to be alive — to have been
reborn — and I'm going to give it all I've got. Will you join me?

And now in age I bud again,
After so many deaths I live and write;
I once more smell the dew and rain . . .

GEORGE HERBERT

REFUGE

It was a dark and stormy night.

EDWARD BULWER-LYTTON

TWO DIFFERENT TIMES COME AROUND SOONER OR LATER: (1) TIMES WHEN WE NEED A REFUGE, AND (2) TIMES WHEN SOMEONE ELSE NEEDS A REFUGE THAT WE CAN PROVIDE. "Dark and stormy nights" are a fact of life, and when we find ourselves in the middle of one, our hearts need a safe place in which to shelter. It's important to appreciate the shelter that others have given us in the past, and even more important to make our hearts a place where they'll find a welcome when they're the ones who are scared of the storm.

Having a heart that provides refuge for others takes some learning. Not many of us have such a heart naturally. Caring perhaps comes naturally, but showing compassion in ways that actually do some good is a skill that has to be learned. It's not rocket science, maybe, but it does take a little education in the school of caregiving. We have to watch and listen. We have to apply good judgment. We have to learn from well-intentioned mistakes that we've made. In short, we have to grow in the quality of the mercy that we extend.

Men, especially, have to learn how to be a refuge to others. Since the simple gift of "nurturance" is not normally our strong suit, we have to exert extra effort to learn it. The strong masculine tendency to "fix" whatever's wrong has to be reined in. To have hearts in which others find refuge, we must learn to see when a safe harbor is all that's needed — and not a dry-dock facility for ship repair.

Who are those that need from you the gift of refuge? The answer would probably surprise you. If you knew the hurts that those around you carry with them every day, you would be astonished. You may never know these hurts. Your friends may never choose to confide in you about them. But you would do well to assume that most of the people you deal with are hurting. Be ready. Be prepared for the time when they might consider seeking some safety in their relationship with you. If that time ever comes, you will have bestowed on you one of life's greatest privileges: the privilege of showing compassion.

Discouraged people don't need critics. They hurt enough already. They don't need more guilt or piled-on distress. They need encouragement. They need a refuge. A willing, caring, available someone.

CHARLES R. SWINDOLL

TOUCH

To touch a child's face, a dog's smooth coat, a petaled flower,
the rough surface of a rock . . . To touch is to communicate.

JAMES W. ANGELL

W E GAIN MUCH — AND WE ALSO GIVE MUCH — WHEN WE
TAKE THE TIME TO TOUCH. Whether it's the people we deal
with or the physical objects that surround us, we need to experience
life more directly and more deeply through the sense of touch.

It's true, there are limits to physically touching other human beings, especially in our litigious culture. We must never touch when our
motives are anything less than pure, and even then, we must govern
ourselves with good judgment and a real respect for others' privacy.
There are some individuals whom we have no business touching.

That said, however, most of us still need to recover the value of
physical touch in our lives. In our age of electronic work, not much
gets manufactured or manipulated anymore except information. We
go through our days without touching much of anything except a
computer keyboard — and we lose touch with many good things that
were meant to be experienced through a direct, physical connection.

How long has it been since you dug in the dirt with your hands?
How long has it been since you stroked an animal and really thought
about what your senses were telling you? How long has it been since
you paid significant attention to a handshake or a hug?

It needs to be kept in mind that no number of indirect connections with people "out there" can take the place of direct connections
with those right around us. When it comes to influence, our main
opportunity is to influence those who're physically close enough that
we may actually touch them. We must not forget this. Rabindranath
Tagore said it well in the form of a prayer: "When one knows thee,
then alien there is none, then no door is shut. O, grant me my prayer
that I may never lose the touch of the one in the play of the many."

Who are those whom you need to touch today? Who are those
whom, eventually, you will wish you had touched more often? The
sense of touch is a unique and powerful gift. Use it appreciatively.

And the stately ships go on
To their haven under the hill;
But O, for the touch of a vanish'd hand,
And the sound of a voice that is still!

ALFRED, LORD TENNYSON

WINGS

Oh! I have slipped the surly bonds of Earth
And danced the skies on laughter-silvered wings;
Sunward I've climbed, and joined the tumbling mirth
Of sun-split clouds, — and done a hundred things
You have not dreamed of — wheeled and soared and swung
High in the sunlit silence . . .

JOHN GILLESPIE MAGEE JR.

HUMAN FREEDOM IS AS MARVELOUS AS IT IS MYSTERIOUS. The ability to envision a more deeply enjoyed life (and then to make choices that lead toward that life) is an ability possessed by no other creatures on the planet except us. The birds may have wings of a sort, but only we have wings that can fly in the firmament of true joy.

Concerning wings, we need to help one another. The pulverizing forces of discouragement tend to destroy our dreams. At times, it takes great effort just to keep going, and the idea of living out our dreams seems silly. So we need to have those who will nudge us out of the nest, so to speak. Each of us needs to believe that our friends are capable of flying — and we need to help them go ahead and do it.

It's a great thing to see others find their wings and begin to fly. And if we've had any role in encouraging them to take flight, that makes the experience all the more gratifying. It is one of life's truest pleasures to witness someone else's discovery of their freedom.

But what about our own wings? All of us have people in our past who have helped us learn to fly. We need to love these people. They may never have gotten any reward for encouraging us except the simple joy of keeping hope alive. We can repay them richly now by living the kind of life they always knew we were capable of. We can determine that their encouragement of us will not have been in vain.

Today, take every chance you can get to go outside and look at the sky. Doesn't its expanse entice you and invite you upward? If you see birds on the wing, aren't you intrigued by their freedom and enriched by the thought of greater possibilities in your life? Let yourself believe in these possibilities, for they are truly yours. Like everybody else, your performance up to now has been less than perfect — but today is the first day of the rest of your life. So take courage. You may have some baggage, but you're not earthbound. Leave the nest and fly.

The sky is the daily bread of the eyes.
RALPH WALDO EMERSON

January 6
SMILES

By Chivalries as tiny,
A Blossom, or a Book,
The seeds of smiles are planted —
Which Blossom in the dark.

EMILY DICKINSON

TOO MANY OF US HAVE FROZEN FACES. We've been in the long, cold battle against life's difficulty for so long that our demeanor has grown hard. We need to unfreeze our faces and smile.

In one sense, a smile is such an easy gift to give, it's a wonder we don't give it to others more often. And yet, in a deeper sense, a smile is not such an easy thing to give. What about those times when we don't feel like smiling? Can we give the gift even when it's not easy?

An insincere smile, of course, is one of the most despicable things in the world. If we smile to make someone think that we mean them well, when in reality we wouldn't be above doing them harm, that's dishonest. A smile is worse than a frown if it misleads another person into thinking that we're more favorably disposed toward them than we really are. The unctuous smile of an enemy is nothing but a lie.

But choosing to smile in the face of difficulty is not insincere. In fact, it's a noble form of courage. Even on our darkest days, there are still many things in this world to be thankful for, and when we choose to take the larger perspective, that's a commendable thing to do.

There are few actions or gestures that communicate any more effectively than a smile. "A warm smile is the universal language of kindness" (William Arthur Ward). Great distances of custom and culture can be bridged by the simple giving of a smile, and we need to build this kind of bridge more often than we do.

But if it's a good thing to smile, it's also a good thing to remember the smiles of others. It is strengthening to conjure up the memory of those whose smiling faces have helped us and encouraged us and kept us moving in the right direction. We need to keep all these smiles in the scrapbook of our hearts. There may come a dark day in the future when it seems that hope is out of reach. On that day, it may be very important to get out the scrapbook and remember those who have been our encouragers. Their smiles will help us to hang on.

If we do meet again, why, we shall smile;
If not, why then, this parting was well made.

WILLIAM SHAKESPEARE

January 7
VOICE

One Christmas was so much like another, in those years around
the seatown corner now and out of all sound except the distant speaking
of the voices I sometimes hear a moment before sleep . . .

DYLAN THOMAS

LIKE THEIR SMILES, THE VOICES OF OTHERS IMPRINT THEM-
SELVES UPON OUR HEARTS. The memory of a distant voice can
connect us to the past in a way more powerful than almost anything
else. To hear someone's voice, either actually or in memory, is to go
through an open door. Voices are sensuous portals through which we
pass into the wide realm of hope, imagination, and shared values.

It is truly fascinating to think about the rich variety of voices
that there are in the world. There are booming bass voices and shiny
soprano ones. Some voices are gravelly while others are silky. One
person's voice tends to excite while that of another person tends to
soothe. Each of these has its place in the world. Each is needed. And
just as we need to pay more attention to the texture of things we
touch, we'd do well to be more interested in the voices we hear. Like
many other physical things, voices were meant to be relished. We miss
much of the interest of daily living when we hear other human beings
speak without savoring the unique timbre of their voices.

With what kind of voice do you speak to those you live and work
with? In truth, each of us is responsible for what is normally called
our "tone" of voice. If, for example, a kind tone of voice is needed
but we speak with a cruel tone, we are responsible. Or if we use an
impatient voice when a longsuffering voice would do more good, we
have no one to blame but ourselves. In every situation, we must accept
responsibility for the manner in which we use our voices.

It's also a fact, however, that even the physical characteristics of
our voices come, over time, to be a reverberation of our character. Just
as our faces eventually come to reflect what's going on inside us, so do
our voices. So there's a sense in which the way to have a more pleasing
voice is not to take voice lessons but to improve our character.

Our voices bear the stamp of our individuality, and crafting a
worthy voice is one of life's better endeavors. So, again, what kind of
voice do you have? And to what benefit are you letting it be heard?

The voice is a second face.
GÉRARD BAUËR

TRUSTFULNESS

*To love involves trusting the beloved beyond the evidence,
even against the evidence . . . the suspicious man is blamed for a
meanness of character, not admired for the excellence of his logic.*

C. S. LEWIS

STRENGTH OF CHARACTER ALWAYS INCLUDES TRUSTFULNESS.
It's not a sign of weakness but rather one of strength to have a
tendency in the direction of trust. Like all other virtues, trustfulness
needs to be balanced and complemented by other qualities of character, but it would be a step in the right direction for most of us even to
admit that trustfulness is a thing to be desired.

Especially with those we love, we need to be more trustful. As
C. S. Lewis wrote, "To love involves trusting the beloved beyond the
evidence, even against the evidence." Just as mercy ceases to be mercy
if it has to be "deserved," trust is not really trust if there's no possibility of betrayal. With our loved ones, if we hold ourselves in reserve
until they've "proven" their worthiness with a long history and lots of
collateral, we're not engaging in love but a business transaction. That's
the way the loan officer down at the local bank "trusts" people.

But isn't the trustful person vulnerable? If we have a tendency to
trust, won't we be taken advantage of? Yes and yes, without question.
But there are far worse things in life than being betrayed. The doubtful lose far more than they gain by doubting, and while it makes good
sense to take reasonable precautions against treachery (don't leave
your keys in the car, read the contract before you sign it, etc.), that
shouldn't be the thing we spend most of our time guarding against.
In fact, there's not anything another human being can do to us that
can hurt us as much as we can hurt ourselves. If we've got any spare
time to spend building defenses, we'd be better off fortifying ourselves
against the failures of our own character, not those of someone else.

Besides, the best way to bring out truth and trustworthiness in
others is to be persons of trust ourselves. Rather than doubting them
and defending against them, we'd accomplish more good if we ex-
tended to others the gift of a trustful character on our own part. Quite
often, people will rise to meet our expectations of them, and most
folks will keep faith with us if we first show some confidence in them.

Trust begets truth.
SIR WILLIAM GURNEY BENHAM

January 9
TURNINGS

It's a long lane that knows no turning.

ROBERT BROWNING

LIFE DOESN'T FOLLOW A STRAIGHT PATH BUT RATHER ONE WITH MANY TURNINGS. None of us gets to live a life of unbroken sameness; we have to accept changes now and then. Life in the real world is varied — and not only varied, but its variety is often unpredictable. As much as we might want things to stay the way they are, that wish is rarely fulfilled for any great length of time.

But life's turnings aren't bad; they're good. As Browning suggests, "It's a long lane that knows no turning." While there is a unique beauty to the plains, where a road can stretch like an arrow all the way to the horizon, I must confess that I like even more to travel through hill country, where the road bends and curves and takes surprising twists. And just as with roads, I also like a *life* that has plenty of turnings. I like to be surprised by what's around the next bend.

The attractiveness of turnings, even unpredictable ones, is one reason we're intrigued by the free life of the hobo, who hops a boxcar to the next town: "Steel rails chase the sunshine 'round the bend / winding through the trees like a ribbon in the wind. / I don't mind not knowin' what lies down the track / 'cause I'm lookin' out ahead to keep my mind from turnin' back" (*Steel Rails* by Louisa Branscomb).

Sometimes, however, the best turnings are those of our own making. The time comes when we need to recast our lives and take a new direction. We need to cinch up our packs and hit the winding trail, walking stick in hand. There is, to be sure, such a thing as recklessness, but there's also such a thing as cowardice, the craven desire for comfort. Comfort is nice — at the end of the day — but during the day there is a path to be followed, a road to be taken. And if the road's a new one, or one with many new turnings, that's not all bad.

The Road goes ever on and on
Down from the door where it began.
Now far ahead the Road has gone,
And I must follow, if I can,
Pursuing it with eager feet,
Until it joins some larger way
Where many paths and errands meet.
And whither then? I cannot say.

J. R. R. TOLKIEN

FRIENDSHIP

> How often we find ourselves turning our backs on our actual friends,
> that we may go and meet their ideal cousins.
>
> HENRY DAVID THOREAU

FRIENDSHIP IS A THING THAT HAS TO BE NURTURED. There are
few people who wouldn't say that friendship is one of life's most
valuable treasures, and yet we don't work on it and take care of it as
we would if we really appreciated its value. And because we don't nurture our friendships, we lose them. We fall into the pattern of losing
friends and gaining new ones, losing friends and gaining new ones,
losing friends and gaining new ones. Surely, friendship was meant to
be a more durable thing than our personal histories make it appear.

As Thoreau observed, we often fail to nurture the real friendships that we have because we spend so much time looking for "their
ideal cousins." In the real world, friends have flaws. Not only can our
friends exasperate us; sometimes they can hurt us deeply. And so we're
always on the lookout for "better" friends, ones that don't have the an-
noying idiosyncrasies of our present ones. Most of the time, however,
this is a poor use of our time. We'd do better to nurture our present
friendships, being grateful for the tangy individuality of each one.

Ideally, what should happen as our lives continue is that the
number of our friends should grow. Old friendships shouldn't have to
be replaced — they should simply be added to. "You date the evolving
of a mind, like the age of a tree, by the rings of friendship formed by
the expanding of the central trunk" (Mary McCarthy).

One of the exciting aspects of friendship is that friends do not
have to be clones of one another. As our minds mature and "rings of
friendship" begin to multiply around the trunk of our character, there
can be an intensely interesting variety in these relationships. As a
favorite teacher told me many years ago, "If two people always agree,
one of them is unnecessary." Indeed, our friendships are beneficial to
us, not because they stroke our sense of self-satisfaction, but because
they challenge us and invigorate our minds with other viewpoints.
Nurturing these friendships means appreciating them, respecting
them, affirming them — and making frequent investments in them.

> The most beautiful discovery true friends make
> is that they can grow separately without growing apart.
>
> ELISABETH FOLEY

January 11
VIBRANCY

Exuberance is beauty.
WILLIAM BLAKE

WOULDN'T MOST OF US LIKE IT TO BE SAID THAT WE HAVE A "VIBRANT" CHARACTER? The word suggests a person who is active rather than passive, someone who is engaged with life, a human being who is awake, alive, and in love with the whole kit and caboodle of good things in the world — and that's how we'd like to be.

But what's the meaning of "vibrancy"? We probably know it when we see it, but what is it? It isn't just a type of personality, although we often think of it that way. Properly understood, vibrancy is a quality of character. It's not the sizzle but the steak, and it can be possessed by people with more than one type of personality. Indeed, some of the most vibrant people I know have personalities that would be described as shy. They shun the limelight and they do more listening than talking, but they still can be said to lead vibrant lives.

Vibrancy has to do with *energy*. It's the intensity of the person who is genuinely, deeply, and inquisitively interested in life. The vibrant person cares passionately about his or her principles, values, and priorities, and this passion produces a way of living that has real impact for good on other people. Samuel Smiles put it this way: "It is energy, the central element of which is will, that produces the miracles of enthusiasm in all ages. It is the mainspring of what is called force of character and the sustaining power of all great action."

If we're not vibrant in our living of life, it's a shame. It's a shame because the world is so full of things that invite our engagement and energy. There are too many beautiful things not to be amazed by them. There are too many powerful things not to be awed by them. There are too many gracious things not to be humbled by them.

We need, as Arthur Gordon reminded us long ago, to "take our raincoats off in the shower." Shedding the protective coverings within which we conceal ourselves so much of the time, we need to expose ourselves to life, letting it wash over us in all its refreshing variety. When we do, things will start to "vibrate" within us. And no matter what our personality might be, we'll engage the world around us in a more powerful, and also a more grateful, way.

And what is energy but liking life?
LOUIS AUCHINCLOSS

HABITS

Moral excellence comes about as a result of habit.
We become just by doing just acts, temperate by doing
temperate acts, brave by doing brave acts.
ARISTOTLE

MORAL EXCELLENCE COMES ABOUT AS A RESULT OF HABIT. Think about that. Do you agree? Aristotle's point is that our character is formed by the things that we frequently do, and I believe he's right. I may think good thoughts, read good books, and even associate with good people, but if I allow myself to engage repeatedly in bad actions, it's silly to suppose that my actions have no bearing on my character. If I allow bad deeds to become my *habitual* manner of acting, that is, if I persist in them to the point where that is my customary and characteristic way of behaving, then I will have qualified myself as having bad character. That is, in fact, the very definition of a bad person: someone who characteristically does bad things.

But, of course, we need not have bad habits; we can choose to have good ones. And what a great choice that would be! There is simply no greater helper in life than good habits. As Elbert Green Hubbard said, "Habits are servants that regulate your sleep, your work, and your thoughts." When our willpower is weak and we need help doing what's right, good habits will support us and sustain us.

Yet good habits aren't easy to come by. I emphatically disagree with the old saying that "good habits are as easy to form as bad ones." If "Habit A" is promptly doing your duty and "Habit B" is procrastination, I must tell you that "Habit A" is the harder one to acquire. Bad habits can be formed by default, by doing nothing. Good habits, on the other hand, almost always require the exertion of extra effort.

But for better or worse, our habits define who we are. A person with bad habits may once in a while "slip up" and do some good deed that is totally uncharacteristic of him, but that doesn't mean his character is good. Before that could accurately be said of him, he'd need to reform his habits. Likewise, we can't realistically expect our friends to have a favorable opinion of us just because we do something spectacularly good on special occasions. It's our habits that define who we are!

The strength of a man's virtue should not be measured
by his special exertions, but by his habitual acts.
BLAISE PASCAL

January 13
WONDER

What happens to the hopes and dreams
and wonder with which every child is born?

JEAN GRASSO FITZPATRICK

IT'S QUITE NATURAL FOR CHILDREN TO HAVE A SENSE OF WONDER. They're easily impressed and delighted, and they find great joy in being amazed. Yet, as Fitzpatrick suggests, the wonder tends to fade as children grow older. There are many reasons for this, I suppose. The older we are, the more we've seen and the more it takes to impress us. The ease with which we can communicate and travel today means that we're presented with such an intricate variety of wonders, we grow accustomed to even the most amazing things. And to top it off, we're so busy, we don't have time to be filled with wonder. We encounter some truly wondrous things, but we hurry past them so quickly that they don't have a chance to work their magic on us.

Yet it's still true that we live in a "wonderful" world: it is filled with wonders beyond count. Many of the most wonderful things that we come in contact with should still be delightful to us even though we've seen them before. And we need to help our children retain their sense of awe in the presence of these phenomena: sunrises and sunsets, full moons, mountains, oceans — and yes, even skyscrapers and theme parks! It's a true tragedy not to wonder at what's wonderful.

Yet we can't become mere thrill seekers, always looking for some new thing "out there" that's more amazing than the last thing we saw. Wonder is essentially an internal characteristic. "We carry with us the wonders we seek without us" (Sir Thomas Browne).

Yet there are external things that can help, and good art is one of them. Whether it's visual, musical, literary, or performance art, art can awe us. Joseph Conrad, the novelist, made this observation: "The artist appeals to that part of our being which is not dependent on wisdom; to that in us which is a gift and not an acquisition — and, therefore, more permanently enduring. He speaks to our capacity for delight and wonder, to the sense of mystery surrounding our lives: to our sense of pity, and beauty, and pain." So find yourself a Beethoven, a Tolkien, or a Michelangelo and let them stir up your astonishment!

Deep into that darkness peering, long I stood there wondering, fearing,
Doubting, dreaming dreams no mortal ever dared to dream before.

EDGAR ALLAN POE

RESPECTFULNESS

Man is still a savage to the extent that he has
little respect for anything that cannot hurt him.
EDGAR WATSON HOWE

IF WE RESPECT ONLY THOSE WHOM WE FEAR, THEN WE'RE NOT
LIVING MUCH ABOVE THE LAW OF THE JUNGLE. Unfortunately,
however, in a world where "might makes right," extending respect to
others often means no more than this: we defer to those who have the
power to punish us if we fail to do their will. Most of us would say we
regret this state of affairs, but what do we do about it? How often do
we show real respect to anyone or anything when we don't have to?

But what if the other person is not "respectable"? If their character or conduct doesn't merit respect, should we go ahead and respect
them anyway, just so that we can have the trait of respectfulness? No,
respect would mean nothing if it were given out indiscriminately. But
with that in mind, consider that the following points are also true:

Our inclination ought to be to extend as much respect as possible.
There may be people whom we'd like to respect more than the facts
presently allow us to, but if we say we'd "like" to respect them more,
that should really be the truth. If we're "respectful," that means our
basic instinct runs in the direction of respect rather than away from it.

People often deserve more respect than we suppose. Just because somebody does something disrespectable, that doesn't mean they deserve no
respect at all. "Reverence [respect] is a good thing, and part of its value
is that the more we revere a man, the more sharply are we struck by
anything in him (and there is always much) that is incongruous with his
greatness" (Max Beerbohm). Respect isn't an all-or-nothing affair; we
may respect a person in some ways even if we can't do so in other ways.

*If there are those who can be respected for no other reason, we can
still respect their humanity.* The bottom line is that we are all human
beings, endowed with a certain dignity as part of our birthright. That
human dignity deserves to be respected no matter how foolishly a
person may have failed. For this reason, we are to love every person
unconditionally. Yes, the love must often be tough love, but it mustn't
ever be anything less than *respectful* love. Respectfulness means wanting to love our neighbors. All of them. Even when we don't have to!

Respect is love in plain clothes.
FRANKIE BYRNE

EXCHANGE

You're exceedingly polite,
And I think it only right
To return the compliment.
W. S. GILBERT

Life is largely a matter of making "exchanges." One person gives us something, and we give them something else. Or perhaps we initiate the transaction, and the other person responds. Either way, a good bit of what we do on an average day consists of exchanging things we have for other things that somebody else has. It is all, as we sometimes say, a matter of "give and take."

A fair exchange is one in which the value of what is given is commensurate with the value of the thing received. For example, you may have paid money for this book. If it delivers to you something as valuable as the money you gave up, then you'd have to say that a fair and honorable transaction has taken place. There's nothing dishonorable about the publisher asking for money in exchange for the book — if the value delivered is worth the value received.

We ought to avoid unfair exchanges, even when the other person is willing to be treated unfairly. Suppose, for example, a man visits a prostitute and pays her a large sum of money for her sexual favors. Is that fair? No, most people would say that what she gave was worth far more than what she received, no matter how much money changed hands. In almost every culture, there is the principle that sexual intimacy is of such value that the only thing it can be fairly exchanged for is a solemn vow of marriage, made in good faith by the other party. If the prostitute received anything less, then she was cheated, and the fact that she was willing to be cheated only makes the matter worse.

The highest and best exchange that can take place, of course, is the exchange of *hearts*. The fair exchange of one heart for another is a beautiful, and transforming, experience. Whether in love or in friendship, no gift is greater to give than one's open, authentic heart — and no gift is greater to receive in return. Heart for heart. Value for value. Such is the stuff of which real and wonderful life is made.

My true friend hath my heart, and I have his,
By just exchange one for the other given:
And I hold his dear, and mine he cannot miss,
There never was a better bargain driven.
SIR PHILIP SIDNEY

POSITIVENESS

I can't say I was ever lost, but I was
bewildered once for three days.

DANIEL BOONE

IT PAYS TO BE AS POSITIVE AS POSSIBLE. We ought never to deny the truth, of course, but that doesn't mean we can't look at the truth from a wide-enough angle to see that there are some good things to be appreciated as well as some bad things to be dealt with. And having looked at the larger truth, we can *choose to focus on its more positive aspects,* those that offer the greater promise of growth and improvement.

The longer I live, the more amazed I am at the extent to which our attitude determines how our external circumstances "feel." People with basically positive outlooks tend to feel that they're surrounded by good circumstances, while those with negative attitudes tend to feel the opposite. As Fulton J. Sheen said, "Each of us makes his own weather, determines the color of the skies in the emotional universe which he inhabits." And Horace Rutledge's comment is also appropriate: "When you look at the world in a narrow way, how narrow it seems! When you look at it in a mean way, how mean it is! When you look at it selfishly, how selfish it is! But when you look at it in a broad, generous, friendly spirit, what wonderful people you find in it."

Since so much depends on our choice of attitude, it's important to make that choice carefully. "The happiness of your life depends upon the quality of your thoughts . . . Take care that you entertain no notions unsuitable to virtue and reasonable nature" (Marcus Aurelius). Cynical thoughts should be shown to the door and told to leave!

But our dreams and goals are also important, and so we should exercise care and make them as positive and worthwhile as possible. "Your imagination has much to do with your life . . . It is for you to decide how you want your imagination to serve you" (Philip Conley).

Positiveness is the outlook of *opportunity.* It deals realistically with what now is, but it's also confident of what *could* be, if energy and intelligence were applied to the situation. Positiveness dares to believe that the future can be better than the past. It's the quality that separates the doers from the doubters, the achievers from the agonizers.

Optimism is the faith that leads to achievement.
Nothing can be done without hope and confidence.

HELEN KELLER

January 17
HEALTHFULNESS

The body manifests what the mind harbors.

JERRY AUGUSTINE

THERE IS AN UNDENIABLE LINK BETWEEN "HEALTHFULNESS" AND "HEALTH." Science may not perfectly understand all the ways our thinking influences our physical condition, but it obviously does. There are choices we can make concerning our attitude that will show up in our bodily state. Wise physicians have always known that healthfulness on the "inside" contributes to health on the "outside": "Since the human body tends to move in the direction of its expectations — plus or minus — it is important to know that attitudes of confidence and determination are no less a part of the treatment program than medical science and technology" (Norman Cousins).

Yet health is not an end in itself; it is not a god to be worshiped. It's a resource over which we should exercise good stewardship, but good stewardship recognizes that the resource is to be used rather than hoarded. George Bernard Shaw was right when he said, "Use your health, even to the point of wearing it out. That is what it is for. Spend all you have before you die; and do not outlive yourself."

But healthfulness also means something else: it means learning to have a healthful impact on others. Over time, each of us has some kind of effect on those who deal with us; the only question is whether the effect will be a healthy one or not. It's a fine thing if others can say that contact with us helps them to be healthier physically, mentally, emotionally, and spiritually. We ought to aspire to that kind of impact — and avoid actions that would pull people in the other direction.

If you've ever tried for very long, you know that it takes a certain amount of discipline and faith to maintain a healthful disposition. Taking the course of least resistance does not result in either healthfulness or health. We are surrounded by powerful forces that will, if we're not careful, turn us into anxious, negatively oriented people who base their lives on the assumption that sickness is the norm. We need to maintain the trust that sickness is not the norm, no matter how prevalent it may sometimes seem to be. We need to discipline ourselves and determine that healthfulness will be a part of our character.

The multitude of the sick shall not make us deny the existence of health.

RALPH WALDO EMERSON

PRIORITIES

> The heavens themselves, the planets, and this center
> Observe degree, priority, and place,
> Insisture, course, proportion, season, form,
> Office, and custom, in all line of order.
>
> WILLIAM SHAKESPEARE

PRIORITY IS A CONCEPT THAT IS GROUNDED IN NATURE. Contrary to the trend today, which is to think of everything as being part of one flat, undifferentiated reality, what we actually see in the objective world is a number of discrete entities arranged and ordered in definite hierarchies. It seems foolish to deny the obvious.

Perhaps it should be noted that lower rank in a hierarchy doesn't necessarily mean inferior *worth*. If some things have priority in a certain hierarchy, that doesn't mean the things that follow it don't matter at all. It just means that, as far as that particular hierarchy is concerned, some things occupy a primary position relative to others.

That said, however, it's still true that we see evidence of priority everywhere we look in the world around us. And that being true, it shouldn't surprise us to find that in the realm of human thinking and activity some things have — or should have — priority over others.

Given the complexity of life, it's probably hazardous to make too many generalizations about the subject of priorities, but here is one that I think most of us would agree with: on the list of things that concern us, *people* ought to have a higher priority than *things*. On our deathbeds, most of us are going to wish we'd spent less time acquiring and playing with the things that caught our fancy, and more time building relationships with the people that crossed our path.

For better or worse, our priorities say a good deal about our character. "Tell me to what you pay attention, and I will tell you who you are" (José Ortega y Gasset). If we chronically focus on "stuff" that is second-rate, there is simply no possibility that our character is going to be first-rate. So the challenge in life is to *recognize* that which is truly important and then to *act* on the basis of that priority. The "main thing" will still be the main thing whether we act on it or not, but if we don't act on it, we'll lose out on the best things in life. And what is worse, those around us may also be hurt by our confused priorities.

The main thing is to keep the main thing the main thing.
ANONYMOUS

ZEST

Zest is the secret of all beauty. There is
no beauty that is attractive without zest.

CHRISTIAN DIOR

ZEST IS AN UNDENIABLY ATTRACTIVE QUALITY. I'm not sure I would go as far as Christian Dior and say that there is no beauty that is attractive without it, for I can think of one or two kinds of beauty that attract with serenity rather than with zest. But even so, zest gets a great amount of favorable publicity and rightfully so.

Most dictionaries indicate that there are two basic meanings of the word "zest" as we use it today. Both of these meanings are suggestive of good things when we speak of zest as a personal characteristic.

(1) Intense flavor, piquancy. Zestful flavors are those that have some zing and some zip to them. The word "zest" comes from an obsolete French word for orange or lemon peel, and we still sometimes use "zest" to refer to the outermost part of the rind of an orange or lemon. As a cook, I love to see zest as an ingredient in a recipe! And I love it no less when I encounter someone who, as a person, has an "intense flavor." People with zest tend to be those who've thought about life and taken a definite stand for some things as opposed to others.

(2) Spirited enjoyment, gusto. People with zest also live with a liveliness and eagerness that is lacking in people who're more bland. There is some "kick" in their outlook and some "gusto" in their manner of living. That doesn't mean that they're unprincipled or immoral; it means that they appreciate that there is much in this world to relish and they've determined to taste it in all of its tanginess.

As I said above, zest may not be the absolute prerequisite for beauty, and likewise, it may not be a personal characteristic that every person in the world should have, at least insofar as their personality is concerned. Yet I believe there is a sense in which every person should look at life in a zestful way. As Bertrand Russell said, "What hunger is in relation to food, zest is in relation to life." Life is too interesting, and too important, for us not to live it with eagerness and enjoyment. In the case of all but a few of us, I reckon we'd do a better job of living if we put a little more "kick" into our philosophy!

Mirth is the sweet wine of human life. It should be
offered sparkling with zestful life unto God.

HENRY WARD BEECHER

FIDELITY

Let us be true: this is the highest maxim of art and of life,
the secret of eloquence and of virtue, and of all moral authority.

HENRI-FRÉDÉRIC AMIEL

FIDELITY MEANS FAITHFULNESS, AND IT'S ONE OF THE MOST IMPORTANT TRAITS THAT WE CAN HAVE. On the other hand, to be guilty of infidelity is to be guilty of a crime as serious as any that can be committed. And while we usually think of marriage when we hear these words, their significance is not limited to marriage. In every department of life, it's important to maintain fidelity.

As we might guess from their spelling, the words "truth" and "trust" are closely linked. In the end, it is always truth that begets trust. When we tell the truth, others come to trust us — they come to expect a high degree of fidelity, or faithfulness, between our words and reality. So in all things, as Amiel says, "Let us be true."

There is an old maxim that says, "Personality may open doors, but it takes character to keep them open." We may dazzle others with our ability to make a positive impression in the short term, but without the character trait of fidelity, the long term will probably reveal a striking number of broken relationships, relationships that sizzled for a while . . . but later fizzled when the need for fidelity arose.

Fidelity requires a strength that not everyone possesses. Everyone *could* possess it, of course, but not all have made that choice. Not all have decided to make commitment-keeping a part of their basic character. But those who've disciplined themselves to do so enjoy one of life's most important strengths: "To be capable of steady friendship or lasting love are the two greatest proofs, not only of goodness of heart, but of strength of mind" (William Hazlitt). Fidelity is not silly or sentimental by any means; it is a quality of strength and stability.

But if fidelity is the measure of a strong mind, it's also the measure of a loving heart. Ultimately, the kind of love that we all want to give and to get is the love that holds up in the face of difficulty and keeps the commitments it has made. This is the kind of love — the kind that is "true" in the sense that it can be "trusted" — that warms us, sustains us, and motivates our very best work in the world.

We should measure affection, not like youngsters by the
ardor of its passion, but by its strength and constancy.

CICERO

MERCY

The quality of mercy is not strained;
It droppeth as the gentle rain from heaven
Upon the place beneath. It is twice blessed —
It blesseth him that gives, and him that takes.

WILLIAM SHAKESPEARE

ALL TOO OFTEN, WE FAIL TO LEARN THE VALUE OF MERCY UNTIL WE OURSELVES ARE IN NEED OF IT. If we've never been guilty of serious moral failure (or if we've never recognized how serious our failures are), we may be among those who major in "justice," making sure that everybody gets just what they've earned, no more and no less. But it only takes about ten minutes as a "defendant" to realize that justice is not the only desirable quality in the world.

When a wrong is committed, there is always some sort of debt that is created. The job of a judge, in effect, is to decide whether to release the debt (mercy) or require that it be paid (justice). And anyone who's ever had to judge someone else's case knows that it's not an easy job. It takes wisdom to know when to extend mercy, and wisdom is a quality that's often in short supply. So when we find ourselves in the role of judge, it's not to be expected that we'll always get the judgment right. We can't avoid errors in judgment, but what we can do is grow. We can improve our attitude toward both justice and mercy.

To learn to be merciful, we must grow in two specific areas: *humility* and *gratitude*. If we don't have the humility to see our own faults, it's not likely that we'll be merciful toward the faults of others. And likewise, if we're not grateful for the mercy that has been shown to us, we won't see the need to pass that mercy on to others. So we must learn two things: a humble recognition of our own failures and a grateful recognition of how tolerant of those failures others have been.

Even when wisdom indicates, as it sometimes does, that mercy must be withheld, there is a sense in which our *inclination* ought to be in the direction of mercy. But when we catch ourselves saying, "I really wish I could be merciful here," we'd better not be lying, because life has a way of getting even with us. In the long run, we need not expect mercy ourselves if we've not been willing to be merciful to others.

We do pray for mercy;
And that same prayer doth teach us all to render
The deeds of mercy.

WILLIAM SHAKESPEARE

INVESTMENT

Goodness is the only investment that never fails.

HENRY DAVID THOREAU

MUCH OF THE QUALITY OF OUR LIVES DEPENDS UPON THE QUALITY OF OUR INVESTMENTS. In the financial world, our return depends not only on how much we invest but on the quality of the enterprises we invest in. The same thing is true of life in general: if we're stingy in the investments we're willing to make or careless in the things we invest in, then we'll be disappointed in what comes back to us. The challenge in life is to find the highest quality things that we can commit ourselves to and then to invest ourselves in them enthusiastically and generously. And in the long run, as Thoreau said, "Goodness is the only investment that never fails."

Worthwhile investments are costly, and by that I mean they require sacrifice. If, for example, we make a serious investment in the principle of love, it will cost us dearly. There is no free lunch, as the saying goes. Likewise, the principles of truth and diligence and service ask us to make investments that are often less than convenient, and sometimes even painful. In the real world, there's just no way around the fact that high-quality dividends require sacrificial investments.

Out of all the worthy things that we may invest in, surely the worthiest are *people*. Yes, we may gain much from sinking our capital into certain principles, projects, and properties, but eventually we discover that it's people who deserve our prime investment. All of us have people in whom we need to be investing more of ourselves; and whoever they are, we need to start increasing our investments *today*.

Even the wisest investments, however, require the passage of time before their value can be seen. Especially when we're investing in people, we need to have the patience to wait. It may be a long time before we see any encouraging result from our efforts. Having made wise investments in people, it's important not to give up on them.

The main thing that we must decide, of course, is not where to invest this or that particular resource that we own; it's where to invest our lives as a whole. We're surrounded by choices, some of which are quite deadly. So invest your life — but think twice before you do it!

I will not just live my life. I will not just
spend my life. I will invest my life.

HELEN KELLER

LOYALTY

When faith is lost, when honor dies,
The man is dead.

JOHN GREENLEAF WHITTIER

IN THE GLUE THAT HOLDS LIFE TOGETHER, LOYALTY IS ONE OF THE MAIN INGREDIENTS. If unity is a good thing, and it usually is, then the loyalty that preserves unity ought to be seen as something important and valuable. Just think of any worthwhile relationship that you're a part of right now. Are there not forces arrayed against that relationship that would tear it apart if you and the other members of the relationship didn't maintain loyalty to one another? If there weren't some truth or some value that mattered more to you than the differences that stand between you, would your relationship stand a chance of survival? No, it wouldn't. Loyalty is one of the main safeguards that keep the good things in life from being torn to pieces.

The concept of "allegiance" is a helpful concept to meditate on. Maintaining allegiance means that we *honor our duty to be loyal.* It might refer to individuals, to groups, or even to causes or ideas, but it always involves the notion of being loyal to the things that we're honorably obligated to support. Blind allegiance, the kind that defends even the faults of that which it supports, is not a good thing, obviously. But rightly understood, allegiance and loyalty are vital virtues.

There aren't many things frowned upon more universally than treachery. Even among thieves, the traitor is despised. And not only is it despicable, but there aren't many things that *hurt* us more than betrayal by those from whom we expect allegiance. So we all pay lip service to the value of loyalty. But if the truth be told, we aren't always as loyal as we should be. Too often, we fail to follow through. We fail to keep promises. We back out of inconvenient commitments.

If loyalty is to mean anything, we must remain loyal even when it is difficult. If our convictions are for sale, then we're not people who can be trusted. And if the only time we root for the home team is when it's having a winning season, then our "support" means very little. Real loyalty maintains its allegiance *through thick and thin!*

Loyalty is still the same,
Whether it win or lose the game;
True as a dial to the sun,
Although it be not shined upon.

SAMUEL BUTLER

SILENCE

The words the happy say
Are paltry melody
But those the silent feel
Are beautiful —
EMILY DICKINSON

SOME MEANINGS EXPRESS THEMSELVES IN WORDS, WHILE OTHERS ARE SIMPLY FELT IN SILENCE. Not everything that we think or feel ends up being clothed with words. Many of the matters in our hearts — even many of the worthiest — are content to rest there silently. And if, as we are told, there is a time to speak and a time to be silent, the time of silence is often more beautiful than the time of speaking. Happy words can hardly compare to the deep joy of meaningful silence. Edward Hoagland said it well: "Silence is exhilarating at first . . . but there is a sweetness to silence outlasting exhilaration, akin to the sweetness of listening and the velvet of sleep."

Amid the noise of our communicative age, I sometimes wonder if many of our friendships wouldn't be improved by a little silence. Emerson once said, "Hospitality consists in a little fire, a little food, and an immense silence." To me, there's something immensely comforting about that image: the silent enjoyment of rich relationship.

But even if friendships wouldn't be helped by silence, I'm quite sure that our thinking processes would. It's hard to learn very much when we're talking, and communication often hinders consideration. "In quiet places, reason abounds" (Adlai Stevenson).

When we express our thoughts and feelings in words, we can hardly avoid limiting them. As wonderful as words are (and as necessary as it often is to utilize their power), our words are imperfect and finite, and they can never fully or perfectly convey all that is in our hearts. The profoundest of our thoughts, those that connect us to the transcendent things that exist beyond us, would be nearly impossible for us to capture in words. And so sometimes the best that we can do when contemplating the most important things is to drink deeply of their meaning in our own minds — resisting the temptation to talk. Indeed, the closer we make an approach to reverence, the less inclined we will be to speak. In the silence of awe, we will *listen.*

Speech is of time, silence is of eternity.
THOMAS CARLYLE

TEACHABILITY

Rebuke is more effective for a wise man
Than a hundred blows on a fool.

THE BOOK OF PROVERBS

IF YOU COULD CHOOSE ONLY ONE CHARACTER TRAIT TO
ACQUIRE THIS YEAR, THE TRAIT OF TEACHABILITY WOULD BE
ONE OF THE WISEST CHOICES YOU COULD MAKE. To be teachable is to be receptive to learning and open to instruction. Unlike the
know-it-all who always ends up learning the hard way, the teachable
person is willing to be warned. He or she is ready to listen and learn
from someone else's experience in the school of hard knocks.

One of the distinctive attributes of our species is that we know
virtually nothing without being taught. Unlike many of the lower
creatures, we are born with very few instincts. In the absence of teaching, we are all but helpless. Pliny the Elder observed this when he
said, "Man is the only one that knows nothing, that can learn nothing
without being taught. He can neither speak nor walk nor eat, and in
short he can do nothing at the prompting of nature only, but weep."
It is true, of course, that we're capable of figuring out many things on
our own, but still, without the willingness to learn from others, our
lives would be so impoverished as to be practically useless.

Yet there is an obstacle to teachability, and it's the old demon of
pride. Even so great a student as Winston Churchill could say, "I am
always ready to learn, but I do not always like being taught." So we
need to put our pride in its place and adopt the humility of the truly
wise ones: those who're willing not only to learn but to be *taught.*

Normally, I suppose, we think of youth as the time when we're
most headstrong and unwilling to listen to others, but unfortunately,
we sometimes become less teachable the older we grow. Perhaps without realizing it, we begin to suffer from "hardening of the categories,"
and we need to go back and regain some of our youthful pliability.
"Better a poor and wise youth than an old and foolish king who will
be admonished no longer" (Book of Ecclesiastes). Maybe we'd even
profit from the wisdom of nursery rhymes like this one:

Oh, that it were my chief delight
To do the things I ought!
Then let me try with all my might
To mind what I am taught.

JANE TAYLOR

January 26

AUTHENTICITY

A cynic might suggest as the motto of modern life
this simple legend — "Just as good as the real."

CHARLES DUDLEY WARNER

SOMETIMES WE HAVE LITTLE CHOICE BUT TO ACCEPT A
SUBSTITUTE, BUT WE OUGHT NOT TO LET OURSELVES GET
TOO COMFORTABLE WITH THAT SITUATION. It's rarely true that the
artificial is "just as good as the real," and we ought to prefer authenticity. True, genuine things are rarely as perfect as a man-made imitation
might be, but for all their ragged edges, authentic things are still best.

Take my Australian shepherd, Wrigley, for example. He's far
from perfect. His behavior sometimes leaves much to be desired, his
physical characteristics fall below the standard for his breed, and he's
considerably more trouble to take care of than a stuffed animal would
be, but despite all of this, he's *genuine.* He's the real deal, and all of his
confoundedness and inconvenience notwithstanding, I'd rather have
him and his every flaw than any number of artificial, dog-like toys.

When it comes to people, I like those who're the real deal
too. I like those who, despite their blemishes, offer themselves to
me genuinely and sincerely, rather than with artifice and pretense.
Unfortunately, people like that often don't "get ahead" in life. As
Aesop observed, "Men often applaud an imitation and hiss the real
thing." But even so, I still prefer those who're authentic.

As soon as we meet people, we begin to construct a mental image
of them. From the little that we actually know, we make huge infer-
ences, and we build up a vision that's more about what we *wish* people
to be than about what they really are. As our relationships unfold,
we discover that real people don't always fit the image that we've
constructed, and so we're disillusioned. But really, which should we
prefer: the artificial image or the real person? Even with their imperfections, aren't real people more satisfying than artificial constructs?

As inconvenient as it is — indeed, as difficult as it is — we need
to keep ourselves open to authenticity. Just because something doesn't
glitter, that doesn't mean it's not gold. And real gold, even when it has
a few impurities mixed in, is a better treasure than imitation gold.

The authentic is almost never found by being pursued;
but there is no missing it when you are in its presence.

EVA HOFFMAN

ABUNDANCE

> The Abundance Mentality . . . flows out of a deep inner sense
> of personal worth and security. It is the paradigm that there is plenty
> out there and enough to spare for everybody. It results in sharing
> of prestige, of recognition, of profits, of decision making. It opens
> possibilities, options, alternatives, and creativity.
>
> STEPHEN R. COVEY

DEPENDING ON WHAT MENTALITY WE ADOPT, WE'LL FIND THAT LIFE EITHER EXPANDS OR CONTRACTS. Seeing life through the lens of abundance, we find that life is, in fact, abundant. It offers us one exciting opportunity after another. But if we look at things through the lens of scarcity, we become defensive and competitive. If there's not enough of the good stuff in life to go around, then we must guard the territory that we've staked out and keep our eye on those who might be plotting to take away from us what is ours. Under those conditions, life becomes a miserable business indeed. So think for a moment what a difference it would make to think "abundantly."

Possessions. An abundant attitude toward material goods would mean that we're not selfish or competitive. It would also mean that we're deeply grateful for the goods that we've been blessed with.

People. Here, an abundant attitude would help us rise above suspicion and jealousy. It would mean eagerly helping others to become all that they can be, with no fear that their success will hurt us.

Possibilities. Abundant thinking sees possibilities where others only see problems. It resists cynicism and keeps hope alive, always willing to work toward an increase in opportunity for one and all.

If life doesn't "seem" or "feel" abundant to us, the problem is most likely inside us rather than outside. It's probably not our circumstances that are scarce but our attitude. As far as the outside world is concerned, there's a great deal of abundance to be enjoyed even in the midst of seemingly scarce circumstances. The happiest folks in the world are not always those who enjoy a wealth of external abundance, but those who've decided to live with the *attitude* of abundance. They've figured out that whatever shortage of some things there may be in the world, there is no scarcity of any of the better things. If those are the things we want, there is plenty for everybody and then some!

> Not what we have, but what we enjoy,
> constitutes our abundance.
>
> JEAN ANTOINE PETIT-SENN

DISCOVERY

Through every rift of discovery some
seeming anomaly drops out of the darkness,
and falls, a golden link into the great chain of order.

EDWIN HUBBELL CHAPIN

DISCOVERIES CAN BE DISAPPOINTING SOMETIMES, BUT MORE OFTEN THEY'RE DELIGHTFUL. Rather than resist or run away from them, we ought to welcome discoveries, even when they require us to make adjustments in the way we think and live. Every true and genuine discovery is always the revelation of a bit more of the "great chain of order." Having discovered some new truth, we're in a better position to see how wonderfully every truth is linked to all the others.

I always enjoy coming to know people who live with the expectancy of delightful discovery. Such people seem to arise every day anticipating that they're going to discover something, and when I interact with them, they whet my own appetite for learning. Someone has said that "the world is brimming with happy thoughts just waiting to be discovered." I believe that's a realistic way to look at life, and it's a viewpoint that most of us would profit from if we made it our own.

J. Robert Oppenheimer made this comment: "Discovery follows discovery, each both raising and answering questions, each ending a long search, and each providing the new instruments for a new search." None of us are completely ignorant, and none of us are completely knowledgeable; we are somewhere on a path between the two. Discoveries move us forward on the path. They show us things we didn't know, but they also point us toward things yet to be learned.

It seems obvious, but it still needs to be pointed out that we won't make discoveries if we don't have *courage*. If we're not willing to leave the safety of our present understanding, we won't enjoy the thrill of seeing new vistas and new horizons. Fearful folks don't forge ahead.

But discovery also takes *faith*. To be discoverers, we have to be willing to "see" some things before they can be seen! On some days, no new discovery will be "in sight," and it's on those days that we must keep our confidence up. Good things are waiting for those who form their hunches carefully and then follow their hunches intently.

They are ill discoverers that think there is no land,
when they see nothing but sea.

FRANCIS BACON

TRIUMPH

The human soul, beaten down, overwhelmed,
faced by complete failure and ruin, can still rise up
against unbearable odds and triumph.

HAROLD RUSSELL

DOWN BUT NOT OUT: THAT IS THE CONDITION IN WHICH WE OFTEN FIND OURSELVES. "Down" means that we've suffered a setback and are perhaps discouraged, but we refuse to be "out" — that is, we refuse to believe the war is completely and permanently over. Having been knocked off our feet, we somehow still know that it's possible to get back up and get back in the fight. The freedom of the human spirit is amazingly irrepressible. It's virtually impossible to defeat a human being so decisively that he or she can't make a comeback. As long as life lasts, human beings are never "out."

And yet, rarely do we triumph without having lost hope once or twice along the way. Discouragement is a thing that must be dealt with by everybody, even those who end up winning the victory. "It is only after an unknown number of unrecorded labors, after a host of noble hearts have succumbed in discouragement, convinced that their cause is lost; it is only then that the cause triumphs" (François Guizot). So when we're discouraged, that's not necessarily evidence of a lack of character. Discouragement is simply a part of the price that must be paid to attain our goals and win our victories.

When we're discouraged, we owe it to those around us not to give up completely. By the choices we make in our own struggles, we either help or hinder others with their difficulties. As any soldier can tell you, individual examples of either courage or cowardice have a powerful effect on the morale of the unit as a whole. We need to make sure that our example has an encouraging effect on the "troops."

Whether we're thinking about our private problems or we're contemplating the larger warfare between good and evil, I believe there's reason for us to have faith. No, the evidence is not unequivocal, but I believe there is sufficient evidence to suggest that persistence will pay off. On any given day, skirmishes may be lost here and there. But the finer things in this world come to those who move forward in confidence — confidence that what's right is stronger than what's wrong.

In the end the good will triumph.

EURIPIDES

STRIVING

Man must strive, and striving must err.
JOHANN WOLFGANG VON GOETHE

MAKING A REAL EFFORT ALMOST ALWAYS MEANS THAT WE WILL MAKE MISTAKES. Yet the possibility (or even the probability) of stumbling is not necessarily an argument for standing still. Errors notwithstanding, it often makes a lot of sense to keep striving.

Athletes know the difference between "playing to win" and "playing to avoid losing." The former is a positive, give-it-all-we've-got force, while the latter is simply a defensive posture, a game plan that has no higher goal than the avoidance of mistakes. Yet in life, as on the athletic field, the conservative attitude that always plays it safe is rarely the one that achieves great results, and most of us realize that there's more honor in striving and erring than in not striving at all. "Far better it is to dare mighty things, to win glorious triumphs, even though checkered by failure, than to take rank with those poor spirits who neither enjoy much nor suffer much because they live in the gray twilight that knows not victory nor defeat" (Theodore Roosevelt).

The word "strife," however, can have a bad connotation, and so we need to consider whether our striving is the good kind. We need to make sure of two things: that our tactics are honorable, and more important, that our goals are worth fighting to achieve. Bertrand de Jouvenel asked the pertinent question when he said, "Year by year we are becoming better equipped to accomplish the things we are striving for. But what are we actually striving for?" Lest we become so preoccupied with the struggle that we forget what the struggle is about, we need to review our goals frequently and upgrade them if necessary.

Some people seem to think that the less pain and difficulty they experience, the happier they will be, and so they never do anything except take the path of least resistance. For them, the main thing in life is to avoid unpleasantness. Yet there's an irony to human life, and it consists in the fact that tranquil things like peace and joy come not from rest but from struggle. The happy life is not the life of constant relaxation; it's the life of conscience-driven *labor*. What we want is not the life of leisure; it's the life of "strife" . . . in the good sense!

> There's life alone in duty done,
> And rest alone in striving.
> JOHN GREENLEAF WHITTIER

REBUILDING

*God strikes at the core of our motivations. He is not interested
in merely applying a new coat of paint, imposing a new set of rules.
He wants to rebuild our minds and give us new values.*

ERWIN W. LUTZER

HAVE YOU EVER CONSIDERED HOW OFTEN WE FIND OUR-
SELVES IN THE "REBUILDING" MODE? Not only do destructive
events occur that require us to rebuild things that have been torn
down, but even when they're just left to themselves, things become
dilapidated and have to be rebuilt. And the "damage" principle is not
just true in the physical realm; it's also true in the realm of personal
character and relationships. Both within our own characters and in
our dealings with other people, much of our most important work
consists of building up again things that have been broken down.

Unfortunately, our rebuilding efforts are sometimes too superficial. When, for example, in our own lives we try to repair the damage
we've done by a past mistake, it's often the case that we don't go deep
enough. We try to talk our way out of problems we've behaved our
way into. We work on fixing our personality when it's our character
that needs renovating. We whitewash our outward behavior when we
should be radically rebuilding our principles, values, and aspirations.

Sometimes our lives have fallen into such disrepair that we're
embarrassed to let anyone know how much rebuilding we need to do.
But really, there's no shame in rebuilding. The shame would be in not
doing so! When we've made a wrong step, it's extremely important
that we choose our next step carefully. That step should be one that
makes our situation better in some way. It should be a rebuilding step.

We should be encouraged by the fact that rebuilt things are often
stronger than they were before. That's because we've been shown
where we're vulnerable, and we've had the chance to do something
about it. Having learned from our failures and reinforced the areas in
which we're weak, we're much less likely to fail in those same areas
again. And of all the things that are stronger when they've been
rebuilt, none are stronger than the human heart. When a broken heart
has been remade into a loving heart, that is a strong strength indeed.

*And ruin'd love, when it is built anew,
Grows fairer than at first, more strong, far greater.*

WILLIAM SHAKESPEARE

MAPS

Thought maps experience; fantasy colors it.
MASON COOLEY

THERE IS SOMETHING IN THE HUMAN MIND THAT MOVES US TO MAKE MAPS. We may not be interested in *road* maps, but even if we're not, we still make "maps." In one way or another, we feel compelled to describe the "territory" that we have traversed. "Thought maps experience," as Cooley says, and "fantasy colors it." Having experienced something, our minds "map" it, and then our fantasy "colors" it: showing what we wish our experience *might* have been and indicating hidden worlds that we hope to experience in the *future*.

If you've never been down a certain road, it often helps to have a detailed description of that road. The unknown is a bit fearful to us, and so before we leave home, many of us like to know exactly what's ahead. But as helpful as certain kinds of maps may be, it's not wise to become too dependent on them. "Even with the best of maps and instruments, we can never fully chart our territory" (Gail Pool). The most joyous people are those who are locked in on such a worthy *destination* that if the *path* takes an expected turn, they simply chalk it up to the "great adventure." There is a sense in which if we have a good "compass" (a good goal based on sound principles), we don't need a "map" (a description of what is going to happen to us along the way.)

Even so, maps are useful, and it's only a fool who will disregard what someone else says who has "been there" before. If necessary, faith and courage will see us through uncharted territory, but if the territory *has* been charted, we are most unwise if we fail to profit from the maps that others have made. And if you've "been there," you'd be foolish not to map that territory for your friends and loved ones.

Maps are wonderful motivators. The best maps make you want to explore the territory they describe; they invite you to experience what the mapmaker has experienced. So be careful which maps you consult. And more important, be careful which maps you *make*. When your mind maps your experience, make sure that it does so *accurately*, and when your fantasy colors the maps you've made, make sure that the fantasies are those that will encourage "adventure" in the *best* sense.

Maps encourage boldness. They're like cryptic love letters.
They make anything seem possible.
MARK JENKINS

REJUVENATION

By no means every destruction has been followed by rejuvenation,
and the great destroyers of life remain an enigma to us.

JACOB BURCKHARDT

EVERYWHERE AROUND US, THE FORCES OF EROSION, DILAPI-
DATION, AND DESTRUCTION ARE AT WORK. Some of these are
forces of nature, while others are of human origin. In the physical
world, nature has a marvelous ability to rejuvenate itself. After a forest
fire, a forest grows back. But in human affairs, rejuvenation is not so
automatic. Rejuvenation ("making young again") requires conscious
choice and hard work, and it's sad but true: not everyone chooses to
engage in that work. Some people are content just to be destroyers.

As important as the concept of rejuvenation is, however, we
sometimes make too much of it, or at least we look at it in the wrong
way. Great social value is placed on youth in our culture, so some
people go to expensive (and ridiculous) lengths to try to rejuvenate
themselves physically, as if the process of aging could be reversed.
Certainly we need to make our bodies last as long as possible (so that
while we live we can get as much good work done as possible), but if
our efforts at rejuvenation spring from a fear of being anything other
than young, then our efforts at rejuvenation will be misguided.

That said, it is also true that many of us should work harder at
rejuvenation. The daily grind will grind us to dust if we don't approach it with the proper attitude, and the destructive tendencies of
modern life will crush and kill us if we don't determine to resist them.

The highest kind of rejuvenation, of course, is the replenishment
that we give to *others*. When the harmful forces of life have worn
someone down, we never do a better thing than when we help them
to be refreshed and reinvigorated. So as far as our reputations are concerned, let's work to be known as rejuvenators rather than destroyers.

There is no good alternative to rejuvenation. If we're not growing
(and growth requires frequent refreshment), then we're simply giving
in to the forces of destruction. Rejuvenation is not something that can
be done once and then forgotten. It has to be repeated as often as we
find ourselves exhausted. The cup of life has to be refilled every day.

We must always change, renew,
rejuvenate ourselves; otherwise we harden.

JOHANN WOLFGANG VON GOETHE

PURITY

I would be true,
For there are those who trust me;
I would be pure,
For there are those who care.

HOWARD A. WHEELER

W E PROBABLY UNDERESTIMATE HOW MUCH OUR CRED-
IBILITY AND POSITIVE INFLUENCE DEPEND ON THE MAIN-
TENANCE OF PERSONAL PURITY. When we indulge in morally
wrongful actions, other people, even the immoral, lose confidence in
our integrity, and that is one of the worst things that can happen.

Unfortunately, many people see purity as nothing more than
"Puritanism." The Puritans considered any sort of physical or temporal enjoyment to be evil, and so the term "Puritanism" came to mean
rejection of any social pleasure at all. But surely that is an unwarranted
view. Whatever good things in the world may have been perverted
and turned into evil, there are still many wholesome things left, things
which ought to be enjoyed in their rightful place. Purity, rightly
considered, does not require us to become ascetics; it means that we
distinguish that which has not been corrupted from that which has,
and commit ourselves to staying away from the latter completely.
Above all, it means that we discipline our *thinking* and acquire habits
of thought that are clean and wholesome and constructive.

Maintaining purity of mind is no easy matter these days. Using
their "freedom of speech," the purveyors of entertainment (and even
information) have surrounded us with stuff that is as toxic to our spirits as any pollutant ever was to the natural environment. Surrounded
by so much dirt, staying clean is hard work, to say the least.

Purity is not a gift that life confers on some and withholds from
others. It is not the result of being born into a certain family or gradu-
ating from a certain university. It does not come from intelligence, talent, or any other natural endowment. It comes from within our hearts
and it's the result of watchfulness and self-discipline by each of us, day
after day. Purity is hard to maintain and easy to lose. So today, let's
not forget its importance or fail to guard the great treasure that it is.

We often pray for purity, unselfishness, for the highest qualities of character,
and forget that these things cannot be given, but must be earned.

LYMAN ABBOTT

MERIT

Charm strikes the sight, but merit wins the soul.
ALEXANDER POPE

MERIT ("EXCELLENCE" OR "VIRTUE") IS AN IMPORTANT CON-
CEPT, BUT IT IS OFTEN MISUNDERSTOOD. Misconceptions
and caricatures seem to crowd out the true meaning of the term.

For example, Christians who believe that salvation is by grace
may recoil from the word "merit." But the religious usage of the word
("spiritual credit granted for good works") is not its only meaning.

Others, who know that "merit" can mean "deserving of approval
or praise," may think those who pursue merit are moved by a desire
for praise. But as Plutarch observed, "Those who are greedy of praise
prove that they are poor in merit." And even Paul the Apostle could
write, "We aim at what is honorable not only in the Lord's sight but
also in the sight of man" (Second Letter to the Corinthians).

It is a false modesty which says that nothing a person does can
have any merit or be worthy of any approval. Augustus William Hare
understood this when he wrote, "True modesty does not consist in an
ignorance of our merits, but in a due estimate of them." When we try
to do what is right — that which has true merit — we don't do it for
the praise, but because it is honorable rather than reprehensible.

But there is another problem. Homer wrote, "How vain, without
the merit, is the name." When it comes to merit, we have a tendency
to take shortcuts, wanting the appearance of merit without having
done the work to acquire any. I have in my library a book entitled
*Faking It: How to Seem Like a Better Person Without Actually Improving
Yourself.* The book is humorous, written tongue-in-cheek, but it
makes a very serious point. We want what Alexander Pope called
"charm" rather than "merit." But in the end, faking it is a losing battle.

There is a world of truth in the simple statement "Time will tell."
In the short run, those who have no real excellence of character may
use outward appearances and personality techniques to get by. But in
the long run, the tests of life will separate the pretenders from those
who have sought true virtue. Right now, it may be hard to tell who has
merit and who has only charm, but take my word for it: *time will tell.*

There is no merit where there is no trial; and until experience stamps the
mark of strength, cowards may pass for heroes, and faith for falsehood.
AARON HILL

GENTLENESS

There is nothing stronger in the world than gentleness.
HAN SUYIN

THERE ARE FEW OF US WHO DON'T NEED TO BE MORE GEN-
TLE. Some of us may not have a naturally gentle disposition,
while others may simply be too hurried and stressed to be gentle. But
whatever the reason, our lack of gentleness can be very costly.

There is a type of person whose gentleness prevents him from
ever acting with strength. This is gentleness to a fault, and it is really
not gentleness — it is weakness. Gentleness does not lack strength,
but it is *strength under control.* The gentle person, while capable of
acting forcefully when the time comes, restrains the impulse to apply
force, applying wisdom to the situation rather than just lashing out.
The gentle do not use any more force than is needed. Like a dentist,
they don't want to inflict any more pain than is absolutely necessary.

In fact, true gentleness of character is what allows us, when need
be, to act strongly. "Be gentle," said Lao Tzu, "and you can be bold."
People will only let you influence them with your strength when you
have earned the right by having shown lots of gentleness on previous
occasions. In your bank account with another person, if you haven't
already made lots of deposits by showing gentleness to them, you are
going to overdraw your account if you hit them with a show of force.

On an even deeper level, however, we see that gentleness and
strength are often identical. Indeed, gentleness is one of the strongest
forces in the world. It is far stronger than the brute force that many
people try to use, which is the point of the Latin proverb: "Power can
do by gentleness what violence fails to accomplish." Frustrated by a
lack of results, we often resort to force (anger, raised voices, and ulti-
matums) when applying a softer touch would be more productive.

So let's lay aside our misconception that being gentle is weak,
and let's work on being more gentle to those around us. It rarely matters whether folks "deserve" gentleness or not — usually they need it
even if they don't deserve it. James Matthew Barrie gave good advice
when he said, "Always try to be a little kinder than necessary." This is
a rough world, and we are all being bruised in the battle. So when you
deal with me, have a care. I am hurting, and I need some kindness.

Feelings are everywhere — be gentle.
J. MASAI

INVOLVEMENT

You can't be detached and effective.

ABBA EBAN

EFFECTIVENESS ALMOST ALWAYS REQUIRES INVOLVEMENT. In sports, for example, the spectators' enthusiasm may be a factor, but basically, the outcome is determined by those who are involved in playing the game on the field, not by those who are just watching. The concept of "involvement" is an interesting metaphor. The Latin verb *involvere* was a compound made up of *in* ("in") + *volvere* ("to roll or turn"). Literally, then, if two things are "involved," they are "rolled together" or "intertwined." With this picture in mind, when we say that a person has gotten involved in some activity, we mean that he or she is "wrapped up" in it. Previously, they may have viewed the activity passively or from a distance, but now they and the activity are intertwined, like the strands of a rope. No longer are they passengers, spectators, or commentators — now they are *involved*.

Don't we need to be more involved with life and its worthwhile activities? I believe we do. In my own life, I constantly battle the temptation to back away from things, to remain passive. And to the extent that I give in to that temptation, I am the loser. What about you? In all honesty, what do you see in your life: a pattern of courageous involvement and engagement, or a tendency to take the easy way out and remain passive? Are you "intertwined" with life or not?

I like to look at the difference between involvement and non-involvement as the difference between going forward and going backward. Am I going to get involved and engage this difficult, unpleasant thing that is on my "to do" list, or am I not? If I go ahead and get involved with the thing, I move forward, but if I back away from it and remain passive, I lose ground. It takes effort to overcome inertia and engage life, but there is no other way to avoid going backward. And if we're going backward, we're not really living; we're dying.

Henry Wadsworth Longfellow wrote, "Act — act in the living present, / Heart within, and God o'erhead." I challenge you to do what Longfellow said: *act.* Be wise and careful, of course, but get involved and *act.* Life's a great drama, so participate and play your part!

To finish the moment, to find the journey's end in every step of the road,
to live the greatest number of good hours, in wisdom.
RALPH WALDO EMERSON

AFFECTION

Affection is responsible for nine-tenths of whatever
solid and durable happiness there is in our natural lives.

C. S. LEWIS

AFFECTION IS NOT THE ONLY KIND OF LOVE, AND IT DOESN'T
HAPPEN TO BE THE HIGHEST KIND, BUT AFFECTION IS
STILL A VERY WONDERFUL THING. It is, as the *American Heritage
Dictionary* describes it, "a fond or tender feeling toward another."
When we feel affection for someone, we not only love them, we *like*
them. We like them with a warm, glowing desire. And the dictionary
is probably right to include the word "tender." When you find that
the thought of being tender to a certain person is an inviting, pleasing
thought, you've probably been bitten by the bug of affection.

Showing affection is indeed one of life's most pleasurable experiences. And the good news is, there's no shortage of people to whom
we may be affectionate. They're there for the finding, if we care to
look. It's certainly a fact that having our affection rejected is a painful
ordeal. When you like someone and they don't like you back, it hurts
as much now as it did in the third grade, if not more. But we shouldn't
let that stop us from finding others — others to whom we can have "a
fond or tender feeling." Those folks are well worth looking for.

Affection, whether we're showing it or receiving it, has a "warming" effect on us. Its enjoyment is like the enjoyment of a fireplace
on a winter's evening. It's a pleasure mingled with many good things:
warmth, security, friendship, fellowship, and, of course, love.

Without affection, many of our other character traits will be
barren, and maybe dangerous. Think, for example, of the harm that's
often done by the person who tells the truth, but without any affection. Or demonstrates courage, but without any affection. Or shows
leadership, but without any affection. Affection is the quality that
keeps our strength and intelligence from becoming brutal. It's one of
the main keys to effectiveness and emotional health. So if we've been
holding back, either in giving or receiving affection, today would be a
great day to get started learning a little fondness and tenderness.

Talk not of wasted affection, affection never was wasted;
If it enrich not the heart of another, its waters, returning
Back to their springs, like the rain, shall fill them full of refreshment;
That which the fountain sends forth returns again to the fountain.

HENRY WADSWORTH LONGFELLOW

UNSELFISHNESS

> There is a life that is worth living now as it was worth living
> in the former days, and that is the honest life, the useful life,
> the unselfish life, cleansed by devotion to an ideal.
>
> HENRY VAN DYKE

AS CHARACTER TRAITS GO, UNSELFISHNESS WOULD HAVE TO BE RANKED SOMEWHERE NEAR THE TOP OF THE LIST. Learning to seek the interests of others, and not merely our own, is one of the primary goals in life. Unselfishness is not only a virtue; it is one of the most basic virtues because it is the key that unlocks the door to so many other qualities that we need to have. It is no small part of what Van Dyke calls the life "worth living." But unselfishness is a trait that is both hard to acquire and hard to maintain.

Acquiring unselfishness. Dag Hammarskjöld once wrote, "To reach perfection, we must all pass, one by one, through the death of self-effacement." Letting go of self-centeredness is so hard that it really can be described as a death. Often it takes some life-altering crisis or trauma to separate us from our selfish concern. This concern is so dominant that it will not give up on us without being "crucified."

Maintaining unselfishness. Learning to be unselfish is a choice that we make. But it's not a choice that can be made and then forgotten — it has to be made and remade every single day. Once we've acquired a measure of unselfishness, we must nurture it, increase it, and recommit ourselves regularly to an outward-focused life.

But when we've paid the price to make unselfishness a part of our character, we possess a treasure of immense value. It's worth every bit of the sacrifice that it takes to learn it and hold on to it. When Jesus of Nazareth said, "It is more blessed to give than to receive," he said something that all of us know is true: those who choose to give are more fortunate ("blessed") than those who do nothing but receive. The unselfish are the richest people on earth, even if they are poor.

Finally, unselfishness is probably the most transformative power in the world. It has the ability to take ordinary duties — even difficult ones — and turn them into acts of joyous love. When we not only "do things" but we do them for someone as a gift, the deeds become extraordinary. For the unselfish, the mundane becomes quite marvelous.

> Unselfishness turns burdens into life!
> ROBERT HAROLD SCHULLER

February 9
TEARS

The soul would have no rainbow had the eye no tears.

JOHN VANCE CHENEY

IT WOULD BE A MISTAKE TO TRY TO AVOID TEARS. As with many other "negative" experiences, we tend to say, "I want as little of that as possible in my life." But tears have a value and a place in our lives that we should not be quick to dismiss. As John Vance Cheney reminds us, "The soul would have no rainbow had the eye no tears."

Those who try to implement a "No Tears" philosophy can only do so by denying the brokenness of the world. If we are honest, we have to recognize this fact: there are many things about the world that can only be responded to with tears, at least if we have any sympathy or tenderness about us. So what should we do concerning the brokenness of the world? Refuse to face the facts or pretend that it isn't so? Live in a make-believe world where "everything is wonderful"?

No, none of these forms of denial are appropriate to engage in. Granted, the heartbreaking aspects of life are never the whole truth about the world, and we should make up our minds to remember the larger perspective — but even so, we should not automatically run away from things that cause us to cry. Unpleasantness is not to be avoided at all costs, and we should not necessarily shun contact with sorrow. As we mature, we come to grips with the fact that life is indeed a bittersweet experience, a mixture of emotions. We learn to be thankful for both the joy of the laughter and the value of the tears.

There is, however, one kind of tears that we should try to keep to a minimum, and that is the tears of other people that result from misdeeds on our part. It is true, as someone has said, that the hardest tears to bear are those that we ourselves have caused, and these should certainly be avoided by refraining from the deeds that cause them.

One remarkable aspect of tears is the way they bond us to other people heart-to-heart. If we had our choice, perhaps we wouldn't want to be crying at all, but when we not only cry but we cry with others, we find the experience to be truly transforming. Tears that, shed in isolation, might harm us may heal us when shed in company.

It is sweet to mingle tears with tears;
Griefs, where they wound in solitude,
Wound more deeply.

SENECA

SOFTNESS

He only is advancing in life whose heart is getting softer, whose blood
warmer, whose brain quicker, whose spirit is entering into living peace.

JOHN RUSKIN

SOFTNESS SUGGESTS MANY THINGS TO MANY PEOPLE. The
American Heritage Dictionary lists a total of seventeen meanings
for "soft," and most of those are divided into several sub-meanings. So
"softness" is a complicated word, but several of the ways it can be used
suggest some character concepts that we would do well to consider.

For example, soft can mean "easily molded." Don't we want to
be teachable and easily influenced by that which is good? Another
meaning of soft is "not loud or harsh." Don't we want to be measured
and reasonable in our speech, rather than be a crank or a loudmouth?
Another meaning is "subdued, not glaring." Wouldn't we rather avoid
being known as "glaring" in our personal characteristics? Another
meaning is "of a gentle disposition, tender." Isn't that the way we
want to be? And finally, soft can mean "affectionate." Who among us
doesn't recognize affection as a positive personal quality?

All of the above attributes suggested by "softness" are admirable
in one way or another. But perhaps many men would say, "That's not
the way I want to be. I want to be masculine." What about that argument? Are masculinity and softness mutually exclusive? I don't believe
so. Using the soft touch may be a bit hard for some men, but even the
strongest of men can learn to be gentle when the need arises. It is a
considerable challenge, but it is not impossible to be a man of "steel
and velvet," as Abraham Lincoln was described by Carl Sandburg.

Softness is one of the most helpful gifts that we can give to others, especially when they are hurting. We all want our doctors and
dentists to be gentle, and most of us want our friends to be that way
too. Balancing our "steel" with a little "velvet" is a friendly thing to do.

It is never a waste of time to act in love and tenderness toward
those around us, that is, to give the gift of softness. When others do
not return the gift, but act harshly toward us, we may be tempted to
respond in kind. But it is still worthwhile to show gentleness — if for
no other reason than that is what will keep our hearts from hardening.

Love is never lost. If not reciprocated it will
flow back and soften and purify the heart.

WASHINGTON IRVING

HONOR

To esteem everything is to esteem nothing.

MOLIÈRE

A PERSON IS NOT HONORABLE IF EVERYTHING THAT PERSON ENCOUNTERS IS GIVEN EQUAL HONOR. The fact is, some things, and even some people, are more praiseworthy than others. Distinguishing what is praiseworthy from what is not, and relating oneself accordingly, is one of life's major responsibilities. True, it takes humility, wisdom, and carefulness to make proper evaluations, and we should all stand ready to be corrected and have our decisions improved. But value judgments must still be made, and the person who won't make them has less regard for honor than he should have.

We live in an age all but obsessed with "self-image." But a healthy self-image doesn't come from being told that we're wonderful regardless of the evidence of our conduct. Instead, it comes from honoring what is honorable outside of ourselves and then keeping our conduct consistent with that ideal. If we know we're not acting honorably, we not only *won't* feel good about ourselves, we *shouldn't* feel that way. Conscience is always the key to self-esteem.

Frankly, we all find ourselves now and then in the position of having acted dishonorably. In this position, the honorable person will act honorably toward the dishonor that he's done! He will acknowledge it without excuse and try to rectify it in every way possible. There is nobody in the world who doesn't fall into dishonor occasionally, but it's the *next* step that's critical. With that step, we either redeem our honor or bury it more deeply in the dirt. In fact, there may be no greater test of our honor than what we do in the face of failure.

Given the difficulty of repairing our honor when it's been damaged, it makes sense to live so that it doesn't have to be repaired very often. When we're tempted to compromise our convictions, we must learn to say no. Our souls must not be for sale. There must be limits beyond which we simply will not go. Based on new learning, we may need to adjust those limits and refine them, but we dare not dispense with them for the sake of expediency or even urgency. If we're wise, we won't let go of our honor — "not no way, not no how."

Never give in — in nothing, great or small, large or petty
— except to convictions of honor and good sense.

WINSTON CHURCHILL

FREEDOM

True freedom is to share
All the chains our brothers wear
And, with heart and hand, to be
Earnest to make others free!

JAMES RUSSELL LOWELL

L IKE MANY OF THE OTHER QUALITIES WE'VE DISCUSSED, FREEDOM IS NOT ONLY A BLESSING TO BE APPRECIATED; IT'S A GIFT TO BE GIVEN. To whatever extent we ourselves are free, we should pause frequently to give thanks for that. But it's almost always true that our freedoms were purchased by the sacrifices of others, and so proper gratitude for freedom has to include deeds as well as words. As a free people, our deeds must be those that lift the burdens of those less free. True freedom, as Lowell wrote, is to share "all the chains our brothers wear." It is to be "earnest to make others free!"

There are many kinds of bondage, of course, and some of them are self-inflicted. Some forms of enslavement are personal, rather than political or social. Some are on the other side of the world, rather than near at hand. But however and wherever human beings languish for lack of freedom, our hearts must be touched by the injustice of their condition. If we ever fail to act with compassion and courage on behalf of the downtrodden and the oppressed, we will have departed from the morality that has made our civilization great.

Abraham Lincoln, whose greatness we remember today, was exemplary in his concern for freedom. Few figures in our history stand out as having sacrificed more for the cause of freedom than Lincoln.

But Lincoln would very likely be disturbed by much that goes on today in the name of freedom. He would be appalled by our softness, our self-indulgence, and our evasion of personal responsibility. He would be shocked by the socially destructive uses to which we put our freedom. He would be saddened to see how selfishly we define freedom and how shortsighted we are in our promotion of it.

To honor freedom — and to celebrate the life of a man like Lincoln — we must do more than join organizations and attend rallies. We must sweat for it, and having defended it for ourselves and others, we must use it as a people who know right from wrong.

We have confused the free with the free and easy.

ADLAI STEVENSON

JOY

Happiness depends on what happens; joy does not.
OSWALD CHAMBERS

WITH REGARD TO JOY, THE FIRST THING WE NEED TO KNOW IS THIS: JOY IS NOT THE SAME THING AS HAPPINESS. As its spelling indicates, "happiness" has to do with "happenings." It is what we feel when what is happening is pleasant. And since what is happening is often beyond our control, happiness is an "iffy" thing. Indeed, the Middle English root from which we get both "happen" and "happy" is *hap* ("luck, fortune, chance"). Sometimes our circumstances may "happen" to be pleasant, but at other times they may not.

Joy, on the other hand, results from the way we think. As Tim Hansel has put it, "Happiness is a feeling. Joy is an attitude." It's the *contentment* that comes from trusting that which is trustworthy — and the *excitement* that comes from doing deeds that are based on that trust. Unlike happiness, which may or may not come our way when we want it to, joy is a quality that can always be ours, and it is a far greater thing to aspire to. "The word 'joy' is too great and grand to be confused with the superficial things we call happiness" (Kirby Page).

To a large extent, joy is a by-product of having aligned ourselves with the true-north principles of right and wrong (honesty, courage, justice, etc.). If our conscience knows that we're guilty of wrongdoing, there can be no true joy for us, even if the present moment may be making us happy. Thomas à Kempis was correct: "No man can safely rejoice unless he possesses the testimony of a good conscience."

So joy (or at least being open to joy) is a choice that we can make for ourselves. But more than that, it's a gift that we can give to others. When we are joyless, we depress and discourage those who have to have dealings with us, and so we greatly honor and benefit our friends and loved ones when we present our "self" to them as a *joyful* self.

Joy is a wonderfully democratic thing. It is available to all, not just the privileged few. And not only is it available to all, but the experience of it is the same for everybody. When one person tastes true joy, the taste of it is no less exquisite than it is for any other person, no matter how different the individuals may be in other respects. In the very highest sense, then, joy is an "equal opportunity" virtue.

Bliss is the same in subject or in king.
ALEXANDER POPE

FRIENDLINESS

It is not, as somebody once wrote, the smell of cornbread that calls us
back from death; it is the lights and signs of love and friendship.

JOHN CHEEVER

WHEN WE MAKE THE CHOICE TO BE FRIENDLY RATHER
THAN UNFRIENDLY, WE OPEN THE DOOR TO ONE OF
THE BEST COMPARTMENTS OF THE GOOD LIFE. "Friends are the
sunshine of life" (John Hay). But it is a choice that we must make.
Friendliness should be more than a mood that comes over us. It
should be an act of the will, a decision to live in a certain way.

"Friendliness," as opposed to "friendship," is a *fondness* for friendship, a *disposition* in that direction, a *determination* to make decisions
that favor friendship. It's an attitude which says, "I see the value of
friends, and I want to do my part to foster friendly relationships."

Friendliness is one of the qualities that we need to have if we
intend to grow throughout life rather than stagnate. Friendly people
are open to new friendships, and as they acquire them, they find their
lives expanding in healthy ways. Without neglecting their old friends,
those who have the quality of friendliness welcome the chance to
demonstrate that attitude to new people in new situations. Sarah
Orne Jewett said it colorfully: "Yep, old friends are always best, unless
you can catch a new one that's fit to make an old one out of."

Today happens to be a day set aside for some special gestures
of friendship. Who are those to whom you will give or send some
Valentine's greeting today? Chances are, they're special people you
need to be thankful for . . . and show friendship to on other days too.

We don't always have to be in close proximity to our friends, but
it's important to know that we have them. It's important to know
that, somewhere, there are those who know us, like us, and trust us.

There is a sense in which friendliness is a measure of character.
By this I don't mean that those with outgoing personalities have a
better character than others, but simply that the choice to welcome
friendships into our lives (along with the work necessary to nurture
them) is an indication of character. In the end, we'll enjoy little else
that we've accomplished if we haven't been fond of friendship.

A man cannot be said to succeed in life
who does not satisfy one friend.

HENRY DAVID THOREAU

EXERCISE

True enjoyment comes from activity of the mind and exercise of the body.
ALEXANDER VON HUMBOLDT

EXERCISE SHOULD BE THOUGHT OF AS A BENEFIT RATHER THAN A CHORE. The very word sounds like something unpleasant, an experience to be endured only because it is good for us. But rightly defined and properly appreciated, exercise is seen to be a privilege. Strictly speaking, "exercise" is part of a group of words that refer to "activities undertaken for training in some skill," but for the purposes of our discussion today, let's think of it simply as "activity." In terms of our character, don't we want to be people of activity rather than inactivity. Don't we want to be people who "exercise" ourselves?

When most people think of exercise, they think only of physical or bodily exercise, and while that is not the only kind (as we shall see in a moment), it is certainly an important kind. In our sedentary society, most of us get far too little physical exercise. Consequently, our bodies atrophy and become less and less capable of doing what needs to be done. We should see our bodies as the instruments through which our minds do their work, and we should be good stewards of our bodies, taking care of them so as to get the maximum mileage out of them. As Socrates said, "We can do nothing without the body; let us always take care that it is in the best condition to sustain us."

But bodily exercise is not the only kind that we need. Our minds need to engage in activity as well, and if we don't exercise them, they will surely become "flabby." If we're wise, we'll put our minds through their paces every day, forcing them to get up and get to work.

Both bodily and mentally, exercise (or activity) is the only way *to improve, to make progress, and to go forward. As* Hugh Blair put it, "Exercise is the chief source of improvement in our faculties." And really, there is no safe middle ground. Either we are, by exercise, going forward or we're sliding backward. To live passively and do nothing is to die. If we would live, we must act, and if we would advance, we must be active. So "exercise" is not such a bad thing after all, is it?

Keep the faculty of effort alive in you by a little gratuitous exercise every day. That is, be systematically ascetic or heroic in little unnecessary points, do every day or two something for no other reason than that you would rather not do it, so that when the hour of dire need draws nigh, it may find you not unnerved and untrained to stand the test.
WILLIAM JAMES

February 16
LIBERALITY

Liberality consists less in giving a great deal than in gifts well timed.

JEAN DE LA BRUYÈRE

SET ASIDE FOR A MOMENT THE CONCEPT OF POLITICAL OR RE-
LIGIOUS "LIBERALISM" AND CONSIDER THAT THE BASIC MEAN-
ING OF "LIBERALITY" IS GENEROSITY. Coming into English from
the Latin *liber* ("free"), the word suggests that in the matter of giving,
a liberal person gives freely rather than in a stingy or miserly way. The
character trait of liberality means that we have open hearts and hands.
When wisdom indicates that a thing is to be done, we do it generously, wanting to do as much (rather than as little) as possible.

But people who have learned the skill of liberality know that it
involves more than just the giving of gifts. As Jean de La Bruyère
noted, "Liberality consists less in giving a great deal than in gifts well
timed." If there is the question of how *much* we should give, there are
also the questions of *when* we should give and in what *manner*. Since
the "how" of giving is every bit as important as the "how much," it
takes wisdom, thoughtfulness, and empathy to be authentically liberal.

Indeed, if we just toss gifts here, there, and everywhere, we are
not being generous but careless. If you give me a gift of money, the
gift will not mean nearly as much if I know that you are wasteful in
the management of your finances. So James Boswell was exactly right
when he said, "If a man is prodigal, he cannot be truly generous."

But real generosity is ironic in that it makes us richer while holding on to our treasures makes us poorer. The Book of Proverbs puts it
this way: "There is one who scatters, yet increases more; and there is
one who withholds more than is right, but it leads to poverty."

Some people think that liberality is a sign of weakness. A judge,
for example, who shows mercy to a guilty defendant might be thought
of as weak in comparison to a judge who takes a tougher approach.
And a nation that deals generously with other nations in its foreign
policy might not be considered as strong as a nation that takes a
military approach to every issue. In the long run, however, individuals
(and nations) who have been generous end up being much stronger
than those who have chosen not to be. It is an undeniable fact of life:
generosity can do many things that brute force is incapable of.

The hand of liberality is stronger than the arm of power.

SAADI

February 17
BLESSING

O God, animate us to cheerfulness.
May we have a joyful sense of our blessings . . .
WILLIAM ELLERY CHANNING

BLESSINGS ARRIVE SO OFTEN IN OUR LIVES THAT IT'S HARD
TO CATCH UP WITH OUR EVER-INCREASING DEBT OF GRATI-
TUDE. Just when we think we've made an appreciative inventory of
the good things we've been blessed with, more good things show up.
As somebody said, counting our blessings is an arithmetic that's hard
to master. We could all use a more "joyful sense of our blessings."

Occasionally we refer to some grace we've received as a "mixed"
blessing. But really, there is no other kind. Most blessings require some
sort of sacrifice. The price is often well worth paying, considering the
benefit, but the fact remains, some things have to be relinquished in
order for other things to be gained. And not only that, most blessings
have some responsibilities attached to them. So, in the real world, very
few of our blessings are pure, unalloyed pleasure — most come mixed
with sacrifice and responsibility. There is, as they say, no free lunch.

Out of all the things that we'd consider our blessings, the best
are surely the *people* we've had the privilege of knowing and interacting with. In each of our lives, there are at least a few people who
have been such a blessing that we'd say it would have been worth
being born into the world just to have the opportunity to know those
people. In most of our lives, in fact, there are *several* such people.

Without a doubt, all of us have been blessed. But more important than the fact of having been blessed is the opportunity to be a
blessing to others. However we would define the "good life," there
should be something in our definition that involves adding a touch
of grace to someone else's life. And of all the skills we might want to
have, none is more valuable than the skill "to soothe and to bless."

Dear Lord, for all in pain
We pray to thee;
O come and smite again
Thine enemy.
Give to thy servants skill,
To soothe and to bless,
And to the tired and ill
Give quietness.
AMY CARMICHAEL

February 18
PERSISTENCE

If you stop every time a dog barks, your road will never end.

ARABIAN PROVERB

MOST OF THE GOOD THINGS IN LIFE ARE ACCOMPLISHED BY PEOPLE WHO KEPT GOING WHEN IT WOULD HAVE BEEN EASY TO QUIT. Persistence is a key that unlocks many wonderful doors, and we would do well to use that key more often. If we don't persist, we won't get to the end of any road that's worth traveling. Among my most favorite quotations is one by A. B. Meldrum. He said, "Bear in mind, if you are going to amount to anything, that your success does not depend upon the brilliancy and the impetuosity with which you take hold, but upon the everlasting and sanctified bull-doggedness with which you hang on after you take hold."

The "everlasting and sanctified bull-doggedness" of which Meldrum spoke requires at least two things: (1) the ability to *visualize* our goals, and (2) the ability to go toward our goals with an unstoppable *determination*. Without the second of these, the first is of little use. "The person who makes a success of living is the one who sees his goal steadily and aims for it unswervingly" (Cecil B. DeMille).

One reason that many of us do not persist in pursuing our goals is that we have not made any real *commitment* to those goals. There is a world of truth in the Chinese proverb which says, "Great souls have wills, feeble ones only wishes." Most of the time, when we think we have set a goal for ourselves, all we have done is to think, "It would be nice if _____ happened." But thinking that a certain thing would be nice is a long way from committing ourselves to it as an actual goal. And the persistence that it takes to reach difficult goals comes from serious commitments. It does not come from wishes.

Persistence would be no great feat if there were no obstacles in our path. But as all of us have noticed, there are many obstacles. We have made mistakes, and those mistakes tend to discourage us. We have failed in the pursuit of some of our goals, and those failures tend to disillusion us. But unless we intend to sit down and give up the journey (which is not an honorable option), our obstacles should not be seen as anything more than temporary delays. As long as our conscience tells us that our goals are good, we must keep going!

Even after a bad harvest there must be sowing.

SENECA

IDEAS

The history of mankind is the history of ideas.
LUDWIG VON MISES

THE THING THAT WE CALL "HISTORY" IS PRODUCED NOT BY EVENTS BUT BY IDEAS. History is a record of events, obviously, but it was ideas that produced the events, and so the real story of the human race is the story of the ideas that have moved people to do the things that they have done. Had the ideas been different, the events would have been different. As the ideas go, so goes the "story."

One reason that ideas are so important is that they produce our personal character. For better or worse, the kind of people we turn out to be is determined by our thinking. Mohandas Gandhi said it well: "A man is but a product of his thoughts; what he thinks, that he becomes." Some ideas produce Adolf Hitlers, while other ideas produce Abraham Lincolns. If we have bad character, we may try to blame it on our ancestors or our environment, but our character has, in fact, resulted from our own thinking (i.e., from our ideas).

Ideas, at least good ones, are not things to be afraid of. I like what Mark Van Doren said about "entertaining" ideas: "Bring ideas in and entertain them royally, for one of them may be the king."

The mistake that many of us make is entertaining only comfortable ideas, and by that I mean those that we already agree with. Especially as we age, we find it more difficult to stretch our minds and to evaluate new ideas. Indeed, one measure of our age is the amount of pain we feel when we come in contact with a new idea. But if we never think anything but comfortable thoughts, we're probably not going to be thinking some new thoughts that we need to think.

Given the far-reaching consequence of our ideas, we need to be careful about the ideas that we allow to take up residence in our minds. Albert Einstein said, "If most of us are ashamed of shabby clothes and shoddy furniture, let us be more ashamed of shabby ideas and shoddy philosophies." Most of us have been too careless in accumulating our ideas. It would do us good to take more responsibility for our thinking and to be more selective in acquiring the ideas that will shape us and bear fruit as the garden of our life grows to maturity.

Good thoughts bear good fruit, bad thoughts bear
bad fruit — and man is his own gardener.
JAMES ALLEN

IDEALS

Ideals are like the stars. We never reach them but, like the mariners
on the sea, we chart our course by them.

CARL SHURZ

IDEALS ARE IDEAS OF A PARTICULAR KIND. They are ideas about
how we think things in the world *ought* to be — and how we *want*
them to be. They are, as Shurz suggests, the "stars" by which we navi-
gate: our principles, values, goals, standards, and aspirations.

Our ideals are very important, to say the least, and because they
are important, they should be protected. From time to time, it is wise
to reevaluate our ideals. Occasionally, we may need to change them or
improve them. But once we have determined what our ideals are, we
should refuse to give them up. Our ideals should never be for sale.

It's a hard world, and all of us face situations in which we are
tempted to sell out and compromise our ideals. But Charles R.
Swindoll was right when he said, "Character is always lost when a
high ideal is sacrificed on the altar of conformity and popularity."

But in addition to guarding our ideals, we need to follow them.
As our guiding "stars," they won't help us if we don't steer by them.
When we are making decisions, especially the big decisions in life, we
need to pay less attention to the difficulties of the immediate moment
and more attention to our ideals. "Never look down to test the ground
before taking your next step: only he who keeps his eye fixed on the
far horizon will find his right road" (Dag Hammarskjöld). So the
thoughts that guide us should be our *highest* thoughts.

If it's important to be mindful of our own ideals, then we should
pay attention to the ideals of others as well. Specifically, we need to
consider people's ideals when we are forming our judgments or assess-
ments of them. As Harold Nicolson said, "We are all inclined to judge
ourselves by our ideals, but others, by their acts." How much better it
would be if, when we are forming judgments of our friends and loved
ones, we took their ideals into account. They may have fallen short of
their ideals (just as we have fallen short of ours), but that which they
are *striving for* should count for something. The thing that matters is
not only where a person is right now but where they *desire* to go.

I love you for what you are, but I love you yet more for what you are going
to be. I love you not so much for your realities as for your ideals.

CARL SANDBURG

FRUGALITY

Frugality includes all the other virtues.
CICERO

FRUGALITY MAY NOT BE A WORD WE USE VERY OFTEN, BUT IT IS AN IMPORTANT WORD AND A GOOD WORD. To be "frugal" is to be economical in the way we use or spend our resources, especially our money. The frugal person is not stingy, but he is, in a prudent way, saving and sparing. Benjamin Franklin, who was known for traits like frugality, summed it up with this advice: "Make no expense but to do good to others or yourself — that is, waste nothing."

It would be possible, of course, to be too frugal. A "miser" is a person who is frugal to a fault; he has carried a good idea to a harmful extreme, having forgotten, perhaps, that our blessings are given to us to be used and enjoyed. Our blessings were not meant to be hoarded.

But not many of us have the problem of being too frugal. We tend more in the direction of wastefulness than miserliness, and so we could stand to be more frugal than we are right now. In the affluent countries where many of us live, there is such an abundance of everything, we are not as careful as we would be if life's necessities were more scarce. When there is a surplus of so many things, we tend to be wasteful, and we need to be reminded of the benefits of frugality.

Cicero said, "Men do not realize how great an income thrift is." At our places of work, most of us would like to get a "raise" more often than we do, but we could give ourselves a raise by being more frugal. It is true, as the saying goes, that "a penny saved is a penny earned." When we save more, we have more resources available when legitimate needs arise, just as if we had received an increase in pay. So being poor is no reason not to be frugal. Indeed, the less we are paid for our work, the more it "pays" us to eliminate wasteful spending.

Finally, we should be reminded that frugality is not opposed to generosity. In fact, it is frugality that opens the door to generosity and makes it possible for us to give to other people. If we wastefully spend everything that comes to us, then we won't have anything to give when the need arises. So one of the best arguments for frugality is that it provides us a fund of resources from which we may draw when the time comes to be generous to those in need.

Because of frugality, one is generous.
LAO TZU

LIBERTY

Those who expect to reap the blessings of freedom
must, like men, undergo the fatigue of supporting it.

THOMAS PAINE

A T THIS LATE DATE, IT IS HARD FOR US TO IMAGINE THE FIRES OF HOPE THAT BURNED IN THE HEARTS OF THOSE WHO FOUGHT FOR OUR LIBERTY AS A NATION. As Pearl S. Buck suggested, "None who have always been free can understand the terrible fascinating power of the hope of freedom to those who are not free." We can hardly identify with the motivation of a man like George Washington, whose birthday is today. But we need to be reminded of the qualities that made him one of the world's legendary liberators.

Service. You don't have to read very far into Washington's letters and private papers to see that he was deeply moved by the concept of service to his peers. Even after the Revolutionary War, when he dreamed of living in well-earned peace at Mount Vernon, his beloved home, he answered the call when his fellow citizens asked him to leave retirement and lead the new nation as its first president. For him, service was not a philosophical theory but an actual way of life.

Self-sacrifice. It is nearly miraculous that Washington was not killed on the battlefield. He fought alongside his men and shared their living conditions. Never do we see him taking thought for his own safety or comfort — for him, the common good had a higher priority. Here was a man who would put his life on the line for liberty.

Steadfastness. The Revolutionary War was not won overnight, and the infancy of the nation lasted a painfully long time. If Washington ever thought about giving up, he apparently said "no" to that thought. The liberties we enjoy were secured by leaders who knew how to stay the course. And today, steadfastness is no less vital to the preservation of our liberty than it was to its attainment in the first place.

Like most of the good things that come to us in this world, liberty is a trust, a stewardship. Its blessings come with duties attached to them, and we must discharge these duties faithfully. Doing so is not a burden; it's a privilege. So let's conduct ourselves in such a way that the work of men like Washington will not have been in vain.

A free man is as jealous of his responsibilities
as he is of his liberties.

CYRIL JAMES

PROGRESSIVENESS

There can be no progress if people have no faith in tomorrow.
JOHN F. KENNEDY

WITHOUT KNOWING YOU, I DON'T KNOW WHETHER "PRO-GRESSIVENESS" SOUNDS LIKE A POSITIVE WORD TO YOU OR NOT. These days, progressiveness means many different things, and not all of the meanings are good. But to simplify matters, let's consider "progressive" to be the opposite of "regressive." At your funeral, would you rather be described as having been a person who was progressive or one who was regressive? Most of us, I expect, would prefer a reputation for having been progressive and forward-looking.

Henry Ford once remarked that a "fever of newness has everywhere been confused with the spirit of progress." Unfortunately, some who consider themselves progressive are not really progressive; they just want change — change for the sake of change, whether it's actually needed or not. But obviously, change is not always progress. "Is it progress if a cannibal uses a fork and knife?" (Stanislaw Lec).

But sometimes change is, in fact, necessary in order to make progress, and moving forward can be frightening. It involves risk, and it takes courage. "All progress is precarious, and the solution of one problem brings us face to face with another problem" (Martin Luther King Jr.). The courage to make progress requires a certain amount of faith and hope. As Norman Cousins said, "Progress begins with the belief that what is necessary is possible." And as John F. Kennedy put it, "There can be no progress if people have no faith in tomorrow." True progress is made not by cynics but by optimists.

Of course, the best kind of progress is *personal progress* — the kind that starts on the inside of us and then moves outward. That's the kind of progressiveness that most of us need to work on. It is fine to lead others in the direction of positive change, but we can hardly do that if we're not making positive changes in our own character. So let's do that. Let's point ourselves forward and strive to do better tomorrow than we did today. Let's not stand still but rather make progress!

I find the great thing in this world is not so much where we stand,
as in what direction we are moving: to reach the port of heaven, we must
sail sometimes with the wind and sometimes against it — but we
must sail, and not drift, nor lie at anchor.
OLIVER WENDELL HOLMES SR.

CLOSURE

You do what you have to do to give people closure.
JOHN SCALZI

SOME PEOPLE ARE NOT BOTHERED BY "LOOSE ENDS" AS MUCH AS OTHERS, BUT ALL OF US, TO SOME EXTENT, FIND INCOMPLETENESS TO BE FRUSTRATING. We like to see unfinished business finished, and we prefer projects to be wrapped up rather than left hanging. In short, we see "closure" as a positive goal worth pursuing.

The fact that most people are this way is no coincidence. I believe that a desire or need for closure is deep within us. We live in a broken world where there is much incompleteness and many of our longings seem to go unfulfilled. Both in the small details of daily living and in the "big picture" of life, we sense that, somehow, things are not as they should be. And so we yearn for a perfection, a completeness that is not ours to enjoy at present. Sometimes our yearning for closure can be so deep that it is painful, but as Augustine of Hippo observed, "Anxiety has its use, stimulating us to seek with keener longing for that security where peace is complete and unassailable."

Of course, if we're looking for some golden age when all of the loose ends will be tied up and everything will be perfect, then we're looking for something that is not going to be found in this world. In the here and now, there is no such thing as complete closure, and we need to come to terms with that. As far as "life under the sun" is concerned, the writer of Ecclesiastes was exactly right: "What is crooked cannot be made straight, and what is lacking cannot be numbered."

Nevertheless, while we sojourn in this world there are specific projects that we can bring to completion, and while we have the opportunity, we should do so. We should finish as much of our work as we can. Not only that, but we need to serve those around us in such a way that we help them close the open loops in their own lives. As John Scalzi said, "You do what you have to do to give people closure."

To sum up, then, we need "initiative" (the ability to get things started) and also "finishiative" (the ability to complete what has been started). Getting started is obviously important, but without closure, many of our good deeds will be less good. "It is well thou hast begun, go on; it is the end that crowns us, not the fight" (Robert Herrick).

The virtue of deeds lies in completing them.
ARABIAN PROVERB

EDIFICATION

Why build these cities glorious
If man unbuilded goes?
In vain we build the world, unless
The builder also grows.

EDWIN MARKHAM

IN TODAY'S READING, WE ARE CONSIDERING AN OLDER WORD THAT HAS FALLEN OUT OF GENERAL USE, BUT ONE THAT STILL HAS SOME GOOD THINGS TO TEACH US. The word "edify" comes from a Latin verb meaning "to build." An "edifice" is a thing that has been "built," so we call it a "building." Figuratively, then, to edify is to "build up." When one person edifies another, he or she *strengthens* the other intellectually, morally, or spiritually. And surely, that's what we should want to do: build others up rather than tear them down.

Modern civilization has many impressive building projects to its credit. As far as physical buildings are concerned, we have excelled. But we have, perhaps, neglected the matter of personal building, the constructing of our citizens' inward character and integrity, and Edwin Markham was right to ask, "Why build these cities glorious / If man unbuilded goes?" Skyscrapers and sports arenas are of little importance if our civilization fails in the upbuilding of its *people.*

To build others up, we have to discipline ourselves for their sake. For example, I will be careful about my speech if my goal is to edify and uplift those around me. Rather than saying everything that is in my mind, I will limit my speech to words that are constructive. My inner thoughts may be truthful, but not every truth needs to be spoken — for the simple reason that not every truth *edifies.*

In the final analysis, it is love that produces edification. Paul the Apostle wrote that "knowledge puffs up, but love edifies" (First Corinthians 8:1). In other words, knowledge makes us proud, but love makes us helpful. When we are moved by real love, we will want nothing for those around us except that which will build them up. Indeed, those who have dealings with us should have the confidence that we will do nothing but strengthen them. When experience has taught them that we will refrain from any word or deed that will not be helpful to them, we will have given them one of life's greatest gifts.

Let each of us please his neighbor for his good, leading to edification.

PAUL THE APOSTLE

SERENITY

We are split personalities. We swear allegiance to one set of principles
and live by another. We extol self-control and practice self-indulgence.
We proclaim brotherhood and harbor prejudice. We laud character but strive
to climb to the top at any cost. We erect houses of worship, but our shrines
are our places of business and recreation. We are suffering from a distressing
cleavage between the truths we affirm and the values we live by. Our souls
are the battlegrounds for civil wars, but we are trying to live
serene lives in houses divided against themselves.

MELVIN WHEATLEY

TO BE SERENE IS TO BE "UNAFFECTED BY DISTURBANCE."
Words like "calm" and "unruffled" describe the person who is
serene, and calmness is surely an admirable thing. It's a more valuable
treasure than many of the things that we spend our time pursuing so
busily. "Serenity of mind and calmness of thought are a better enjoyment than anything outside of us" (Benjamin Whichcote).

But as Melvin Wheatley suggests in the quotation above, when
we aspire to serenity but live in "houses divided against themselves,"
we set ourselves up for disappointment. Even when we achieve a
measure of outward serenity, if there still remains a conflict between
"the truths we affirm" and the "values we live by," we find that we can't
enjoy the external tranquility that surrounds us. As long as we're at
odds with ourselves, we'll be at odds with everyone else, and until we
find peace within our own hearts, we won't find it elsewhere.

Yet the world around us is a distinctly unpeaceful place — disturbance and disruption seem to be the norm rather than the exception.
And even within ourselves, we find it hard to maintain serenity for
very long. Try as we may, our conduct sometimes falls below the standard set by our principles, and so our conscience is unsettled. In the
world as it now is, there is no avoiding conflict either within ourselves
or without. That being true, our confidence — and hence our serenity
— must be based on something other than our own efforts at self-
improvement or the ability of the human race to fix the brokenness of
the world. Science can be helpful, and so can self-improvement. But if
there is nothing more to help us than science and self-improvement,
then frankly, there can be none of the peace that we so deeply desire.

All men who live with any degree of serenity
live by some assurance of grace.

REINHOLD NIEBUHR

ROOTS

To be rooted is perhaps the most important and
least recognized need of the human soul.

S I M O N E W E I L

ALL OF US HAVE ROOTS, BUT NOT ALL OF US APPRECIATE
THEM. Behind us lie many antecedents and ancestors. When we
were born into the world, we were born into the midst of a unique set
of circumstances, and there were even older circumstances that preceded the ones that we were born into. But few of us have bothered
to learn about the people and the events that preceded us. And to the
extent that we do know about these things, we are often unapprecia-
tive of them — as if we would have preferred to have different roots.

But there is another way in which we use the word "roots," and
that is in reference to the depth of our character. When a person has
learned the enduring principles that have proven their value over
many centuries, we say that his or her character is solidly "rooted."
Compared to others, that person will be better able to withstand the
difficulties of life. So, in this sense, each of us needs to be putting
down new roots. We need to ground our character more deeply in the
lasting truths of life and, beyond that, in the eternal verities.

George Herbert said, "Storms make the oak grow deeper roots."
If we haven't already sunk our roots deeply into the soil of life, it may
be that some crisis will force us to do so. And if storms make us grow
deeper roots, then storms serve a useful purpose in our lives.

But if roots are important to us as adults, they are no less important to our children. In the often-remembered words of Hodding
Carter Jr., "There are two lasting bequests we can give our children.
One is roots. The other is wings." As parents, most of us work might-
ily to give our children "wings," and that is as it should be. It would
be well, however, if we also gave them "roots." Without roots, our
children will be cut off from their heritage, not knowing the people
who came before them in the chain of generations or the sequence
of events through which things came to be as they are now. The
"weather" of the world can be perilous, to say the least. So let's give
serious thought to our roots — and also the roots of our children.

The old that is strong does not wither,
Deep roots are not reached by the frost.

J. R. R. T O L K I E N

HONESTY

A commentary of the times is that the word *honesty*
is now preceded by *old-fashioned.*
LARRY WOLTERS

OF ALL THE VIRTUES DISCUSSED IN THIS BOOK, HONESTY IS
THE LEAST TRENDY. But despite being old-fashioned, honesty
is still one of the main components in the character of a moral person.

Honesty has to do with both our words and our deeds. When
most people think of honesty, they think only of those who tell the
truth: to speak honestly means that we never lie, mislead others, or
misrepresent the truth. But as important as it is to tell the truth, it
is no less important for us to "do" the truth. We must not only speak
truthful words, but our *actions* must be based on nothing but truth.
We must conduct ourselves in ways that are consistent with *true principles* — rather than erroneous concepts or false information.

Unfortunately, some people have given honesty a bad name
by using it as a cover for unkindness. Richard Needham was probably right when he said, "The man who is brutally honest enjoys the
brutality quite as much as the honesty. Possibly more." We should
work hard to rise above that kind of honesty. True honesty never uses
the truth as a blunt instrument to bludgeon others into submission to
our viewpoint. "The genius of communication is the ability to be both
totally honest and totally kind at the same time" (John Powell).

To be honest, we must first learn to be honest with *ourselves* —
and this requires an admission of our own frailties and foibles. When
we've learned to face the (sometimes painful) truth about ourselves,
we'll be in a much better position to deal honestly with others.

Some virtues are so high and exalted that they seem out of reach
to ordinary people, but honesty is within the reach of everybody. That
doesn't mean it's easy, for it can sometimes be very hard. But honesty is a choice that every person can make. And when we make the
choice to be honest in all of our dealings (both "telling" and "doing"
the truth), we place ourselves among the greatest people in the whole
world. If our friends and associates know us to be consistently honest,
what higher reputation could we aspire to than that?

I hope I shall always possess firmness and virtue enough to maintain what I
consider the most enviable of all titles, the character of an "Honest Man."
GEORGE WASHINGTON

MUSIC

I know only two tunes: one of them
is "Yankee Doodle," and the other is not.

ULYSSES S. GRANT

IS IT TOO MUCH OF A STRETCH TO THINK OF MUSIC AS A CHAR-
ACTER TRAIT? Well maybe, but who wouldn't feel complimented
if a friend said, "There's music in your eyes" or "You make me want to
sing" or "What you're saying is music to my ears"?

As a force and an influence in our lives, music is both powerful
and wonderfully varied. There are so many different kinds of music,
almost every person can find something to like, and within each type
of music, there is something for every time and mood. The ways in
which we respond emotionally to music are rich and complex. We can
be stirred to sorrowful tears or turned upside-down with laughter. We
can be encouraged and emboldened, or sobered and made more sensitive. Music can be celebratory or frivolous or enlightening or reverent.
It can both educate and entertain. It can lift us higher and keep us
going. All things considered, music packs a more powerful punch in
more different directions than anything it might be compared to. The
ability to make music is one of our highest human endowments.

If you'll think about it, you'll probably agree that the people you
find the most interesting — and the most refreshing — are those in
whose lives there is a lot of music. Those who, like Ulysses S. Grant,
"know only two tunes" may be people we respect, but we tend to think
of them as being a bit grim. On the other hand, those who've learned
to enjoy a wide variety of music seem to be lighter. They like to listen
to music as often as possible, and when they're not listening, they're
usually whistling or humming or singing. These "musical" folks are
undeniably fascinating. We usually find them easier to like.

It's a rare person whose life wouldn't be made better by the inclu-
sion of a little more music in it. Our mission in life may be quite serious, and we may be working our way toward the accomplishment of
some weighty goal, but most of us could still stand to lighten up now
and then. There's no worthwhile destination we can aim toward that
isn't reached better by those who have a song in their hearts.

Light quirks of music, broken and uneven,
Make the soul dance upon a jig to heaven.

ALEXANDER POPE

IDENTITY

You are, when all is done — just what you are.

JOHANN WOLFGANG VON GOETHE

WHAT WE ARE RIGHT NOW STANDS BETWEEN WHAT WE USED TO BE AND WHAT WE WILL BE. Our "identity" consists of the characteristics that we actually possess. It may change and be different tomorrow, but our identity is not what we ought to be or plan to be: *it is a description of the facts about us at the present moment.* In Goethe's words, "You are, when all is done — just what you are."

These days, many individuals, especially the young, are concerned about "finding themselves." This may or may not be a useful endeavor. If we're trying to learn self-honesty and gather objective information about the characteristics that we currently possess, that can be helpful. And if we're trying to decide what set of characteristics we want to have in the future, that kind of introspection and goal-setting can also be helpful. But if we imagine that there is some sort of "identity" floating around in space, just waiting for us to "find" it, then we are sadly mistaken. Good identities are not found; they have to be built.

Some of us have the problem of trying to have too many identities. Like the author who wants to write a book that *everybody* will enjoy, we try to please everybody with our identity. But this is futile. When we try to please everybody, we please nobody. That is the moral of the Aesop fable *The Bat, the Birds, and the Beasts:* "He that is neither one thing nor the other has no friends." None of the "animals" will appreciate us if we try to be every kind of animal all at once.

But obviously, we do need to know who and what we are. We need to be in touch with our true identity. As Djuna Barnes pointed out, "A strong sense of identity gives man an idea he can do no wrong; but too little accomplishes the same." If there is such a thing as too much concern for our identity, there is also such a thing as too little.

Yet many people spend too much time working on the *appearances* of their lives and too little on their *character.* Eager to be thought of in a particular way, we concentrate on projecting a certain image. But our character — that is, our real identity — is of far more consequence than our image. And, in fact, the most efficient way to acquire an acceptable image is simply to *be* what we wish to *appear* to be.

It matters not what you are thought to be, but what you are.

PUBLILIUS SYRUS

HELPFULNESS

Don't point a finger — hold out a helping hand.
ANONYMOUS

AS A CHARACTER TRAIT OR VIRTUE, HELPFULNESS IS ONE OF THE GREATEST. It is easy to aspire to but hard to acquire. We may, without much effort, learn how to be helpful in certain lesser ways, but becoming *skillful* at helping takes a lifetime of experience. So here are three suggestions for growth in our helpfulness:

Helping with humility. There is no worse helper than the person who thinks that he never needs any help with his own life. So to become effective helpers, we need to humble ourselves and realize our own neediness. The right to help others has to be earned, and one of the principal ways we earn it is by being willing to *receive* help.

Helping without humiliating. Some people will never let you pick up the check in a restaurant. They insist on being the giver every time, and one begins to suspect that some kind of power game is being played, in which you are expected always to play the subservient role. These people "help" with a help that is overwhelming and overpowering; it is not helpful so much as it is humiliating in its "generosity."

Helping with hopefulness. It is a tough world that we live in, and at times it is hard not to become cynical about whether it does any good to help others. Sometimes we give help with an attitude that says, "I know this help is going to be wasted on you, but I'm going to help you anyway," and the one being helped senses that we don't have any confidence in them. But we must discipline ourselves to rise above cynicism. Whether we can see the results or not, it always does good to do good, and love requires that we believe the best in people and interpret the facts in the best way that we possibly can.

As we've said, helpfulness is a trait that has to be learned; we get better at it as we go along. So we need to seize every opportunity to work on our helpfulness, and the fact is, we get many such opportunities every day. Unfortunately, we let many of these go by because we're waiting for some "big" opportunity to help someone. But the person who is not helpful in the little things is not going to be helpful in the big ones either. So let's work on our helpfulness *every chance we get.*

Great opportunities to help others seldom come,
but small ones surround us every day.
SALLY KOCH

INTEREST

We are raising a generation that has a woefully small stock
of ideas and interests and emotions. It must be amused at all costs,
but it has little skill in amusing itself. It pays some of its members to do
what the majority can no longer do for themselves. It is this inner
poverty that makes for the worst kind of boredom.

ROBERT J. MCCRACKEN

WHICH CONCEPT IS MORE APPEALING TO YOU: BEING "IN-TERESTING" OR BEING "INTERESTED"? Would you rather people find you interesting or you find life interesting? Most people, it seems, prefer the former: they want to be interesting to other people. But today, let's consider the value of being interested. Let's look at interest in the world around us as a good character trait.

As Robert J. McCracken points out, the trend today is toward hiring others to interest us. We call them "entertainers." There have always been entertainers, obviously, but think how many more there are today than ever before. Is this not an indication that we are less capable of entertaining ourselves? Has it come to the point where we have so little personal interest in the world around us that we have to employ professionals to interest, amuse, and entertain us?

There is much to be said for becoming an interested person, one who takes the initiative to be interested in what is around him. This is true even with respect to our work. As George C. Hubbs said, "You may know for a certainty that if your work is becoming uninteresting, so are you; for work is an inanimate thing and can be made lively and interesting only by injecting yourself into it. Your job is only as big as you are." And as it is with our work, so it is with life in general — interested people find the world to be a fascinating place.

So here is some old-fashioned advice: "To insure good health: eat lightly, breathe deeply, live moderately, cultivate cheerfulness, and maintain an interest in life" (William Louden). In the end, how interesting we find the world is determined by a fundamental choice that we make: the choice to go out and engage life inquisitively!

[I] ask myself what God is saying through that star that I am
looking at, through this friend who is speaking to me, through this
difficulty that is holding me up, or through this trouble that befalls me.
Once awake to this way of thinking, one discovers the true savor
of life. Everything becomes throbbing with interest.

PAUL TOURNIER

FORGIVENESS

When you forgive, you in no way change the past —
but you surely do change the future.
BERNARD MELTZER

FEW ABILITIES THAT WE POSSESS ARE ANY MORE POWERFUL THAN THE ABILITY TO FORGIVE. It is remarkably transformative in its power to do good for others, to change our own situation, and to open up doors that would otherwise remain closed. When we forgive someone who has wronged us, we create wonderful possibilities.

Forgiveness is not easy, even under the best of circumstances, but we sometimes make it harder than it has to be. We do this by thinking of forgiveness merely as an emotion. Finding it hard to *feel* a certain way about an adversary, we suppose that we can't forgive them. But forgiveness is a *choice*. It is a decision of the will, and it can be made even in the absence of forgiving feelings.

The best way to think of forgiveness is to think of it as canceling a debt. Henry Ward Beecher described it this way: "A forgiveness ought to be like a canceled note — torn in two and burned up, so that it can never be shown against the man." If you owe me money and I forgive the debt, that means the debt is canceled. You don't have to repay it. And similarly, if you have wronged me and I forgive you, then I am saying, "The debt is canceled. You owe me nothing. Rather than pursue payment, I am releasing you from the obligation."

Doing this, of course, requires the extension of mercy and grace. Whereas justice would demand full repayment of the debt, mercy rises above justice and forgoes the repayment. This is hard to do, as anyone who has ever tried it knows. But mercy becomes easier when we realize that no mercy will be shown to us if we have not been merciful to others. "He that demands mercy, and shows none, ruins the bridge over which he himself must pass" (Thomas Adams).

One thing is certain: if we make the choice not to forgive, we doom ourselves to an existence that can hardly be called "life." So we must decide to forgive. Having done so, resentments will creep back into our minds now and then, and the decision to forgive may have to be remade many times. This is hard work. But if we take the easy way out and wallow in bitterness, then we sell ourselves into bondage.

Life lived without forgiveness becomes a prison.
WILLIAM ARTHUR WARD

March 5
STUDY

If it's heads, I go to bed.
If it's tails, I stay up.
If it stands on its edge, I study.

ANONYMOUS

A S A WRITER, AND ONE WHO LIKES TO STUDY, IT'S HARD FOR ME TO UNDERSTAND THIS FACT: MOST PEOPLE DON'T ENJOY THE ACT OF STUDYING. I think I know some folks who would rather go to the dentist than sit down and study. So in today's reading, I am trying to be realistic and fair. Not everybody needs to be a scholar. But even so, "study" is a positive word, and I want to recommend it.

It is certainly true that some people spend too much time studying and not enough time working. In fact, study can sometimes be an evasion of work. No matter how hard he is studying, if the student should be doing something else, then by studying, he is just being lazy.

But few of us have that problem. We tend more in the direction of the opposite problem, that of too little study. Cicero, the Roman orator, once listed the "six mistakes of man." Mistake No. 5 was, he said, "neglecting the development and refinement of the mind, and not acquiring the habit of reading and study." There is simply no way around the fact that there are some important truths that need to be known by everybody, and we help ourselves greatly by studying to learn these truths. To neglect "the development and refinement of the mind" is to make a mistake that we will regret if we live very long.

Mao Tse-Tung was probably not far wrong when he said, "Complacency is the enemy of study." Most of the study that is done in the world is done by people who, in one way or another, are trying to change something. That being true, it may be that we don't study any more than we do because we are content with the way things are. If we saw study as a means to an end that was very important to us, then we would study to learn how the end or goal could be reached.

Usually, our study should be a means to a very personal end. We ought to study with a view to upgrading our own character and conduct. If we study to improve the world and give no thought to improving ourselves, there's a good chance that we're wasting our time.

Forasmuch as many people study more to have knowledge than to live well therefore ofttimes they err and bring forth little fruit or none.

THOMAS À KEMPIS

RESTORATION

Tired nature's sweet restorer, balmy sleep!

EDWARD YOUNG

MOST BIOLOGICAL ORGANISMS, INCLUDING OUR OWN BOD-IES, REQUIRE A CERTAIN AMOUNT OF REST. No machine can run indefinitely without any downtime for repair, and so it is with us: if *exhaustion* is not followed by *restoration,* trouble arises.

It is easy to see the need for physical restoration. Our bodies run down and have to be allowed to recharge. But other kinds of restoration are just as important, if not more so. For example, our minds will "wear out" if we don't allow them to rest on a regular basis. The same is true with our emotions and our spirits. When we feel "spent," we need to allow our inner resources to be refilled and replenished.

To say that people are busy these days is to say the obvious. And since we're busy doing things that we deem important, we may feel that we can't take time for restoration. But renewal and restoration aren't luxuries; they are essentials. If we neglect the restorative side of life, we destroy the very tools by which our work has to be done.

We give a great gift to those around us when we make restoration a priority in our own lives. When we wear ourselves out and never experience any refreshment, not only do we become tired ourselves, but we become tiresome to others. So doing what is necessary to replenish our bodies and spirits is not a selfish act; it has a refreshing effect on everyone who comes in contact with us.

Many of us are engaged in work that involves restoration in one way or another. In the world around us, everything tends to degrade, and so there is a constant need for restoration. Houses have to be repaired, and cars have to be fixed. Social problems have to be solved, and human institutions have to be revitalized. When you think about it, much of the activity of the human race is for the purpose of restoring something that has diminished or become dilapidated. But as important as it is to try to "make the world a better place," we miss the real value of restoration if we don't work on ourselves. We're fighting a losing battle if we're concerned with restoring the external world, yet we neglect the restoration of our own hearts and minds.

The problem of restoring to the world original and
eternal beauty is solved by the redemption of the soul.

RALPH WALDO EMERSON

ACCURACY

If I were to prescribe one process in the training of men which
is fundamental to success in any direction, it would be thoroughgoing
training in the habit of accurate observation. It is a habit which every
one of us should be seeking ever more to perfect.

EUGENE G. GRACE

THE LATIN VERB *CURARE* MEANT "TO CARE FOR." From it we
get several English words, such as "care," "cure," and "curator."
We also get the word "accurate," which literally means "done with
care." So if "accuracy" is one of our values, several things will happen:

(1) We will describe things accurately. An accurate statement is one
that conforms to fact. It is consistent with reality. It should be obvious, then, that our words should be as accurate as we can make them.
When we describe something we know or saw or experienced, the
report should be trustworthy. And when we relate something that
somebody else said or did, the report should be factual. Accuracy is
nothing more than simple, everyday *truthfulness.* Accurate people go
to great lengths not to pass on false information . . . about anything.

(2) We will adhere to worthy standards as closely as possible. At
the gas pump, if the meter says you bought 10.5 gallons, you expect
that reading to be accurate, that is, to conform to the governmental
standard of weights and measures that defines a gallon. But there
are many other standards that need to be adhered to, and the most
important are those that govern our relationships with other people.
Those around us need to know that our conduct toward them will be
accurate, in that it conforms closely to *the standards of morality.*

(3) We will be meticulous in our work. I once applied for a job that
involved some very detailed, precise work. In the interview, I was
asked how important accuracy was to me, and the questioner's tone of
voice clearly indicated that if I was not a meticulous person, I would
not be happy in this work. When it comes to being meticulous, some
people overdo it, obviously. But most of us would profit from an extra
dose of accuracy in what we do: *being more careful in our work.*

Basically, then, *accuracy* is a function of *honesty.* Both traits have
to do with *factualness* — and that is something we dare not neglect!

Accuracy is the twin brother of honesty;
inaccuracy is a near kin to falsehood.

NATHANIEL HAWTHORNE

SUPPORTIVENESS

We love those who know the worst of us and don't turn their faces away.
WALKER PERCY

NONE OF US CAN SAY THAT WE NEVER NEED TO BE SUP-PORTED. Lacking some necessity, we need to be helped. In danger of falling, sinking, or slipping, we need to be propped up. On the verge of weakening — or even failing — we need to be strengthened.

Out of all the people whom we love, those who have supported us may well be the easiest to love, especially if we are conscious of the grace that was involved in their support. As Walker Percy wrote, "We love those who know the worst of us and don't turn their faces away." Those who fought for us when we were under attack and unable to defend ourselves are unique friends. And those who supported us in the face of strong opposition, running a risk to stand with us when no one else was doing so, have a special place in our hearts. There is really no love quite like that of a supportee for a supporter.

Support runs in both directions, of course. Sometimes we need to receive support, but at other times we need to give it. And giving support engenders a special love also. In fact, as Eric Hoffer suggests, "We probably have a greater love for those we support than those who support us." This is partly why parents love their children so much.

We need to have the *character* to engage in support — both to receive it and to give it. It's obvious that giving support requires the virtue of generosity, but receiving support requires a particular virtue also: that of humility. If we have the generosity to help others but are too proud to let ourselves be helped, then our character is not yet fully formed. We must learn to acknowledge our own neediness.

But as givers of support, one of life's greatest mistakes is withholding our encouragement from people we dislike or disagree with. Yet if we never support anyone but our friends, we aren't doing anything more than the average criminal would do. Would it not be better to rise above this limited kind of support and learn to be encouraging, strengthening, and helpful to all those who come within our circle of influence — whether they see "eye to eye" with us or not?

> The real . . . is always checkered with failure, imperfection, and even wrong. So instead of biting and devouring one another, let's support individual freedom as we serve one another in love.
>
> CHARLES R. SWINDOLL

PLEASURE

> Life is to be enjoyed, not simply endured. Pleasure and
> goodness and joy support the pursuit of survival.
>
> WILLARD GAYLIN

WHAT IS YOUR BASIC ATTITUDE: DO YOU SEE LIFE AS SOMETHING TO BE ENDURED OR SOMETHING TO BE ENJOYED? Granted, there are some things that have to be endured, but the endurance of these doesn't mean there aren't some pleasures that can be enjoyed along the way. It comes down to a choice as to where we're going to place the emphasis: on the unpleasant side of life or on the pleasant? I am no hedonist (pleasure in this world is definitely not the *summum bonum,* the ultimate good), but even so, I want to recommend pleasure to you as a good thing that is to be appreciated.

Before we go any further, we should be reminded of one thing: *unprincipled* pleasure is not a good thing. We must not seek pleasure at any price, for whatever honest and honorable pleasures there are in the world, these must be enjoyed within the boundaries of justice, goodness, and rightness. Cicero said it well: "If you pursue good with labor, the labor passes away, but the good remains; if you pursue evil with pleasure, the pleasure passes away, but the evil remains."

Yet when it can be enjoyed rightly, pleasure should be . . . *enjoyed!* We err foolishly when we let the joyous aspects of life slip by untasted and unappreciated. But if some of us are guilty of this, others are guilty of seeking pleasure too deliberately. "Pleasure is seldom found where it is sought," wrote Samuel Johnson. "Our brightest blazes of gladness are kindled by unexpected sparks." And one other thing that would enhance our pleasure in life is to put more emphasis on the *giving* of pleasure. Pleasures given are often the most pleasant of all.

Søren Kierkegaard said, "Most men pursue pleasure with such breathless haste that they hurry past it." If there is one tendency we all share, it's the tendency to ignore the enjoyment of pleasure until something "big" comes along or until some idyllic period of perfect pleasure arrives. But if life is to be tasted with any joy at all, it must be tasted daily — in the unexpected and unplanned pleasures of home and hearth and honorable work. These pleasures are not unmixed with sorrow, but they are very real. And they were meant to be enjoyed.

> Think big thoughts but relish small pleasures.
>
> H. JACKSON BROWN JR.

METICULOUSNESS

Discipline is based on . . . meticulous attention to details.

GARY BLAIR

IF YOU CALLED A FRIEND "METICULOUS," THEY MIGHT TAKE IT AS A CRITICISM RATHER THAN A COMPLIMENT. The word just means that one has a "careful regard for details," but most people use it to mean pickiness or *excessive* regard for details. Yet meticulous can also mean *constructively* careful, and in all of the more important areas of life, we understand that carefulness is a positive trait. You may poke fun at a friend for being picky, but you probably don't want your architect, your accountant, or your anesthesiologist to have anything less than a "careful regard for details." Being meticulous is good, isn't it?

As Gary Blair points out, "Discipline is based on . . . meticulous attention to details." Granted some people spend so much time on details that they forget the purpose of what they are doing (they "can't see the forest for the trees"), but many others fail to achieve excellence in their activities because they are undisciplined in dealing with the details. It is well and good to contemplate the "big picture," but if we never get around to working carefully on the details, then the big picture is probably not going to be realized. Perhaps you had a grandfather who told you, "If you take care of the pennies, the dollars will take care of themselves." If so, your grandfather was right.

Some people shy away from being meticulous because they fear it will inhibit their freedom. They think that if the details are planned too specifically, they won't be able to be spontaneous. But genuinely meticulous people are not uptight and rigid. In fact, it is attention to detail that enables us to be truly free in our choices. For example, if I have planned a trip with some attention to detail, that planning will help me rather than hinder me. If I need to change plans spontaneously, I can do that more easily than the person who didn't do his homework. Almost always, meticulous people have more options!

Other people suppose that they're too busy doing "important" things to worry about details. But experience has probably taught most of us that we can't be negligent in the small matters of daily living and still shine when the big occasions come along. So the more important our goals are, the more it helps us to be meticulous.

He that would climb the tree must take care o' his grip.

SCOTTISH PROVERB

CANDOR

Candor is a compliment; it implies equality. It's how true friends talk.
PEGGY NOONAN

CANDOR REQUIRES A CERTAIN KIND OF COURAGE. To be frank and sincere in the expression of our thoughts is to risk rejection, and sometimes even retaliation. So we are sometimes less than candid in our communications. Nevertheless, when we open up our hearts and speak honestly, we honor those with whom we communicate in this way. As Peggy Noonan suggests, "It's how true friends talk."

We can't discuss candor, however, without remembering that caution is in order. As Wilhelm Stekel said, "Candor is always a double-edged sword; it may heal or it may separate." When wisdom tells us that being candid would do more harm than good, we ought to keep our silence. Just because a thing is true, that doesn't mean it should be verbalized. "Not every sheer truth is better for showing her face," wrote Pindar. "Silence also many times is the wisest thing for a man to have in his mind." Some truths are damaging while others are constructive, and those that merely do damage should be kept to ourselves.

Ideally, we should speak with both candor and courtesy, but doing this is very hard. Indeed, it is one of life's greatest challenges. Most of the time, we go overboard in one direction or the other. Either we speak unkindly and hurtfully in the name of "candor," or we fail to communicate things that really need to be communicated because we value "courtesy." I believe that it's possible to be both candid and courteous, but consistently doing this is beyond most of us. Even the very wise sometimes fail to get the balance right. All we can do is make the necessary adjustments when we see we've erred.

When we have the need or the desire to be candid with someone, it pays to make sure that what we have to say is really the *truth*. When a friend listens to us, thinking that we're being frank, and what we say turns out to be untrue, we have done them a great disservice. It is better not to be candid than to be candid about a falsehood!

But when it is honestly and compassionately practiced, candor has a cleansing, refreshing effect on our relationships. We spend so much time being superficial with one another, our relationships become dingy. But a little heart-to-heart candor makes them shine.

A frank talk is good soap for hearts.
ARABIAN PROVERB

WHOLESOMENESS

To meet the great tasks that are before us, we require all
our intelligence, and we must be sound and wholesome in mind.

ELWOOD HENDRICKS

WHOLESOMENESS HAS AS MUCH TO DO WITH THE MIND
AS WITH THE BODY. While things that are wholesome in a
physical sense are obviously important, our minds are no less in need
of wholesomeness than our bodies. Both physically and mentally, our
ability to function and deal with the challenges that come our way
depends on our state of health — and our state of health depends, to a
large extent, on our nourishment. It is foolish to think that we can in-
gest an unwholesome "diet" and our abilities not be affected. "Garbage
in, garbage out" is not only true of computers but of human beings.

But wholesomeness — especially mental wholesomeness — is not
a quality that modern people admire. If a person said that he wanted
to think only wholesome thoughts, he would brand himself as being a
small-town simpleton, out of touch with the coolness of pop culture.
It is regrettable, but we may as well face it: wholesomeness is not hip.

But think of what wholesomeness means. It means "healthfulness." Wholesome food, wholesome activities, and wholesome
thoughts are those that promote *well-being*. They are salutary and
conducive to soundness of mind and body. Open any dictionary
and look at the synonyms for "wholesome." You will see words like
"healthy," "hardy," "hale," "robust," and "vigorous." How can we think
of these as positive conditions and not be interested in wholesomeness? Faced with a choice between what's hip and what's healthy, why
does healthfulness have to be such an unappealing alternative?

At the risk of being written off as unsophisticated, I'm going to
come down firmly on the side of wholesomeness. Frankly, most of us
live in a culture that's awash in unhealthfulness. At every point on the
spectrum from physical to mental to spiritual healthfulness, we are
surrounded by unhealthful influences. To maintain our wholeness and
wellness, we must resist the junk — especially the mental junk. And
let me say it: *nowhere is this more important than in our homes.*

The home should be a self-contained shelter of security,
a kind of school where life's basic lessons are taught . . . a place where
wholesome recreations and simple pleasures are enjoyed.

BILLY GRAHAM

ANSWERS

Most of us ask for advice when we know
the answer but want a different one.

IVERN BALL

NOT EVERYBODY WHO ASKS US A QUESTION IS REALLY LOOK-
ING FOR AN ANSWER. In fact, as Ivern Ball suggests, people
who ask for advice are often running away from what they already
know is the true answer to their question. They are just looking for
someone who will give them another answer: one more to their liking.

But now and then, it does happen that someone will ask us an honest
question, and if we're able to give them a helpful answer, we experience one of life's most gratifying moments. It feels good to be helpful.

To be helpful, we don't need to have the answers to every question that might be asked. In fact, the most helpful people in the world
are those who have the humility to admit when they don't know the
answer to a question. "It is a sign of strength, not of weakness, to
admit that you don't know all the answers" (John P. Loughrene).

Usually, it's not the scholar, the expert, or the know-it-all who
is most helpful to us — it's the person who has lived with a healthy
sense of curiosity about life, the person who has kept his eyes and
ears open and thoughtfully observed what has happened around him.
Practical wisdom, the kind that is most often able to help people,
comes from actively and observantly living life to the fullest. So as the
years come and go, if we find that we've not become helpful to others,
it may be that we haven't been paying attention and life has slipped by
us. When we don't thoughtfully look and listen to what happens, we
don't learn anything that will help us or be useful to those around us.

If we've grown in wisdom, however, there is another problem that
we may face, and that is the problem of being wise for others but not
for ourselves. If we expect to be helpful to others, we had better be living by our own advice and not just telling others what they should do.

But finally, questions have a way of testing our integrity. There
is an old proverb that says, "He who asks questions cannot avoid the
answers." To ask a question is to place ourselves under this judgment:
what will we do about the answer when it is given to us? It is easy to ask
a question, but the answer often entails a serious responsibility.

Answer me this!
ANONYMOUS

PARTNERSHIP

Partnership is a synallagmatic and commutative participation in profits.
CIVIL CODE OF LOUISIANA, 1808

HAVE YOU EVER BEEN IN A "SYNALLAGMATIC" RELATIONSHIP WITH ANOTHER PERSON? Well, you probably have and just didn't know it. In civil law, a synallagmatic contract is one in which each party is obligated to provide something to the other party. The word comes from the Greek *synallagma* ("mutual agreement").

So what does this have to do with the concept of "partnership"? Just this: a partnership is a relationship in which two or more parties agree to work together "synallagmatically" — each helping the other in certain ways, so that a result is reached that is beneficial to all. And without a doubt, this idea is one of the most important ideas in history.

In business, it used to be that there was a hard line drawn between "partners" and "competitors." But nowadays, businesses are much more likely to see the benefits of partnership, even with companies that are competitors. It is not unusual now to hear of companies partnering on specific projects while still competing in other areas.

This trend is refreshing to me. And frankly, I wish that more of us could see the value of this approach in our personal lives. We tend to think only in terms of "allies" and "adversaries," and when we take an adversarial approach to anyone who seems to be in "competition" with us, we lose the advantages that come from the paradigm of partnership and mutual benefit. Granted, there are some non-negotiable areas in which we may find ourselves on opposite sides of a question. But wouldn't it help if we made an effort to see others as partners as much as possible and as competitors as little as possible?

The indisputable fact is this: *none of us is completely independent.* We need the help of others. We need partnerships in life. And we need to be people with whom others are delighted to partner.

What needs to be cultivated among men interested in social relationships whether as owner, manager or employee, producer or consumer, seller or buyer, partner or competitor, is self-control, refraining from unfair advantage, determination to give value as well as to take it; the appreciation that immediate gain is not the principal consideration; that one group cannot continue to profit at the expense of another without eventual loss to both; that all classes of men are mutually dependent on the services of each other; that the best service yields the greatest profit.

PRESTON S. ARKWRIGHT

WELFARE

> No society of nations, no people within a nation, no family can
> benefit through mutual aid unless good will exceeds ill will; unless the
> spirit of cooperation surpasses antagonism; unless we all see and act
> as though the other man's welfare determines our own welfare.
>
> HENRY FORD II

EVERYBODY WANTS TO "FARE WELL" IN LIFE, BUT NOT EV-
ERYBODY SEEKS THE "WELFARE" OF OTHERS. Yet these two
can hardly be separated. When it is "dog eat dog" and "every man for
himself," nobody fares well for very long. Unless people are willing to
seek each other's welfare, life degenerates into intolerable enmity. As
Henry Ford II points out, the spirit of cooperation must surpass that
of antagonism. We must understand that our welfare depends, to a
very great extent, on whether our neighbors are faring well.

Helping one another's needs. Relationships, organizations, and
communities thrive when people help people. If anybody has a need
that somebody else can help with, everybody benefits when that need
is taken care of. Certainly, we don't want to help people in ways that
enervate them or sap their initiative, for our purpose is to encourage
and to empower. But still, we need to help one another whenever we can.

Building opportunity for everybody. When privileged or powerful groups keep others from moving upward, they eventually destroy
themselves. But when everybody works for conditions of maximum
opportunity for every participant, the relationship itself prospers. Life
is not a zero-sum game. Your gain is not my loss — it's my gain too.

Advancing the common good. When we commit ourselves to the
welfare of those around us, certain sacrifices will be necessary. There
will be times when I'll need to exercise restraint and self-discipline
for the common good. If getting what I want for myself would not be
good for the group of which I'm a part, then I must restrain my will.

In the highest sense, it is love that moves us to seek the welfare
of those around us, and if our love does not move us in this direction,
we need to question what kind of love we have. And true love doesn't
work just for the benefit of friends — it labors for the benefit of all.
Whoever you may be, I can't love you and not desire your highest good.

> [Love] is rather a condition of the heart and will that causes us
> to seek the welfare of others — including people we don't particularly
> like, and even people who have done us harm.
>
> LOUIS CASSELS

LIVING

Excess on occasion is exhilarating. It prevents moderation
from acquiring the deadening effect of habit.

W. SOMERSET MAUGHAM

SOME PEOPLE ENGAGE IN THE ART OF LIVING, WHILE OTHERS
MERELY EXIST. To live, we must go out and meet life, experiencing it actively, deeply, and gratefully. We must taste the tang of life — in all of its sweetness and bitterness. But many of us are reluctant to do that. We adhere to our daily caloric intake even on Thanksgiving. We never stay up late or sleep in. We never splurge on a gift for a loved one. With unmitigated moderation, we simply . . . exist.

Since time immemorial, people have thought and written about "the art of living." It would be a step in the right direction if some of us would acknowledge that life is, indeed, an art rather than a science.

Sydney J. Harris said, "The art of living consists in knowing which impulses to obey and which must be made to obey." It takes wisdom to discern when we may follow our desires, but the "wisdom" that says our desires should *never* be followed is mere foolishness.

In a similar vein, Havelock Ellis said, "All the art of living lies in a mingling of letting go and holding on." In this broken world, many goodbyes have to be said. Yet while some good things are still ours to enjoy, we should not fail to hold on to them with heartfelt joy.

One thing is certain: whatever we are to make of life, it must be made *today* — and it must be made out of the *materials already at hand.* It does no good to postpone real living until later on or until we acquire some material possession or privilege that we think will make us happy. How we spend our days is how we spend our lives.

So are you living or just existing? If you're not living, I recommend that you start doing so. Decide to do more than take up space on the surface of the planet. Live it up! You will need to stay within the boundaries of morality and justice, of course, but within those limits, you shouldn't hesitate to "walk in the ways of your heart" (Book of Ecclesiastes). So grasp the cup of life with both hands, turn it up, and drain it to the dregs. You may still be in this world a long time from now or you may depart from it today. But whether your stay is long or short, while you're in this world, be truly *present* here.

Presence is more than just being there.

MALCOLM S. FORBES

March 17
OBEDIENCE

It is right that what is just should be obeyed.

BLAISE PASCAL

ONE OF LIFE'S MAJOR DECISIONS IS DECIDING WHETHER WE WILL ADOPT AN OBEDIENT ATTITUDE OR NOT. To obey means to "carry out a command, order, or instruction," and an obedient attitude would be one that is *willing* to do that. Such a disposition would mean that we are humble enough to take direction, and that we're willing to subordinate ourselves to someone who is in a position of authority over us. Willing to be compliant rather than resistant, we put self-will and stubbornness aside and work cooperatively with those whose job it is to lead us. Obedience, then, is the decision to *yield to authority* — not because it is easy but because it is right.

Great consequences flow from our decision concerning obedience. It's an unavoidable fact that many of the good things in life require a willingness to obey. "Justice is the insurance we have on our lives, and obedience is the premium we pay for it" (William Penn).

One clarification is certainly in order: we must never violate our conscience in order to obey someone else. Even if it is the highest law of the land, when we are instructed to do that which we believe is morally wrong, we must respectfully decline to obey and accept the consequences. "I was told to do it" is never an excuse for wrongdoing.

But barring the violation of our conscience, we should not refuse to obey those who occupy a position of authority over us. Nearly every important activity in life requires that someone be in authority. Without hierarchies and the authority that goes with them, life would soon collapse into chaos. So we need to see the usefulness and the goodness of legitimate authority — and we need to see that there's nothing dishonorable about adopting obedience as a basic attitude.

Hierarchy and authority can be carried too far, obviously, but that is a discussion for another day. Today, let's meditate on the value of rightful authority and rightful obedience. These are sometimes difficult concepts, but they are absolutely essential to the good life.

A man's true greatness lies in the consciousness of an
honest purpose in life, founded on a just estimate of himself and
everything else, on frequent self-examinations, and a steady
obedience to the rule which he knows to be right . . .

MARCUS AURELIUS

March 18
VERSATILITY

Time is a versatile performer. It flies, marches on,
heals all wounds, runs out and will tell.

FRANKLIN P. JONES

VERSATILITY HAS TO DO WITH "TURNING." The "verso" of a
piece of paper, for example, is the "reverse" side: you have to
"turn" the page over to see it. So a versatile person is one who is able
to "turn" in more than one direction. He or she can do a variety of
things competently and serve others in more than one capacity.

Usefulness is a worthy aim in life. Our relationships should be
more than serviceable and utilitarian, of course, but they should certainly not be any less. It's a simple fact that there is work to be done
in the world, and we need to equip ourselves to do some of it. We are
not merely passengers or consumers of that which others produce —
we are responsible for doing a certain amount of the work ourselves.

If you've ventured out into the world lately, you will have noticed
that there is a complex array of *different* things that need to be done.
The world is not a simple place anymore, if it ever was. The needs
that have to be filled and the problems that have to be solved are
extremely varied. And even in our own individual lives, the issues that
challenge us are demanding in many different directions. So we have
to be able to "turn." To live effectively, we have to be versatile.

But more important, if we want to help others with their needs,
we're going to need some versatility. Life is not about selfish indulgence; it's about service, and the more varied our capabilities are, the
more kinds of service we can render. Yes, we do need to specialize, but
there is no reason we can't have more than one specialty!

Last, but not least, when we acquire a healthy measure of versatility, we make ourselves more interesting to our friends and loved
ones. And we should *want* to be interesting and enjoyable to others
— not for our sake but for theirs. We should want to offer ourselves
as individuals who are not "flat" but have some "texture" to our lives:
some variation and some variety. When we work on our versatility, we
give a pleasant gift to those who have to deal with us from day to day.

A man so various, that he seem'd to be
Not one, but all mankind's epitome;
. . . in the course of one revolving moon,
Was chemist, fiddler, statesman, and buffoon.

JOHN DRYDEN

PURPOSE

Man can endure almost any suffering if he can see a purpose or meaning in it.
Conversely, he will be miserable even amidst great luxury if he cannot relate
his life to some larger context which makes it meaningful.

VIKTOR E. FRANKL

THERE IS AN IMPORTANT SENSE IN WHICH OUR SURVIVAL DEPENDS ON OUR PURPOSE. Viktor E. Frankl, a survivor of the Nazi concentration camps and the author of *Man's Search for Meaning*, wrote powerfully about this matter. He learned firsthand what is obvious to any of us if we think about it seriously: we can deal with any set of external circumstances if we have inside of us a strong sense of purpose. Seeing a meaning to our existence in this world and living in the direction of an all-important goal is not just nice — it is crucial.

But it's not just crucial to our survival; it's crucial to our enjoyment. As Frankl put it, a person will be "miserable even amidst great luxury if he cannot relate his life to some larger context which makes it meaningful." Henry J. Golding said it this way: "What our deepest self craves is not mere enjoyment, but some supreme purpose that will enlist all our powers and will give unity and direction to our life. We can never know the profoundest joy without a conviction that our life is significant." If we're not living for some purpose that is meaningful to us, then even the highest joys will become tiresome.

People who know about achievement and success will tell you quickly that excellence requires tenacity in the pursuit of a purpose. Billy Sunday, who was a professional baseball player before he become an evangelist, was right when he said, "More people fail through lack of purpose than through lack of talent." To get to any place worth going to, we have to visualize our purpose and then pursue it tenaciously.

But pursuing our purpose tenaciously requires that our purpose be extremely important, and so I want to recommend something to you. You need to have a purpose that is of such all-encompassing importance that you would give up anything and everything for it, even your life. This old world is full of tradeoffs and exchanges, and "purpose" presents us with the biggest of them. So my wish for you is simply this: *I hope that you will have a purpose for living that is so valuable that you will spend everything else in order to attain it.*

The only true happiness comes from squandering ourselves for a purpose.
JOHN MASON BROWN

March 20
SINCERITY

Sincerity and competence is a strong combination.
PEGGY NOONAN

IT IS HARD TO HOLD BACK A PERSON WHO IS BOTH SINCERE AND SKILLFUL. One of these qualities without the other may not be very effective, but when a person does what they do "from the heart" and they have also acquired a good deal of know-how and experience, then the results are often nearly incredible.

But if being sincere is dynamic, being insincere is draining. It takes considerable effort to pretend to be something that we're not, and the exertion of that effort usually leaves us with little energy for anything more constructive. As Anne Morrow Lindbergh once remarked, "The most exhausting thing in life is being insincere."

In a world where "image" has become so important, we are surrounded by insincerity. From a practical standpoint, we need to be able to recognize real sincerity when we see it, but it is an interesting fact that "the sincere alone can recognize sincerity" (Thomas Carlyle). Just as the honest are the best at detecting honesty in others, the sincere are the best at detecting sincerity. It's not easy to pass off a fake or a counterfeit to someone who is familiar with the real thing.

The main thing in life is not to prey upon people but to render them service. And sincerity is the key to service. If we want to help those around us in significant ways, we must offer them something that money cannot buy: genuineness. Actually being what we appear to be is such a simple thing, but it is often overlooked when we're being taught how to make a contribution to the world. It is the key, however, to service. It alone opens the door to a beneficial life.

If we're not sincere, we will find, in the long run, that it's futile to try to influence other people. In the short run, you may use personality and communication techniques to sway people, but sooner or later the real "you" is going to surface. And long before then, those whom you try to influence will probably sense that you are not the real deal, and they will not give you the privilege of impacting them at the deepest level. To influence people where it really counts, we have to be utterly sincere. There is simply no shortcut to someone else's heart.

What is uttered from the heart alone
Will win the hearts of others to your own.
JOHANN WOLFGANG VON GOETHE

RESURRECTION

Wag the world how it will,
Leaves must be green in Spring.
HERMAN MELVILLE

NEW LIFE! With the arrival of springtime, we're surrounded by renewal and the reappearance of life. What has been drab now bursts into color. What seemed to be dead now reasserts itself with greenery and new growth. The warming days invite us to come outdoors and shake off the sleepiness of winter. The world is being reborn once again, and it's time to stretch ourselves and bring to life the plans we made during winter's hibernation by the fireside.

It would take a person with a somewhat unusual outlook not to look forward to spring. Most folks are just naturally drawn to it. We may disagree in our preferences for summer or winter, but I don't recall hearing many people complain about spring. It's the easiest of the seasons to enjoy. And isn't that because it's the season of rejuvenation and new life? Summer is the time of growth, fall is the time of reaping, and winter is the time of reflection — but spring is the time of resurrection! Spring points us *forward*. It holds out the promise that in the months ahead we can be more fully alive than we've ever been before!

It's a good thing that spring comes "wag the world how it will," as Melville put it. The years that we need springtime the most are probably the years that it wouldn't come, if it were up to us. But we can be thankful that as long as we live and the earth continues to orbit the sun, spring will always give us a chance to make a fresh start.

Most of the renewal that we see this time of year is more or less automatic. Maple trees don't have to think about whether to put forth fresh leaves this spring. Birds, newly arrived from the south, don't have to decide whether to build nests and lay eggs again this year. But for us, the experience of new life is usually a choice. We have the ability to be renewed at a deeper level than any of the creatures around us, but we also have to exercise a greater degree of volition. Without a conscious choice to grow, our lives tend to decline. If we don't decide to be refreshed, we won't be. So while the sap is rising in the world of nature, it's a good time to make some thoughtful commitments of our own. This spring, in what ways shall we be "new"?

I'll turn over a new leaf.
MIGUEL DE CERVANTES

March 22

ACCESSIBILITY

You never know till you try to reach them how accessible men are;
but you must approach each man by the right door.
HENRY WARD BEECHER

SOME PEOPLE WILL GIVE US ACCESS TO THEIR HEARTS AND MINDS MORE READILY THAN OTHERS. By their personality, some are less inclined to be accessible than others, while others deliberately put up their guard in order to keep anyone from influencing them. Assuming that our motives are honorable and that we have something to communicate that would be worthwhile for others to receive, it takes wisdom to know the right "door" by which each individual may be approached. A particular approach may succeed with some and fail with others. Gaining helpful access to others' thinking is one of the fascinating challenges of human communication.

But perhaps we should be less concerned about whether others are accessible to us and more about whether we are accessible to them. It's easy to criticize another person for being unapproachable, but if we're not careful, we may be guilty of the very same thing.

Consider two important qualities we will have if we are accessible:

Communicative. When we've learned to be accessible, we will welcome communication with our fellow human beings rather than run away from it. One dictionary defines "accessible" as "easy to talk to or get along with; friendly." Those are, I suggest, admirable qualities.

Influenceable. Another meaning of "accessible" is "receptive, responsive, able to be persuaded," and those are admirable qualities too. Granted, we need to be careful what ideas we allow to become fixtures in our minds, but if we are resistant and unwilling to be influenced at all, then we've cut ourselves off from the good influences as well as the bad ones. People whom others can't influence are people who don't grow.

So I want to be accessible. If someone needs to say something to me, I don't want them to be afraid to approach me and say it!

Do not be inaccessible. None is so perfect that he does not need at times the advice of others . . . Even the most surpassing intellect should find a place for friendly counsel. Sovereignty itself must learn to lean. There are some that are incorrigible simply because they are inaccessible: they fall to ruin because none dares to extricate them. The highest should have the door open for friendship; it may prove the gate of help. A friend must be free to advise, and even to upbraid, without feeling embarrassed.
BALTASAR GRACIÁN

MANAGEMENT

Lots of folks confuse bad management with destiny.

KIN HUBBARD

MOST OF THE POSSESSIONS, ABILITIES, AND OPPORTUNITIES THAT ARE AVAILABLE TO US CAN BE CONSIDERED AS "RE-SOURCES." These things are the "raw materials" with which we work as we seek to be productive, contributing members of society. But resources, even when they are abundant, have to be managed carefully. That is, good stewardship has to be exercised so that the resources are not wasted but used to accomplish their intended purpose.

It often happens that people blame fate or destiny for their less-than-desirable circumstances when, in reality, their circumstances would be different if they had managed their resources differently. That is not to say that there aren't some circumstances beyond our control, for there surely are many of those. But even so, most of us would have to say that our lives would be very different today if we had more carefully managed the resources that *were* under our control.

Management is not easy, of course, and it's easy to excuse our failings by complaining that we just don't have any talent in that area. Some people do seem to have a knack for good management, but for the most part, management consists of skills that anyone can learn. Whether it's managing our finances, our time, our relationships, or anything else, we can profit from the wisdom of other managers in learning how to be better stewards of our own resources. We can't be perfect managers, but most of us could easily find ways to improve — and continuous improvement is a major part of good management.

The more limited our resources, the more important it is to manage them well. And let's face it: all of our resources in this world are limited. We don't have an infinite supply of any of them. So it behooves us to get every ounce of good out of them that we can.

But if it's hard to manage our "external" resources, it's even harder to manage the "internal" ones. Our thoughts and our habits have to be managed just as surely as our money and our time. But the level of difficulty here is much higher. Out of any one hundred "external" managers, there might be only one or two who are good at "internal" management. But if the difficulty is greater, so are the rewards.

The most difficult thing we have to manage is self.

HANNAH WHITALL SMITH

CONNECTIONS

> The family the soul wants is a felt network of relationship,
> an evocation of a certain kind of interconnection that
> grounds, roots, and nestles.
>
> THOMAS MOORE

MODERN LIFE CROWDS US INTO CITIES WHERE WE HAVE PHYSICAL PROXIMITY TO MILLIONS OF OTHER HUMAN BEINGS, BUT VERY LITTLE REAL CONNECTION TO ANY OF THEM. Our longing for ties to others is just as deep as ever, but we seem to be losing the ability, or perhaps just the opportunity, to make those ties.

You don't have to have lived in the world very long to know that connections can sometimes be painful. We're surrounded by people who're just as imperfect as we are, and our connections to them will, at least some of the time, involve some discomfort. But even so, we're better off being connected than disconnected. If there's a price to be paid for relationship and involvement, it's a price worth paying.

It is hard, of course, to maintain the right balance between "individuality" and "community." Both in our own lives and the life of society as a whole, we see the pendulum constantly swinging. After a period of over-emphasis on the individual, there is usually a swing toward the groups of which the individual is a member. Then, when that has gone too far, the pendulum swings back in the other direction. Life would probably be a dull affair if every important thing were emphasized equally all the time. But even so, we probably do need to strive for a little more balance in our lives. We need to be careful not to become so involved with our individual concerns that we neglect the connections through which we can show love and render service.

Most of us, from time to time, need a little humility added to our mindset. Whatever we think we're achieving in this world, our work should be seen within the context of something much larger than our own endeavors. We're not alone. We live in a world of other people. And if we'll do right toward our connections, our part in the human story, however small, will be a much more interesting part.

> Nothing worth doing is completed in our lifetimes; therefore, we
> must be saved by hope. Nothing true or beautiful or good makes complete
> sense in any immediate context of history; therefore, we must be saved by
> faith. Nothing we do, however virtuous, can be accomplished
> alone; therefore, we are saved by love.
>
> REINHOLD NIEBUHR

CHASTITY

> There is no getting away from it: the old Christian rule is "Either marriage,
> with complete faithfulness to your partner, or else total abstinence." Chastity
> is the most unpopular of our Christian virtues.
>
> C. S. LEWIS

I DO NOT BELIEVE C. S. LEWIS WAS EXAGGERATING. Chastity is indeed the most "unpopular" of the virtues — and if it was unpopular in Lewis's day, it is much more so today. This is somewhat ironic, as Rosalie de Rosset observed: "There is little praise for the consistently sexually controlled single. Too often, it is mixed with granulated pity or powdered condescension. Ironically, while discipline and self-control are encouraged and admired in scholarship, athletics, music, and ministry, their absence is strangely excused in sexual matters."

The basic meaning of chastity is "purity," but we use the word in various ways. Most people think of chastity as virginity or abstinence from sexual intercourse before marriage. But it can also refer to celibacy, the choice to remain unmarried and forgo sexual intercourse altogether. And finally, chastity can mean virtuous character in general.

In all three of these meanings, the idea of purity is prominent. But let's be careful. The impure thing that chastity abstains from is not sexual intercourse, but rather sexual intercourse with anyone other than the mate that one is rightfully married to at the present time. Chastity is about protecting the *boundaries* of sexual pleasure.

This principle is important not only for single people but also for married ones. Chastity, or purity, for single people means waiting until marriage, and for those who are married it means not violating the exclusiveness of the relationship. Sexual purity is important for every person in the world, whether married or unmarried. And chastity does not only have to do with physical actions — if we are to be chaste, purity of thought and motive must also be maintained.

Contrary to popular opinion, the argument in favor of chastity is not based on a low view of sex. Indeed, it is based on the highest view possible. It is not a denigration of sex to say that its purity should be protected; it is a concern to protect the "walls" that surround this, the most beautiful pleasure garden that a mortal being is capable of entering.

> There is a tendency to think of sex as something degrading;
> it is not, it is magnificent, an enormous privilege, but because of that
> the rules are tremendously strict and severe.
>
> FRANCIS DEVAS

SACRIFICE

> I believe that the rendering of useful service is the common duty of mankind
> and that only in the purifying fire of sacrifice is the dross of selfishness
> consumed and the greatness of the human soul set free.
>
> JOHN D. ROCKEFELLER JR.

SELF-CENTEREDNESS, THE PROMOTION OF OUR OWN INTER-
ESTS AT ALL COSTS, IS THE WORST MISTAKE WE CAN MAKE.
And it is an exceedingly hard problem to eradicate. Rockefeller was
right: the only thing that can get rid of it is "the purifying fire of sacrifice." We will not learn — indeed we cannot learn — how to serve
the needs of others until we have learned the art of letting go.

For our purposes, let me define "sacrifice" in this way: when we
sacrifice something, we give up one thing of great value for something
that is of even greater value. It is not uncommon, for example, to hear
of individuals who have been trapped in an accident and have severed
an arm or a leg to free themselves. Surely, an arm or a leg is of great
value. But one's life is of even greater value, and faced with the choice,
most of us would sacrifice a limb in order to save our life.

Obviously, we need to be more disciplined when it comes to giving up the lesser things for the greater. We need both the *wisdom* to
properly evaluate things (both seen and unseen, present and future),
and the *strength* to sacrifice the minor treasures for the major ones.

But even more important, we need to learn the difficult habit of
self-sacrifice. We must be able to let go of what we want for ourselves
in order to serve other people, seeing their needs as having a higher
value than our own. And we must learn to make *costly* sacrifices for
others, letting go of things that we desperately need and can hardly
do without, so that others will have what they need. "He who gives
what he would as readily throw away, gives without generosity; for the
essence of generosity is in self-sacrifice" (Sir Henry Taylor).

But if we give up what we highly value and desperately need,
don't we doom ourselves to impoverishment? No, we don't. If there is
something in this world that has such a hold on us that we could not
bring ourselves to part with it, then we do not own it — it owns us.
As C. S. Lewis aptly put it, "Nothing that you have not given away
will ever really be yours." It is, indeed, more blessed to give than to receive.

> That which one sacrifices is never lost.
>
> GERMAN PROVERB

ATTENTIVENESS

Skillful listening is the best remedy for loneliness,
loquaciousness, and laryngitis.
WILLIAM ARTHUR WARD

MANY PEOPLE LISTEN WHEN OTHERS SPEAK, BUT NOT MANY LISTEN SKILLFULLY — OR ATTENTIVELY. The sounds of others' words may enter our ears, but we may not concentrate on them or make any effort to exclude other thoughts while we listen. If we are attentive to what others say to us, the *purity* of our attention is often lacking. But when we fail in our attentiveness to others, look at the benefits that we lose. Skillful listening really is, as Ward humorously suggests, the best cure for "loneliness, loquaciousness, and laryngitis."

But attending to the words of others is only a species of attentiveness in general. Not only do we need to pay attention to what others say, but we need to pay attention to life. Life in this world is too precious — and too full of joy — to let it flow past us unobserved, unenjoyed, and unappreciated. Our attention must be selective, of course, for not everything in the world deserves being focused upon, but there are many fascinating things that are worthy of our concentration, and we need to learn the habit of attending to these things.

Memory experts tell us that memory is a function of attentiveness: we remember longest the things we pay the most careful attention to. In my experience, I have found this to be only partially true. To remember something, we have to do more than pay attention; we have to pay attention with *interest*. I agree with Tryon Edwards, who said, "The secret of a good memory is attention, and attention to a subject depends upon our interest in it. We rarely forget that which has made a deep impression on our minds." So to remember someone's name, you're going to have to be genuinely interested in them!

One meaning of "attentive" is "marked by devoted attention to the pleasure or comfort of others" (*American Heritage Dictionary*). In the end, that's why attentiveness is so important. It gets us out of ourselves and our own little world. It connects us to the larger reality that we're a part of and opens our hearts to active, other-centered love.

Pleasure-seeking is a barren business; happiness is never found
till we have the grace to stop looking for it, and to give our attention
to persons and matters external to ourselves.
J. I. PACKER

DEFINITIONS

A definition is that which so describes its object
as to distinguish it from all others.
EDGAR ALLAN POE

IF A WORD OR A CONCEPT IS "ILL-DEFINED," THAT IS MORE OF A PROBLEM THAN YOU MIGHT THINK. To be "finite" is to have limits or boundaries, and so to "define" something is to describe its limits. As Poe put it, a definition "describes its object as to distinguish it from all others." When we define a word, we, in effect, show how it is unique: we specify the semantic territory the word can cover and show how that territory is different from that covered by other words. By describing its limits, then, we show what makes it special.

Now think with me for a moment. Is it not a fact that our communications with one another suffer from a lack of "definition"? By failing to think carefully and specifically, don't we tend to convey vague meanings, those that have no definite limits but are fuzzy and foggy instead? I believe we do. I had a very helpful editor years ago who used to say, "Gary, unclear writing is almost always the result of unclear thinking. You can't write clearly if your thoughts are not sharply defined in your own mind." This is advice that we can all profit from. We can improve our communications by clarifying (or "defining") our thoughts before we verbalize them to other people.

But many of us make a worse mistake: the lives that we lead are ill-defined. Wanting to be all things to all people, we have not defined the limits of our principles and values. And not having decided to be any specific kind of person, distinct from all others, we drift through life. Maybe we're afraid to accept any precise set of characteristics because we're afraid this will restrict our usefulness, but in the real world, just the opposite is true. A tool that "does everything" will never be as useful as one that is more sharply defined in its characteristics.

To sum up, then, it is no small thing to be able to think and speak rationally. Thought and communication are among our highest endowments — and they should be used carefully. So when we speak, let's communicate clearly defined thoughts. And when we act, let's act as people who know exactly what we are — and also what we are not.

The light of human minds is perspicuous words, but by exact
definitions first snuffed, and purged from ambiguity.
THOMAS HOBBES

STRENGTH

Things will probably come out all right,
but sometimes it takes strong nerves just to watch.
HEDLEY DONOVAN

LIFE IN THIS OLD WORLD IS A CRAZY MIXTURE OF DELIGHT AND DIFFICULTY. Some days are easier than others, of course, but on most days the delight is so mixed with difficulty that the result can be intimidating. Sometimes it takes strong nerves just to watch!

Clearly, "strength" is something that all of us need. But like physical strength, inner character is not easily obtained. "It takes courage to live — courage and strength and hope and humor. And courage and strength and hope and humor have to be bought and paid for with pain and work and prayers and tears" (Jerome P. Fleishman). We need not expect to grow strong if we take the course of least resistance.

Acquiring strength is a gradual process, and so is losing strength. If we're doing the things each day to build strength, we probably won't see the results until later. And similarly, if we're defaulting on life's responsibilities, growing weaker each day by taking the easy way out, we probably won't see the results of that until later, either. But eventually we will meet some great test of our character, and when that time comes, it will be plain whether we've grown strong or not. As B. F. Westcott wrote, "Great occasions do not make heroes or cowards; they simply unveil them to the eyes of men. Silently and imperceptibly, as we wake or sleep, we grow strong or we grow weak, and at last some crisis shows us what we have become."

So right now, we need to be very honest about both our strengths and weaknesses. We need to appraise accurately the points at which we've gained some strength, and we need to identify carefully the areas in which we're weak. Most of all, we need to make sure we don't mistake our weaknesses for strengths, which is what many people do.

Finally, gaining strength requires two things that we're reluctant to do: looking "upward" and looking "outward." Looking upward means placing our faith in the unseen things, the eternal verities, and looking outward means doing what is right toward those around us.

For strength to bear is found in duty alone,
And he is blessed who learns to make
The joy of others cure his own heartache.
M. V. DRAKE

ENTHUSIASM

Give me a man who sings at his work.

THOMAS CARLYLE

IT'S SIMPLY A FACT THAT THOSE WHO ARE ENTHUSIASTIC DO BETTER WORK THAN THOSE WHO ARE NOT. A mediocre attitude produces mediocre workmanship. If we're not feeling well and we make an effort to go ahead and do what needs to be done, that's honorable. Necessary work done unenthusiastically is preferable to defaulting on our duties. But often, the problem is not that we don't feel well or that we're having a bad day; it's that our *attitude* has gotten out of line. In that situation, we can make the choice to ratchet our enthusiasm up a notch or two. We can recall the real reasons why we do our work and put more of our heart into our undertakings.

As everybody knows, enthusiasm is contagious. Those who live with enthusiasm have an energizing effect on the people who come in contact with them. What we may not recognize, however, is that the opposite is also true. When we slog through our days as if we couldn't care less what happens, that also has an effect on others — and it's not one we're going to feel good about as we look back on our lives.

It's time we took personal responsibility for the degree of enthusiasm we've been living with. If we've been less than grateful for life and that's been showing up in a less-than-enthusiastic manner of living, it doesn't do much good to blame it on our external circumstances. Circumstances certainly do have an impact on our enthusiasm, but the more important question is what we do with our circumstances. We can choose to respond with more eagerness and interest, rather than less. Our choice can make a significant difference.

Our family, friends, and coworkers deserve the best that we can give them. Indeed, life itself deserves our best. Nothing less than an enthusiastic approach will produce the quality of life that a human being is capable of. There comes a time when we simply have to step up to the issue and decide what kind of people we're going to be. We have the freedom of our will, and we've been blessed with an abundance of raw materials to work with. It comes down to the question of whether we're going to go "all out" to achieve excellent results or be content with the meager products of lazy, lackluster living.

Do it big or stay in bed.

LARRY KELLY

COMMENDATION

Whenever you commend, add your reasons for doing so;
it is this which distinguishes the approbation of a man of sense
from the flattery of sycophants and admiration of fools.
RICHARD STEELE

I ONCE KNEW A MAN WHO SAID HE WAS ALWAYS SUSPICIOUS OF ANY COMPLIMENT BECAUSE HE NEVER KNEW WHAT THE GIVER'S MOTIVE MIGHT BE. It's a fact that those who commend us sometimes have ulterior motives, but surely we can rise above suspicion long enough to appreciate — and give — genuine commendation. Commendation is one of the most refreshing things in life, and it's one of the most powerful gifts that we can give to others.

As Richard Steele pointed out, the best kind of commendation is usually that which has reasons attached to it. As a writer and speaker, I can tell you without hesitation that the compliments that have meant the most to me over the years are not the vague, generic remarks like "Good article" or "Good talk," but the specific ones in which somebody told me exactly what they liked or benefited from.

That said, even very general commendation is sometimes a great gift. Years ago, a friend called me one day ("out of the blue," as the saying goes) and simply said, "I was thinking about you and wanted you to know that I appreciate you for being the person that you are." That's about as general as a commendation could be, but coming from that particular person, it meant a great deal to me, and it still does.

But as we've already suggested, to avoid the perception of flattery, our commendation of others must be sincere. When we praise another person, we must be absolutely sure (a) that we mean what we say, and (b) that we're not saying it merely to get "points" for having said it.

In general, most of us are too quick to criticize and too slow to commend. And worse, we tend to criticize in public, letting as many people as possible know everything we're dissatisfied with, but we keep our commendations private. In other words, we are more vocal about our displeasures than about our delights. But shouldn't the proportion be reversed? If we have to criticize, shouldn't we keep that as private as possible? And when we have the opportunity to commend someone, shouldn't that be the "news" that we want to publicize?

Reprove thy friend privately; commend him publicly.
SOLON

PLAYFULNESS

It is a happy talent to know how to play.
RALPH WALDO EMERSON

PLAYFULNESS MAY NOT BE ONE OF THE CARDINAL VIRTUES THAT WE NEED TO STRIVE FOR, BUT IT'S STILL SOMETHING WE NEED TO PAY ATTENTION TO. It's a part of good character, and those who know only how to work and not how to play are not only missing out on much of the joy of life; they're missing one of the qualities that enable us to make a contribution to the lives of others.

Traditionally, this date on the calendar is marked as a day when we give a little freer rein to the playful spirit than we do at other times. Personally, I think it says something good about our civilization that we have such a day. It says that we understand the need for some lightheartedness and laughter — and even a little mischief!

How will you respond today if someone plays you for an "April Fool"? I hope it won't be with irritation or impatience. I hope you won't look down on the "immaturity" of the jokers. I hope, instead, that you'll laugh with those who're having an innocent laugh at your expense. A moderate application of embarrassment is good for us now and then, because it breaks up the ruts that we tend to fall into. It humbles us and frees us to respond to life in a more flexible way.

Actually, it's a compliment when someone thinks enough of us to play a joke on us or invite us to join them in joking with someone else. When we were children, those with whom we played were usually our friends, and it's much the same way as adults. When people show us their playful side, they may be inviting us to be friends, and more often than not, we need to say "yes."

When we're playful, we tend to be more honest. At play, we let down our defenses and relate to people more transparently. And while sometimes that freedom can get out of hand and be abused, normally it's a good thing. If we think we don't have time for play, that's probably an indication that some playfulness is overdue. And if, in all honesty, we have personalities that shy away from play, we probably have a greater need than the next person to get out and do some playing. Life in this world is serious business, it's true, but those who're prepared to deal with it the best are those who're a little mischievous!

In our play we reveal what kind of people we are.
OVID

SURPRISES

Wherever life takes us,
there are always moments of wonder.
JIMMY CARTER

MORE OFTEN THAN NOT, SURPRISES SHOULD BE WELCOMED. Occasionally, the unexpected will turn out to be hurtful or harmful, but for every such unwelcome surprise there are many more that we should be glad to experience. The completely predictable life would be a dull one that few of us would enjoy for long.

It's important to be people who are "surprise-able." We need to be more like the children we once were, eager to be astonished and amazed. Even being startled would be good for us now and then. The life of joy is always the life of *wonder* and the life of *growth*. Whatever opens our eyes and expands our experience is to be embraced rather than avoided. Most of us tend in the direction of mental sleepiness, and so we need an occasional thunderbolt to wake us up. "Surprise," as Boris Pasternak said, "is the greatest gift that life can give us."

But if it's important to value surprise in our own lives, it's also important to be people who bring surprises into the lives of others. We'd do our friends and family a great favor by becoming more imaginative in our interaction with them. Pleasantly surprising others is a sign of thoughtfulness, for one thing. It says that we're not taking those around us for granted but are looking for fresh, invigorating gifts we can give them. But being a person who surprises others is also a sign that we're fully engaged with life. It's evidence that we're moving forward, glad to taste more of the fascinating variety of life.

Real life is a good deal more unpredictable than the safe existence that many of us have settled for. Granted, we couldn't get along without the help that good habits give us, but too much habit can be deadly. If we never leave our comfortable ruts, the surprises that can turn us into wise and joyful people won't be able to reach us. And so real life calls us to come out of our comfort . . . into a realm where our hearts can be pierced by the beauty of unexpected truth.

"Pass in, pass in," the angels say,
"In to the upper doors,
Nor count compartments of the floors,
But mount to paradise
By the stairway of surprise."
RALPH WALDO EMERSON

CULTURE

Culture is the acquainting ourselves with the best that has been known and said in the world, and thus with the history of the human spirit.

MATTHEW ARNOLD

IF SOMEONE SAID THAT YOU WERE "CULTURED," WOULD YOU CONSIDER THAT A COMPLIMENT OR A DISPARAGEMENT? For today's meditation, let's set aside the stereotype of the cultured person as a pretentious "highbrow" and consider culture in its better sense. It is, as Matthew Arnold suggests, "acquainting ourselves with the best that has been known and said . . . and thus with the history of the human spirit." Is that a bad thing? Is it undesirable to know at least a little of what human beings have experienced and felt about life down through the ages? Only a person who values ignorance would say so.

Obviously, we need to avoid pride and pretense. If we've had the privilege of learning a little about history and culture and civilization, there's no need for us to look down on those who haven't. There may be good reasons why they haven't, and there may be, in fact, some advantages to their situation. The world would be a dull place if we all had the same interests, so let's not assume that wider experience necessarily makes a person a superior human being. Often it does not.

But let's face it: when we have the opportunity, we do need to get out of our own life and learn something of how life has been experienced by people at different times and places. The basic challenges have always been the same for every person, but people have had to deal with these from within very different circumstances. To be cultured is to have had some curiosity about other people's lives.

So Harold W. Dodds said, "Be sure to find a place for intellectual and cultural interests outside your daily occupation. It is necessary that you do so if the business of living is not to turn to dust and ashes in your mouth." So read and travel. Visit museums and art galleries. Attend lectures and concerts. *Explore "the history of the human spirit."*

We should do these things not to become "highfalutin'" but to be better informed — and by being better informed, to make better choices. True culture is not for show. It's for personal improvement.

The value of culture is its effect on character. It avails nothing unless it ennobles and strengthens that. Its use is for life. Its aim is not beauty but goodness.

W. SOMERSET MAUGHAM

April 4
ONENESS

All for one, one for all!
ALEXANDRE DUMAS

ONE OF THE BEST KINDS OF ONENESS, OR UNITY, IS COMMIT-
MENT TO A COMMON CAUSE. When two or more people place
a high value on some goal, they will work together to advance that
goal. They may have differences, but they will try to keep those differences from interfering with the shared goal. The group is committed
to the good of each individual, and each individual is committed to
the good of the group. The attitude is: *all for one, one for all!*

Identical robots have no trouble maintaining oneness, for they
have "oneness" in the most literal sense. Manufactured to the same
specifications, they have no differences. But people are not robots.
They vary from one another, often radically. And so the unified pursuit of common goals is a significant challenge for human beings. We
have to keep our personal preferences in their place, and we have to
see which differences are unity-breakers and which are not. All of this
takes wisdom, and wisdom is an exceedingly hard thing to acquire.

But there are many worthy goals to which we may commit
ourselves, and the higher up the scale of worthiness we go, the bigger
a difference would have to be to keep us from working together. If a
goal is perceived as being important enough, it will outrank almost
any difference. For example, when one nation is attacked militarily by
another nation, its citizens will set aside almost every private difference in order to defend themselves against the public foe.

It should be obvious that oneness requires humility and unselfishness. If I am so bent on advancing my personal agenda that I am
willing to ride over you roughshod, then you and I will probably not
be able to work together for very long. But if I am willing to subordinate my personal preferences to yours — and even make sacrifices for
the sake of your desires — then oneness is a possibility in our work.

It is often surprising to see what obstacles can be overcome when
people are unified in their labors. There is a transformative power that
comes from working together that almost never comes from individual effort. This does not come from fake or pretended oneness, but
when the unity is real, the results are electrifying.

Weak things united become strong.
ENGLISH PROVERB

April 5
DELEGATION

> Surround yourself with the best people you can find, delegate authority, and
> don't interfere as long as the policy you've decided on is being carried out.
>
> RONALD REAGAN

GOOD LEADERS PRACTICE THE ART OF DELEGATION. That is,
they are willing to entrust others with a part of the work that
is being done. Those delegated are given the authority, the resources,
and, if necessary, the training to carry out the delegated duty on
their own. This is called "division of labor." Someone has to lead the
endeavor, but the leader can't do all of the work alone. If the work is
of any size at all, parts of it have to be delegated to others. And the
principle of delegation is important not just in the business world; it's
important in nearly every group activity that human beings engage in.

The unwillingness to delegate is often a *pride* issue. Perhaps we
want to get all the credit for the work ourselves. Perhaps we don't
think anyone else can complete the task as well as we could. Or perhaps we're just so independent and self-sufficient that we don't trust
anyone else. These are all variations on the same theme: we believe
ourselves to be the most important person involved in the project.

Sometimes, however, the issue is not pride but *control.* Some of
us are afraid of situations that we can't control, and so we're reluctant
to delegate any serious work. If we did that, we would relinquish a
significant measure of control, and so we simply don't do it. Or we do
it and then still try to control the outcome by micromanaging the one
to whom the work has been delegated.

But if we're willing to learn *humility* (letting go of pride) and
trust (letting go of control), then great good can come from the division of labor and the delegation of responsibility. Working together,
even two or three people can achieve wondrous results, but not if
everybody is equally involved in everything the group is doing. For
"synergy" to take place, different people have to do different jobs.

One thing, however, must not be forgotten: leaders do not escape
responsibility by delegating work to others. The captain of a ship has
to entrust many different duties to his sailors, but he is still responsible for what happens to the ship. So let's be wise enough to delegate
some work to others, yet big enough to accept a leader's responsibility.

> You can delegate authority, but you cannot delegate responsibility.
> STEPHEN W. COMISKEY

April 6
AWARENESS

Great eaters and great sleepers are
incapable of anything else that is great.
HENRY IV OF FRANCE

THERE IS A MALADY THAT AFFLICTS MANY OF US THAT MIGHT
BE CALLED "DULLNESS." I don't mean that we ourselves are dull,
but rather that our attention to life has been dulled. Maybe we have
experienced so much that we're jaded, maybe we've been beaten down
by too many problems, or maybe we're just tired or sleepy or bored.
Whatever the reason, many of us do not live our lives with much
awareness. Our days — and our experiences — flow by us without
much conscious attention on our part. It's as if we're only half-awake.

As I said, the problem may be that we've had too many difficulties to deal with. But on the other hand, maybe we've had it too easy.
As Karl Ritter said, "People need resistance, for it is resistance which
gives them their awareness of life." It's a fact that dealing with difficulty enhances our awareness. Pain concentrates our attention, and if
that's what it takes to wake us up, then maybe pain is not all bad.

I can't discuss awareness, however, without mentioning a particular failure that characterizes our age, and that is a failure to be aware
of those around us. Manners expert Emily Post has said, "Manners are
a sensitive awareness of the feelings of others." If so, that is probably
why our age is ill-mannered. We are so self-centered that we feel no
need to "tune in" and be aware of anyone else's feelings. Unconcerned
and oblivious, we act in ways that a more aware person would not.

Henry Miller once wrote, "The aim of life is to live, and to live
means to be aware." As a statement of the meaning of life, that does
not go nearly far enough, but it does contain an important grain of
truth. There is a sense in which if our consciousness and our awareness have been dulled, we are not really living. If we fail to taste life
fully, both the bitter and the sweet, then we're losing the experience
that life was meant to be. So the advice of Thomas Mann is well
worth considering, and I heartily recommend it to you: "Hold every
moment sacred. Give each . . . the weight of thine awareness."

Hold fast the time! Guard it, watch over it, every hour, every minute!
Unregarded it slips away, like a lizard, smooth, slippery, faithless, a pixy wife.
Hold every moment sacred. Give each clarity and meaning, each the weight
of thine awareness, each its true and due fulfillment.
THOMAS MANN

SERVICE

*If things are not going well with you, begin your effort at correcting
the situation by carefully examining the service you are rendering,
and especially the spirit in which you are rendering it.*

ROGER BABSON

A FAILURE TO RENDER SERVICE IS AT THE ROOT OF MANY OF OUR DISSATISFACTIONS WITH LIFE. Frequently, when we get ill-tempered and out of sorts, the reason is that we've gotten so bogged down in our own concerns that we've quit serving those around us. When this happens, we come dangerously close to missing the main point of our lives. "No one has learned the meaning of life until he has surrendered his ego to the service of his fellow men" (Beran Wolfe).

One obvious thing about service is that it has to be rendered to actual people. There is no such thing as abstract service to "humanity." Either we serve those we actually come in contact with or we don't serve. It's usually just as simple as that. But therein lies the problem. Those we actually come in contact with are always fallible, imperfect people. They often have unpleasant habits and irritating responses to our help. So we tend to put off serving until we find some people to serve who are more congenial. But just as we don't get to pick our families, we don't usually get to pick those whom we have the opportunity to serve. Life (I would use the word "providence") brings us into contact with certain people and presents us with the opportunity to serve them. We don't choose whether to serve them or to serve someone else. We choose whether to serve or not serve, period.

There is an old saying that "the smallest good deed is better than the grandest good intention." Most of us mean no harm. We have good intentions. But if our good intentions don't show up in service, then they serve no useful purpose beyond making us feel better about our intentions. So let's quit making excuses and get busy finding someone to serve. Even if we don't see the results with our own eyes, we must never doubt this fact: *it always does good to do good.*

Give me the power to live for mankind;
Make me the mouth for such as cannot speak;
Eyes let me be to groping men and blind;
A conscience to the base; and to the weak —
Let me be hands and feet;
And to the foolish, mind.

THEODORE E. PARKER

GRACIOUSNESS

Amazing grace! How sweet the sound!
JOHN NEWTON

FEW THINGS IN LIFE ARE FINER THAN THE DAILY DEMONSTRA-
TION OF GRACIOUSNESS. When the things that are done are
not only correct from a legal or technical viewpoint but they're also
warmed with the goodness of grace, that's a beauty that makes us glad
we're alive! A friend compassionately notices that we're struggling. A
coworker kindly covers a task for us. A neighbor beautifully remembers our birthday. A child charmingly says thank you. A spouse tact-
fully helps us with a weakness. *Amazing grace! How sweet the sound!*

Attentiveness and thoughtfulness. The most basic element of graciousness is that it pays careful attention to another person. It's considerate in the literal sense of the term, that is, it considers the other
person. When we act graciously, we're saying that we've taken thought
for someone else and that their needs are important to us.

Kindness and courtesy. To be gracious, however, we must not only
take thought for others; we must do so with a desire to be merciful.
The essence of kindness is that it is compassionate; it desires to deal
gently with other people, even when they've not done their best. And
that's why the help that gracious people offer actually does help.

Charm and beauty. Good manners are not a waste of time, nor are
they finicky or pretentious. To endow our deeds with a bit of charm
— and even elegance once in a while! — is to say to those around us
that we think enough of them to act graciously for their sake. The
beauty of gracious conduct is one of life's happiest pleasures.

Many people have the resources to be gracious but lack the character to carry it out. On any given day, most of the opportunities for
people to act graciously toward other people are probably lost. So when
we encounter that rare person who cares enough to have acquired the
qualities of kindness, courtesy, and beauty, we are deeply refreshed by
them. Thank goodness for the gracious ones! Like daffodils peeking
out from a spring snow, they strike us with hope and happiness. Our
days would be dreary indeed if it weren't for their gift of graciousness.

Riches may enable us to confer favours,
but to confer them with propriety and grace
requires a something that riches cannot give.
CHARLES CALEB COLTON

IMPORTANCE

There was a time when I had all the answers. My real growth
began when I discovered that the questions to which I had the
answers were not the important questions.

REINHOLD NIEBUHR

IN THIS LIFE, WE'RE ON A JOURNEY: AN ODYSSEY ON WHICH WE
LEARN, LITTLE BY LITTLE, WHAT THE IMPORTANT THINGS ARE.
The further we go, the more obvious it becomes that at the beginning we had no clear idea concerning life's real priorities. We were full
of answers, but as it turns out, we had not even discovered what the
main questions were. It begins to dawn on us that "importance" is a
thing much easier understood at journey's end than at its beginning.

If we wish to see what's truly important, the main requirement
is to overcome our sense of *self-importance*. Each of us is important,
certainly. But our self-centered concerns are nowhere near the most
important thing in life. As R. M. Baumgardy said, "Man must realize
his own unimportance before he can appreciate his importance."

T. S. Eliot once wrote, "Half of the harm that is done in this
world is due to people who want to feel important . . . They do not
mean to do harm . . . They are absorbed in the endless struggle to
think well of themselves." Too often, we are like Ed Koch who in a
famous conversation said, "But enough about me. Let's talk about you.
What do you think of me?" As long as we are stuck in this mode of
thought, we will never appreciate the things that matter most.

But even when we rise above self-importance, we still have the
challenge of multiple priorities. Not all of the things that we have to
deal with are equally important, but many of them are important to
some degree, and it takes wisdom, courage, and no small amount of
discipline to separate the less important from the more important.

And finally, all of us need to have something that is of *ultimate*
importance. In other words, we need to cherish some value that is
such a surpassing treasure that we would, if necessary, sacrifice everything else for that one value. When we possess such a value, we can
arrange all the lesser values in their proper order, and we're motivated
to give our first and finest effort to that which is at the top of the list.

The most important thing in life is to live your life
for something more important than your life.

WILLIAM JAMES

FOCUS

Concentrate on finding your goal,
then concentrate on reaching it.
MICHAEL FRIEDMAN

WHEN WE LEARN WHAT THE IMPORTANT THINGS ARE, THE CHALLENGE IS TO KEEP FOCUSED ON THEM. It is not easy to keep the most important things in the center of our concern, even when we see what those things are. So today, let's think about the importance of focus. It's one of the keys to effective living.

As life becomes more complex, the more tempted we are to dilute our attention. With so many fascinating concerns competing for our recognition, we tend to be distracted from the few that should be our focus. But as enticing as all of these things are, we must resist the urge to dabble in them. With a limited amount of energy, we must make some hard choices and concentrate on our highest priorities.

Samuel Johnson wrote, "A man may be so much of everything that he is nothing of everything." Poorly focused people end up making less of a contribution to the world than those who have narrowed their interest. To attempt too much is to accomplish too little.

When we summon the courage to concentrate, focusing like a laser beam on what is most important, many of our practical problems disappear. For instance, focus tends to drive away worry and anxiety. Lady Bird Johnson was on the right track when she said, "Become so wrapped up in something that you forget to be afraid."

But how do we learn to concentrate? Where does focus come from? I believe it comes from two things: (a) deciding what our greatest goals are, and (b) giving ourselves passionately to the accomplishment of those goals. Walter J. Johnston said it well: "Many people who wonder why they don't amount to more than they do have good stuff in them, and are energetic, persevering, and have ample opportunities. It is all a case of trimming the branches and throwing the whole force of power into the development of something that counts."

So how long has it been since you "trimmed the branches" in your life? And are you "throwing the whole force of power" into what matters most? If not, you're probably drifting through life without any certain destination. I can tell you from experience: you need to *focus*.

This one thing I do . . . I press toward the goal.
LETTER OF PAUL TO THE PHILIPPIANS

AID

Knowing sorrow well, I learn the way to succor the distressed.
V I R G I L

FROM TIME TO TIME, ALL OF US NEED TO RECEIVE AID AND ALSO TO GIVE IT. At any given moment we may need to be doing one more than the other, but before our lives are over, we will have had to do both: receive aid and give aid. And learning to think rightly about the subject of aid is one of life's great challenges.

It is an interesting fact that the things that best equip us to give aid are those that are often painful to experience. None of us wants to suffer any more than necessary, but there is no denying that suffering puts us in a position to help others who are suffering. As Virgil put it, "Knowing sorrow well, I learn the way to succor the distressed." If we could see the long-term benefits of difficulty and see how it makes helpers of us, we would accept our sufferings with a greater strength.

Most normal people have the urge to help others, but the problem is we don't act on the urge as consistently as we should. In the story of the Good Samaritan, the man who rendered help to the injured traveler might have had no more of a generous attitude than the other two men. But unlike them, he *acted* on the impulse to give aid. As the saying goes, "a little help is worth a great deal of pity."

In the Book of Genesis, there is the story of Joseph and his brothers who sold him into slavery. Later, when events had sharpened their conscience considerably, they made this statement: "Yes, now we are suffering the consequences of what we did to our brother; we saw the great trouble he was in when he begged for help, but we would not listen." Truly, there is no regret in life worse than looking back and knowing that you did not help someone who was pleading for it.

Unfortunately, it is often pride that hinders our urge to give aid and to receive it. If we're honest, we have to admit that there are limits on whom we would aid and whom we would want to receive aid from. But shouldn't aid be unprejudiced? Sometimes the greatest benefit of aid comes from helping someone outside our comfort zone — and having the humility to receive aid from the last person on earth we would want to be helped by is humility indeed. So since the need for aid is universal, let's look at it that way.

Everyone needs help from everyone.
B E R T O L T   B R E C H T

CREDIBILITY

*A credible message needs a credible messenger
because charisma without character is catastrophe.*

PETER KUZMIC

MOST OF US UNDERESTIMATE THE IMPORTANCE OF CRED-
IBILITY. In our interactions with other people, not much can
be done without credibility. Our words may be true and our work may
serve a worthy cause, but if we've not gained credibility (or if we've
damaged our credibility), it's going to be an uphill climb trying to
influence those around us. Whether we like it or not, almost every
activity in this world involves persuasion in one form or another, and
without credibility, persuaders find it hard to persuade anybody.

If we give "credence" to something, that means we believe it.
So "credibility" means believability. People who have credibility are
those whom others find it easy to believe. They are trusted by those
who have dealings with them, and their words carry weight. Having
proven themselves reliable, in both word and deed, they are worthy of
confidence. So when the time comes to persuade or influence someone else, people with credibility find that others are willing to listen.

Several things are involved in building credibility, but the most
important factor is also the most obvious: if we want to be perceived
as being credible, we need to *be* credible. If we want others to think
of us as trustworthy, we need to *be* worthy of their trust. No effective
shortcut has ever been found to credibility. It can't be built by quick
fixes or maintained permanently by personality techniques. It doesn't
result from the smoke-and-mirrors manipulation of others by tricks
of the communication trade. No, if others are to trust us and listen
seriously when we speak, we're going to have to establish a pattern
of telling the truth in every situation. Rome wasn't built in a day, and
credibility won't be acquired in a day either. It takes time.

But if it takes time to build credibility, it can certainly be lost
quickly. A lifetime of painstaking effort to become trustworthy can
be thrown away in a moment of carelessness, and once lost, credibility
is extremely hard to regain. So if we want others to listen when we
speak, let us carefully, scrupulously, and consistently . . . *tell the truth!*

*Every exaggeration of the truth once detected by others destroys
our credibility and makes all that we do and say suspect.*

STEPHEN R. COVEY

INTEGRITY

This above all: to thine own self be true,
And it must follow, as the night the day,
Thou canst not then be false to any man.
WILLIAM SHAKESPEARE

INTEGRITY HAS TO DO WITH "ONENESS." It can be thought of in several different ways, as we shall see, but integrity always involves some kind of unity or wholeness. A person who has integrity is not fractured, divided, or conflicted, but instead is a person of consistency. He or she is *one* person rather than two or three different persons fighting for control of the same mind and body.

Here are three ways that people of integrity maintain oneness:

Alignment of principles with truth. "To thine own self be true" is not good advice if our principles aren't valid. (Think of Adolf Hitler.) So to have integrity, we must adhere to time-tested moral principles.

Consistency between principles and conduct. Having adopted valid principles, we must then keep our conduct in line with our principles. Integrity means that we refuse to violate our conscience. In Plato's *Gorgias*, Socrates said, "And yet, my friend, I would rather . . . that the whole world should be at odds with me, and oppose me, than that I myself should be at odds with myself and contradict myself." We must have a solid confidence in ourselves that we will do what is right.

Agreement between public and private life. The person who lives one life in public but contradicts that life in private is a hypocrite. Integrity means that our public and private lives are harmonious.

Without integrity, life is worth very little. Unfortunately, many people sell out and sacrifice their integrity in order to gain some temporary advantage. But if we violate our principles to acquire things like fame, fortune, power, safety, security, or social acceptance, what have we gained in the long term? Yes, the temptations are strong, and it can be hard to hold on to our convictions. But we must guard our integrity even when it is hard — I would say *especially* when it is hard. "He has honor if he holds himself to an ideal of conduct though it is inconvenient, unprofitable, or dangerous to do so" (Walter Lippmann). So come what may, let us heed the quiet voice of our conscience.

Hold it the greatest wrong to prefer life to honor
and for the sake of life to lose the reason for living.
JUVENAL

SECURITY

With all its alluring promise that someone else will guarantee
for the rainy day, Social Security can never replace the program that man's
future welfare is, after all, a matter of individual responsibility.

HAROLD STONIER

THESE DAYS, WE TEND TO THINK THAT OUR SECURITY IS THE RESPONSIBILITY OF SOMEONE ELSE TO PROVIDE. The government program in the United States called "Social Security" is a good example. Whatever its original merits may have been, it has come to be thought of as an entitlement. We think we have a right to be financially secure in old age, and it's the government's responsibility to take care of us. Personal responsibility has been lost in the shuffle.

That said, it is also true that security is a goal we must pursue together with those around us. While I must assume personal responsibility, I must also take my neighbors into account because security that is gained by selfish means is always a shaky security. "Ultimately there can be no freedom for self unless it is vouchsafed to others; there can be no security where there is fear, and a democratic society presupposes confidence and candor in the relations of men with one another and eager collaboration for the larger ends of life instead of the pursuit of petty, selfish, or vainglorious aims" (Felix Frankfurter).

So even in terms of our own security, we can't afford to leave our neighbors out of the equation. What is more, we must be actively involved in providing for the security of those around us. It is not enough to *receive* security; we must also be those who *give* it. Here is an area where it is truly more blessed to give than to receive. And there are few gifts that we can give any better than the gift which says to someone, "In every possible way, I want to help make you secure."

In the end, however, there is no such thing as real security in this world. If our peace of mind depends on our ability to provide everything we will ever need, we are bound to be disappointed. How much better it would be if we redefined security and sought it spiritually rather than financially. As far as this world is concerned, we will never be secure if there is anything we think we have to have, and the sooner we loosen our grip on these things, the more truly secure we will be.

Security depends not so much on how much you have,
as upon how much you can do without.

JOSEPH WOOD KRUTCH

LABOR

It is only by labour that thought can be made healthy,
and only by thought that labour can be made happy,
and the two cannot be separated with impunity.

JOHN RUSKIN

LABOR, ESPECIALLY WHEN IT'S THOUGHTFUL LABOR UNDER-
TAKEN ON BEHALF OF THOSE WE LOVE, IS ONE OF THE MAIN
THINGS THAT MAKE LIFE GOOD. We may forget it while we're
working, but it only takes a period of sickness or enforced inactivity to
remind us: the ability to work is a blessing, not a curse.

Labor is not inherently good, of course. Whether it's good or
not depends on the object of our endeavors. As far as character traits
go, it's better to be industrious than not industrious, but it makes a
big difference whether we're trying to achieve honorable ends or not.
Judging from the evidence, the devil has a diligent work ethic, but for
all his hard work, he still has some serious public relations problems!

To be satisfying, our labor must be based on valid principles. It
must be aligned with truths that are known to produce helpful results,
rather than harmful ones. And not only that, it must be motivated by
something more than self-centered aims. We're at our best when we're
laboring to create something someone else will enjoy or profit from.

If you don't have somebody for whom you love to work, you need
to find somebody like that. You need to have one or more persons
whose needs it gives you great pleasure to fulfill. There really is a
great deal of truth to the saying that "it's more blessed to give than to
receive." By nature, we're producers, and we derive a deeper pleasure
from that than from consuming that which others have produced.

Since we're all connected to a vast array of relationships in the
world, we also need to see our labor as being connected to the labor
of others. Whatever our work is, our activity impinges on others in
some way; it affects their work, either positively or negatively. Since
that's true, one of the most ennobling things in life is to aspire to the
making of a positive contribution, one that will add a little quality
or excellence to the world's output. When we labor toward that end,
gratefully and enthusiastically, good things can be expected to happen.

No task, rightly done, is truly private.
It is part of the world's work.

WOODROW WILSON

PHILANTHROPY

A man of humanity is one who, in seeking to establish
himself, finds a foothold for others and who, desiring attainment
for himself, helps others to attain.
CONFUCIUS

IT WOULD BE IMPOSSIBLE TO HAVE A VIRTUOUS CHARACTER AND NOT BE CONCERNED ABOUT THE PUBLIC WELFARE. As Confucius observed, an honorable man does not climb without helping others to find a foothold. And that is what philanthropy is all about: *helping our fellow citizens to attain what we're trying to attain.*

There are, obviously, many problems associated with philanthropy, problems that cause many to shy away from the whole idea. First, there is the problem of less-than-honorable motives. As Friedrich Nietzsche said, "If all alms were given only for pity, all beggars would have starved long ago." And then, there is the problem of unintended consequences. Sometimes our generous impulses lead us to give help in a way that ends up doing more harm than good. And these are just two of the problems; there are many more. All things considered, genuine philanthropy requires a great deal of wisdom, perhaps more wisdom than any of the other virtues.

But although philanthropy is fraught with difficulty, we must not let ourselves become cynical about it. Steering clear of the problems, we don't want to swing to the opposite extreme and come to be known for practicing *misanthropy.* The old Chinese proverb is true: "It is better to light a candle than to curse the darkness." The difficulty of doing good wisely is no excuse for not doing any good at all.

There are two things that we need to understand about philanthropy. First, it is not just for the rich. Our means may be more limited than the fabulously wealthy, but we are still responsible for doing what we can. Second, philanthropy is not just about money. Things like time and effort are often more needed than our financial help.

Good deeds must be done outwardly, but philanthropy is as much a matter of the heart as it is of the hands. It has to do with a spirit, an attitude, a way of thinking. And in the end, the best philanthropy comes from a high-quality character on the *inside* of us.

The place to improve the world is first in one's own heart and head
and hands, and then work outward from there.
ROBERT M. PIRSIG

RELIEF

Can I see another's woe,
And not be in sorrow too?
Can I see another's grief,
And not seek for kind relief?

WILLIAM BLAKE

IF A BEAST OF BURDEN IS STRUGGLING UNDER ITS LOAD, "RELIEF" WOULD CONSIST OF LIFTING OR LIGHTENING THE BURDEN. In a similar way, we speak of "relief" among human beings. Relief is "the easing of a burden or distress, such as pain, anxiety, or oppression" (*American Heritage Dictionary*). Our burdens may not be physical, but they are no less oppressive, and when one person provides relief for another, something happens that is wonderful indeed.

It's obvious that we live in a "burdensome" world, but it's not always obvious why that is so. None of us understands completely all of the whys and wherefores of suffering, but even in the absence of understanding, we still have the opportunity to help specific people. Francis of Assisi was probably putting the emphasis in the right place when he said, "I do not aspire . . . to understand pain or suffering. I aspire only to relieve the pain and suffering of others."

One of the finest reputations that we can have in this world is to be known as somebody that others can confidently turn to in their hour of distress. We can't make the suffering of others go away, but we can learn the skills, the wisdom, and the courage to *lighten* their load.

But what about our own relief? When we are distressed, may we desire that someone will help provide relief for us? Yes, we may desire it and even long for it. But relief in the form of help from others may not come, and so it's wise to take responsibility for our own situation. We may not be able to free ourselves from pain completely, but there is one thing we can do and it's a great help: *we can determine that we'll follow our conscience.* Whether relief from others comes to us or not, if we can end the day confident that we've done our best, then our hearts will find some relief. And if we've not done our best, the first order of business tomorrow should be rectifying our wrongs and moving ahead. *At the end of the day, the key to relief is conscience.*

A man is relieved . . . when he has put his heart
into his work and done his best; what he has said
or done otherwise shall give him no peace.

RALPH WALDO EMERSON

THOUGHTFULNESS

> Only when we turn thoughtfully toward what has already been thought
> will we be turned to use for what must still be thought.
>
> MARTIN HEIDEGGER

A S BUSY AS WE ARE THESE DAYS, BEING THOUGHTFUL IS NOT EASY. Thinking requires time, and we don't have much of that left over after we've ticked off the items on our "To Do" list. So looking back, we often realize that we've been thoughtless in various situations, simply because we were too hurried to be otherwise. At the pace life is lived in this age of the world, those who remain thoughtful are usually those who have more self-discipline than the rest of us. The thoughtful are those who deliberately slow down and . . . think!

One of the things that we need to think about is that which others have thought before us. Heidegger's point is well taken: "Only when we turn thoughtfully toward what has already been thought will we be turned to use for what must still be thought." We hurt ourselves when we commit the sin of "chronological snobbery" and dismiss the value of anything that is not new or contemporary. But that said, think with me now about two different kinds of thoughtfulness:

Careful thought. One meaning of "thoughtful" is "contemplative." The thoughtful person is one who ponders and considers what is the best path to follow. He or she might be described as being "pensive." Some are more inclined in that direction than others, obviously, but if we never take the time to consider (a) what is true, and (b) what we ought to do, then our deeds are going to do damage sooner or later.

Concern for others. To be thoughtful also means to be considerate of others. And this, I believe, is the highest kind of thoughtfulness. It involves not only stopping to think of others but anticipating their needs and wishes. So thoughtful people, in this sense, are those who think of others with a noticeable degree of wisdom and sensitivity. Deep down, of course, this concern is a product of love. It comes from "charity" in the older sense. And if we're too busy to anticipate the needs of others and serve them, then we're simply too busy to love.

> What is charity?
> It's silence when your words would hurt
> It's patience when your neighbor's curt
> It's deafness when scandal flows
> It's thoughtfulness for another's woes.
>
> ANONYMOUS

MOVEMENT

The flowering of the person is not a state at which we arrive,
it is the movement that results from perpetual incompleteness.

PAUL TOURNIER

WITHIN US ALL, THERE IS A DEEP, INSTINCTIVE URGE TO MOVE AHEAD. We are creatures who dream and aspire. We set goals and reach toward them. We are not content to stay put. That being true, it's all the more strange that many of us do stay put! We make ourselves miserable when we stand still, but we do it anyway. What we need is a more powerful appreciation of "movement."

Change. To live is to change, and so if we are living, we are changing. "Our nature lies in movement; absolute rest is death" (Blaise Pascal). But change is frightening as well as inconvenient. Most of us tend to resist significant change. But in our more serious moments, we realize that resisting change is resisting growth. Even where our hearts are concerned, we need to embrace the idea of moving forward. As Paul Tournier said, "Love is not a state, it is a movement."

Progress. While change and movement can be good ideas, a word of warning is needed: not all change is good. There is no inherent value in change; it is good only when it moves us in the direction of true progress. As the pace of change around us increases, we need this warning all the more. It's easy to let ourselves be swept along by the latest "new" thing, but before we move in any direction, let's honestly inquire whether that change is moving us upward or downward.

Engagement with life. This is a different kind of movement, but it is nonetheless important. Some people back away from any real engagement or involvement with life because that kind of movement requires effort. They would rather lie down and remain passive than move out onto the battlefield where the action is. But when we take the easy way out, we lose the opportunity to learn new skills and equip ourselves for useful work. When we stay put, we fail to serve.

So let me come right out and ask you: are you a person who is characterized by movement? Are you going toward any worthy destination? And are you actively and interestingly engaged with the people and circumstances around you? If not, I urge you to get moving. The static life is no life at all. It is a death worse than death itself.

The great affair is movement.

ROBERT LOUIS STEVENSON

VULNERABILITY

> To suffering must be added mourning, understanding, patience, love,
> openness, and the willingness to remain vulnerable.
>
> ANNE MORROW LINDBERGH

T O BE VULNERABLE IS TO BE SUSCEPTIBLE TO INJURY, AND THAT DOES NOT SOUND LIKE A GOOD THING. The word "vulnerable" has a negative, and even fearful, connotation to us, as every insurance salesman knows full well. But think more carefully about our vulnerability. Is it really something that we should try to escape?

The fact is, we are vulnerable in many ways, and there is no use pretending otherwise. And there is no use trying to protect ourselves from every conceivable loss or injury. There are just too many possibilities. Try as we may, we can never achieve perfect safety in this world. So if we're going to have any peace of mind, it will have to be by some means other than playing it safe in every situation.

In most people's lives, a certain stage of maturity has to be reached before they are willing to accept their vulnerability and not be afraid of it. But what a liberating experience when we reach that point! The "willingness to remain vulnerable," as Lindbergh puts it, is one of the finest fruits of thoughtful and honest living. It is quite a relief when we quit making the effort to be strong — and to *appear* to be strong — in every circumstance. Having moved beyond the need for constant safety, we are free to work on more productive projects.

Sadly, some of us never get to that point. We remain bogged down in futile efforts to protect ourselves from any possible hurt, and we have no higher goal in any endeavor than to do what is safe. But while wisdom prompts us to take reasonable precautions (only a fool "throws caution to the wind"), it is not wisdom that makes us obsess over safety. Safety is a value, certainly, but it is not the ultimate value.

In matters of the heart, above all, we must accept our vulnerability. Real love is always attended by the possibility of being hurt. Indeed, love carries with it the *probability* of being hurt, since there is no one we may love in this world whom we will not have to say goodbye to. But should we protect ourselves by avoiding love? No, down that path lies nothing but death. *Love is a chance well worth taking.*

> Vulnerability, attachment, uprooting, tenderness, interest,
> anxiety, expectation, anguish — all these are nothing else but love.
>
> LOUIS EVELY

CIRCUMSPECTION

The necessity of the times, more than ever, calls for our utmost
circumspection, deliberation, fortitude, and perseverance.
SAMUEL ADAMS

SOME WORDS CONVEY AN IDEA BY MEANS OF A MENTAL PIC-
TURE, AND "CIRCUMSPECTION" IS SUCH A WORD. Literally, it
means to "look in a circle" or to "look around," and the picture is that
of a person walking through a dangerous area and looking around
before he takes each step. Think of a soldier walking across a minefield: he would look around carefully and watch where he stepped. To
live circumspectly, then, is to live carefully. The main idea is what we
might call *heedfulness* — paying attention to where we "step."

The more hazardous the times in which we live, the more important it is to make careful decisions about our lives. And if the "necessity of the times" called for circumspection in Samuel Adams's day,
the age in which we live is no less perilous. If we don't "watch where
we're going," some very unpleasant surprises are going to shock us.

As we discussed in yesterday's reading on "vulnerability," it is
possible to be too concerned with things like prudence and risk-
avoidance. In this matter, we need to strive for balance, and balance
can only be achieved by wisdom. Life's issues are not all equal; some
are weightier and deserve more circumspection than others. So we
need to grow in the wisdom that is required to tell the difference.

Without circumspection, we're going to hurt ourselves, but what
is worse, we're going to hurt others. Our concern for others is mainly
what should make us want to be circumspect. Thomas à Kempis
spoke truly when he said, "Love is watchful." The more we love those
around us, the more careful we'll be in the way we live our lives. In an
interconnected world, carefulness is a great gift that we can give.

But in deciding what to be circumspect about, most of us should
be less concerned about physical issues and more concerned about
spiritual and moral ones. Too much of the time, we lavish great care
on the former and are shockingly careless about the latter. So my
advice to you is this: however prudent you are in doing what is *safe*,
watch your step even more in doing what is *right*. Let the question of
moral integrity be the one where you "watch your step" most carefully.

Watch that you do what you should do.
OSWALD CHAMBERS

April 22
SERIOUSNESS

It is not so important to be serious as it is to be
serious about the important things.
ROBERT MAYNARD HUTCHINS

IS SERIOUSNESS A QUALITY THAT YOU WOULD LIKE TO ADD TO YOUR CHARACTER? Many people would rather be lighthearted than serious, but before you reject the idea of seriousness, think what the alternatives are. Would you rather be known as a silly, foolish person? Would you like to be one who deals only with the trivial, inconsequential side of life? Probably not, but those are the opposites of true seriousness. The stereotype of the serious person as being "humorless" is only a mockery and a caricature of seriousness. Genuine seriousness may be something more valuable than you have thought.

These days, we have trouble rightly considering seriousness because of our culture's overemphasis on frivolity. Years ago, Neil Postman powerfully described this phenomenon in his *Amusing Ourselves to Death*, a book that was written long before the entertainment business had grown to today's gigantic proportions. Postman's argument was not that mirth and merriment are wrong, but that we have overdosed ourselves on these things — and seriously damaged our culture in the process. Having come to see everything in terms of entertainment, we have lost the ability to deal seriously with serious things. We have been, in his words, amusing ourselves to death.

The crucial thing is not just to be serious but to be "serious about the important things" (Hutchins). In our culture, we desperately need a sense of proportion and relative value. Not everything should be measured by the values of entertainment and fun; some things are more important and deserve our serious regard. We should want to be people who have a reputation for that kind of seriousness. We should aspire to having the capacity for careful thought and consideration. Rather than dabbling, we should become deeply interested and involved with the big issues. We should know what diligence means. And we should even know when gravity and solemnity are in order.

In short, seriousness should be a prominent part of our character. That doesn't mean that we're humorless or never playful. It does mean that our lightheartedness serves a higher function than mere fun.

Play so that you may be serious.
ANACHARSIS

CLEANLINESS

The forcefulness of simplicity.
The winsomeness of courtesy.
The attractiveness of modesty.
The inspiration of cleanliness.

ROLLO C. HESTER

IT IS POSSIBLE TO BE OVERLY CONCERNED WITH CLEANLINESS, BUT NOWADAYS NOT MANY PEOPLE HAVE THAT PROBLEM. As a virtue and a character trait, cleanliness is old-fashioned. It has gone out of style. With the possible exception of bodily cleanness, modern people think of cleaning activities as a waste of time. They either pay someone else to do it or it doesn't get done. The "inspiration of cleanliness" sounds like language that comes from another universe.

But isn't cleanliness a function of stewardship? I happen to believe that it is, and I will give you an example. Many years ago, I bought a house from an older couple who had built the house and raised their rather large family in it. Considering its age, the house was in immaculate condition. Rather than being hastily cleaned up before being placed on the market, it had been well cleaned and maintained as long as its owners had lived in it. I remarked on this to my real estate agent, and she said, "Yes, these owners were very old-school. They came from a time when people believed that if you bought something, you took care of it." That house was kept clean not because its owners were obsessive-compulsive, but because they understood the concepts of gratitude, responsibility, and stewardship.

The same real estate agent made another interesting comment. She said she was always amazed at the great morale boost that people get when they clean their houses before putting them up for sale. "Clean windows do wonders for the psyche," she said. "It makes you feel so good, why don't people clean their houses more often?"

But in regard to cleanliness, the most important kind is that which has to do with our inner persons. I believe we do need to keep things clean outwardly, but however much we're concerned about that, we need to be even more concerned about our inward life. Too many of our *hearts* are disheveled and dirty. They're overdue for a cleaning!

Better keep yourself clean and bright;
you are the window through which you must see the world.

GEORGE BERNARD SHAW

MOTIVES

To act in everything with the highest motives . . .
HELEN KELLER

THOSE WHO ACT WITH HONORABLE MOTIVES ARE ADMIRED
FOR DOING SO. Even when someone's deeds have been less than
satisfactory, we understand that it makes a positive difference if we
can say "They meant well" or "Their intentions were good." Why is
that so? Is it not because a person's "heart" is more basic to their character than their "hands"? What we do is important, without a doubt,
but what we are trying to do is even more important. That being true,
it's a healthy exercise to examine our motives from time to time. Why
are we doing what we do? Are our reasons as good as they can be? Are
there any adjustments that we need to make in our motives?

Aristotle said, "All that we do is done with an eye to something
else." Every action is prompted by some motive, and we must accept
that fact. The question is not whether we have any motives but only
what they are. Rather than deny that we have any motives, we need
to be honest about their nature . . . and then work on improving them
if necessary. There is no improvement better than the improvement of
our motives, but we can't improve them if we're in denial about them.

But (and here is where it gets tricky) what are our motives for
wanting to improve our motives? Do we wish others to think well of
us? Do we wish to think well of ourselves? Neither of these is necessarily wrong, but there is a higher consideration, and that is *the objective, unchanging standard of what is right*. We should want to think and
do what is right because it is right. And it is right to want to do so!

There are few things more powerful or beneficial than "motive
force." When a person's actions are fired by motives that are important
to them, there is virtually no limit to what they can accomplish. And
if their motives are not only important to them but right in regard to
the universal moral code, the results are even more astounding. For
that reason, it pays to be careful about our motives. If we want to be
more highly motivated, we need to elevate the quality of our motives.
The higher they are, the more powerful they will be. And when we
operate from the very highest motives of all, great mountains become
moveable and unbearable burdens become easy to carry.

When the will is ready, the feet are light.
GEORGE HERBERT

ENDS

The question should be, is it worth doing, not can it be done?
ALLARD K. LOWENSTEIN

MOST OF US WOULD DO WELL TO CONSIDER MORE CARE-
FULLY THE "WHY" OF OUR ACTIONS. In other words, what is
the *purpose* of what we do? What are we trying to *accomplish* with our
various activities? If we concentrate solely on our "means" and not on
our "ends," we are bound to do harmful things. We may do them efficiently, but if they shouldn't be done at all, then our efficiency simply
gets us to the wrong place faster. Lowenstein's point is a good one:
"The question should be, is it worth doing, not can it be done?"

Our point in today's reading is that "ends" are important. But
the first thing that needs to be recognized is that ends are not *all*-
important. There is no such thing as a goal so great that it justifies any
means that might be used to achieve it. No matter how glorious the
goal, principles of right and wrong must be taken into account when
we're deciding what our tactics are going to be. We are not free to "do
evil that good may come," to borrow the words of Paul the Apostle.

But to return to the importance of our ends, I suggest that we
need to think more about our *ultimate* ends. We do need to have
short-term objectives to keep us working, but these lesser ends should
always be examined in the light of our long-range purpose. When we
focus totally on our smaller goals, we lose touch with this bigger purpose. So we must step back and recall what end we're working toward.

Also, I suggest that we must maintain consistency between our
means and our ends. If we're not careful, we may find ourselves paying
lip service to very noble ends but engaging in actions that are directly
opposed to those ends. Integrity and wholeness consist, in large part,
of harmony between our professed ends and our actual means.

You can be sure of one thing, however, and that is that the means
you employ in your life will take you to whatever destination is *the
logical result of those means*. You can't travel the road to one city and arrive at another city. To get to that city, you'll have to change roads. So
the question of our ends — and the means we use to get there — is a
question of tremendous consequence.

The means prepare the end,
and the end is what the means have made it.
JOHN MORLEY

PROMISES

I believe in the sacredness of a promise, that a man's word
should be as good as his bond; that character — not wealth
or power or position — is of supreme worth.

JOHN D. ROCKEFELLER JR.

FEW THINGS ARE MORE VALUABLE, OR MORE ADMIRABLE,
THAN A PROMISE WHEN IT IS KEPT. Yet by the same token,
there are few things more destructive than a promise when it's not
kept. Treachery and betrayal are among the worst things we know.

Unfortunately, we live in an age when commitment-keeping
seems to be on the decline. Indeed, some forms of promise-breaking
seem almost trendy and fashionable. One thinks, for example, about
the frightening frequency with which the marriage promise is set
aside in our culture, or the explosion of legal litigation in our society
in which someone claims that someone else has violated a contract.
We seem to have gotten to the point where a promise only indicates
what we'll do until a better deal comes along or the commitment becomes an inconvenience to us. Rarely will anyone now honor a promise if that promise stands between them and something else they've
come to want. Indeed, we go so far as to applaud those who have the
"courage" to stand up and do what's right "for them," regardless of
what promises have to be broken in the process. And as a result, there
is human wreckage nearly everywhere we look.

One of the saddest consequences of the modern approach to
promises is that few of us have any confidence in our own reliability
anymore. We've broken so many commitments that we no longer
trust ourselves to do what we say we'll do. In a pinch, we're not sure
that we'd do the right thing. And that's a tragic loss, because confidence in our own integrity is one of the basic foundations of life.

But if we chose to do better, we could improve, and that's exactly
what we ought to do. Honor is such a simple thing, really, but it's a great
thing nevertheless. It's a nobility that's available to every man, woman,
and child: the living of a life that's based on everyday believability.

Greatness is a matter, not of size, but of quality, and it is
within the reach of every one of us . . . There is greatness in patient
endurance; in unyielding loyalty to a goal; in resistance to the temptation to
betray the best we know; in speaking up for the truth when it is assailed; in
steadfast adherence to vows given and promises made.

SIDNEY GREENBERG

KINDNESS

Kindness in words creates confidence.
Kindness in thinking creates profoundness.
Kindness in giving creates love.

LAO TZU

IF THERE IS A GIFT THAT PEOPLE ENJOY RECEIVING ANY MORE THAN KINDNESS, I DON'T KNOW WHAT IT IS. Anytime another person deals kindly with us, we like that experience very much.

Unfortunately, when we experience the opposite behavior and are treated unkindly, we tend to remember that longer. Grudges seem to stick in our minds more than gratitude does. But shouldn't we rather "write injuries in sand and kindnesses in marble" (French proverb)?

I think most people would agree that appreciation for kindness grows as we mature. We can relate to the sentiment of Abraham Joshua Heschel, who said, "When I was young, I admired clever people. Now that I am old, I admire kind people." Perhaps this is true because we need acts of kindness more when we're old than when we're young. But as we age, our value system changes as well as our needs. While we're young, our attention is captured by treasures that sparkle outwardly. It is only when the shine has worn off of these things that we learn to appreciate the more homely virtues like kindness.

As the quotation from Lao Tzu indicates, there are many different species of kindness. In addition to kind words, there are kind deeds, kind gestures, kind gifts, and many others. But what about kindness in *thinking?* You may not have tried to keep your thinking kind, but that's the root of the matter. Most of the time, what we do outwardly is simply the overflow of what is in our hearts. So if kind behavior is our goal, then we need to make kind thinking a habit.

Most ordinary people have the impulse to be kind, at least occasionally. But too few of us act on that impulse. Busy to the point of distraction, we slip into the practice of postponing our kindnesses. But while having kind intentions is certainly better than not having them, the intentions themselves do little good if they are not acted upon, at least as far as the recipient is concerned. Let's not pile up regrets in our lives by failing to be kind when we have the opportunity.

You cannot do a kindness too soon,
for you never know how soon it will be too late.

RALPH WALDO EMERSON

SENSITIVITY

> The very nature of intelligence is sensitivity, and this sensitivity is love.
> Without this intelligence there can be no compassion. Compassion is not
> the doing of charitable acts or social reform; it is free from sentiment,
> romanticism and emotional enthusiasm. It is as strong as death. It is like
> a great rock, immovable in the midst of confusion, misery, and anxiety.
>
> JIDDU KRISHNAMURTI

OUR "SENSES" ARE IMPORTANT BOTH PHYSICALLY AND EMO-
TIONALLY. In the physical realm, if our fingertips are insensitive
(that is, they can't feel anything), that is a significant problem. But
emotionally, if we have a low degree of sensitivity (our hearts can't feel
anything), that is an even greater problem. Our senses, whether physical or emotional, are meant to give us feedback from the external world,
and if they don't do so, then we are isolated within our own selves.

As Krishnamurti suggests, sensitivity is closely linked to love.
Love is an outward-moving force that urges us in the direction of
others. It causes us to want to serve their needs. But to act responsibly,
love must be preceded by sensitivity. We must be able to "feel" with
our hearts the experiences and needs of those around us. It is difficult
to imagine how a person could love and not make an effort to be sensitive. We may love and not be as sensitive as we ought to be, but love
will make us want to improve our sensitivity, at the very least.

Sensitivity requires paying conscious attention to those around
us. "It means 'tuning in' to the thoughts and feelings of [others], listening to the cues they give us, and reacting appropriately to what we
detect" (James C. Dobson). For busy people like us, that is not easy.

Not only does sensitivity require conscious effort; it is somewhat
dangerous. It requires openness, receptivity, and even the willingness
to be vulnerable. It can't be practiced very well by "protective" people.

In the end, it is usually suffering that teaches us what sensitivity
means and how to practice it. It is the taste of tears that makes our
hearts more responsive to the tears of others. And it is the struggle to
overcome difficulty that makes our "senses" more alive and alert.

> The most beautiful people we have known are those who have known
> defeat, known suffering, known struggle, known loss, and have found their
> way out of the depths. These persons have an appreciation, a sensitivity, and
> an understanding of life that fills them with compassion, gentleness, and
> a deep loving concern. Beautiful people do not just happen.
>
> ELISABETH KÜBLER-ROSS

ACKNOWLEDGMENT

In comparing various authors with one another, I have discovered
that some of the gravest and latest writers have transcribed, word for
word, from former works, without making acknowledgment.

PLINY THE ELDER

IN ANY BOOK, THERE IS NO MORE IMPORTANT SECTION THAN
THE "ACKNOWLEDGMENTS." As readers, most of us probably skip
that section, but from the writer's perspective, that is the place where
he or she expresses appreciation for the help that others have given,
including those who have shared their inspiration and their ideas. To
stand on the shoulders of others, particularly other writers, and not to
acknowledge one's debt to them is a serious crime.

Recognition. One of the greatest types of acknowledgment is that
which says, "I recognize your presence. I am aware of you. I am taking
thought for you at this moment." This sounds like a simple thing,
but it is a gift that we fail to give when we walk in front of someone
without speaking or acknowledging their presence, when we "listen"
to someone without giving them our full attention, and so forth.

Honor. There are many times when we need to go beyond the
bare acknowledgment of someone else's presence. If what another
person has said or done is praiseworthy, then acknowledgment means
verbalizing the fact that we see their deed as good and honorable.

Gratitude. Just as honor goes beyond recognition, gratitude goes
beyond honor. Gratitude is an active, personal *appreciation* of someone else. It includes recognition and honor, but it adds the personal
element which says, "What you have done is meaningful to me, and I
want you to know that you have helped me." It takes not only thankfulness but also humility to acknowledge that we have been helped.

There is simply no such thing as greatness of character without
the acknowledgment of others. No matter what the endeavor, the
person who says "I did this all by myself" is usually telling a lie. In
telling this lie, we diminish ourselves. So let us increase the amount of
acknowledgment that is in our lives. Let us recognize the presence and
the contribution of others, let us give honor where honor is due, and
let us never be afraid to say "thank you" to those who have helped us.

There is as much greatness of mind in acknowledging
a good turn, as in doing it.

SENECA

QUICKNESS

The quick brown fox jumps over the lazy dog.
<small>PRACTICE SENTENCE USED IN TYPEWRITING</small>

O N AN AVERAGE DAY, WHICH ONE ARE YOU: THE QUICK
BROWN FOX OR THE LAZY DOG? While there are certainly
times when taking a nap is the right thing to do, more often the
brown fox who is "quick" has an advantage over the dog who is "lazy."

Consider two areas of life where quickness might be considered
a virtue. First, there is a well-known proverb which says, "Be slow to
promise and quick to perform." When we are thinking about making a commitment, slow deliberation is in order, but when the time
for keeping the commitment arrives, quickness is what we need. But
second, The Epistle of James says, "Let every person be quick to hear,
slow to speak, slow to anger." Too often, we reverse the order and are
quick to speak, especially in anger. If we're going to be quick, however,
quickness in hearing is the better policy. Seeking to understand the
other person is the thing that we ought to be the most eager to do.

But here is something else: there is a sense in which life will escape us if we don't enjoy it quickly. Martial, the Roman poet, went so
far as to say, "No man is quick enough to enjoy life." That may be an
exaggeration, but it is certainly true that life slips by us at an astonishing rate, and if we postpone the enjoyment of it until some future
date, we may find that life has passed us by before we had a chance
to enjoy it. Our childhood, our youth, our young adulthood, our kids,
and even our grandkids — these are all things that must be enjoyed
"quickly." As for life's true enjoyment, he who hesitates is lost.

If we think of quickness as "promptness," it is obvious that there
is a great value in it. "Well done is quickly done," said Augustus
Caesar. (He also said, "More haste, less speed.") There is a small, flat,
polished stone that I often keep in my pocket. Aquamarine in color,
it is engraved with the word "Now." I find that the presence of that
stone in my pocket is a very helpful reminder to act . . . quickly.

Quickness is especially important when the opportunity arises to
give to others or to serve them. There are times, no doubt, when we
can't give as quickly as we would like, but whenever possible, we should
increase the benefit of a gift by giving it sooner rather than later.

He gives twice who gives quickly.
<small>ENGLISH PROVERB</small>

GIVING

It is more blessed to give than to receive.
JESUS OF NAZARETH

ONE OF LIFE'S MOST BASIC DECISIONS IS THE DECISION BE-
TWEEN GIVING AND RECEIVING. During our lifetimes, each of
us will do a good bit of both: sometimes we will give, while at other
times receiving will be our lot. But by the time we die, each of us will
have established one or the other as our predominant pattern. That is,
our friends and family will know that one pattern — either giving or
taking — has prevailed over the other in our lives. Deciding which of
these modes of living will be ours is a decision of huge consequence.

Most of us struggle to be as giving-oriented as we would like to
be. Why is that? There are many reasons, I suppose, but one is that
we tend to put off giving until we have become more "prosperous." In
other words, we delay giving because, at the moment, we feel that we
just can't afford it. And this is true with our time and energy as well as
with gifts that are more monetary. We operate on the assumption that
being a consistent giver requires that we have ample resources.

But Harold Nye was undoubtedly correct when he said, "If you
are not generous with a meager income, you will never be generous
with abundance." So to become givers we need not wait until we
reach some stage in life when giving will have become easy. Indeed,
when we give out of an abundance, we hardly miss what has been
given, and our giving means less than when it requires real sacrifice.
Since sacrifice makes giving more gratifying, people of less means
are in a position to be more blessed in their giving than others. As
George Eliot said, "One must be poor to know the luxury of giving."

But the very best giving is the giving of ourselves, and here is
where we should be the most generous. Indeed, nothing else that we
can give to others matters if we withhold the gift of a gracious self. As
Shakespeare put it in *Hamlet,* "Rich gifts wax poor when givers prove
unkind." Before the opportunity escapes us, may we learn to be givers
more than takers — and givers of ourselves most of all.

That man may last, but never lives,
Who much receives but nothing gives;
Whom none can love, whom none can thank,
Creation's blot, creation's blank.
THOMAS GIBBONS

MATURITY

To exist is to change, to change is to mature,
to mature is to go on creating yourself endlessly.
HENRI-LOUIS BERGSON

IN A YOUTH-ORIENTED CULTURE, IT MAY SEEM STRANGE TO
DESCRIBE MATURITY AS AN "ENTHUSIASTIC IDEA." Maturity
has the aura of old age about it, and while most people want to live as
long as possible, they never want to become "old people." Yet moving
in the direction of maturity is the natural progression of life. If we are
aging but not becoming more mature, something is seriously wrong.
Maturity is not something to be resisted but rather welcomed.

But what is "maturity"? The word itself simply means "full development" or "maximum excellence." But chronologically, maturity
is the stage between youth and old age: the period after we've learned
the lessons of youth but before our physical and mental powers have
started to decline. It's the stage in life when our powers are at their
peak, the time when we do the work that our youth has prepared us
for. But more generally, we use the word "maturity" to describe the
wisdom and *good judgment* that come with the passing of years. It is
a mental state and not just a physical one. In fact, mental and physical maturity don't always go together. It's possible for a young person
to be quite mature, just as it's possible for an aged person to have
remained immature. Normally, however, maturity grows with age.

One of the salient characteristics of maturity is that we begin
to take personal responsibility for our actions. The more mature we
are, the less we blame external factors for our problems. "We have
not passed that subtle line between childhood and adulthood until
we move from the passive voice to the active voice — that is, until we
have stopped saying 'It got lost' and say 'I lost it'" (Sydney J. Harris).

All things considered, maturity is the most desirable stage in
life. The only way to avoid it is to die young or to grow old without
becoming mature. Sadly, the latter is what many of us have done. But
it's not too late. We may be behind schedule in acquiring the wisdom
that goes with maturity, but we can start working on it right now.
We can make up for lost time. And the best way to do that is to start
listening — with an open mind — when mature people are speaking.

You are never too old to grow up.
SHIRLEY CONRAN

GOALS

Establishing goals is all right, if you don't let them
deprive you of interesting detours.

DOUG LARSON

Two extremes are possible concerning goals: not setting any and being obsessed with them. Both of these are counterproductive. If we don't have any goals, we're probably going to wander haphazardly from one activity to another. But if we're so focused on our goals that we can't allow ourselves an occasional diversion, that is wrong-headed also. Both of these extremes diminish the good that can come from worthy goals wisely pursued.

Generally speaking, goals are good, but we need to be reminded that not all goals are equal. To be worthy of our pursuit, our goals must be principle-based, grounded in the standards of what is right and just. And since all of us are in the process of learning these standards, our goals can always be improved. There is much wisdom in revisiting our goals now and then to make adjustments in them.

Those who have dealings with us will appreciate us for seeing the value of goals and for working to improve our goals as time goes by. Learning to be goal-oriented is a great gift that we can give to others, and this is especially true when the goals have to do with the common good. Personal goals are beneficial, but we live on a higher plane when we frequently set goals with other people — and then commit ourselves to working with them to turn these goals into reality.

Every one of us has wasted some of the time that has been given to us in this world. Whether because of negligence, irresponsibility, or outright wrongdoing, we haven't made the progress toward our goals that we should have. Nevertheless, we are not captives of our past. "What is important is not where you came from but where you are going" (Bernie Rhodes). If our goals are good ones, then committing ourselves to them will point us toward a future that is better than our past. But if that is to happen, we're going to have to do more than say, "Well, I know I need to do better about some things." The question is: how *specific* are you willing to be about that? Exactly *what* do you need to do better about? And by what *date* do you plan to have done better? It's a fact: *the goals that are powerful are those that are specific!*

Goals are dreams with deadlines.

DIANA SCHARF

UNDERSTANDING

O divine Master, grant that I may not so much
seek to be consoled as to console; to be understood
as to understand; to be loved as to love.

FRANCIS OF ASSISI

To "UNDERSTAND" MIGHT MEAN SEVERAL THINGS. For our meditation today, let's select three of the more important definitions. First, understanding indicates that we grasp the meaning or significance of something. (I "understand" English grammar.) Second, it indicates that we know something thoroughly by close contact or long experience. (I "understand" my best friend.) And third, it indicates that we comprehend the meaning intended by another person. (I "understand" your objection to the plan.) All three of these kinds of understanding are valuable. They are good goals to strive for.

The third kind of understanding is especially valuable, and we need to spend more time trying to gain it. In our communications, we don't listen very carefully, we don't ask clarifying questions, and then we walk away assuming that we have gotten what the other person was saying. Many times, however, we've missed the point. All of us want to be understood when we're doing the talking, but not many of us are as concerned as we should be about understanding others. So Francis of Assisi's prayer is appropriate: "O divine Master, grant that I may not so much seek . . . to be understood as to understand."

Understanding others is not easy. As with academic subjects, we must "study" those who communicate with us. "It is profound philosophy to sound the depths of feeling and distinguish traits of character. Men must be studied as deeply as books" (Baltasar Gracián). But the effort is well worth making. As Oliver Wendell Holmes Sr. said, "A moment's insight is sometimes worth a life's experience."

The important thing is to be *growing* in our understanding. We will never understand everything about the world, but what understandings we do gain should be enjoyed. And since almost every understanding corrects some previous misunderstanding, growth in our understanding requires humility. Indeed, the prime difference between the wise man and the fool is that the wise man is correctable.

Once we realize that imperfect understanding
is the human condition, there is no shame in being wrong,
only in failing to correct our mistakes.

GEORGE SOROS

KNOWLEDGE

We do not know one millionth of one percent about anything.
THOMAS ALVA EDISON

ONE OF THE GREAT ADVENTURES IN LIFE IS THE EXPLORA-
TION OF NEW KNOWLEDGE. Learning things that we have
never known before is tremendously exciting. But just as the explora-
tion of previously uncharted physical territory is hard work, the attainment of new knowledge requires considerable effort. Perhaps that
is why many do not bother about it. But the rewards of new knowledge are well worth the exertion of ourselves to gain it.

The current "explosion of knowledge" may lead us to believe that
there is not much new territory to be explored, intellectually speaking.
But there is! Edison lived well before our times, but his words are just
as true today: "We do not know one millionth of one percent about
anything." And even in subject areas that we think are well-trodden,
there is still much that we might profitably give our minds to. As a
writer, I agree with Dostoevsky's observation: "There is no subject so
old that something new cannot be said about it."

I believe that there is a special benefit that comes from stretching
our minds to study topics that we do not presently have much interest
in. If you've never tried it, do this: go to a good bookstore, find a well-
written book on a topic that you know absolutely nothing about, and
read it seriously, just for the intellectual workout that it gives you.

And if you're really serious about learning, I want to recommend two other practices: *listening* and *teaching.* In regard to listening, a good listener "is not only popular everywhere, but after a while
he knows something" (Wilson Mizner). It's amazing what you can
learn by listening. And as for teaching, there is no better way to know
anything than to teach it to others. So do both of these things. Listen
every chance you get, and never turn down an opportunity to teach.

Finally, remember that we do not accumulate knowledge simply to be smarter; we do it so that we can make better choices in the
living of our lives. Our quest for *truth* (right knowledge) is for the
purpose of *goodness* (right conduct). The ultimate question, therefore,
is not what we know but what we are doing about what we know.

Whoever acquires knowledge and does not practice it
resembles him who plows his land and leaves it unsown.
SAADI

May 6
DIRECTION

He flung himself from the room, flung himself upon
his horse, and rode madly off in all directions.
STEPHEN BUTLER LEACOCK

AMONG THOSE WHO HAVE NO DIRECTION IN LIFE, THERE
ARE TWO TYPES OF INDIVIDUALS. One is the person who has
no goal at all. But the other is the fellow in Leacock's description: he
rides off "in all directions" at once. In these days of complexity and
choice, many of us suffer from this syndrome. Wanting to pursue so
many different interests, we have no sharply focused commitment to
any of them. We suffer from a serious lack of direction.

But before you settle on the main direction of your life, let me
caution you about the dangers of a wrong direction. One of my favorite quotations from William Barclay is this one: "However far you go,
it is not much use if it is not in the right direction." Couple that insight with Charles Caleb Colton's distinction between ignorance and
error: "Ignorance is content to stand still, with her back to the truth;
but error is more presumptuous and proceeds in the wrong direction. Ignorance has no light, but error follows a false one." Obviously,
deciding on our life's direction is a matter of extreme importance.
And if we're contemplating changing direction, that's an important
matter also. It's better to think slowly about changes in direction than
to make quick changes that will have to be undone later. F. Scott
Fitzgerald was right: "Once a change of direction has begun, even
though it's the wrong one, it still tends to clothe itself as thoroughly
in the appurtenances of rightness as if it had been a natural all along."

Perhaps because people of clear direction are so rare, those who
do have a strong sense of direction are strikingly noticeable. They
stand out. I don't recommend that you decide on your direction
merely for competitive reasons, but I can tell you this from experience:
if you want to be different from your peers, just know where you are going.
That will distinguish you clearly. And not only that, but when you
decide on your direction and commit yourself to following it, you'll
find yourself filled with a motivation that you've probably not known
before. "To grow and know what one is growing towards — that is the
source of all strength and confidence in life" (James Baillie).

The world stands aside to let anyone pass who knows where he is going.
DAVID STARR JORDAN

MAKING

Man unites himself with the world in the process of creation.
ERICH FROMM

IN ONE SENSE, WE CAN'T REALLY "MAKE" ANYTHING; WE CAN ONLY REARRANGE WHAT'S ALREADY BEEN MADE. But what marvelous rearrangements we can sometimes achieve! A world in which things like the Eiffel Tower or the Egyptian Pyramids can be made is a world that easily qualifies for the term "amazing."

In the taxonomy of living things, we categorize ourselves as *homo sapiens,* the species that "knows." But we could just as accurately designate ourselves, *homo faber,* the species that "makes." We're a "making" bunch of creatures if ever there was one. Never content with what is, we're always taking what we find at hand and making something new out of it. It's instinctive to us, and we find great pleasure in it.

Have you ever wondered why we make so many things and why we derive such satisfaction from doing so? What motivates us in our making? Igor Stravinsky said, "In order to create there must be a dynamic force, and what force is more potent than love?" I think he's right. In the end, it's almost always love that drives us to create. We love the process of making, we love the thing made once it's finished, and we love, especially and most powerfully, those for whom it is made. Of all the things we make, none are of greater quality and worth than those we make out of love and dedicate to another person.

It is good for us to keep alive the urge to bring new things into being. For many obvious reasons, we tend to take on fewer new projects when we reach old age, but even then it's healthy to keep pushing ourselves to create. Every day there is something new we can make, even if it's only a small thing, and it's good for us to keep on trying.

Some of the most honorable traits that can be built into the human character come from the effort to create. Makers (as opposed to those who only consume what others make) have good reasons to keep their integrity. They tend to be trustworthy, and we'd do well to borrow a little of their motivation. When we're making, we're moving forward, and more often than not, that's the direction we need to go!

Let a human being throw the energies of his soul
into the making of something, and the instinct
of workmanship will take care of his honesty.
WALTER LIPPMANN

May 8

HOME

A child on a farm sees a plane fly overhead
and dreams of a faraway place. A traveler on the plane
sees the farmhouse . . . and dreams of home.

CARL BURNS

IF OUR LANGUAGE HAS ANY MAGICAL WORDS IN IT, "HOME" IS
SURELY ONE OF THEM. Few can say the word thoughtfully and
remained unmoved. But if the homes from which we came are important to us, the mothers who made those homes shouldn't be forgotten.
Fathers matter too, of course, but if it's patriarchs who beget families,
it's matriarchs who make homes. And with the approach of Mother's
Day, we ought to be thinking of generous ways to say "thank you."

Modern mothers, unfortunately, are often seduced into believing that "home" is not as important a concept as their grandmothers
thought it was. To the great detriment of our culture and our civilization, too many good women have come to think of childbearing and
child-nurturing as inconvenient obstacles that stand between them
and the happiness they deserve "out there." Modern fathers are not
without their own share of blame, to be sure, but there's a special
sense in which the loss of a motherly presence in our homes is tragic.
I'll go so far as to say this: a home can more easily survive the loss of
Dad's presence than it can Mom's, and Moms these days need to be
honestly confronting the extent to which their absence is voluntary.

But one of the wonderful virtues of this thing that we call "home"
is how resilient it is. None of us had homes that were perfect, but despite that fact, most of us can look back with a good deal of gratitude.
Somehow we survived the mistakes that were made, and now it's nourishing to remember the environment where we got our start. It's not
often possible to "go back home," at least physically, but it's a mighty
good thing to go back home emotionally every chance we get. Those
who get "above their raising," so to speak, lose many of the best things
in life. So we need to reconnect with our origins, however humble they
may have been. We have to go forward in this world; that's just the
way life works. But the time will surely come, if it hasn't already, when
our hearts will need to go back home . . . for a visit.

I have come back again to where I belong;
not an enchanted place, but the walls are strong.

DOROTHY H. RATH

INDIVIDUALITY

The reason a polar bear wears a fur coat
is because he'd look funny in a woolen one.
ANONYMOUS

ERIC FROMM SAID, "MEN ARE BORN EQUAL BUT THEY ARE ALSO BORN DIFFERENT." In our more serious moments, we realize that this is a good thing, but much of the time we act as if standardization of the human race were the ideal. We spend foolish amounts of time trying to be just like other people — or trying to convince them to be just like us. Some differences among people should be removed, of course, but differences of personality, taste, and native ability ought to be appreciated as marks of individuality.

It should be noted that individuality is quite different from individualism. Individualism is an imbalanced, self-centered lack of regard for groups and relationships and communities. It's an attitude which says, "I only care about one thing, and that is doing my own thing." If adopted by enough people, this attitude would destroy human society.

But individuality is not self-centered. It's a healthy appreciation of our uniqueness, and it has a strong sense of duty to others. Sydney J. Harris said it this way: "Every single person has one thing that he can do a little better than most people around him, and he has a sacred obligation to himself to find out what that thing is and to do it."

Igor Sikorsky once said, "The work of the individual still remains the spark that moves mankind forward." So individuality helps us to make a better contribution to the relationships that we're a part of. "In proportion to the development of his individuality, each person becomes more valuable to others. There is a greater fullness of life about his own existence, and when there is more life in the units there is more in the mass which is composed of them" (John Stuart Mill).

Two things, then, are necessary. The first is that we develop our own individuality, and the second is that we accept the individuality of others. This does not mean condoning wrongdoing or immorality. Within the limits of what is right, it means rejoicing in variety.

Cultivate your own capabilities, your own style. Appreciate the
members of your family for who they are, even though their outlook
or style may be miles different from yours. Rabbits don't fly. Eagles don't
swim. Ducks look funny trying to climb. Squirrels don't have feathers.
Stop comparing. There's plenty of room in the forest.
CHARLES R. SWINDOLL

GUIDANCE

It is better to ask the way ten times
than to take the wrong road once.

JEWISH PROVERB

MOST OF US SUFFER FROM A LACK OF GOOD GUIDANCE. Like the pioneers of yesteryear who migrated to California in covered wagons, we are passing through unfamiliar (and often dangerous) "territory" these days, and without guidance, we are apt to get lost. Frequently, we're like the fool who says, "I don't need to consult a guide. I can figure this out myself." And so we err, often needlessly.

When we do seek guidance, however, we tend to make two mistakes. First, we consult only our peers, those who are close to our own age and socio-economic bracket. These people may sometimes give good guidance, but because they are our peers, they probably don't know much more about life than we do. To get better guidance, we need to find someone older, or at least someone who looks at life from a different angle than we do. But second, the only people we ask for guidance are those who are likely to tell us what we want to hear. We may say that we're seeking wise people, but who are those whom we consider wise? Isn't it usually those who think the same as we do?

Both of these difficulties illustrate that there is a strong personal element to guidance. If we're honest, we'll have to admit the truth of this statement by John White: "Deep in your heart it is not guidance that you want as much as a guide." When the path before us is uncertain, we need not only facts and information; we need a friendly person who will guide us by leading us and supporting us.

Ultimately, we should want our guidance to be based on truth. Whether we're giving guidance to others or seeking guidance for ourselves, our desire should be both to advise and to do what is right. And truth's guidance would be more clear to us if we listened more honestly to our conscience. Conscience is not an infallible guide, of course, because our conscience may be misinformed. But more often than not, our conscience will give us helpful guidance. The problem is, we don't listen. And not even the best guidance can help the "deaf."

Everywhere, O Truth, dost thou give audience to all who ask counsel of thee,
and at once answerest all, though on manifold matters they ask thy counsel.
Clearly dost thou answer, though all do not clearly hear.

AUGUSTINE OF HIPPO

PREVENTION

An ounce of prevention is worth a pound of cure.
OLD PROVERB

IT HARDLY SEEMS NECESSARY TO SAY IT, BUT PREVENTING A PROBLEM IS BETTER THAN REPAIRING ONE. Prevention can be difficult and costly, but in truth, it is nowhere near as difficult and costly as repair. Surely, we need to do more prevention and less repair.

I hesitate to recommend prevention, though, because some people overdo it. There is a certain type of person who is so prudent and conservative that the thought of doing anything risky never enters their mind. They are obsessed with the prevention of anything unpleasant. So please understand: in recommending prevention, I don't want you to be like these *overly* cautious folks. They know nothing of adventure or joy — and they do very little good in the world.

Rightly defined, however, prevention includes two ingredients:

Patience. There is a Chinese proverb that says, "One moment of patience may prevent disaster; one moment of impatience may ruin a life." When you think about it, it's clear that many damaging things happen because we aren't patient enough. We rush ahead, ignore the warning signs, and suffer harm that patience would have prevented.

Promptness. Many of the costly mistakes we make are in areas where we put off doing "preventive maintenance." If you own a house or a car, you know how this works. Because you didn't promptly tend to that "little problem," it grew worse and ended up costing a fortune to fix. The big problem could have been prevented by fixing the little one promptly. And so it is with many of our personal problems.

To err is human, and looking back, all of us can see damage that was done because we failed to engage in the work of prevention. But that is not cause for despair. Indeed, there is some hope in it. If it weren't for the mistakes that we've made — and the painful consequences that got our attention — we would likely have made more serious mistakes later on. The "live and learn" maxim is based on the fact that making one mistake can prevent the making of another one. So let's not be morbid about having failed to prevent certain things from happening. Instead, let's learn everything we can from our failures. Doing so is the very best way to prevent worse things from happening.

A stumble may prevent a fall.
THOMAS FULLER

REALITY

The real world is not easy to live in.

CLARENCE DAY

FACTS ARE STUBBORN THINGS, AS JOHN ADAMS ONCE TOLD THE JURY IN A FAMOUS TRIAL. We may deny reality, run away from it, or suppress it, but the facts are still there to be dealt with. Philip K. Dick defined reality this way: "Reality is that which, when you stop believing in it, doesn't go away." What this means, in practice, is that there is a certain hardness to reality. "The real world is not easy to live in," as Clarence Day said. It presents us with challenges that call for intelligence, determination, and fortitude.

Truth is more than appearances. Most of us are world-class athletes when it comes to the sport of conclusion-jumping. We leap to erroneous conclusions very quickly. But if we're committed to reality, we will look a little deeper. In any situation, what is really going on is probably different from what seems to be going on. First impressions, outward appearances, and superficial judgments can be misleading.

Truth is more than personal preferences. "How reluctantly the mind consents to reality!" exclaimed Norman Douglas. It's true. When our wishful thinking collides with reality, rather than yielding to reality, we simply pretend that it is whatever we want it to be. But make-believe is foolish. As hard as it is, we have to come to grips with reality.

Truth is more than opinion polls. As a student of philosophy, I used to have a hard time understanding why, if some things are real, everybody doesn't agree that they are real. But there is no reality that commands universal assent, and as the Danish proverb says, "The sky is not less blue because the blind man does not see it." We can't afford to reduce our beliefs to the little, if anything, that everybody believes.

So we must be willing to deal with what is, in fact, true. What is true may not be what we prefer, it may not be what we first thought was true, and it may not be what many other people accept. But if a thing is true, then we need to have both the humility and the courage to acknowledge it. We are free to work toward a better reality and move any situation closer to what it ought to be, but we dare not lose touch with the reality of our circumstances as they *presently* are.

Mental Health Rule No. 5 — *Balance fantasy with fact.*
Dream but also do; wish but build; imagine but ever face reality.

JOSEPH FETTERMAN

May 13
CRITERIA

Nothing is more difficult, and therefore more precious, than to decide.
NAPOLEON BONAPARTE

DECISIONS ARE AN EVERYDAY REALITY, AND SOMETIMES THEY ARE HARD TO MAKE. In some instances, they are hard because we don't have all the information we need. But at other times, our decisions are difficult because we aren't sure what criteria ought to be applied in making the decision. A criterion is a standard, rule, or test by which a decision can be made. It is, as we say, a "deciding factor." Suppose a recent college graduate has two job offers. Which will he accept? The decision will have to be made on the basis of some criteria. Selecting what criteria are going to be used is very important.

The criteria that a person uses in making decisions says a good deal about his or her character. In our example, let's say that one job will be more lucrative, but it will require lying on behalf of the company. When the candidate selects one of these to be the deciding factor — money or honesty — we will learn something about his character.

Unfortunately, many people have no higher criteria than their own experience or their own preferences. "The accepted philosophy of today . . . emphasizes meaningful experience as the criterion for truth. Facts are considered irrelevant, except insofar as they 'turn us on'" (Erwin W. Lutzer). But I want to suggest that there are some objective standards by which our decisions can be made. When we are deciding what is true, what is right, and what is good, there is far more to consider than "whatever works for me," to use the popular lingo. Personal experience can be misleading, and personal preference is notoriously fickle. Are there no higher and better criteria? Yes, there are!

As a species, we are distinguished by our moral faculty. We are capable of deciding between right and wrong, but unfortunately, we don't often consider rightness as a criterion in our decisions. Frequently, we make crucial choices using no higher criteria than pleasure, social benefit — or worse, economic benefit. In a materialistic, capitalistic culture like ours, it is hard to keep in mind that there is more to think about than the mere question of monetary advantage. But if that is hard to keep in mind, we need to keep it in mind anyway.

Every act of every man is a moral act,
to be tested by moral, and not by economic, criteria.
ROBERT MAYNARD HUTCHINS

PERFECTION

Aim at perfection in everything, though in most things it is unattainable.
However, they who aim at it, and persevere, will come much nearer to it than
those whose laziness and despondency make them give it up as unattainable.

LORD CHESTERFIELD

JUST BECAUSE PERFECTION IS OUT OF OUR REACH RIGHT NOW, THAT DOESN'T MEAN WE SHOULDN'T PURSUE IT. There are many goals that are unachievable but still worth trying to achieve because the effort itself is beneficial. Perfection is one of them. We exert a greater effort and see better results when we aim high rather than low. As Ralph Barton Perry said, "A man can do his best only by confidently seeking (and perpetually missing) an unattainable perfection."

What is commonly called "perfectionism" is not a good trait, of course. That's the picky, neurotic impulse to accept nothing but absolute perfection. Such thinking is not beneficial. Indeed, the "pursuit of perfection often impedes improvement" (George Will).

But we are not recommending perfectionistic intolerance. We are simply suggesting that striving for perfection (call it "excellence" if you wish) is an uplifting exercise. Along the way, we'll have to accept a good deal of imperfection in our own lives and that of others.

The pursuit of perfection involves us in two disciplines: the discipline of *waiting* and the discipline of *hardship*. In regard to waiting, Voltaire said, "Perfection is attained by slow degrees; it requires the hand of time." The higher our standards are, the more patient we will have to be. And as for hardship, we must understand that the process of being perfected is not easy. "The gem cannot be polished without friction, nor man perfected without trials" (Chinese proverb).

Finally, may I suggest something you may not have thought about. We often think perfection would mean filling in the gaps and adding to our lives things that are not there right now, but the truth is often just the opposite. I believe Antoine de Saint-Exupéry was right: "Perfection is finally attained, not when there is no longer anything to add, but when there is no longer anything to take away."

So where would you be if your innermost character had reached its perfect culmination? I recommend that you strive to go there.

We are fallible. We certainly haven't attained perfection.
But we can strive for it, and the virtue is in the striving.

CARLOS P. RÓMULO

AIM

A novelist must know what his last chapter is going to say
and one way or another work toward that last chapter.

LEON URIS

IN WRITING, THE FIRST THING AN AUTHOR DECIDES IS WHAT TO PUT LAST. Once he knows the definite point that he is aiming for, he can figure out how to hit that target. But without a target, his writing is going to be "aimless" in the very worst sense of the term.

But if aimless writing is bad, aimless living is worse. Little good comes from wandering through life with no particular point in mind that we are trying to get to. As Epictetus said, "First say to yourself what you would be, and then do what you have to do." The various activities in which we engage from day to day ought to be the means that we have decided upon to accomplish our intended aim.

Living without an aim is actually dangerous. Great damage can be done to ourselves and others by following the *Ready! Fire! Aim!* philosophy. Simply rearranging the order to *Ready! Aim! Fire!* is one of the best precautions we can take as we make our way through life.

There is another danger, however, and that is the danger of losing sight of our aim in the midst of making our effort. Even when we have carefully decided what goals and aspirations are worth working toward, we may become so obsessed with the "what" of our work that we lose our grip on the "why." This is dangerous because it leads to blind, uncritical zealotry. "Fanaticism consists in redoubling your effort when you have forgotten your aim" (George Santayana).

But the word "aim" can mean not only the target toward which one's efforts are directed; it can also mean skill in hitting the target. A person with "good aim," then, has two characteristics: (1) he has a good target in mind, and (2) he is good at hitting the target. The second of these characteristics is where many of us fail to take personal responsibility. We blame our "poor aim" on everything and everybody except ourselves. But we can do better than that. So today, let's evaluate the worthiness of our aim (or goal) in life — and then let's work on improving whatever skills we need to hit the mark.

When an archer misses the mark, he turns and looks for the fault
within himself. Failure to hit the bull's-eye is never the fault
of the target. To improve your aim, improve yourself.

GILBERT ARLAND

NATURALNESS

*I want to be seen here in my simple, natural, ordinary fashion,
without straining or artifice; for it is myself that I portray.*
MICHEL DE MONTAIGNE

GENERALLY SPEAKING, IT IS BETTER TO ACT NATURALLY
THAN TO ACT UNNATURALLY. But naturalness is a somewhat
complicated issue. Before you take someone's advice to be "yourself,"
you need to know that, as the advertisers say, "some restrictions apply."

For one thing, your natural self may need some improvement. If,
for example, dishonesty is one of your personal characteristics, it won't
do for you to lie, cheat, and steal from your neighbor, and then say,
"Well, I was just being myself." No, many things that come naturally
to us are things that need to be changed, and naturalness is no excuse
for wrong conduct. If we want to "be ourselves" and feel good about
it, we need to adjust our habits in the direction of what is *right*.

But in the second place, there is nothing hypocritical about
doing our best in special situations. If your house is like mine, it is
not always kept in immaculate condition. There is a sense in which,
when people come to see me, I ought to be content for them to see
my house in its natural condition. But in another sense, I honor those
who are my guests by getting the place in tiptop shape before they arrive. That's not being hypocritical — it is giving someone a gift which
says, "I care enough about you to give you my very best effort."

With these two cautions in mind, however, consider the benefit
of naturalness in our dealings with others. We ought not to be so
embarrassed or vulnerable to social pressure that we engage in fake or
phony behavior. That kind of behavior is called "affectation," and John
Locke was right when he said, "Affectation is an awkward and forced
imitation of what should be genuine and easy, lacking the beauty
that accompanies what is natural." The truth is, unnatural behavior
is hardly ever successful. It doesn't fool anybody. So why don't we lay
aside our artificiality, our pretense, and our pride? Yes, we need to improve ourselves in every way that we can, but if we're doing our best,
then there is no need for us to hide the natural person that we are.

How majestic is naturalness. I have never met a man whom I really
considered a great man who was not always natural and simple.
Affectation is inevitably the mark of one not sure of himself.
CHARLES G. DAWES

AMBITION

*Ambition is neither a virtue or a vice, although it may easily
become either. It derives whatever moral quality it possesses from
its object and from the means employed in its attainment.*

JAMES T. WHITE

IN ITS MOST BASIC SENSE, AMBITION SIMPLY MEANS A STRONG
DESIRE TO ACHIEVE SOMETHING. But this is a word with two
very different uses: one strongly positive and one strongly negative.

Negatively, ambition describes the selfish, competitive, and often
ruthless attributes of the person who is bent on getting to the top.
Sometimes called "selfish ambition," this trait is driven by pride (and
often, to tell the truth, a sense of inferiority). It is the social-climbing,
status-seeking motivation described by one writer as "the mind's immodesty," and it should have no place in any honorable person's life.

But ambition need not be of that sort. On the positive side, ambition can indicate a character trait that is very desirable. As someone
has described it, it is simply "looking to the heights." Aspiring to
goals that are worthy and right in themselves, we pursue these goals
passionately. In its positive sense, ambition means that whatever we
do, we aim to do well. We are not content to slouch through our lives.

Surely, ambition must be governed by conscience — and not just
conscience but a well-educated conscience, grounded in the valid,
unchanging principles of right and wrong. True ambition will never
pursue any goal that fails the test of rightness. But more than that,
ambition will not pursue even a right goal by *means* that are not right.
And this, it seems to me, is what chiefly distinguishes right ambition from wrong ambition. Thinking that the end justifies the means,
wrong ambition will do whatever it takes to get ahead. It would stab
its best friend in the back for the sake of personal advantage. But
right ambition understands that he who "sacrifices his conscience to
ambition burns a picture to obtain the ashes" (Chinese proverb).

Within the limits of a principled conscience, then, we need to
have ambition. The "height of our ambition" needs to be high indeed.
"Good enough" is simply not good enough, and if we ever quit trying
to do the best things to the best of our ability, then we will have sold
our souls to the devil of mediocrity. So let's not sell out. Let's aspire!

Hitch your wagon to a star.

RALPH WALDO EMERSON

GENEROSITY

Giving is a joy if we do it in the right spirit. It all depends on whether
we think of it as "What can I spare?" or as "What can I share?"
ESTHER YORK BURKHOLDER

GENEROSITY, LIKE MANY OTHER THINGS, DEPENDS ON OUR ATTITUDE AND OUR MOTIVATION. If our heart is not in the right place, what could be a good thing will end up being not so good.

So let's ask ourselves: where is our heart when we're being generous? Unfortunately, it's often on some payoff that we suppose might come from our generosity. We scratch the backs of those who have it within their power to scratch our backs in return. Or maybe we just want the psychological payoff of feeling good about ourselves. Either way, we need to be careful. Such motivations are self-centered. To be truly generous, a gift must be one for which nothing is expected in return. "A generous action is its own reward" (William Walsh).

When we purify our motivation, however, what we begin to realize is that generosity is one of the most uplifting things in the world. When we forget about whether we're being benefited, great benefits flow our way — not as the aim of our generosity but simply as a by-product. For example, Karl Menninger, the well-known psychiatrist, once said, "Generous people are rarely mentally ill people." All in all, there is nothing in the world that contributes to personal balance and well-being any more than becoming outward-oriented and generous.

If honesty indicates that we've not been generous in the past, we need to begin retraining ourselves. But I would suggest that you start small. Look for little gifts that you can give. Next, do this more frequently, and then gradually learn to give bigger gifts. In time, generosity will be more than a once-in-a-while gesture. It will be a habit.

At some point, our generosity needs to become sacrificial in nature. Lesser giving certainly has its place, but the act of giving means the most when it is costly — that is, when we give that which we can't afford to lose. And there is no shortcut to this kind of generosity. So sale-shoppers and coupon-clippers, be advised: generosity is a thing that never goes on sale. It is always expensive. Generosity is measured in terms of sacrifice, and so truly generous gifts are never affordable.

We'd all like a reputation for generosity,
and we'd all like to buy it cheap.
MIGNON MCLAUGHLIN

May 19

ENDEAVOR

Every human soul is of infinite value, eternal and free. No human being,
therefore, is so placed as not to have within his reach, in himself and
others, objects adequate to infinite endeavor.

ARTHUR JAMES BALFOUR

I BELIEVE THAT "ENDEAVOR" IS ONE OF THE MOST BEAUTIFUL WORDS IN THE ENGLISH LANGUAGE. Living in a world that, despite its goodness, is tragically broken and where many of our desires and goals seem frustratingly out of reach, the fact that we continue to endeavor speaks volumes about the nobility of the human spirit. In the face of such discouragement, lesser creatures would give up. But we do not. We persevere. We stay the course. We endeavor!

To endeavor is to make an earnest effort to reach a goal or fulfill a purpose. It is to strive conscientiously toward an end. But does anything we do make any difference? Are there any purposes worth working for? I, for one, believe that there are. I refuse to give in to the nihilism and cynicism that are so fashionable. Doesn't the fact that we continue to struggle say something about us? Deep down, we know that all is not lost. We know that endeavor is worthwhile.

But let me clarify something. As a philosopher, I agree with the Book of Ecclesiastes. In the grand scheme of things, we are not going to change this world by anything that we do. As individuals, when we have lived and died, the world will be pretty much the same as it was when we got here. *But that doesn't mean our endeavors are useless!* It means that we do good not to change the world, but to lessen the suffering of specific people in specific ways. We have the opportunity to make a difference in our own generation. And that's worthwhile!

Even in the short term, however, we don't always know what's going to happen. We endeavor, we work, and we do our best, but most of the time we have no guarantee as to the outcome. Yet we endeavor anyway. "There are some things that it is better to begin than to refuse, even though the end may be dark" (J. R. R. Tolkien).

So today, I hope you will ponder the word "endeavor." It is a rich word, suggestive of some of the highest thoughts that we can think. It reminds us that there is value in trying to do our best. No matter what.

Despite the success cult, men are most deeply moved not by
the reaching of the goal but by the grandness of the effort involved
in getting there — or failing to get there.

MAX LERNER

May 20
SWEETNESS

Out of the eater came something to eat,
And out of the strong came something sweet.
THE BOOK OF JUDGES

MOST OF US COULD STAND A LITTLE SWEETENING. To be
described as sweet is not a criticism but a compliment, even for
men. And in these days of stress and strain when life tends to make us
hard, a bit of sweetness added to our character would be welcomed by
those who have to deal with us. When you consider the opposites of
sweetness — sourness, bitterness, unpleasantness, grouchiness, etc. —
isn't it clear that sweetness is an attribute we should aspire to?

Sweetness can be overdone, of course, and that is probably what
most people have in mind when they think of the word negatively.
Just as foods can be too sweet, so can people. Personally, I appreciate
being called sweet, but I wouldn't care to have it said that I am "sug-
ary" or "saccharine." That would mean there is an imbalance in my
makeup and that I am missing some qualities meant to complement
sweetness, such as seriousness, realism, and strength. But balanced
with other qualities, sweetness should be one of the traits for which
we're known. It simply means we have a pleasing disposition and are
kind and gracious in our dealings with others.

But in addition to sweetness of disposition, there is also the
sweetness of life itself. At least two things need to be said about this.
One is that we often fail to appreciate it because of our abundance.
For many of us, sweetness is a very ordinary, unexceptional thing, and
as Shakespeare said, "Sweets grown common lose their delight."

The other thing, closely related to the first, is that our hearts may
have to be broken before we can understand the sweet side of life. As
an old Jewish proverb puts it, "The man who has not tasted the bitter
does not know what the sweet is." And not only that, but it may take
hardship and suffering to bring out the sweet side of our disposition.
You may not think of yourself as being very sweet, and others may not
think of you that way either. But when you have been deeply hurt, all
of that may change. It will depend on how you choose to respond.

Aromatic plants bestow
No spicy fragrance while they grow;
But crushed or trodden to the ground
Diffuse their sweetness all around.
OLIVER GOLDSMITH

AMIABILITY

To those who knew Kropotkin, the man seemed more important
than his works, and throughout our account we have had to record
the strong impressions of amiability and goodness left by him.

GEORGE WOODCOCK

YESTERDAY WE TALKED ABOUT "SWEETNESS," AND TODAY OUR
TOPIC IS "AMIABILITY." Today's word, a good one although we
don't use it very often, is one of several English words that come from
the Latin noun *amicus* ("friend'). Amicable ("characterized by friendship or goodwill") and amity ("peaceful relations") are two others.
All of these words have to do with friendship. Amiability means a
friendly disposition or outlook. The amiable person tends to think of
other people as friends, and this shows up in two characteristics:

(1) *Likableness.* This is the most basic feature of amiability. It
suggests the person who is agreeable in temperament. The expression
"good-natured" is probably an apt synonym. The amiable person's
natural bent or inclination is to like people — and he or she is easy for
others to like in return. Friendly people have friends!

(2) *Cordiality.* The second aspect of good-natured people is that
they enjoy the company of others. Words like "cordial" and "congenial" describe them. They see the value of social relationships, and
they enjoy time spent interacting with friends. They also see the value
of relating to strangers and newcomers in a friendly, welcoming way.

Although most people think of these two things — likableness
and cordiality — as personality traits, they are much more than that.
Indeed, these two characteristics have little to do with personality.
They are *chosen ways of thinking,* and having been chosen, they will
show up in ways appropriate to each of our various personalities.

In general, we need to give higher priority to simple traits like
amiability. Judging by our schedule books, we spend more of our daily
time chasing the goals of "intelligence" and "talent" and "success." But
when the final accounting is made, wouldn't we rather be remembered
for characteristics like amiability? Without qualities like these — the
ones that connect us joyfully to other human beings — what will we
have achieved by all of our "accomplishments"?

Good nature is more agreeable in conversation than wit, and gives
a certain air to the countenance which is more amiable than beauty.

JOSEPH ADDISON

SELF-CONTROL

Whoever has no rule over his own spirit
is like a city broken down, without walls.

THE BOOK OF PROVERBS

IF WE FAIL TO LEARN SELF-CONTROL, WE LEAVE OURSELVES DEFENSELESS AGAINST THE WORST ENEMIES OF THE HUMAN SPIRIT. It is simply a fact that some things have to be refused, and while we may sometimes err in distinguishing between what should and should not be refused, the inability to say "No" to anything is a disastrous deficiency. Without the power of "No," we are doomed.

Consider anger, for example. While not inherently wrong, anger is a form of emotional dynamite that most of us are not capable of handling without hurting ourselves and others. Anger requires restraint, but it is extremely hard to restrain. The person who can do it is a person of uncommon strength and courage. As another text from Proverbs says, "He who is slow to anger is better than the mighty, and he who rules his spirit than he who takes a city."

Ultimately, self-control means that we yield to the commands of our conscience. I like how W. K. Hope described it: "Self-discipline is when your conscience tells you to do something and you don't talk back." But since following our conscience is not always what we want to do, it's a hard habit to acquire. For most of us, subordinating our impulses and desires to our conscience takes years of practice.

Life is full of tests, and some are bigger than others. Before we die, two or three situations are probably going to arise that will test us far beyond the limits of life's normal trials. Some people think they can repeatedly default on life's little responsibilities, but when the big moment arrives (and the spotlight is on), they'll be able to rise to the occasion and do what's right. But H. P. Liddon was telling the truth when he said, "What we do upon some great occasion will probably depend on what we already are; and what we are will be the result of previous years of self-discipline." So if honest evaluation indicates that we're "a city broken down, without walls," now is the time to work on our self-control. When we've mastered our impulses, we'll be rulers over a treasure-city with riches no enemy is strong enough to take from us.

Lord of himself, though not of lands;
And having nothing, yet hath all.

SIR HENRY WOTTON

PREPARATION

Luck is a matter of preparation meeting opportunity.
OPRAH WINFREY

WHEN GOOD THINGS HAPPEN TO THEIR NEIGHBORS, SOME PEOPLE JUST SHAKE THEIR HEADS AND SAY, "SOME FOLKS HAVE ALL THE LUCK." They assume that life's blessings are only for the lucky. But while fortuitous circumstances do occur, the thing that most people call "luck" is not luck at all. It is, as Oprah Winfrey said, a matter of "preparation meeting opportunity." Oprah herself gave a number of writers their "big break" by putting them on her television show. But there is nothing lucky about that process. These were people who had worked long and hard at their writing craft, and when Oprah called, they were prepared and ready to take advantage of the opportunity. For the unprepared, such a "break" would be useless.

In our instant society, the whole concept of preparation is often short-circuited. If a situation requires any preparation at all, we can't see why it should take very long. The idea of preparing for something by working diligently over a period of many years sounds crazy to us.

The truth, however, is that all serious work requires preparation — sometimes over a long span of time. Indeed, the time of preparation may exceed the time of the work itself. And not only does it take time, but it often requires considerable hardship and pain. Those who finally succeed are usually those who have experienced many failures along the way. So I encourage you to take a broader view of preparation. *There is not much that you will ever learn or experience that won't help prepare you for some worthy work that you could do in the future.*

My good friend Curtis Byers, who knows the science of physics, tells me that "potential" is the amount of "work" that can be done by an elevated object. But its potential (the work that it can do) is no greater than the work that was required to elevate it in the first place! So in life, as in physics, there is no free lunch. Those who have the greatest *potential* are those who have worked the hardest at *preparation.* Instead of luck, it's a matter of being ready when opportunity knocks.

Men who have attained things worth having in this world have worked while others idled, have persevered while others gave up in despair, have practiced early in life the valuable habits of self-denial, industry, and singleness of purpose. As a result, they enjoy in later life the success so often erroneously attributed to luck.
GRENVILLE KLEISER

SOLACE

Many a green isle needs must be
In the deep wide sea of Misery,
Or the mariner, worn and wan,
Never thus could voyage on.

PERCY BYSSHE SHELLEY

IF IT WERE NOT FOR SOLACE, MOST OF US WOULD HAVE GIVEN UP LONG AGO. Solace is comfort. It comes from the same Latin root as the word "consolation." And what wonderful things comfort and consolation are. Where would any of us be without them?

In our culture, it is assumed that all of the painful emotions should be avoided. Feelings like sorrow, shame, and discouragement are defined as being inherently undesirable. If possible, they are to be kept out of our lives, and if they do appear, they are to be gotten rid of as soon as possible. As a result, most of us have the notion that giving solace or comfort to someone means helping them to hurry up and feel better. If they don't snap out of it, we tend to lose patience.

But the painful emotions have their place, and they are not to be avoided. (Getting "stuck" in these, of course, is undesirable, but that is a discussion for another day.) The old saying is true: *we can only heal what we've allowed ourselves to feel.* So solace doesn't necessarily mean ceasing to feel sorrow or pain. It means being comforted, encouraged, and supported while we feel those emotions. In time, we will feel better, but for the time being, we simply need . . . solace.

Sometimes, we are in the position of *giving* solace. The art of consolation is a high art, and not many of us are adept at it. We would do well to work on our comforting skills. But at other times, we are the ones *seeking* solace. At such times, it's easy to assume that we need another person to console us. And that may be true, but the fact is, there are many other rich sources of solace. Depending on our makeup, we may find comfort in books, music, or other things. The best one of all is the outdoors. "Nature has been for me, for as long as I remember, a source of solace, inspiration, adventure, and delight" (Lorraine Anderson). Ultimately, however, it is within our own hearts that comfort must be found. And find it we will, if we are patient.

There is nothing so bitter that a patient mind
cannot find some solace for it.

SENECA

PEACE

All men desire peace, but very few desire
those things that make for peace.

THOMAS À KEMPIS

PEACE IS HARDER TO WORK FOR THAN TO WISH FOR. Whether
it's peace within our own hearts or peace with other human beings, peace does not result from wishful thinking or pious platitudes.
A price has to be paid, and it's a price that many people are simply not
willing to pay. Yes, it sounds good to quote Jesus' statement, "Blessed
are the peacemakers." But this blessing is not upon peace-*lovers*. It is
upon peace-*makers* — and we would do well to notice the difference.

Peacemaking work. Pursuing peace is not a sentiment; it is an
activity. Steps have to be taken to remove the barriers to peace.

Peacemaking patience. As a rule, the longer an enmity has lasted,
the longer it takes to overcome it. If we're committed to peace, we
should be prepared to persevere in its pursuit. Usually, it is slow work.

It must be said, however, that no matter how patiently we work
for peace, the results do not depend entirely on us. There is much
truth in the Dutch proverb which says, "No man can have peace
longer than his neighbor pleases." No matter how peaceful our desires
and our efforts may be, we are always vulnerable to the unpeaceful
actions of others, and it is nothing but naive to suppose that if we will
just be nice to other people, they will want to have peace with us.

I am a lifelong student of J. R. R. Tolkien's work, and one of my
favorite Tolkien lines is the one where Aragorn, surprised to see how
well Éowyn handles a sword, says to her, "You have some skill with a
blade." And Éowyn replies, "The women of this country learned long
ago, those without swords can still die upon them." Those who think
that "unilateral disarmament" is the key to peace are sadly mistaken.

That is why we must pursue peace internally as well as externally.
As far as it depends on us, we should certainly have peace with others. But despite our efforts to avoid it, a certain amount of conflict is
going to sweep over us. When it does, there can be within our hearts a
calm, peaceful place of refuge. If we can't choose to avoid conflict, we
can at least choose how to respond to it. Therein lies our freedom.

Peace is not an absence of war; it is a virtue, a state of mind,
a disposition for benevolence, confidence, justice.

SPINOZA

AGE

Forty is the old age of youth; fifty is the youth of old age.
FRENCH PROVERB

ARE YOU AN "AGED" PERSON YET? Even if you are, you may not realize it. It's true, as Oliver Wendell Holmes Sr. said, "A person is always startled when he hears himself seriously called an old man for the first time." It takes most of us about ten years to get used to being the age we are, and by that time, of course, we are well past that age. But if we have, in fact, reached old age, what is our attitude about that? Are we embarrassed? Resentful? Appreciative? Enthusiastic?

To be sure, there is no inherent value in age. When she was asked about having lived a long time, Katharine Hepburn said, "I have no romantic feelings about age. Either you are interesting at any age or you are not. There is nothing particularly interesting about being old — or being young, for that matter." Neither youth nor age is anything we can take credit for. As Tom Wilson observed, "Wisdom doesn't necessarily come with age. Sometimes age just shows up on its own."

But normally, we do grow wiser as we age. That is something to be grateful for, and if we're not there yet, it's something to look forward to. In youth, we learn, but in age, we understand. And if we miss having the physical vitality of our younger days, it's worth remembering this observation by Richard Needham: "It's easier to have the vigor of youth when you're old than the wisdom of age when you're young." After all, everybody in the world has been young, but not everybody has been old. What that means is that the old have two benefits — the benefit of having been young and the benefit of now being old. The young have only one of these . . . for the time being.

One thing is sure: age has a certain "definiteness" that youth does not. When we are young, our lives are filled mostly with possibilities, but as we age, the real characteristics of our lives begin to emerge. "A young boy is a theory; an old man is a fact" (Ed Howe).

Victor Hugo once wrote, "When grace is joined with wrinkles, it is adorable. There is an unspeakable dawn in happy old age." I agree, and I would add that age is best seen as a *goal.* The years of our youth were not meant to be hoarded. They were meant to be spent!

I can't think of anything better to do with a life
than to wear it out in efforts to be useful to the world.
ARMAND HAMMER

REPUTATION

A good name is more to be desired than great riches.
THE BOOK OF PROVERBS

REPUTATION IS A CONCEPT THAT IS EASILY MISUNDERSTOOD. Some people live their lives with an "I-don't-care-what-anyone-else-thinks" arrogance, while others judge every action they take in terms of whether it will boost their approval ratings. Neither of these extremes is wise or healthy. Still, reputation is a matter that deserves our serious attention — and a good reputation is a treasure more valuable than most people realize. Love and respect are goals worth pursuing. Indeed, they are worth making significant sacrifices for.

We must understand, first, that there is a difference between reputation and character. Reputation is what others think we are, but character is what we really are. Character is the sum total of our actual attributes. It's what a person would know if they knew everything about us, even our innermost thoughts and motives. But obviously, our reputation may not be congruent with our character. In fact, the two are never completely congruent. Because others can know us only based on what we have revealed to them outwardly, their assessment of us may be either more positive or more negative than the "inside story" would bear out. As Elbert Green Hubbard said, "Many a man's reputation would not know his character if they met on the street."

So what should we do? If our reputation is better than our character (which, frankly, is the case with most of us), then we need to work on actually being the good person that others perceive us to be. And if our reputation is worse than our character, then we should not waste any time complaining about that. We should simply live the best lives we can and trust that, ultimately, the truth will be known.

In the end, the "law of the farm" will always prevail: we will reap as we have sown. There are no tricks, techniques, quick fixes, or personality shortcuts that will give us a good reputation if we haven't earned one by honest, rightful living. If we don't have real substance, people will eventually see through the appearances that we've conjured up. So let's work on having a good name, but let's do it the old-fashioned way. Let's make sure that we deserve the reputation that we desire.

The way to gain a good reputation is
to endeavor to be what you desire to appear.
SOCRATES

RELEVANCE

Relevance describes how pertinent, connected,
or applicable something is to a given matter. A thing is
relevant if it serves as a means to a given purpose.

WIKIPEDIA

IN OUR DAY, MANY OF US WANT TO BE "RELEVANT" — BUT WE OFTEN APPROACH IT FROM THE WRONG ANGLE. It is easy to define relevance, but not so easy to pursue it wisely. The word simply means that our actions have a bearing on "the matter at hand." In other words, a thing is relevant if it has a significant connection to what we're trying to do. For example, at this moment I am trying to write a book. Relevant activities would be those that are connected to getting the book written; irrelevant activities would be those that are not, such as watching television, talking on the telephone, or taking a nap.

Now, here is the problem. If relevance means a connection to "the matter at hand," then what is the matter at hand? What is it that we are trying to do? Nothing can be relevant if we don't have a clear idea of the object of our endeavor. And frankly, many people don't. They want to be relevant, but they are not sure what to be relevant to.

Years ago, Neil Postman made this comment: "We no longer have a coherent conception of ourselves, and our universe, and our relation to one another and our world. We no longer know, as the Middle Ages did, where we come from, and where we are going, or why. That is, we don't know what information is relevant, and what information is irrelevant to our lives." His point is well-taken. Being able to judge what is relevant requires a well-defined worldview, and in particular the acceptance of objective truth and goodness. Without these standards to judge by, relevance becomes irrelevant! If there is no objective "reality" and "truth" is anything we want it to be, then there is no "matter at hand" worth our trying to be relevant to.

So do you want to be relevant? I hope you do. But you can't judge what you should do by judging what is relevant. To judge that, you will first have to determine what is true and good. These are the primary considerations. Once we've locked in on these goals, then we can figure out which actions are connected to them and which are not.

Never question the relevance of truth,
but always question the truth of relevance.

CRAIG BRUCE

ENTERPRISE

On the neck of the young man sparkles
no gem so gracious as enterprise.
RALPH WALDO EMERSON

AS AN ECONOMIC PHILOSOPHY, "FREE ENTERPRISE" IS FAMIL-
IAR TO US, BUT WHAT IS "ENTERPRISE" ITSELF? A typical dictionary might say something like this: "industrious systematic activity."
But enterprise is more than an activity; it is the spirit or attitude that
motivates such activity. The attitude is often related to profit-making,
but it can be seen in a wider sense as well. I suggest there are four or
five interesting characteristics of the enterprising person.

Goal orientation. Those who are enterprising have formulated
clear goals that strongly direct the way they spend their time. And
not only that, but their goals tend to be imaginative and venturesome.
They are looking to do much more in life than play it safe.

Initiative. Enterprising individuals are self-starters. They don't
have to be held by the hand and encouraged to get busy. Active rather
than passive, they can often be described as bold. They go out to meet
life head-on because they are stirred by aspiration and hope.

Energetic effort. Enterprise is a hard-working trait. The enterprising are industrious and earnest in their endeavors. They build their
lives on the principle that if a thing is worth doing, it is worth doing
well. They will get up early and stay up late working on their goals.

Systematic effort. To be enterprising, one must not only "work
hard" but also "work smart." These are the folks who are eager to learn
how to accomplish their goals in the most advantageous way. They are
eager, inquisitive students of the "best practices" in their line of work.

These four characteristics are crucial to success in nearly every
endeavor. Whether the goal is economic or not, being enterprising is
important if we wish to go places that are worth going to in life. But
enterprise has a fifth characteristic, and I have deliberately saved it
until last: *enterprising people take personal responsibility for their goals.*
They don't wait for someone else to improve their lot. They understand what the fellow meant who said, "Go, wake up your luck."

Neither a wise man nor a brave man
lies down on the tracks of history to wait for
the train of the future to run over him.
DWIGHT D. EISENHOWER

ENDOWMENTS

*We hold these truths to be self-evident — that all men are created equal;
that they are endowed by their Creator with certain unalienable rights . . .*

THE DECLARATION OF INDEPENDENCE

HUMAN BEINGS ARE MARVELOUSLY UNIQUE. The question
is, where did all of this uniqueness come from? Are our intellect, emotions, free will, and other attributes merely the accidents of
nature? Historically, many have believed that our unique traits are *gifts*
— that is, that we have been "endowed" with these characteristics by
a Creator. We may not think much about it, but we hear the language
of endowment nearly every day. Someone might say, "She is a *gifted*
student." Or someone else might say, "He has a natural *gift* for music."
This language expresses what we know to be true: *many of the things
that we enjoy most in life are endowments.* They are gifts.

Rights. If the framers of the Declaration of Independence were
correct, we have been endowed with certain rights by our Creator.
Some people may live in cultures where these rights are not respected,
but all human beings have these rights nonetheless. They are endowments, given to every person at birth, and they should be respected. In
addition, as a result of being created by a Creator, we have an unalienable human worth. This inherent worth and dignity of every human
being is a "given," an endowment. "The worth of an individual is not
ascribed by law . . . it's endowed by the Creator" (James C. Dobson).

Abilities. Not only do we have rights and worth, we are endowed
with amazing abilities and talents. Not a day goes by that we are not
astonished to hear of some new thing that some human being has accomplished — and the abilities that make these achievements possible
are all the more wondrous because they are gifts. Truly, we've been entrusted by our Creator with endowments of a high and noble nature.

When you stop to consider it, there is not much that we enjoy in
this world that is not a gift. Paul the Apostle asked the Corinthians
a probing question when he asked, "What do you have that you did
not receive?" This means that when we're thinking clearly, we'll be
humbled by a profound sense of gratitude, and our gratitude will show
up in a serious desire to be responsible stewards of our endowments.

*I do not feel obliged to believe that the same God who has endowed us with
sense, reason, and intellect has intended us to forgo their use.*

GALILEO GALILEI

CONSISTENCY

Consistency:
It's the jewel worth wearing;
It's the anchor worth weighing:
It's the thread worth weaving;
It's the battle worth winning.

CHARLES R. SWINDOLL

CONSISTENCY IS A CHARACTER TRAIT WORTH STRIVING FOR. Some kinds of consistency may not be helpful, as we shall see, but if there is no consistency at all in our lives, it's going to be hard for us to accomplish any worthwhile goals. And not only that, but we will be extremely frustrating to those who have dealings with us. Our unpredictability will be a constant source of strain in our relationships.

At the outset, however, let's admit that consistency is not always a virtue. Emerson, for example, said, "A foolish consistency is the hobgoblin of little minds," and he was right. Sometimes we lessen the quality of our work by being picky and pedantic. But worse, if we fail to make positive changes in our lives because we don't want to be in-consistent with what we've done in the past, that is extremely foolish.

The kind of consistency that we ought to admire and emulate, however, is the consistency of *people who can be counted on.* Their behavior is predictable enough that their friends know what to expect. They keep their commitments. They finish what they start. There is a *dependable uniformity* in their character and conduct. And surely, this kind of consistency is one of the highest goals in life. "To be capable of steady friendship or lasting love, are the two greatest proofs, not only of goodness of heart, but of strength of mind" (William Hazlitt).

Yet I believe there is an even higher goal, and that is *consistency to truth and goodness.* This type of inner consistency often requires outward changes in our lives, but our goal is not to keep our *behavior* unchanged; it's to follow our *conscience* consistently. As we learn more of what's right, we may have to break with how we've done things in the past, and following our conscience may sometimes leave us open to the charge of inconsistency. But we shouldn't worry about that too much. Come what may, our goal is to be able to say, "I did what I believed was right." That's the one thing that should be consistent.

He does not believe who does not live according to his belief.

THOMAS FULLER

STRATEGY

Divide the fire, and you will the sooner put it out.
PUBLILIUS SYRUS

STRATEGY MEANS FINDING THE WISEST WAY TO DO WHAT WE WANT TO DO. When a sports coach has a game to win, he carefully considers his game plan, and we're foolish if we don't think about ours.

Admittedly, strategy can sometimes seem a little shady. If a person has no higher goal in his or her relationships than using good strategy, that's a person we would probably want to stay away from. The conniving, scheming individual who is always calculating and plotting his next selfish move is hardly a person that we admire.

We may as well face it: strategy without character does more harm than it does good. General Norman Schwarzkopf once said, "Leadership is a potent combination of strategy and character. But if you must be without one, be without the strategy." That sounds like an extreme statement, but I believe it's true. I'd much rather deal with someone who has good character but little common sense than someone who knows a lot about strategy but has no conscience. Nobody is more dangerous than the "strategic" person who has no principles.

But strategy can be both balanced and principled, and when it is, we ought to value it. When we don't, we often defeat ourselves. For example, think about this observation from the Book of Ecclesiastes: "If the ax is dull, and one does not sharpen the edge, then he must use more strength." The wood-chopper who has no time to waste on things like sharpening the ax blade will have to work much harder than the fellow who first gives a little thought to strategy.

Strategy has to do with expediency. It thinks not only about what is to be done but how it may be done in the wisest way. It considers ways and means, pondering the possible consequences of reaching the goal by different paths. Strategy can't tell us much about the worthiness of the goal itself (our conscience will have to tell us that), but once the goal is determined, strategy can get us there more wisely.

Strategy is necessary because brute force is not enough to take us where we want to go. When an obstacle confronts us, a battering ram is not always going to remove it. So as inconvenient as it is, we have to stop and think: *Here is our goal. Now what is our plan for getting there?*

To win by strategy is no less the role of a general than to win by arms.
JULIUS CAESAR

June 2

QUESTS

It is only possible to succeed at second-rate pursuits . . . First-rate
pursuits — involving, as they must, trying to understand what life is
about and trying to convey that understanding — inevitably result in
a sense of failure . . . Understanding is forever unattainable. Therein
lies the inevitability of failure in embarking upon its quest, which
is none the less the only one worthy of serious attention.

MALCOLM MUGGERIDGE

IF THERE ARE NO QUESTS THAT INSPIRE US, THEN WE'RE LIVING
LIFE FAR BELOW THE LEVEL THAT WE SHOULD ENJOY. There
is no poorer person than the one without any dreams. If you fall into
this category, you'd do yourself a favor by finding something to live for
— and even something to die for. There are many worthy quests you
might consider, some more challenging than others. Look into some
of the "first-rate pursuits," as Malcolm Muggeridge calls them.

But just as there are those who have too few quests in their lives,
there are some who have too many. There is a certain type of person who, like a kid in a candy shop, can't make up his mind what he
wants; he wants one of each! If you fall into this category, you need to
concentrate your mind and clarify your quest. You need to learn about
focus. We can have anything we want, but not everything we want!

One thing that all of us can do is be more appreciative of the
goals that give our lives meaning. It's a wonderful thing, really, to
be able to dream as we do and work toward the realization of those
dreams. We ought not to take our free minds and wills for granted.

But finally, we can work on improving the *quality* of our quests.
We can elevate our aims and our ambitions, making them, in particular, less self-centered and more outward-oriented. As Keith Yamashita
has said, "All meaningful change starts with right aspiration." If we
want to change our lives in significant ways, we need to take a long,
hard look at (1) *what* it is that we want, and (2) *why* we want it. Is our
goal honorable and worthy of aspiration? Are we committed to our
quest with all our hearts? Is the quest we've embarked upon one we'd
give our lives to try to achieve? If so, we're among the fortunate few!

Whither, O splendid ship, thy white sails crowding,
Leaning across the bosom of the urgent West,
That fearest not sea rising, nor sky clouding,
Whither away, fair rover, and what thy quest?

ROBERT BRIDGES

WORTHINESS

I urge you to live a life worthy of the calling you have received.
PAUL THE APOSTLE

WORTHINESS DOES NOT MEAN ARROGANCE OR IGNORANCE OF GRACE. It simply means that we "practice what we preach." When there is an obvious inconsistency between the things we stand for and the way we live, it causes people to dismiss what we stand for. For that reason, we try to maintain conduct that is considered worthy or fitting for a person who believes what we do. Looking at it the other way around, we try to avoid "unbecoming" behavior — that which is not in accord with the standards implied by our position.

In a culture very much concerned with self-esteem, the concept of worthiness comes up in many discussions. In general, people want to have a sense of self-worth. Within limits, there is nothing wrong with that, but the question is: how do we obtain it? I suggest that it is not by having others constantly "affirm" us by telling us how wonderful we are. It comes, instead, from living in a way that is consistent with our principles — in other words, it comes from doing our duty. I agree with Edgar Friedenberg, who said, "What we must decide is perhaps how we are valuable rather than how valuable we are." When you can go to bed at night and know that you have made yourself useful to other people by conduct that is worthy of your calling, you won't have any trouble going to sleep. You'll know what you're worth.

This applies to every single one of us, no matter what our calling may be. All of us have some responsibilities and some relationships. Worthiness means managing our behavior in such a way that we reflect a positive light on these responsibilities and relationships. If I'm a farmer, I need to farm in such a way that people will think more highly of farming. If I'm a father, I need to be such a father that others will think more highly of fatherhood. But shame on me if I bring discredit upon the work that I do or upon any of the roles that I fill!

Finally, let's be reminded that worthiness is, first and foremost, an inward matter, a matter of the heart. If I strive for worthiness, I must do more than work on appearances. In the end, I won't be able to deceive others by adopting a worthy style or form. I must be a person of worth and not just one who seems to have that quality.

Outside show is a poor substitute for inner worth.
AESOP

FIRMNESS

With malice toward none; with charity for all; with firmness in the right,
as God gives us to see the right, let us strive on to finish the work we are in . . .
ABRAHAM LINCOLN

WOULD THOSE WHO KNOW YOU DESCRIBE YOU AS "FIRM"? I
hope they would. The old saying is true: "You've got to stand
for something or you'll fall for anything." But I hope that when you
show firmness it will be carefully considered and rightly motivated.

La Rochefoucauld, who liked to look on the cynical side of
things, said, "Often we are firm from weakness, and audacious from
timidity." As much as I hate to admit it, he was telling the truth. Too
many times, our firmness comes not from the steady assurance of a
strong, well thought-out conviction, but from the suspicion that we
may be in an indefensible posture. When we are secretly unsure of
ourselves, we tend to mask our insecurity by bluster and bravado. In
such cases, we need to calm down. Rather than raise our voices, we
need to strengthen our arguments, as G. K. Chesterton once said.

One of the most destructive forces in the world is *unthinking*
firmness. When our intellect and our firmness become disconnected,
many bad things begin to happen. As Saadi put it, "Intellect, without firmness, is craft and chicanery; and firmness, without intellect,
perverseness and obstinacy." What this means is that there is a time
to be firm and a time not to be so. Charles Hole summed it up well:
"Deliberate with caution, but act with decision; and yield with graciousness, or oppose with firmness." At the thinking stage, we should
take plenty of time, and if our decision is to yield to another, then we
should yield. But if our decision is to take a stand and oppose something that is wrong, then that should not be done weakly but firmly.

In summary, then, we need to be firm and we need to be careful:
careful in how we form our convictions and careful in how we defend
them. But with that in mind, let's go back to Abraham Lincoln. On
the question of slavery, he had patiently considered the matter and
would act with "malice toward none" and "charity for all." But he was
not a wimp when it came to defending what was right. He was firm.

Renew the courage that prevails,
The steady faith that never fails,
And makes us stand in every fight
Firm as a fortress to defend the right.
HENRY VAN DYKE

KINSHIP

When brothers agree, no fortress is so strong as their common life.
ANTISTHENES

OUR "KIN" ARE OUR RELATIVES, THOSE TO WHOM WE ARE RELATED BY BIRTH, MARRIAGE, OR ADOPTION. But the word "kinship" suggests something different — and much better — than the mere state of being related to someone. It is an affinity, or attraction that we feel, to other people with whom we share important things, whether we are kin to them or not. And it happens to be one of the deepest sources of joy available to us in this disconnected world.

First, it needs to be said that we should work on having a greater feeling of kinship for those we are actually kin to. These days, families become scattered geographically, and the tendency is for us to become detached emotionally from our relatives. It takes a special kind of work to maintain our family ties, and it often takes disciplining our thoughts to retain an appreciation for our kinfolks, whoever they may be. We lose many of the best things in life when we don't do this work.

But second, we may enjoy a feeling of kinship with many others besides our physical family. For every person on our physical family tree, there are many more people to whom we are related by sharing common joys, sorrows, interests, experiences, and places. At whatever points our lives overlap with the lives of other human beings, ties are created and kinship is brought into being. The highest of these kinships is that which we feel for those who share our spiritual lives.

In the very broadest sense, of course, there is a kinship that all human beings ought to feel for one another. Despite our differences, we have many commonalities that ought to make us feel as if we were kin. Mohandas Gandhi was widely known for this kind of thinking, and he said, "I feel kinship with everyone in the world and feel that I cannot be happy without the humblest of us being happy."

In addition to the strength that comes from kinship ("When brothers agree, no fortress is so strong as their common life"), there is really no earthly happiness that equals the feeling of kinship. It is the "heart to heart" likeness with other people that gives us gladness!

It is not the level of prosperity that makes
for happiness but the kinship of heart to heart
and the way we look at the world.
ALEXANDER SOLZHENITSYN

June 6

TALENT

If you have a talent, use it in every way possible.
Don't hoard it. Don't dole it out like a miser. Spend it lavishly
like a millionaire intent on going broke.

BRENDAN FRANCIS

HENRI-FRÉDÉRIC AMIEL APTLY DEFINED TALENT AS THE ABILITY TO "DO EASILY WHAT IS DIFFICULT FOR OTHERS." If, for example, your mind processes mathematical information easily, or you find it easy to do woodwork, or you have a knack for empathizing with others, then those are talents that you have. All of us have a unique set of such natural abilities and aptitudes, and we need to be using them. As Emerson put it, "Each man has his vocation. Talent is the call."

It's important for us to identify the things we can do more easily than we can do other things. We can't use our talents productively if we aren't sure what they are. So I advise you to think about your strengths and weaknesses, talk with others who know you, and explore the things that you have a personal flair for. An excellent book to help you in that investigation is *StrengthsFinder* by Tom Rath.

Having identified our talents, we then need to pursue work that uses those abilities to their maximum advantage. Grateful for our talents, we need to devote ourselves to their use. "Whatever you are by nature, keep to it; never desert your own line of talent. Be what nature intended you for, and you will succeed; be anything else and you will be ten thousand times worse than nothing" (Sydney Smith).

No matter what our talents may be, we won't be effective in their use without discipline and hard work. "Discipline," as Roy L. Smith said, "is the refining fire by which talent becomes ability." Talent alone doesn't guarantee success in any endeavor. That takes hard work!

Lastly, remember this: with every talent comes responsibility. If there is something you can do more easily than somebody else could do it, you have more responsibility in that area than they do. That is the main reason why we need to find our talents — and also help others to find their talents. Right now, it may seem far in the future, but eventually there's going to be an accounting in which we'll face the question, "What have you done with what you were given?"

The real tragedy of life is not in being limited
to one talent, but in the failure to use the one talent.

EDGAR W. WORK

DECISIVENESS

*Decision is a sharp knife that cuts clean and straight. Indecision is
a dull one that hacks and tears and leaves ragged edges behind.*

JAN MCKEITHEN

WE'D PROBABLY BE SHOCKED IF WE COULD SEE HOW MUCH OF LIVES WE WASTE EITHER PROCRASTINATING DECISIONS THAT NEED TO BE MADE OR UNDOING DECISIONS THAT HAVE ALREADY BEEN MADE. Rather than getting good traction and moving ahead, we spin our wheels. We fret. We delay. We divert our own attention. We do everything in the world except the one thing that would make a difference: decide. Our indecision "hacks and tears and leaves ragged edges behind" — sometimes tragically so.

There is simply no way to dodge this truth: building a quality character requires decisiveness. And Charles Millhuff was correct, I believe, in identifying the three main areas where our decisions determine the kind of lives that we create: "Many of life's circumstances are created by three basic choices: the disciplines you choose to keep, the people you choose to be with, and the laws you choose to obey." So write it down and remember it. You decide your character (and consequently, your quality of life) by this: *the disciplines you choose to keep, the people you choose to be with, and the laws you choose to obey.*

Someone has said that one of the most exhausting things in the world is the continual hanging on of an unmade decision. Indeed. All of us are familiar with the burst of energy that comes from finally making a decision that we've been running away from. Can we imagine what life would be like if we were to go ahead and make all of the decisions that are presently draining our energy and debilitating us?

When a decision is ready to be made, the best thing to do is go ahead and make it. In other words, when our conscience has clearly indicated what course of action we should pursue, we should pursue it. There may be times when the thing that holds us back is laziness, but more often it is fear (which comes, of course, in many different varieties). On the very brink of doing something that would be good to do, we . . . hesitate. And as a result, much that could have graced our lives and that of others is lost. Let's do better than that. Let's decide!

*Half the failures in life arise from pulling
in one's horse as he is leaping.*

JULIUS CHARLES HARE

JUDGMENT

Wisdom is knowledge tempered with judgment.
LOUIS RITCHIE-CALDER

THERE IS NO WAY TO AVOID THE MAKING OF JUDGMENTS. They are a fact of life. We make them every day, from very little judgments all the way up to very big ones. The challenge that we face is not to avoid judgments, but to make them carefully and wisely.

To "judge" is simply to distinguish or make a difference. In a court of law, for example, a judge distinguishes between guilt and innocence, and between justice and injustice. But there are many other kinds of judgments that have to be made in life. As consumers, we have to judge between good products and bad ones. In the business world, we have to decide between productive policies and those that would be counterproductive. In entertainment, we have to decide between excellent performances and those that are inferior. And, of course, in the greater issues of life, we have to judge between right and wrong, truth and falsehood, wisdom and folly, and so forth.

Usually, our judgments are no better than our information. So before forming our judgments and making our distinctions, we need to acquire all the facts that we can. The better informed we are, the better our judgments will be. This is especially important when our judgments involve other people, as they often do. Before I make a decision whether your character is good or bad, I need to look past first impressions and outward appearances. The real truth about you may take a little digging to find out — so before I judge the quality of your character, I need to check and double-check my information. Above all, I need to be fair and evenhanded: I must not judge you by a standard any stricter than those I am willing to be judged by myself.

Just as an art critic gets better at judging paintings by going to lots of museums, we get better at making judgments by exercising our powers of discernment over and over again. As we grow older, we find that making useful distinctions gets easier. And that's good. Because in a mixed-up world, there are many things that have to be sorted out.

Grant to us, O Lord,
To know that which is worth knowing,
To love that which is worth loving . . .
Grant us with true judgment
To distinguish things that differ.
THOMAS À KEMPIS

CONSTRUCTIVENESS

Some people are constructive. Others are destructive. It's this
diversity in humankind that results in some making positive
contributions and some negative contributions.

JONAS SALK

LIKE ANY OTHER WRITER OR SPEAKER, I ENJOY PEOPLE'S EXPRESSIONS OF APPRECIATION. But in my opinion, there is no higher compliment that anyone can pay than to say, "That was helpful." If something I said or did was interesting or engaging, that's all right. And if someone says it was enjoyable or delightful, that's okay. But more than anything, I want to be *constructive.* That is, I want to be useful and beneficial. My aim is to build up or construct.

Most often, when we hear the word "constructive," we think of constructive criticism. Criticism can indeed be constructive, but unfortunately, the constructive kind is extremely rare. If criticism is unjustified or inappropriate, or if it's delivered unwisely, it does not build up; it simply tears down. Learning to offer the kind of criticism that "constructs" is one of the most difficult goals in the world.

But in addition to criticism, there are many other forms of constructiveness. In a world where so many of those around us have needs that we can help with, opportunities to strengthen and build up are plentiful. Acts of encouragement, aid, and assistance can always be constructive, if they are infused with wisdom and kindness.

But if we desire to be constructive, we have to acquire the ability to be that way. Most of us wish to be constructive, but good intentions can carry us only so far. At some point, we must learn how to be constructive. Wisdom asks not only *What needs to be done?* but also *How can it be accomplished?* The second question is harder than the first. We have to learn how to help without doing further harm, and the truth is, it often takes years of practice to become adept at that art.

So constructiveness is a steep mountain to climb. But climb it we must, for if our lives have not been constructive, in the long run they will have been destructive. There is no middle way. Either we gather with those who are building up or we scatter with those who are tearing down. So which will it be: destructiveness or constructiveness? Of all our choices in life, very few are more far-reaching than this.

Taking to pieces is the trade of those who cannot construct.

RALPH WALDO EMERSON

ORGANIZATION

Every great man exhibits the talent of organization
or construction, whether it be in a poem, a philosophical
system, a policy, or a strategy.
JOHN BULWER

LEFT TO THEMSELVES, THINGS TEND TO DISINTEGRATE. Your garage is a good example. If you don't exert the effort now and then to organize it, it descends into a random, chaotic mess — and let's face it: the mess is not really all that pleasant. But "exerting the effort" is the key concept. Left to itself, your garage is not going to keep itself organized. For that to happen, effort has to be expended.

But is it worth it? Does organization, or order, really matter? Some folks crave order so much they spend most of their time organizing . . . just for the sake of organizing. As neatness freaks, they lead imbalanced lives, organizing when they should be doing other things. At the other end of the spectrum is the person who spends no time at all on organization. His life is totally chaotic, and as a result of his negligent randomness, the contribution that he makes to the world is far below what he's capable of. Somewhere between these extremes, however, is a balanced view of organization: a view that appreciates the value of order and pursues it reasonably and responsibly.

Think about the difference between these two words: *chaos* and *cosmos*. They are opposites. A cosmos is what you have when order is introduced into a chaos. Coming from the Greek *kosmos* ("order"), cosmos is the result of organization. And let me tell you: a cosmos is a much better place to live in than a chaos! A measure of informality is good, and a bit of randomness is nice now and then. But none of us wants to be surrounded by total chaos. Because order is a part of beauty and goodness, we have a built-in need for these things. The good life is impossible without ordering, arranging, and organizing.

Organization multiplies the good that we can do. We don't have to be neatness freaks, but organizing our lives increases our output in doing good works. It's not the whole journey, but ordering our re-sources is a step that has to be taken on life's pathway. Otherwise, the chaos of our ideas never becomes the cosmos of our accomplishments.

First comes thought; then organization
of that thought, into ideas and plans;
then transformation of those plans into reality.
NAPOLEON HILL

OBSERVATION

You can observe a lot by watching.
YOGI BERRA

MANY OF THE BEST THINGS IN LIFE SLIP BY THOSE WHO ARE NOT OBSERVANT. And sadly, most of us would have to plead guilty. Our powers of observation have been dulled by lack of use, and we're not as attentive as we should be. We overlook much and ignore even more. The most remarkable things around us go unnoticed. But when we start working on our observation habits, great things begin to happen. You really can, as Yogi said, "observe a lot by watching."

Our observation of life's details can be hindered by two opposite problems. We may not see what we need to see because we're not involved enough. Sometimes discovery requires rolling up our sleeves and digging in, actively and personally entering into an experience. But at other times, our observation is hindered by being too involved. We can't see what we should because we are too close and not objective enough. "A stander-by may sometimes, perhaps, see more of the game than he that plays it" (Jonathan Swift). So it takes wisdom to know when to "move in" and when to "back up" for a better view.

Most of us are surrounded by people who would appreciate it if we became more observant. Observation is, indeed, a great gift that we can give to our friends, family, neighbors, and coworkers. Being aware and alert — just *noticing* them — says to another human being, "You are significant. In this moment, I am paying attention to you."

I am probably a little crazy about this, but I love to observe and "drink in" what I am observing. (People hate to go to museums and art galleries with me.) A friend asked me the other day what I do when I go to New York, and I was too embarrassed to tell him that I just enjoy going to interesting places and . . . observing! I could spend hours atop Rockefeller Center, for example, just listening, looking down on the city, noticing details, savoring curiosities, relishing wonders, thinking, pondering, meditating, and . . . observing!

But of course, the human race is the most curious phenomenon in the world, and if you want to get better at observation, I suggest that you start noticing people — beginning with those right around you.

Let observation with extensive view
Survey mankind, from China to Peru.
SAMUEL JOHNSON

June 12

FELLOWSHIP

No man is an island, entire of itself;
every man is a piece of the continent,
a part of the main.

JOHN DONNE

WE ARE "FELLOWS" WITH OTHER PEOPLE WHEN OUR LIVES OVERLAP THEIRS IN SOME WAY. If, for example, two people are both physicians, then they have "fellowship" in that profession. That which they have in common — in this case, their vocation — creates a comradeship, a sharing of interests, ideals, and experiences.

Obviously, there are many different areas in which our lives overlap the lives of others. We may be in the same physical family or live in the same community. We may share a recreational interest or a philanthropic cause. We may have a common spirituality, ethnicity, or nationality. In each of our lives, there are innumerable points at which similar characteristics create bonds of fellowship with others. The largest of these, of course, is that we're all members of the human race.

The challenge is to *cherish* our various fellowships in ways that are wise. And in the fellowships that involve joint activity or collaboration, the challenge is to *participate constructively*. Serious differences may have to be dealt with, but even in the act of working through these, we can remember the things that we have in common, realizing that these things often outweigh the things about which we differ.

At the deepest level, we show appreciation for fellowship when we serve our fellows. And ultimately, we must be ready to serve any of our fellow human beings, not just the nice ones who are in our same social niche and are easy to serve. As Aldous Huxley pointed out, "A man may have strong humanitarian and democratic principles; but if he happens to have been brought up as a bath-taking, shirt-changing lover of fresh air, he will have to overcome certain physical repugnancies before he can bring himself to put those principles into practice."

Too often, our high-sounding talk about fellowship in the human race is just talk, mostly about people we've never met. But what would those who are closest to us, the ones we actually come in contact with, say? Is our fellowship with them what it ought to be? Think about it.

A low capacity for getting along with those near us often goes hand in hand
with a high receptivity to the idea of the brotherhood of man.

ERIC HOFFER

June 13
ELEMENTS

The world today is sick to its thin blood
for lack of elemental things, for fire before the hands,
for water welling from the earth, for air,
for dear earth itself underfoot.

HENRY BESTON

IT IS A COMPLICATED WORLD IN WHICH WE LIVE, AND IT'S GETTING MORE COMPLICATED ALL THE TIME. Science combines simple ingredients into artificial substances and technologies of increasing complexity, and society presents us with extremely involved circumstances rather than simple scenarios. No wonder we find ourselves, as Beston suggests, "sick . . . for lack of elemental things." In an intricate world, we long for the deep-down comfort of the basics.

That's what the "elements" of a thing are: its basics, the blocks out of which it is built. If we say something is "composite," that means it's "composed" of different parts. Elements, then, are the fundamental, irreducible parts that go together to make up a composite entity.

Now think with me for a moment. Almost every "thing" we deal with is composite rather than simple. These days, most of the chemical substances and mechanical gadgets that we encounter are made up of many elements — but the same thing has to be said about the ideas and objectives and activities that we're concerned with from day to day. Simplicity in anything is rare in the modern world. And that being true, it helps us to see, as much as possible, the elements of everything.

For one thing, we understand things better when we can identify their elements and see how the elements relate to one another. When we gain a little insight into how things are "put together," we can do a better job of working with them in positive and productive ways.

But paying attention to elements helps us in another way also. Many of our problems are the result of imbalances. In other words, the elements of a thing are competing rather than working together. The more complicated our problems, the more we need to break them down into their parts — and then see how these can be balanced in a better way. So how good are you with the "elements" of life? I hope that you're good with them . . . and getting better all the time.

Harmony means that the relationship between
all the elements . . . is balanced, is good.

KARLHEINZ STOCKHAUSEN

GOVERNMENT

The proper function of government is to make it
easy for people to do good and difficult for them to do evil.
JIMMY CARTER

IN ITS MOST BASIC SENSE, "GOVERNMENT" MEANS CONTROL OR GUIDANCE. And while the word has a distinctly negative ring to many people nowadays, the fact is there are very few things that are dynamic or forceful that don't need to be governed. Even the physical forces that have the greatest potential for good must be harnessed and controlled. Despite its many beneficial uses, fire, for example, can be horribly destructive when it's allowed to do whatever it pleases.

We shouldn't be surprised, then, that human beings need to be governed. Whether individually, in small groups, in large groups, or in nations, we need limits that will channel our energies in positive directions. A human being is far and away the most powerful force in the natural world, but in the absence of any restraints at all, a human being can do more harm than fire ever could, even at its most destructive. So John Ruskin's observation is consistent with what we know to be true: "Government and cooperation are in all things the laws of life; anarchy and competition the laws of death."

Yet if we need government, it's a marvelous fact that we're often able to supply much of that government ourselves. We need to work within boundaries and limits, but we've been endowed with a capacity called *self-discipline* — which means that we can govern our own activity. And oftentimes, the amount of *external* government that ends up being imposed upon us is determined by how willing we've been to exercise *internal* government. "It is for men to choose whether they will govern themselves or be governed" (Henry Ward Beecher).

There are very few of us who wouldn't make a better contribution to the world if we'd discipline our abilities more productively. We have more powers than we bother to use and more resources than we've ever tapped into. And the question each of us must eventually answer is not what we accomplished in life, but what we could have accomplished if we'd governed ourselves and been better stewards.

For better or worse, man is the tool-using animal,
and as such he has become the lord of creation. When he is lord also
of himself, he will deserve his self-chosen title *homo sapiens.*
WILLIAM RALPH INGE

FAMILY

This expression of ours, "father of a family" . . .
PLINY THE YOUNGER

THE LATIN WORD *PATERFAMILIAS* ("FATHER OF A FAMILY") SHOULD BE OF MORE THAN PASSING INTEREST TO US. When a man becomes a father, it's a family that he becomes the father of, and that's a truth that's both sobering and encouraging.

It's sobering because it reminds us that our actions have consequences for better or worse. When a man fathers a family, what he does reverberates down many generations. The lives of numerous other people will be made easier, or else more difficult, by the manner in which he chooses to live his life. If he's a good man, his family will appreciate his goodness long after he's gone, and if he's evil, his family will feel the effects of that evil for many years to come.

But it's also encouraging to think about the family that a man fathers. The connections that link us together constitute one of life's richest treasures, and any man who is blessed with children (and grandchildren, great-grandchildren, great-great-grandchildren, etc.) needs to drink deeply of the joy that comes from those connections. In truth, we're all part of a huge web of relationships whether we're a father or not — and we need to be encouraged by that fact.

My great-grandfather Jairus A. Copeland is buried beside his beloved wife, Georgia, in the old church cemetery at Pleasant Home in Pike County, Arkansas. A few years ago, I was able to reserve my own burial plot just three spaces over from "Papa" Copeland. He and Georgia had twelve children who lived to adulthood, and by this time their descendants number in the thousands all over the world. What an honor it will be to be laid to rest just a few feet away from this great *paterfamilias,* a good man from whom I have descended.

It is largely by looking backward and forward that we come to understand who we really are. When a man carefully considers his ancestors, he learns some important things about himself. But when he contemplates his descendants — the family he will have *fathered* — he has an even better opportunity to become educated.

Family faces are magic mirrors. Looking at people
who belong to us, we see the past, present and future.
We make discoveries about ourselves.
GAIL LUMET BUCKLEY

FULFILLMENT

Whenever we are faced with a crucial decision,
our generation has been taught to ask, What's in it for me?
Will it give me pleasure? Profit? Security? Fulfillment?

ERWIN W. LUTZER

THE CONCEPT OF "FULFILLMENT" IS SO WIDELY MISUNDER-STOOD, I ALMOST HESITATE TO SAY ANYTHING GOOD ABOUT IT. In the self-centered, narcissistic age in which we live, many people have bought into the foolish idea, promoted by the psychological establishment, that there are no higher goals in life than "self-fulfill-ment" and "self-actualization." I certainly don't want to encourage that kind of thinking. Nevertheless, fulfillment is an enthusiastic idea, and we need to consider it rightly. Let's try to do this by considering what some of the things are that need to be fulfilled in our lives:

Desires. We would all like to have our desires fulfilled. And as long as our desires are within the boundaries of moral integrity, there is nothing wrong with this. What some don't understand, however, is that the best way to doom our desires is to make them our primary focus. "I doubt that there has ever been one recorded case of deep and lasting fulfillment reported by a person whose basic mind-set and only question was: what am I getting out of this?" (John Powell).

Responsibilities. As we move higher on the scale of value, another form of fulfillment is the fulfillment of our responsibilities. However much I am concerned about getting what I want, I should be more concerned about doing what I should. Life "under the sun" is not just about enjoyment; it's about doing our duty and finishing our work.

Potential. This, finally, is the fulfillment that we should be seek-ing the most passionately. Each of us is a unique "package" — we have a very particular set of abilities, gifts, and opportunities. These personal characteristics are not merely for our personal indulgence; they are meant to point us in the direction of some worthy goal that we have the unique ability to reach. So are we going there? Are we headed in that direction? Are we fulfilling the potential that we've been given? "The important thing is this: to be able at any moment to sacrifice what we are for what we could become" (Charles du Bos).

Do not seek death. Death will find you.
But seek the road which makes death a fulfillment.

DAG HAMMARSKJÖLD

RESONANCE

Things we do and experience have resonance ... The present
is filled with past experience ringing in various ways and now
is colored by this symphony of resonance.

PAUL LANSKY

RESONANCE IS A WORD THAT COMES TO US FROM THE SCI-
ENCE OF ACOUSTICS. When the sound-producing vibrations
of one body (such as a violin string) produce sympathetic vibrations
in another body (such as the wood of the violin body), the result is
resonance. And when one set of vibrations creates similar vibrations in
another body, the result is not only a bigger sound but a richer sound.

Another way of looking at resonance is to say that one thing
"resounds" to another. That is, one thing responds to the sound of
another by sympathetically "re-sounding," or sounding again, the first
sound, thus making it more interesting and impactful than the first sound
would be all by itself. So resonance increases the quality of sounds.

Figuratively, then, we speak of resonance as the effect produced
when something that one person says or does creates a deep, sympathetic response in another person. The second person is the "sounding
board" that receives a message and then "sounds it again," connecting
to it emotionally and reflecting it back in a rich and meaningful way.

Surely, we ought to welcome experiences like this. They can
be positively life-changing. Musician Rita Coolidge said, "I choose
things by how they resonate in my heart." Some messages and some
experiences produce no effect within us; they make no deep connection. But others resonate, and these are the ones that matter most.

And since we have the ability to influence one another, we should
always seek to resonate with those around us. We do this by first listening to others sympathetically and learning their needs. Then we are
able to send "sounds" that resonate with them, impacting them richly.

It is marvelous to see how things are connected in our world. In
the realm of human activity, just as with physical objects, what happens in one place can create a sympathetic vibration in another. The
fact of this connectedness is sobering — we will answer for it if our
impact on others was not helpful. But it's also encouraging. What a
wonder that one heart can "sound again" the music of another heart!

... like a resonance of sound in the clearest grain of a violin.

NORMAN MAILER

HEALING

The wish for healing has ever been the half of health.
SENECA

THERE IS NO PERSON WHO NEVER NEEDED HEALING — AND NO PERSON WHO NEVER LONGED FOR IT. Wounded by the hurts of this world, we yearn to be made whole again. When our injuries and ailments do not produce outright pain, we still sense a vague longing for a wholeness that is not ours right now. And when these things do produce pain, we are acutely aware of our need for healing.

As much as we long for healing and health, however, it is self-defeating to become obsessed with it. Whatever damage we may have suffered, whether self-inflicted or otherwise, we will recover from it better if we get the focus off ourselves and onto other people. One of life's ironies is that we ourselves experience the greatest healing when we concentrate on being the agents of healing for others. Healing comes to us as a by-product of serving the health of those around us.

The major mistake many of us make nowadays, however, is thinking that healing comes from pleasure. Wounded and world-weary, we throw ourselves into mirth, merriment, and sensual indulgence, seeking to "drown our sorrows." But Billy Graham was right when he said, "The river of pleasure, though it flows through lush meadows and beautiful glens, contains no healing for the soul." When true healing is what we need, mere pleasure will not suffice.

What then will suffice? Although you don't want to hear it, the truth is that nothing will suffice — at least if what you have in mind is the perfect, complete healing of every grief and emptiness before you die. My personal belief is that spiritual truths are available that can put us on the road to such healing, but the perfection of that healing must await the completion of this life and our graduation to the next.

That said, it's encouraging to know that progress can be made on our healing in the here and now. But healing is a process that takes time. Rarely is there any quick fix that is available to us. So we can wear ourselves out reading the latest self-help analysis of our problems, trying to figure out the solution, but in the end, "time heals what reason cannot" (Seneca). To be healed, we must be willing to wait.

How poor are they that have not patience!
What wound did ever heal but by degrees?
WILLIAM SHAKESPEARE

INGENUITY

A common mistake that people make
when trying to design something completely foolproof
is to underestimate the ingenuity of complete fools.

DOUGLAS ADAMS

WHEN YOU HAVE A PROBLEM, WHAT IS YOUR FIRST IN-
STINCT? Do you expect a friend or family member to fix it for
you? Do you begin looking for a professional or an expert to hire? Or
do you first bring your own ingenuity to bear upon the problem?

Certainly, there is a time and a place to rely upon others. Indeed,
the person who is so stubborn that he won't ever ask for help (or too
witless to know he needs to ask) has a serious problem. But many
people have the opposite problem: that of asking too quickly for help.
Today, let's think about the value of increasing our own ingenuity. If
we can learn to be more imaginative and inventive, displaying more
skill in solving our own problems, many benefits will come our way.

(1) Ingenuity makes us less dependent. When we show resourcefulness in finding solutions to our difficulties, we're able to survive in
situations where no outside help is available. *(2) Ingenuity helps us
to take personal responsibility for our lives.* Rather than look to others
to make our problems go away, we take responsibility and apply our
own creativity. *(3) Since help is one of the things that is more blessed to
give than to receive, we should be more interested in helping than in being
helped.* Ingenuity puts us in a better position to do that. When others
are in need, our ingenuity can sometimes lift their burdens.

But finally, consider two specific areas where ingenuity can help us:

Education. For too long, many of us have assumed that it is somebody else's responsibility to educate us. But isn't education a personal
project? If all you know is what you've been taught, you don't know
much. So show some ingenuity in exploring ways to educate yourself!

Entertainment. A very bored society is what has resulted from the
assumption that other people should keep us entertained. So I encourage you to go back to your childhood. Be ingenious. Be imaginative. Be
clever and resourceful in having fun. Learn how to entertain yourself!

Growing up, I didn't have a lot of toys, and personal
entertainment depended on individual ingenuity and imagination.
I would think up a story and go live it for an afternoon.

TERRY BROOKS

RESTFULNESS

> "Holy leisure" refers to a sense of balance in the life, an ability
> to be at peace through the activities of the day, an ability to rest
> and take time to enjoy beauty, an ability to pace ourselves.
>
> RICHARD J. FOSTER

MANY OF THE CRACKS IN OUR CULTURE ARE "STRESS FRAC-TURES." We are a driven people, almost frantic in the pace of our lives. And we're not only busy, but we're proud of our busyness, as if our involvement in so many activities indicated that we are more "with it" than those who are less busy or that we have a greater sense of responsibility. Whatever the reason may be, our overcommitment has cost us dearly. Many of our less-than-desirable social characteristics are the traits of people who are seriously short of rest.

Rest. All work requires some sort of "fuel," and doing the work uses up the fuel. At that point, the fuel has to be replenished, and that is the point of rest: it is meant to renew us and recharge our energies. In a sense, our resources (whether physical or mental) are not permanently ours — they have to be "re-created" by regular periods of rest and repose. Taking care of this is not being lazy. Laziness is, as someone has said, resting before we are tired. But when we are tired, it is not lazy to rest. In fact, when we are tired, it is dangerous not to rest.

Restfulness. In addition to periods of rest, we also need restfulness, which is something a little different than mere rest. Restfulness is a mode of thinking and a manner of living, even when we are busy. It is, as Richard J. Foster said, "an ability to be at peace through the activities of the day." Restfulness is knowing how to hasten leisurely.

In a culture like ours, both rest and restfulness require discipline. Without a certain amount of training and self-maintenance, we won't take the time for rest. It is a choice that we must learn to make.

Yet the discipline of restfulness is a discipline that pays great dividends, not the least of which is that *we do better work*. It's only a fool who thinks that he can be more productive by never turning the machinery off for maintenance. Wise people know better.

> Cultivate the habit of doing one thing at a time with quiet
> deliberateness. Always allow yourself a sufficient margin of time
> in which to do your work well. Frequently examine your working methods
> to discover and eliminate unnecessary tension. Aim at poise, repose,
> and self-control. The relaxed worker accomplishes most.
>
> H. W. DRESSER

GROWTH

Winter is cold-hearted,
Spring is yea and nay,
Autumn is a weather-cock
Blown every way.
Summer days for me
When every leaf is on its tree.

CHRISTINA GEORGINA ROSSETTI

TO ME, THERE IS SOMETHING JOYFUL ABOUT SEEING A LUSH FIELD OF CORN IN THE MIDDLE OF THE GROWING SEASON. I'm not sure why, but a field full of something so obviously "growing" fills me with a strange mixture of comfort and motivation. It's reassuring to see what nature can do — and sobering to remember that I'm also a part of nature, with some growing of my own that I need to do.

We need to be people who are growing. Granted, we don't have to make significant progress in our lives every single day of the year — there will be seasons of growth for us, periods when we make more progress than at other times. Intentionally or otherwise, our fields will often lie fallow. But over time, we need to be growing.

Even in old age, when we're on the downside of the physical life cycle, there is still a sense in which we need to keep pressing ahead. There are still things to be learned. There are still new frontiers to be explored in our hearts and minds. And, yes, there is probably still some work to be done, good work that can enrich the lives of those around us. We can't escape our mortality — it's foolish even to try — but we can keep going forward . . . and avoid drifting backward.

One of our most valuable beliefs is the conviction that progress and improvement are possible. They're not inevitable, of course. Most of us have learned the hard way that our own decisions can keep us from growing. Yet whatever setbacks we may have dealt ourselves in the past, we still believe that growth is possible in the future. That's a vital belief and we dare not let any naysayer take it away from us.

We have this belief because we are *personal* beings, endowed with free minds. We're free moral agents, and so we hold on to this thought in defiance of short-term disappointments: *the courage to make right choices will lead us, sooner or later, in the direction of healthy, life-enhancing growth.* If we don't believe this, then we're dead already.

Growth is the only evidence of life.
JOHN HENRY NEWMAN

INTEGRATION

All true educators since the time of Socrates and Plato have agreed that
the primary object of education is the attainment of inner harmony, or, to put
it into more up-to-date language, the integration of the personality. Without
such an integration, learning is no more than a collection of scraps, and the
accumulation of knowledge becomes a danger to mental health.

ALFRED ZIMMERN

INTEGRATION MEANS BRINGING ALL THE PARTS OF SOMETHING
TOGETHER, THEREBY MAKING A UNIFIED WHOLE. The verb
"disintegrate" means to tear apart, and so to "integrate" means to put
back together what has been broken or fractured or separated.

In a world of strife and discord, the goal of social integration is
obviously desirable. What a better world it would be if all the parts of
humanity could be integrated into a more unified whole! But I want
you to think about something: we are fighting a losing battle trying
to bring other people together socially if we are not integrated within
ourselves privately. That is, social harmony or oneness will always be
an elusive goal for people who have no unity inside of themselves.

The psychologists talk a good deal about the "integration of the
personality," and, in fact, most people's personal traits and tendencies
are not integrated. They are at odds, and often at war, with one another. So counselors would like to help us bring our various attributes
into a more harmonious whole. And whether a psychologist helps us
with that or not, personal integration is certainly a project that we need
to work on. In plain language, we need to "get ourselves together."

But the importance of this goes beyond just feeling better emotionally. As you may have noticed, the words "integration" and "integrity" are related. They both come from a Latin root meaning "whole"
or "complete." So if we have no personal integration, then we have no
integrity. For example, if there is no unity between our conscience and
our conduct, or if our "preaching" and our "practice" are not in agreement, then this lack of integrity is a serious problem (one that goes
by the name of "hypocrisy"). So we need to get busy integrating our
personal characteristics. *If life is to be good, the parts have to harmonize!*

No truths are simple . . . But as we pursue them
and participate in them more fully, they begin to reveal
to us a life deeper and more integrated than we ever
could have known otherwise.

TIM HANSEL

June 23
INCLUSIVENESS

> He chose to include the things
> That in each other are included, the whole,
> The complicate, the amassing harmony.
> WALLACE STEVENS

INCLUSIVENESS LEADS TO A VERY DIFFERENT LIFE THAN EXCLUSIVENESS. Those whose basic instinct is to "include" end up with different circumstances than those whose first thought is to "exclude," so our decision between these two outlooks is far-reaching.

Ideas. The lens through which most of us look at ideas has a pretty narrow focus. We tend to consider very specific ideas, and we don't think about how those ideas are connected to other ideas. Intellectually, we would do well to use a wider-angle lens. We need to back up and see more of the big picture. Viewing ideas in their larger context will help us to prevent errors in our thinking and judgment.

Interests. Our interests are often as narrowly focused as our ideas. Intensely practical in our interests, we have little time for anything that doesn't solve an immediate problem. But truly, the world in which we live is a fascinating world. For those who are fully engaged with life, there is not much that is not interesting. And the more inclusive our interests are, the more useful we'll be to other people.

Activities. In these days of specialization, many of us spend so much time in our individual silos that our activities begin to be very narrow and predictable. While it is certainly possible for a person to be too busy for his own good, I believe most of us would profit from a greater variety in our activities. I urge you to look for things to do that will stretch you — widening your imagination and your experience.

People. If we would profit from more inclusiveness in our ideas, interests, and activities, we would profit even more from a richer variety in our relationships. This is, by far, the most important kind of inclusiveness to strive for. There is a tendency for us to limit our contacts to individuals within a narrow profile, but if we would make an honest effort to be more inclusive, the results would surprise us pleasantly. With human beings, inclusiveness is hard, but it's worth it.

> The three hardest tasks in the world are neither physical feats
> nor intellectual achievements, but moral acts: to return love for hate,
> to include the excluded, and to say, "I was wrong."
> SYDNEY J. HARRIS

June 24
TASKS

Nothing is so fatiguing as the
eternal hanging on of an uncompleted task.
WILLIAM JAMES

ALL OF US SUFFER FROM TASK-RELATED FATIGUE, BUT THE INTERESTING THING IS THAT MOST OF OUR FATIGUE COMES FROM UNFINISHED TASKS. Emotionally, we exhaust ourselves with the weariness that comes from putting off our tasks until tomorrow.

Strictly defined, a task is simply a piece of work that one must do. But we normally think of tasks as unpleasant work or work that we don't want to do — and those are the tasks that we procrastinate.

Yet very few tasks are inherently unpleasant. They're only unpleasant because we make them so; having erected mental barriers against them, they are unwelcome. But if we looked at our tasks in a more positive light, we would find them less tedious. "The difficult tasks to be performed are not the ones that mean physical and mental labor, but the ones that you dislike, or the ones that you do not love. There are unpleasant angles to nearly every important job to be done in this world, but there must be an overall love for doing each, else precious time and effort are uselessly wasted" (George Matthew Adams).

One of the best gifts that we can give to those around us is learning to have a brighter, more grateful view of our tasks. As Helen Keller expressed it, "This world is so full of care and sorrow that it is a gracious debt we owe to one another to discover the bright crystals of delight hidden in somber circumstances and irksome tasks."

But how do we learn this way of thinking? *We do it by connecting our tasks to our vision in life.* If there is any task that duty calls us to complete, then that task is linked, however remotely, to our purpose in life. To finish that task is to take one step toward our vision, and truly, there are no small steps if they are connected to our reason for living. This point was captured beautifully in the inscription on an eighteenth-century cathedral in Sussex, England: "A vision without a task is only a dream, a task without a vision is drudgery, but a vision with a task is the hope of the world." There is, indeed, no limit to the energy that can be unleashed by putting *ourselves* into our tasks.

Set me a task in which I can put something of my very self,
and it is a task no longer; it is joy; it is art.
BLISS CARMAN

DEPENDABILITY

The world is a collection of cogs; each depends on the other.
JEWISH PROVERB

IN THE REAL WORLD, WE CAN'T AVOID BEING DEPENDED ON.
Whether we like it or not, we are connected to others in ways that
involve dependencies. Human beings have to count on other human
beings to do certain things. And the road runs both ways — before
we die, each of us will have depended on others and others will have
depended on us. *It's a simple fact: people have to have other people!*

But this is not a fact to be regretted; it's one to be appreciated.
It is nothing less than a privilege to have others who look to us to
perform deeds that are important to them. Serving others who need
us is a blessing. When we're thinking rightly, we'll see this blessing as
a stewardship, a sacred trust. But the principle also works in reverse. It
may go against our pride, but depending on others is also a blessing. If
there are others whom we truly need, that fact is not to be regretted.

But if dependence is an unavoidable fact, then we need to make
sure that dependability is also a fact. If others are counting on us,
then we should be "count-on-able," as a friend of mine used to say.
Words like *steady, reliable, trustworthy,* and *unfailing* should come to
mind when people think of us. That will only be the case if we have
established a track record of keeping promises and commitments, of
following through, and of finishing what we start. It takes more than
a short spurt of good intentions to gain a reputation for dependability.

But if our record of dependability is spotty, what should we do?
I suggest that we start by honoring small commitments. There is a
Persian proverb which says, "Do little things now; so shall big things
come to thee by and by asking to be done." That contains not only
great wisdom but great common sense. Dependability in big things
is built up, bit by bit, as we learn faithfulness in the little things of
everyday relationships. So look for some small commitment that you
can keep today. Then look for another one tomorrow, and keep doing
that day after day. In time, you'll see that you've become dependable.

Commitments can sometimes be hard to make. But in the end, it
is not the making of commitments that counts — it is the keeping of
them. So let's be people on whom others are not afraid to depend!

An acre of performance is worth the whole world of promise.
JAMES HOWELL

June 26

CONFIDENCE

All social life, stability, and progress
depend upon each man's confidence in his neighbor,
a reliance upon him to do his duty.

A. LAWRENCE LOWELL

THINK WITH ME TODAY ABOUT HOW MUCH DEPENDS ON OUR
HAVING CONFIDENCE IN ONE ANOTHER. Doubt and cynicism
are corrosive forces. They not only eat away at us internally, but they
destroy the foundations of our social relationships. If I don't trust you
and you don't trust me, then any "community" we build together is
going to be a perilous place. It's frightening to think what would happen if nobody in the world had any confidence in anybody else.

But if it's important to maintain confidence in one another, it's
also important to encourage each other's self-confidence. Many of the
most important things in the world won't get done if those who are
responsible for them don't believe that they can do them. Just as an
absence of mutual trust would destroy society, the work of the world
would collapse if nobody had any self-confidence. So if you don't
care whether your neighbor has any confidence in himself, please be
advised that his self-doubt may cost you more than you think.

It was John Dryden who said, "They can conquer who believe
they can." In a more modern context, baseball players say that "a
pitcher is only as good as he thinks he is." It happens very often in
life that the doing of a thing depends on our believing that we can do
it, and when we're not sure, our doubts are often self-fulfilling. So a
certain level of self-confidence is essential to our survival. "In a world
where survival is always seen as a struggle, and in which some pitfalls
always exist, if something brings into question our confidence in our
own coping ability, it will threaten our safety" (Willard Gaylin).

What, then, about your friends and family? Are they confident?
And if they are not, do you share part of the blame for having failed
to encourage them? These are some of the most crucial questions in
life. In this world, we are unavoidably connected. That being true, discouragement is more than a personal problem — it's a social problem.
When we encourage anybody's confidence, we help everybody.

We blossom under praise like flowers in sun
and dew; we open, we reach, we grow.

GERHARD E. FROST

June 27
EMOTION

Emotion cannot be cut out of life . . . There are many dangers of false
emotionalism, but that does not rule out true emotion and depth of feeling.

BILLY GRAHAM

LIKE ALL OF OUR OTHER ENDOWMENTS, OUR EMOTIONS ARE
THINGS THAT WE CAN EITHER PAY TOO MUCH ATTENTION TO
OR TOO LITTLE. Wisely managed, our emotions can be a powerful
ally, but when we give them either too much or too little space, harmful results usually follow. The challenge is to steer a middle course.

These days, when emotional experience tends to trump all other
considerations, one thing we need to acknowledge is that our emotions are poor managers of our lives. How we feel flows quite naturally from how we think, and our feelings can be a wonderful support
for our thinking, but feelings alone can never tell us right from wrong.
They shouldn't be allowed to jump in the driver's seat of our lives; that
place should be reserved for our conscience. As Robert Benson said,
"Emotions should be servants, not masters — or at least not tyrants."

Most of us would do well to allow ourselves a wider range of
emotions. In particular, I believe that we shouldn't be in such a hurry
to get rid of the so-called "painful" emotions. All of our emotions
have their place and should be given a chance to enhance our lives
and help us. "The experience of the whole gamut of emotions is a part
of the human condition, the inheritance of every man" (John Powell).

Generally, our emotions come to us unbidden. We can't help
what we feel. What we can do is govern our intentions and our actions, and we must do that. We are responsible not for our feelings
but for what we do with our feelings. And when we do what is right,
our feelings will adjust themselves appropriately in due time.

Earl Riney wrote, "Our emotions are the driving powers of our
lives. When we are aroused emotionally, unless we do something
great and good, we are in danger of letting our emotions become
perverted." As one of the natural endowments that we've been given,
our emotions are meant to help us. I would go so far as to say that our
emotions cannot successfully be neglected or misused. If our heart is
not involved in our effort to live rightly, that effort is bound to fail.

The heart has such an influence over the understanding
that it is worthwhile to engage it in our interests.

LORD CHESTERFIELD

VIEWPOINT

Your point of view is everything:
the pond is an ocean to a tadpole.

ANONYMOUS

WHAT WE "SEE" DEPENDS LARGELY ON WHAT "ANGLE" WE ARE LOOKING FROM. If our viewpoint is quite limited, we may, like the tadpole, mistake the pond that we're in for an ocean.

There are several ways that our viewpoint can be improved:

(1) *Moving from side to side.* When you are looking at a painting in an art gallery, it helps to move around, seeing it from one side and then the other. Similarly, we can vary the "angle" from which we look at almost everything in life. We just have to make mental adjustments.

(2) *Backing up.* It sometimes helps to see more of what we're look-ing at. We do that by mentally "backing up," so that our view is more comprehensive. Very often, the most helpful view is the bigger one.

(3) *Looking more intently.* Seeing things accurately requires work, and so we often fail to see what we should because we haven't really concentrated on it. There is a Chinese proverb that says, "You must scale the mountain if you would view the plain." If we haven't paid the price, we shouldn't expect any improvement in our perspective.

(4) *Looking more honestly.* The one thing that hinders our view-point the most is our lack of honesty. Too often, we only see what we want to see. As J. Oswald Sanders said, "Eyes that look are common, but eyes that see are rare." Moving from side to side, backing up, and looking more intently can't help us if we're not willing to see what we need to see. Ultimately, our "heart" is what determines our "vision."

As finite creatures, we won't ever be able to see everything. But we can certainly improve our viewpoint, and we're foolish not to do that when we have the opportunity. Our Creator, of course, sees all things from a perfect viewpoint. To whatever extent we can adopt His perspective, what we see will help us to exercise better judgment — especially when it is other human beings that we are judging.

Man judges from a partial view.
None ever yet his brother knew;
The eternal eye that sees the whole
May better read the darkened soul,
And find, to outward sense denied,
The flower upon its inmost side!

JOHN GREENLEAF WHITTIER

KEEPING

To everything there is a season, a time for every purpose under heaven . . .
A time to gain, and a time to lose; a time to keep, and a time to cast away . . .
THE BOOK OF ECCLESIASTES

B Y OUR NATURE AND INDIVIDUAL PERSONALITY, SOME OF US ARE KEEPERS AND SOME ARE NOT. The keepers are those who never throw anything away ("I might need it someday"). At the other extreme are those who get rid of everything except what they need right now ("If I don't need it today, I won't ever need it"). Neither trait is inherently right or wrong, but today let's meditate on the fact that some things in life do need to be kept — and kept carefully.

It takes wisdom, of course, to know what to keep and what not to keep, and wisdom always seems to be in short supply. If we knew what we were going to need and not need in the future, it would be easy to manage the matter of keeping and not keeping. But none of us knows the future, so decisions about keeping have to be made using our best judgment. Dinah Maria Craik laid down one of the most challenging principles in life when she said, "Keep what is worth keeping, and then with the breath of kindness blow the rest away."

Whatever should be kept, should be kept gratefully and faithfully. Our blessings ought to be maintained with a stewardship that indicates our appreciation of the value of what's in our keeping.

There is even a sense in which our inner lives have to be "kept." Just as our houses and our physical bodies can be "unkept" (or "unkempt"), so our hearts can be also. There is a certain amount of maintenance that goes into the keeping of our inner lives, and poor heartkeeping is a far worse habit than poor housekeeping. As Mark Twain said, "Be careless in your dress, if you must, but keep a tidy soul." That echoes a sentiment from the Book of Proverbs: "Keep your heart with all diligence, for out of it spring the issues of life."

On the highest level, however, that which must be kept is our *duty*. All of us have responsibilities that are attached to the various roles that we fill. Almost always, these responsibilities are privileges — we are blessed to have these duties to carry out. So we live life at its best when we faithfully maintain (or "keep") our commitments. Whatever else we throw away, we must not discard our duties.

A charge to keep I have . . .
CHARLES WESLEY

COMPETENCE

The end of education is to see men made whole,
both in competence and in conscience.
JOHN S. DICKEY

TO BE COMPETENT IS TO BE QUALIFIED TO DO A JOB — ABLE TO COMPLETE THE TASK SKILLFULLY. The competent are those who can be trusted to carry out a responsibility in an adept manner.

It should go without saying (but these days we often forget) that competence must always be governed by conscience. Not everything that can be done should be done, and the fact that we have the ability to do something is often dangerous if we don't have the moral judgment to evaluate what we're doing. John S. Dickey, who said that the goal of education is to see us "made whole, both in competence and in conscience," also said that "to create the power of competence without creating a corresponding direction to guide the use of that power is bad education." So *know-how* without *know-why* is only half an education. Allan Bloom, who has written trenchantly on these matters, observed that fathers and mothers "have lost the idea that the highest aspiration they might have for their children is for them to be wise — specialized competence and success are all that they can imagine."

What we should aim for are the twin towers of *character* (who we are in our principles) and *competence* (what we can do in our practice). When these two are combined, we have the makings of a real person. It's the blending of these that should be our goal.

But if competence without conscience is dangerous, conscience without competence is not much good either. Being honorable people and having good intentions will not suffice. We'll have to gain some actual skills if we want to make a worthy contribution to the world. And when we learn how to do some things that the world needs to have done, we give a great gift to all the people who care about us.

In this life, we need the humility to recognize our limitations. But we also need the courage to pursue competence in the work that's within our reach. Rather than settle for mediocrity, or spin our wheels in frivolous pastimes, we'd do better to invest in the mastery of some solid skills. Expertise is a gift that keeps on giving for a very long time.

Superfluity comes sooner by white hairs,
but competency lives longer.
WILLIAM SHAKESPEARE

ACCOMPLISHMENT

No matter what accomplishments you achieve, somebody helps you.
ALTHEA GIBSON

IT IS GOOD TO REMEMBER THAT WHEREVER WE ARE, WE'VE HAD TO HAVE HELP IN GETTING THERE. There is no such thing as a completely independent achievement, and each of us needs to acknowledge our indebtedness to those who have helped us.

But while humility and gratitude are in order, it's also in order to emphasize accomplishment. Even with the help of others, some people never do anything. Grace is shown to them, but it's wasted. They pass through life dreaming, planning, and promising — but never doing.

There is a Persian proverb that says, "Thinking well is wise; planning well is wiser; but doing well is wisest and best of all." At times, we are nothing more than dreamers and talkers. We envision great accomplishments, and we talk about how wonderful they would be. But maybe instead of dreaming of worthy accomplishments, we should just stay awake and do them! I still chuckle when I remember a literary agent who once told me, "Gary, when you get done dreaming about your great book, send me some hard copy. That's all I can sell."

Our accomplishments are often hindered because our motivation is wrong. We fail to do things because we're not sure we'll be *rewarded* as we wish. (Will people appreciate this? Will they praise it? Will it make me rich and famous?) But many things have an inherent worth, and we should accomplish them simply because they're worth doing. As Emerson said, "The reward of a thing well done is to have done it." It is, after all, better to be a nobody who accomplishes something than a somebody who accomplishes nothing. At the end of the day, accomplishment has little to do with what the world calls "celebrity."

So each of us needs to heed the advice of Theodore Roosevelt, who said, "Do what you can with what you have where you are." Our accomplishments won't be those of someone else — they will be those we were uniquely gifted to accomplish. And yes, we'll make mistakes and blunders. But as Samuel Smiles put it, "He who never made a mistake never made a discovery." Our lives in this world are too short to waste. Enthusiastic ideas should lead to energetic action.

The great accomplishments of man have resulted from
the transmission of ideas and enthusiasm.
THOMAS J. WATSON

HEARING

*O God, give us sympathy for those who are deaf. They live in a silent
world so remote and so different from ours. We take for granted speech and
music and the ceaseless sounds of ordinary life — to them all is silence,
they cannot even hear the voices of their dearest friends.*

SID HEDGES

IT WAS THOMAS TRAHERNE WHO SAID, "IS NOT SIGHT A
JEWEL? IS NOT HEARING A TREASURE?" One of the saddest facts
about us is that we take for granted the gifts of seeing and hearing —
and of the two, hearing may be the one we undervalue the most. It
would only take a day of being deaf to remind us how blessed we are
to be able to hear the voices of those around us. Yes, we can read the
written words "I love you," but there is really nothing like the music of
hearing them said. There is no lonelier world than the silent world.

But it is not only sweetness that we should want to hear. We
should also be willing to hear truth — especially truth that calls for us
to change our behavior. As a people, Americans are typically religious,
but we're often guilty of what one writer called "the sin of sermon
listening." We listen, and even praise the presenter, but we don't truly
hear. The words don't sink in. We don't act on them. And this kind of
"hearing problem" is not physical. It is moral and spiritual.

Peter Drucker once said, "The most important thing in communication is to hear what isn't being said." Hearing what "isn't being
said" is not an impossibility; it occurs when we wisely and sympathetically listen with our hearts as well as our ears. As Jeremy Taylor
put it, "It is not the eye that sees the beauty of the heaven, nor the ear
that hears the sweetness of music, but the soul." If all we hear are the
sounds that enter our physical ears, we will miss many of the most
important messages in life. And this is true even within ourselves. It
takes skillful listening to hear what our own hearts are saying.

Whether it's our own heart or the hearts of others that we are
hearing, what we often hear are the groanings of a broken heart. Even
at its best, this life still deals out hurtful experiences to us and leaves
our hearts longing for comfort. We never meet anyone who is not
carrying some private burden, and we never do any better hearing than
when we hear the cry of a fellow human being for understanding.

[Love] has ears to hear the sighs and sorrows of men.

AUGUSTINE OF HIPPO

RECEPTIVENESS

It is part of the photographer's job to see more intensely than
most people do. He must have and keep in him something of the
receptiveness of the child who looks at the world for the first
time or of the traveler who enters a strange country.

BILL BRANDT

WHAT WE RECEIVE IN LIFE DEPENDS, TO A LARGE EXTENT,
ON HOW OPEN WE ARE. Just as the photographer in Bill
Brandt's illustration may not see his subject clearly if he doesn't retain
"the receptiveness of the child," we may not receive some very good
things because we're not ready to receive them. All sorts of things can
shut down our receptiveness: things like closed-mindedness, resistance, stubbornness, skepticism, pride, or even complacency. It takes
constant work to resist these tendencies and maintain open minds and
hearts, eager to receive the good things life has to offer.

Receptiveness is a trait that can be cultivated, but it takes more
self-honesty than most of us are accustomed to. We must be willing to
see when a lack of receptivity is hurting us and then have the humility
and courage to make the necessary correction. Being receptive is, after
all, frightening. It requires a certain amount of vulnerability and trust.
Perhaps that is the reason so many of us no longer have "the receptiveness of the child." Having grown up, our guard is up.

But we can't be emotionally healthy without being open. William
James often wrote about this, as when he said, "The transition from
tenseness, self-responsibility, and worry, to equanimity, receptivity, and
peace, is the most wonderful of all those shiftings of inner equilibrium
. . . and the chief wonder of it is that it so often comes about, not by
doing, but by simply relaxing and throwing the burden down." Love is
the key ingredient to health, and while love can be given, it can never
be taken by force. It must be received. As Karl Menninger said, "Love
cures people — both the ones who give it and the ones who receive it."

But finally, consider the importance of a point made by Judah
Halevi: "Divine Providence only gives man as much as he is prepared
to receive; if his receptive capacity be small, he obtains little, and
much if it be great." Closing our minds to God is the worst unrecep-
tiveness of all. By it, we impoverish ourselves in the most tragic sense.

So much God would give . . . so little is received.

FRANCES J. ROBERTS

PATRIOTISM

*The mind supplies the idea of a nation, but what gives
this idea its sentimental force is a community of dreams.*

ANDRÉ MALRAUX

IN THE UNITED STATES, TODAY IS THE MOST PATRIOTIC DAY OF THE YEAR. There is, however, a growing chorus of voices, here and elsewhere, that decry the whole notion of "nationalism." Is patriotism a bad thing? Let's take a moment to get a clearer idea of what it is (or at least what it should be) and what it isn't.

The word "patriot" comes from the Greek *pater* ("father"). In Greece, the *patris* is the "fatherland," the land of one's forefathers or ancestors. The United States, of course, is largely a nation of immigrants; for most of us, the land of our distant ancestors is somewhere else. So for us, "patriotism" would be not so much the love of our ancestral lands as it would be the love of our present nation. It means to appreciate and be devoted to the country of which we're citizens.

So is patriotism not a good idea? Well, it certainly can get out of hand and become a negative force. If by patriotism we mean "my country, right or wrong," then we need to rethink our principles. But just as tenants take better care of a house if they own it, most folks are better citizens when they're able to think of "our" country.

The very best use of July 4th would be to refine and purify our concept of patriotism, to make it more worthy. For one thing, we'd do well to make our patriotism more of a yearlong thing. As Adlai Stevenson said, "Patriotism is not short, frenzied outbursts of emotion, but the tranquil and steady dedication of a lifetime."

In its finest form, patriotism is the spirit of those who make up a "community of dreams." It's the common ideals and aspirations of those who, living in a particular section of the world, band together with a healthy sense of "ownership" of their unique society and commit themselves to the improvement of that society and the world at large. True patriots are always conscious of a stewardship: a responsibility to handle carefully the good things they've inherited (making them even better, if they can) and then to pass them on to others. Patriots worthy of the name are never bullies. They're caretakers.

*Patriotism is not so much protecting the land of our fathers
as preserving the land of our children.*

JOSÉ ORTEGA Y GASSET

Tactfulness

The point of tact is not sharp.
COLLEEN CARNEY

I DON'T KNOW OF ANYTHING MORE WIDELY PRAISED YET RARELY PRACTICED THAN TACT. Nearly everybody thinks tact is a good idea, but hardly anybody uses it. This may be because tact is such a hard habit to learn. It's one of the biggest challenges in the world.

Tact would be much easier if it only meant remaining silent and leaving some things unsaid. But while there is more to tact than this, as we shall see in a moment, most of us have room for improvement even at this preliminary stage. Just because a thought enters our head, that doesn't necessarily mean it should be verbalized. It's only a fool (and a rude one at that) who says everything that comes into his mind. Common sense tells us some things are better off left unsaid.

But there is more to tact than silence. As Samuel Butler said, "Silence is not always tact and it is tact that is golden, not silence." If there is something you think about me — perhaps a criticism — you've got to decide whether to say it. After considering the matter, you may decide not to say it: perhaps it's not clear whether the criticism is justified, it's not very important in the greater scheme of things, or it's simply not your place to talk to me about it. By your silence, you've been tactful. But if you remain silent about something you *should* talk to me about, that's not tact. As Frank Medlicott wisely noted, "Some people mistake weakness for tact. If they are silent when they ought to speak and so feign an agreement they do not feel, they call it being tactful. Cowardice would be a much better name."

When we speak, however, it takes wisdom to know *how* to speak. "Tact," as Henry W. Newton said, "is the art of making a point without making an enemy." And as Franklin P. Jones put it, "Tact is the art of building a fire under people without making their blood boil." Doing these things is hard. It calls for great earnestness and effort.

But we must try. We must learn tactfulness. And I want to conclude with this observation: it is with those who mean the most to us that we should be the most tactful. *Closeness is no excuse for rudeness.*

Don't flatter yourself that friendship authorizes you to say disagreeable things to your intimates. The nearer you come into relation with a person, the more necessary do tact and courtesy become.
OLIVER WENDELL HOLMES

RIGHTNESS

We have heard enough about being practical and efficient and prudent.
We heard it preached through several decades that these things would save
the world. I think that, with the salty taste of blood and sweat on our lips, we
are learning that we had best talk again about doing what is right.

ELLIS ARNALL

A S YOU KNOW BY NOW, I AM VERY OLD-FASHIONED. So you'll
hardly be surprised to hear me say that the question of rightness
is the supreme question in life. As we make our decisions, especially
the complex ones, many questions have to be asked, but the one that
matters the most has never changed — *what is the right thing to do?*

There is no denying that doing the right thing often requires
courage. Following our conscience can have short-term consequences
that are fearful, but I agree with A. W. Tozer, who said, "If a course is
right, [one] should take it because it is right, not because he is afraid
not to take it. And if it is wrong, he should avoid it though he lose
every earthly treasure and even his very life as a consequence."

Those who tend to be pragmatic need to avoid defining what is
right solely in terms of consequences. The possible consequences of
our decisions must surely be taken into account (Jesus of Nazareth
called it "counting the cost"), but we must not define what is right in
terms of what works the best from a practical standpoint. Rightness
often requires going against the counsels of prudence and practicality.
Following our conscience can be inconvenient, to say the least.

But whatever obstacles stand between us and doing what is right,
we need to be bold and believe that if a thing is right, there will always be a way to do it. So rightness requires not only courage but also
confidence. "Progress in every age results only from the fact that there
are some men and women who refuse to believe that what they know
to be right cannot be done" (Russell W. Davenport).

In our postmodern age, the question of feelings is usually the
main question. But again, I'm old-fashioned. I still believe in the su-
premacy of what is right. Good feelings aren't always at our command,
but no matter which direction the emotional breezes are blowing, there
is one thing that's always within our power — *we can do what is right.*

You cannot make yourself feel something you do not feel,
but you can make yourself do what is right in spite of your feelings.

PEARL S. BUCK

CONQUERING

O Father, who hast ordained that in stern conflict we should find
our strength and triumph over all, withhold not from us the courage by
which alone we can conquer. Still our tongues of their weak complainings,
steel our hearts against all fear, and in joyfully accepting the conditions
of our earthly pilgrimage, may we come to possess our souls and
to achieve our purposed destiny. Amen.

ANONYMOUS

IT CAN HELP US TO THINK OF THIS WORLD AS A BATTLEFIELD.
The military metaphor is not the only way to illustrate life, of
course, but it is a helpful one, given the problems we have to deal
with. There is simply no denying that we face difficulties that must be
conquered. We may ignore these difficulties, but they don't go away.

Let me speak plainly: as far as our hardships in this world go,
there is no safe middle ground. "You must either conquer the world or
the world will conquer you. You must be either master or slave" (John
Henry Newman). Those of us who are theists believe God is our
helper, but even so, we must fight the problems that beset us or we'll
be overcome by them. The risks are real. The stakes are high.

Our foes are of various kinds. Some of our enemies are personal,
while others are impersonal (natural disasters, financial reverses, and
such). Some are external, while others are internal (thinking problems,
self-discipline problems, and such). I believe our internal problems —
those that have taken up residence inside our hearts and minds — are
our most challenging, and I agree with Aristotle, who said, "I count
him braver who overcomes his desires than him who conquers his
enemies; for the hardest victory is the victory over self."

When I was younger, I used to suppose that, at some point,
life could be figured out and straightened out. I thought that one's
battles could be won decisively, and then one could live out the rest
of his days in peace and tranquility. What I now see is that, as long as
we live in this world, the challenges never go away. The business of
conquering is an ongoing project. "Of freedom and of life he only is
deserving who every day must conquer them anew" (Goethe).

But ultimately, conquering is not a matter of our own strength —
it's a matter of aligning ourselves with the principles of truth and goodness. If we side with what's right, we'll enjoy its triumph eventually.

I believe that in the end the truth will conquer.

JOHN WYCLIFFE

COMMITMENT

If you start to take Vienna, take Vienna.
NAPOLEON BONAPARTE

THERE IS A BIG DIFFERENCE BETWEEN "COMMITMENT" AND MERELY "GIVING IT A TRY." For every failure that results from a lack of skill, there are millions more that result from a lack of commitment. We almost guarantee defeat by the fine print we write into our promises. Trying to keep our options open, we lose the benefit of radical choice. And too often, when we look back we see a trail of broken promises, unfinished business, and dreams that didn't work out. Our lives are littered with might-have-beens, justified in our minds with excuses about what happened to us. All along, however, the problem was simply that we weren't willing to close the back door.

Commitment is especially important when two or more people are trying to reach a mutual goal. Lou Holtz, who knows a thing or two about how to get a job done, said this: "It's tough enough getting the boat to shore with everybody rowing, let alone when a guy stands up and starts putting his life jacket on." To which I simply say, "Amen!"

Vincent van Gogh is one of my favorite artists. When I look at his paintings, I, along with many others, feel a powerful pull into his imaginative world. And it's no coincidence that he could say, "I am seeking, I am striving, I am in it with all my heart." Great art, like anything else great, is the result of bolting the back door shut.

Over the years, I've read a good bit about commitment, but I've never seen its real meaning expressed more clearly than by Robert Moorehead: "My face is set, my gait is fast, my goal is heaven, my road is narrow, my way is rough, my companions are few, my guide is reliable, my mission is clear. I cannot be bought, compromised, detoured, lured away, turned back, diluted, or delayed. I will not flinch in the face of sacrifice, hesitate in the presence of adversity, negotiate at the table of the enemy, ponder at the pool of popularity, or meander in a maze of mediocrity. I won't give up, shut up, let up, or slow up."

If those words don't describe the pursuit of your goal, you don't have a goal — you just have a wish. Go get yourself a goal and commit yourself to it with the soul of a warrior who will, in the words of General George S. Patton, "either conquer or perish with honor."

You can't try to do things; you simply must do them.
RAY BRADBURY

WILLPOWER

Willpower is being able to eat just one salted peanut.
PAT ELPHINSTONE

FEW THINGS ARE MORE POWERFUL THAN WILLPOWER. If there are situations that require the use of physical power, there are many more that require intellectual, emotional, and volitional power. And when willpower is brought to bear, the results can often be astonishing. Indeed, there are not many problems that won't yield to the power of a concentrated will ("Where there's a will, there's a way"). But unfortunately, not many of us see that kind of power at work in our own lives. Learning, and then exerting, willpower is exceptionally hard, and very few people pay the price to acquire it and use it.

Actually, there are two kinds of willpower. One is the strength of will to do something that needs to be done when the thing is unpleasant or difficult. ("I'll do it tomorrow" is often our consolation.) The other is the power to resist temptation, the ability to refuse things that shouldn't be done. ("Just this once" is usually our excuse.) Frankly, I don't know which is harder: moving ourselves to do difficult things or refraining from doing wrongful things. Both of these scenarios present a serious challenge to our willpower.

I do, however, know one thing: most of the failures in the world result from someone's lack of willpower. Occasionally, we may falter because of insufficient opportunity, skill, etc., but more often, it is our willpower that is deficient. "Lack of willpower has caused more failure than lack of intelligence or ability" (Flower A. Newhouse).

By every decision we make, even the "little" ones, we either gain or lose willpower. When we enforce the dictates of our conscience, our willpower grows, and the next test will be somewhat easier to manage. But when we back away from our decisions and default on our duty, our willpower is weakened. The next time we're tested, we will be even less able to do the difficult thing. *Every decision we make either strengthens our will or diminishes it.* So we need to be very careful. If honesty compels us to admit we don't have the lives more willpower would have given us, then right now is the time to start strengthening our will. Excuses never produced progress in anyone's life.

We have more ability than willpower, and it is often an excuse to ourselves
that we imagine that things are impossible.
FRANÇOIS DE LA ROCHEFOUCAULD

INWARDNESS

> In proportion as our inward life fails, we go more constantly and
> desperately to the post office. You may depend on it, that poor fellow who
> walks away with the greatest number of letters, proud of his extensive
> correspondence, has not heard from himself this long while.
>
> HENRY DAVID THOREAU

WE DON'T GET OUR LETTERS AT THE POST OFFICE ANY-
MORE. Still, Thoreau's point is well taken. As our "inward life
fails," we depend all the more obsessively on external communications.
And is there not a suggestion here as to why the many social media
of our day are so popular? If there was a healthy inwardness about us,
would we need such an outward avalanche of tweets and texts?

Don't misunderstand me. Social connections are vitally important. We need to maintain our relationships and empathize with other
people. But I believe our understanding of others is impoverished
when we spend too little time meditating inwardly. Walter Lippman
made the point well: "We forge gradually our greatest instrument for
understanding the world — introspection. We discover that humanity
may resemble us very considerably — that the best way of knowing
the inwardness of our neighbors is to know ourselves."

But introspection (at least the healthy kind) is hard. As Dag
Hammarskjöld said in *Markings,* "The longest journey is the journey
inwards." Inwardness requires not only concentrated thought but also
honesty. Many years of meditation wouldn't do a person any good if he
didn't deal honestly with the truth that he discovered about himself.

With these cautions in mind, however, let's go back to our original point: inwardness is important. It should be given more priority
than we usually give it. "Goodness consists not in the outward things
we do, but in the inward thing we are" (Edwin Hubbell Chapin). The
busier we are, the more we need to be reminded that as important as
"doing" (or conduct) is, "being" (or character) is even more important.

The challenge, of course, is to bring our inward and outer lives
into alignment, so that our private introspection produces a public
persona consistent with the principles we cherish inwardly. Integrity,
which basically means "oneness," is one of life's great goals.

> Give me beauty in the inward soul,
> and may the outward and inward man be one.
>
> PLATO

EXECUTION

The prayer of the chicken hawk does not get him the chicken.
SWAHILI PROVERB

IN A BOOK ABOUT ENTHUSIASTIC IDEAS, WE NEED TO EMPHA-SIZE THE IMPORTANCE OF "EXECUTION." To execute an idea or a plan is to carry it out, and it should be obvious that if our ideas are not executed, they will be fruitless. It is not enough to think good thoughts; we have to do something about them. "Life happens at the level of events, not words," as Alfred Adler said. And as Curtis Grant colorfully put it, "Having the world's best idea will do you no good unless you act on it. People who want milk shouldn't sit on a stool in the middle of a field in hopes that a cow will back up to them."

In the business world, there is a keen recognition of the importance of execution. Organizations engage in strategic planning, but then the plans have to be implemented. And, in fact, the word "executive" simply means one who helps to carry out the organization's mission. The "chief executive officer" is the person who has been given the highest authority to carry out the plans of the owner or directors.

In our personal lives, I would suggest that execution is the key to having a positive self-image. Self-esteem is often overrated in our culture, but it is certainly important, and the way to get it is to get out of our easy chair and start executing our good ideas. "The only way to get positive feelings about yourself is to take positive action. Man does not live as he thinks, he thinks as he lives" (Vaughan Quinn).

Ultimately, execution is the main measure of our character; it is what reveals our true convictions. Ashley Montagu bluntly summed it up in these words: "The only measure of what you believe is what you do. If you want to know what people believe, don't read what they write, don't ask them what they believe, just observe what they do."

Will Rogers once said, "Even if you're on the right track, you'll get run over if you just sit there." He wasn't exaggerating. Life ruthlessly rolls over those who do nothing but think and plan and prepare. So while our dreams are vitally important — as I've written elsewhere — it's even more important that we implement our aspirations. If they are not soon acted upon, our best impulses will vanish.

Inspirations never go in for long engagements;
they demand immediate marriage to action.
BRENDAN FRANCIS

IMMUNITY

Immune: not affected by a given influence.
AMERICAN HERITAGE DICTIONARY

IF IMMUNITY IS IMPORTANT TO OUR PHYSICAL HEALTH, IT'S EVEN MORE IMPORTANT EMOTIONALLY AND SPIRITUALLY. There are certain influences we need to be resistant to, both physically and mentally, or else these will harm us. And just as there are things we can do to strengthen our physical immunity, there are things we can do intellectually to shore up our defenses.

Immunity does not mean it's impossible for us to be affected; it means we're *resistant*. If we're immune to a certain influence, it's *less likely* we'll be affected by it. My father was a watchmaker, and when I was a child, I remember him pointing out that most watches claim to be water-resistant, not water-proof. But let me tell you: *resistance is an important plus*. With some things in life, being even a little more resistant to them is a valuable benefit.

I'm afraid, however, that many of us wrongly identify the things we want to be resistant, or immune, to. In a culture where feelings are all-important, many people, if they had their wish, would want to be immune to suffering, pain, sorrow, and difficulty. But while these things are unpleasant, they often serve useful purposes in our lives. Not infrequently, they produce significant growth in our character. So it's not these things that we should want to be protected from, but rather those that are morally wrong. More than every other malady, the one we should most want immunity from is the influence of evil, the violation of the timeless standards of right and wrong.

There is, of course, no vaccination against evil. There is no insight we can gain that will make us proof against its influence for the rest of our lives. But we can increase our resistance by meditating daily on what is right and making consistent choices in that direction.

Without a doubt, the main ingredient in our immunity to evil is love — not the sentimental thing many call love, but a strong, passionate commitment to seek the highest good of everyone around us. If there is anything that will immunize us against evil, this is it. Real love is a powerfully protective shield, one we can hardly do without.

The only power which can resist
the power of fear is the power of love.
ALAN STEWART PATON

MEMENTOS

Surrounding ourselves with reminders of who we are and
where we've been is another simple way we have found to make
our home uniquely ours. The walls, shelves, floors, and windowsills
of both our home and my studio are full of objects that tell the stories
of where we've been and what we've done and enjoyed together.

THOMAS KINKADE

OBJECTS HAVE THE POWER TO EVOKE HEALTHFUL MEMORIES.
When there is some physical remnant of a past event, seeing or
touching that object connects us to the event, and the people associated with it, in a "sensuous" way, that is, by means of our senses. That's
why we make scrapbooks and keep souvenirs. That's why we hold on
to otherwise worthless pieces of paper that bear the signature of some
admired person. And that's why, above all, we treasure objects that
have been given to us by some especially beloved person. However
ordinary those objects might be in themselves, they are mementos,
tangible reminders of a relationship that has enriched us.

For many years, I have kept on my desk two rocks. You couldn't
tell by looking at them that there is anything special about them.
They are only special to me because I picked them up in two special
places while I was with two special friends. One came from the burning floor of Death Valley one July Fourth many years ago when I was
there with a friend to whom I'm deeply indebted. The other came
from the stony beach at Scotts Head on the little island of Dominica,
when I was there with another special friend. This particular friend, a
native of the Caribbean, shook his head in amusement at the thought
of my going back through customs with rocks in my bag. But to this
day, the stone connects me to the island and to him. It's a memento.

There is, I think, great value not only in keeping mementos but
also in picking them up and handling them from time to time. The
sense of touch is a powerful connector to things we need to stay connected to, and we ought to use it more than we do. So while we keep
some things for their usefulness, we ought to keep others for their his-
toricalness. Mementos are pegs upon which we can hang memories.
And in our occasional housecleaning fits, let's be careful not to throw
away the things that our best memories are attached to.

Keep some souvenirs of your past, or how will
you ever prove it wasn't all a dream?

ASHLEIGH BRILLIANT

PERSEVERANCE

Drudgery is as necessary to call out the treasures of the mind
as harrowing and planting those of the earth.
MARGARET FULLER

WITH EVERY PIECE OF INTERESTING WORK IN THE WORLD,
THERE IS ALWAYS SOME LESS-THAN-INTERESTING WORK
THAT GOES ALONG WITH IT. If a person can't persevere, the work
won't be finished, no matter how interesting or valuable it may be.

Perseverance is not the primary consideration in our work, of
course. Other factors must be considered first. For example, wisdom
must precede perseverance. Being persistent in a foolish project is
not good. So before we apply perseverance to a task, we must wisely
consider whether what we're doing is *right*. If it is, we may commit
ourselves to the undertaking — and persevere until we reach the goal.

There is hardly anything worth doing that is not fraught with
difficulty, so it takes perseverance to push our way through the
hardships and finish the job. In fact, the level of difficulty is often a
measure of how worthwhile a project is. Free things are usually worth
about what we pay for them, and jobs that don't involve any resistance
aren't usually worth any more than what they cost us. So before we
complain about how hard it is to persevere, we should ask whether
we'd rather be doing something easy . . . and relatively insignificant.

I hesitate to recommend stubbornness as a character trait, but
there is a sense in which it is virtuous. If by stubbornness we mean
the dogged determination to keep on working, most of us need to be
more stubborn. As someone has said, "We must overcome stubborn
facts with a stubborn will." The good things in life are accomplished by
those who were just too tenacious and bullheaded to give up.

James T. White said, "Perseverance is the statesman's brain, the
warrior's sword, the inventor's secret, and the scholar's open sesame."
Very often, we find it to be the critical hinge on which everything else
turns. And truly, perseverance is a matter of character. Do we have
what it takes to keep going when weaker individuals would lie down
and quit? So the next time you are tempted to give up, I urge you to
stop and ask yourself, "What kind of stuff am I made out of, anyway?"

Perseverance is the grindstone saying to the axe,
"You are hard, but I am harder. I will wear you away."
JAMES T. WHITE

July 15
HOPE

The leaders of men are those who are full of some great and fruitful idea.
And he who is thus possessed sees clearly, and maintains a cheerful courage,
where common men tremble and rebel.

JAMES T. WHITE

THANK GOODNESS FOR LEADERS. They are the ones whose imaginations are fired up with great ideas, and they blaze the trail ahead of us, undeterred by whatever obstacles may block the path. The grinding forces of discouragement and pessimism would often be too much for us if it weren't for leaders who keep hope alive. *Our ideas are our possibilities* — and leaders are those who keep us believing that our ideas are worthwhile and they can actually be carried out.

Hopeful leaders have an impact on us because hopefulness is contagious. When a crowd is discouraged, it only takes one brave, optimistic leader to give them hope. Discouragement is contagious too, of course, but I believe hopefulness is stronger than discouragement. The influence of one truly hopeful person can often counteract the gloom of many pessimists. For that reason, all of us need to be people of hope. Blind hope is not worth much, obviously, but when hope is built on a foundation of solid evidence, we can make the choice to maintain hope even in the midst of momentary darkness. When we do that, others will very likely "catch" our hope.

Some people are more naturally prone to hopefulness, but it is a quality that can be cultivated by all of us. It takes disciplining our minds to remember the evidence that our hopes are built on — refusing to let temporary discouragements distract us. And when we cultivate hope continually, it turns into an enthusiasm that is unquenchable.

Despair — the loss of all hope — is one of the worst things in the world. It robs us of the courage to take the next step, the one that is right in front of us at the present moment. Despair kills us by paralyzing us, preventing us from doing the very doable thing (the next step is always a step we can take) that would move us in a better direction. So as a matter of principle, let's reject despair and refuse to give up our ideals. Come what may, let's keep moving forward!

Let us beware of losing our enthusiasm. Let us ever glory in something,
and strive to attain our admiration for all that would ennoble, and our interest
in all that would enrich and beautify our life.

PHILLIPS BROOKS

RATIONALITY

Because we are intelligent creatures — meaning that we are
freed from instinctive and patterned behavior to a degree unparalleled
in the animal kingdom — we are capable of, and dependent on,
using rational choice to decide our futures.

WILLARD GAYLIN

O UR ABILITY TO THINK RATIONALLY IS A TRULY MARVELOUS
ENDOWMENT. In the natural world, we alone possess it. As
personal beings, we can differentiate between truth and untruth, and
between right and wrong. We can weigh multiple courses of action
and choose the one that is best to follow. And with this ability to reason, we have a great deal of freedom. To a much greater extent than
the lower creatures, we can choose our own future.

Things like "logic" and "reasoning" and "propositions" may be out
of fashion in these days of postmodernism. But in practical affairs, we
can't do without these things. In fact, the postmodernist has to use
rational propositions to persuade us that rational propositions are bad.

We may as well face it: our feelings flow from our thinking, so
the quality of our thinking is critically important. If, for example, a
man thinks his wife is being unfaithful to him, he will have certain
feelings that are quite natural to that thought. But what if the thought
itself is irrational? What if he has misinterpreted certain things she
has said or done? If his wife is, in fact, not being unfaithful to him,
the feelings he has are inappropriate, and they will be destructive to
his relationship with her. So before we grant sovereign authority to
our feelings, we would do well to ask whether the thoughts that have
produced those feelings are true.

Something else also needs to be given priority, and that is our
principles. For example, if my highest principle is pleasure, certain
actions will seem logical and reasonable. But if my highest principle is
justice, then logic will dictate a radically different set of actions. Our
principles form the starting point for our reasoning processes — so
our principles need to be chosen very, very carefully.

The gift of rationality is a stewardship. We need to use it more
often — and more skillfully. It takes practice, but we can learn to base
our choices on wisdom rather than folly. We can learn to be reasonable.

So for the hairsbreadth of time assigned to thee, live rationally . . .
MARCUS AURELIUS

EQUITY

There is but one law for all, namely, that law which governs all law,
the law of our Creator, the law of humanity, justice, equity . . .

EDMUND BURKE

EQUITY IS JUSTICE OR FAIRNESS. But equity emphasizes one particular aspect of justice, and that is its impartiality. The word "equity" comes from the same Latin root as the word "equal." It refers to the equal application of the rules of justice to one and all. And that, as we all know, is one of the leading qualities of genuine fairness.

Double standards are, I fear, more of a plague upon our society than we realize. We simply don't see how often we apply a stricter standard to others than we apply to ourselves. We don't see how often we criticize "the other side" for actions that, if we did the very same thing, would not be thought objectionable. And we don't acknowledge how often certain segments of our society get preferential treatment.

Equity, however, gets rid of double standards. "What's good for the goose is good for the gander" — so I should be willing to apply to myself the exact same rules I apply to everybody else.

It's easy to say these things, but in practice, equity is often hard to determine because it requires sorting out many different factors, conflicting priorities, and competing claims. If you think a judge's job is easy, you've probably never had to do it. The difficulty of justice and equity is why Solomon, when he became king of Israel, asked God for wisdom. His prayer is recorded in the First Book of Kings: "So give your servant a discerning mind so he can make judicial decisions for your people and distinguish right from wrong. Otherwise no one is able to make judicial decisions for this great nation of yours" (NET).

In our daily affairs, we all need the same thing Solomon needed: *wisdom.* And there is no shortcut to wisdom. It takes, first, seeing its value, and then acquiring it patiently. As with most skills, we get better at judging by doing it — *and we had better be doing it.* There is no more important work. We can't live well in this world without equity, and we can't learn equity without constant practice.

To know wisdom and instruction,
To perceive the words of understanding,
To receive the instruction of wisdom,
Justice, judgment, and equity.

THE BOOK OF PROVERBS

ALMSGIVING

Give, if thou canst, an alms; if not, afford,
instead of that, a sweet and gentle word.
ROBERT HERRICK

AN OLDER WORD, "ALMSGIVING" IS STILL A GOOD WORD AND ONE THAT CONVEYS AN ENTHUSIASTIC IDEA. Almsgiving is what we would call charitable giving, such as the giving of aid to a poor person who is begging in a public place. The word comes from the Greek noun *eleos* ("pity, mercy"), and the giving of alms was an act much more highly regarded in ancient times than it is today. We would do well to recover some of the old attitude toward almsgiving.

In an affluent society where "welfare" has become a way of life for many who could be working, it is easy to become cynical about the poor, but we must resist that temptation. Yes, it does take wisdom these days to know when and how to help, but we dare not become so "wise" that we overlook those in genuine need. And if we're going to err, wouldn't it be better to err on the side of generosity?

Concerning almsgiving, Jesus of Nazareth raised the issue of our motivation: "But when you give alms, do not let your left hand know what your right hand is doing." When we give, it should not be simply to get credit for being generous, so our giving should, if possible, be kept private. As Henry Ward Beecher advised, "Do not give, as many rich men do, like a hen that lays her egg and then cackles."

And speaking of motivation, what about the enrichment we receive from giving? It's true, as an English proverb says, that alms "never make the giver poor." All things considered, we gain more than we lose when we give. But that shouldn't be our primary motivation.

The bottom line is that many important things hinge on our decision concerning the poor. Robert Southey said of a certain person, "His alms were money put to interest in the other world." And John Donne made a sobering point when he said, "The rich have no more of the kingdom of heaven than they have purchased of the poor by their alms." Almsgiving is an issue with very serious implications.

But for all of us, life is a mixture of giving and receiving. I may give to you today, but tomorrow I'll be in need of something you can give.

There is not a soul who does not have to beg alms of another,
either a smile, a handshake, or a fond eye.
EDWARD DAHLBERG

July 19
COMPREHENSION

There exists a passion for comprehension, just as there exists
a passion for music. That passion is rather common in children,
but gets lost in most people later on.
ALBERT EINSTEIN

MOST NORMAL HUMAN BEINGS WANT TO COMPREHEND THE WORLD. That is, we want to understand ourselves and our surroundings. In particular, we are curious about two questions: how things got to be the way they are and how they work now that they're here. So most folks have some interest in history and in science. These two disciplines add to our comprehension of the world. They help us understand where things came from and how they operate.

Children have an obvious interest in these things, of course, as Einstein observed. Children naturally ask questions about both history ("Where did we live before we lived in this house?") and science ("What makes the grass grow?"). They want to figure things out. They want to understand how and why. They want to comprehend.

Adults are curious also, but with a significant difference. When we grow up, we begin asking how and why for a different reason. It is no longer a childlike sense of awe and wonder that makes us curious about the world; now we're interested in fixing the parts of the world that aren't what we want them to be. The only things we want to comprehend are those we wish to control and bend to our will. As adults, we've become "practical." We're not curious about anything that won't help us solve the problems that interfere with our "happiness."

I see this as a sad state of affairs. For one thing, it's sad that we lose the pure fascination children enjoy. Not yet into fixing the world, they revel in the mystery of life. They want to comprehend not for utilitarian purposes, but simply for the amazement of it all. But second, our "comprehension and control" mentality is sad because of its pride. We've figured out so many things, we now believe everything is controllable. And in our pride, we're bored. As Thomas à Kempis said, "If the works of God were of such sort that they might easily be comprehended by human reason, they should no longer be called wonderful or unspeakable." We'd comprehend more (and enjoy more) if we bowed in awe before some things that can't be comprehended.

A finite creature can never fully comprehend that which is infinite.
THOMAS MANTON

July 20
STEADFASTNESS

Security is never the friend of faith.
It is peril that produces steadfastness.
CALVIN MILLER

IT IS FOOLISH TO THINK THAT WE'D BE MORE STEADFAST IF WE HAD AN EASIER LOT IN LIFE. For one thing, we wouldn't need to be steadfast if we didn't have any difficulties. (It's no great feat to keep going when there's no resistance.) But more important, it is difficulty that teaches us to be steadfast. It is only through dealing with hardship, and sometimes failing the test, that our steadfastness has a chance to grow. When there's no pain, there will be no significant gain.

As virtues go, steadfastness may seem rather unspectacular. It's not very flashy, and it doesn't get a lot of press. But in reality, there is no more critical ingredient in success. Most of the important work in the world is done by those who are steady, not by those who are flashy. The "hare" may grab the headlines, but the "tortoise" goes the distance — and often gets to the finish line first. "Slow and steady wins the race" is not just old-fashioned advice from Aesop. It's true to real life.

When the hard demands of life call on us to be steadfast, it helps to remember that hardship, like everything else in this life, is temporary. If we hold steady, the situation will eventually change. It may be later rather than sooner, and we must avoid setting deadlines for our hardships to go away, but eventually, circumstances are going to shift.

Many difficulties require steadfastness, but the most important, by far, is the difficulty of keeping promises, vows, and commitments. In the real world, commitments almost always turn out to be harder to keep than we thought they would be, but having *character* means keeping our word even when it costs us dearly. Tempted to break our commitments, we remain steadfast. We forge ahead.

If steadfastness seems mundane in comparison to other virtues, we need to remember its worth. It is one of the supreme aspects of the good life — none of us can claim to have "arrived" until we've learned it. And yes, it is hard. To keep on keeping on, when everybody else is quitting, is not easy. But in the end, the quitter's life is even harder.

Give me, O Lord, a steadfast heart, which no unworthy
affection may drag downwards. Give me an unconquered heart,
which no tribulation can wear out. Give me an upright heart,
which no unworthy purpose may tempt aside.
THOMAS AQUINAS

POSSIBILITIES

Nothing ever built arose to touch the skies unless some
man deemed that it should be done, some man believed
that it could, and some man willed that it must.
CHARLES F. KETTERING

WHAT ARE THE POSSIBILITIES? That is one of the trickiest
questions we ever have to answer. When faced with a difficult
decision, it often helps to focus not on theoretical possibilities but on
the real alternatives we're actually faced with. On the other hand, we
often sell ourselves short. We fail to see that what seems impossible
might actually be achievable. Sometimes our aim is too low.

It is especially important not to underestimate other people. Their
possibilities are often far greater than we think. And this is often true
of those from whom we expect the least. As Harry Emerson Fosdick
was fond of saying, there are "extraordinary possibilities in ordinary
people." We give a great gift to our friends and loved ones when we set
aside our preconceived notions about what they can do and let them
actually show us. Very often, we are pleasantly surprised.

These days, the achievement of things that were previously
thought impossible is a common occurrence. If we haven't learned
it already, we should learn it now: *the word "impossible" is a word that
should be used with great caution.* What seems impossible today may be
very possible tomorrow, based on new knowledge about the way the
world works. Much that appears impossible is actually doable — we
just don't know it yet. And this is as true at the personal level as it is
in the area of science and technology. Before you say, "That's impossible; I can't do it," hold your tongue. *Don't underestimate your possibilities.* There's a great deal of truth in Jim Goodwin's remark, "The
impossible is often the untried." So give it a try. Aim high, and aspire
to things you think are beyond your reach. You may surprise yourself.

I encourage you, therefore, to do the "impossible." But on a
lighter note, you should be forewarned: once you've pulled it off,
the impossible will become routine. If you ever do something other
people thought couldn't be done, you'll be expected to do it from then
on. To stay fresh, you'll have to find some other windmills to joust at!

Accomplishing the impossible means only that
the boss will add it to your regular duties.
DOUG LARSON

SIGNIFICANCE

The most basic need is a sense of personal worth, an acceptance
of oneself as a whole, real person. The two required inputs are *significance*
(purpose, importance, adequacy for a job, meaningfulness, impact) and *security*
(love — unconditional and consistently expressed; permanent acceptance).

LARRY CRABB

THERE IS NO USE DENYING THAT "SIGNIFICANCE" IS ONE OF THE MAIN QUESTIONS WE HAVE TO WRESTLE WITH. First, we want to know that the world in which we live has a meaningful significance. But second, we also want to have a personal significance. Larry Crabb speaks for every one of us when he says, "I long to know that someone sees something in me that's valuable."

As Crabb suggests in the beginning quotation, our sense of personal worth rests on two pillars: significance and security. Men seem to need significance more, while women appear to need security more. But the truth is, we all need both of these, and we need significance no less than security. If a person's presence in the world didn't make any difference to anyone — that is, he or she was completely insignificant in every way — it would be an existence hard to bear. So it's important for each of us to find truthful answers to these questions: *What difference does it make that I am in the world? Why do I matter?*

In this book, however, we're paying special attention to gifts we can give to those around us, so I want to suggest that we should be concerned not only about our own significance but also that of others. We never do a finer thing than when we help another human being see why they matter. Indeed, to the extent we focus on encouraging others, our own significance tends to take care of itself.

One of the saddest facts in the world is our tendency to go down so many dead-end streets looking for significance. Desperate to believe our lives are meaningful, we look to popular culture for answers. We let the advertisers and entertainers tell us what makes a life significant — and in the end, we find out we've been misled.

But make no mistake, the question of our significance is critical. Our lives in this world are either more than they seem or less than they seem, and the difference is huge. The stakes are unimaginably high.

We begin to lose our humanity as soon as we begin to lose
the emphasis that what we do makes a difference.

FRANCIS SCHAEFFER

CONVERSATION

The best of life is conversation, and the greatest success is confidence,
or perfect understanding between sincere people.
RALPH WALDO EMERSON

THE GIFT OF LANGUAGE CAN BE USED ON HIGH OCCASIONS, BUT IT CAN ALSO BE USED IN EVERYDAY CONVERSATION. Our lives would be enriched if we learned more of the value of good conversation and more of the skill that's required to engage in it.

Sydney J. Harris once wrote, "The two words 'information' and 'communication' are often used interchangeably, but they signify quite different things. Information is giving out; communication is getting through." Conversation falls into the category of "communication" rather than mere "information." It calls for an investment of *ourselves*.

Good conversation is challenging because it requires that we balance so many elements and avoid so many extremes. It should be "pleasant without scurrility, witty without affectation, free without indecency, learned without conceitedness, novel without falsehood" (Shakespeare). Consider two particular areas of concern:

(1) *We should avoid saying some things at all.* Earl Wilson was right when he said, "If you wouldn't write it and sign it, don't say it." Gossip is tempting, but it furnishes poor material for genuine conversation.

(2) *We should avoid saying too much.* Most of us have a tendency to keep talking when we should take a breather. Many a thought has been suffocated by being expressed in too many words. And many a conversation has been destroyed by one person's domination of it.

All in all, good conversation is a challenge. It's an art that has to be learned. But oh, what a delightful art once we've learned a bit of it! Few things equal the simple pleasure of "conversing." In the words of Samuel Johnson, "That is the happiest conversation where there is no competition, no vanity, but a calm quiet interchange of sentiments."

Conversation is but carving!
Give no more to every guest
Than he's able to digest.
Give him always of the prime,
And but little at a time.
Carve to all but just enough,
Let them neither starve nor stuff,
And that you may have your due,
Let your neighbor carve for you.
JONATHAN SWIFT

SENSIBILITY

Nothing is little to him that feels it with great sensibility.
SAMUEL JOHNSON

SENSIBILITY REFERS TO OUR ABILITY TO FEEL OR PERCEIVE THINGS. Just as our "senses" enable us to experience physical stimuli, "sensibility" allows us to be affected by things of an intellectual or emotional nature. As personal beings, we can perceive and feel and respond with a will that is free. The gift of consciousness allows us to be "in touch" with reality in ways that are truly wonderful.

The ability to feel is a blessing, obviously, but it is a mixed blessing. Physically, we can't feel pleasure without also being able to feel pain, and the same thing is true emotionally. "The heart that is soonest awake to the flowers is always the first to be touched by the thorns" (Thomas Moore). But we wouldn't want it any other way, would we? It is the more sorrowful (and even the more painful) emotions that give depth and contrast to our character. If we weren't sensible to these things, our emotional lives would be impoverished.

It is interesting, however, that our sensibility either grows or diminishes as we live. If we don't open ourselves up to that which we ought to feel, or "sense," then our sensibility begins to atrophy. Without an effort to keep them open and receptive, our hearts begin to shut down — which is to say, we begin to lose our humanity.

Blaise Pascal pointed to another potential problem when he wrote, "The sensibility of man to trifles, and his insensibility to great things, indicates a strange inversion." Just as we need to enhance our sensibility and keep it in good working order, we also need to make sure it has a good sense of priorities. Ideally, we want to be more sensible to that which is most important in life, and less sensible to all the rest. Some things should affect us more keenly than others.

Life involves more than our feelings, of course, but it should never involve less. We may do great deeds and witness extraordinary events, but if we've not had the sensibility to enjoy them (tasting them with full awareness and wakefulness), we've lost much of what's available to us in the temporal world. So let's not allow life to simply wash over us. Instead, let's be deeply and joyously *sensible* to it.

The man who has lived the longest is not he who has spent the greatest number of years, but he who has had the greatest sensibility of life.
JEAN-JACQUES ROUSSEAU

STILLNESS

Be still, my soul.
KATHARINA VON SCHLEGEL

OF ALL THE QUALITIES CONDUCIVE TO DEEP CHARACTER, STILLNESS MAY BE THE HARDEST ONE TO HOLD ON TO. Our modern environment is anything but still, and it takes discipline to maintain a quiet center in the midst of our lives.

Silence. Our work in the world requires a good deal of communication, obviously, but as time goes by, we suffer if we never engage in silence. This, perhaps, is the greatest form of stillness. Turning off all the noise (physically going to a secluded place, if necessary) and soaking in the silence is a truly transformational practice.

Meditation. One of the main reasons why silence is so helpful is that it allows us to meditate — and by meditation I do not mean that which is devoid of any cognitive content. I refer to the contemplation of truthful thoughts, those which not only refresh us but instruct us and send us back to our active lives having been edified.

Trust. Many of the demands of life require faith and confidence. As Corrie ten Boom said, "When a train goes through a tunnel and it gets dark, you don't throw away your ticket and jump off. You sit still and trust the engineer." So when confronted with doubtful and worrisome challenges, there is a great value in knowing how to "sit still."

Calmness. Faced with danger, or even distraction, most of us become frantic. In desperation, we lash out and flail at the problem. But stillness means we've learned to keep our heads and control our responses. The ability, as Tim Hansel puts it, "to be still, to be present, and not to panic or lose perspective" is a valuable skill.

Courage. Compared to other kinds of stillness, this one is a bit more active, but it's no less important. It means that on the battlefield of life we "stand still" and refuse to retreat before the onslaught of evil. Merely standing our ground may not seem very heroic, but it is. There is a bravery to standing still that is nothing short of noble.

There is a familiar English proverb which says, "Still waters run deep." Words and deeds are fine; indeed they are necessary. But let us not become so wordy and so busy that we lose our balance. The good life consists not only of fruitful activity but also of nourishing stillness.

The greatest events are not our noisiest, but our stillest hours.
FRIEDRICH NIETZSCHE

July 26
TEMPERANCE

Temperance and labor are the two best physicians of man.
JEAN-JACQUES ROUSSEAU

MOST PEOPLE THINK OF TEMPERANCE AS SELF-CONTROL. If we're temperate, that means we're able to govern our desires and moderate our impulses, restraining ourselves when we need to. But think with me today about what that really means. One of the most basic definitions of the verb "temper" is "to modify by the addition of a moderating element." Self-control almost always involves this kind of temperance. If I say no to a second helping of chocolate pie, for example, I am not just saying no — I am saying yes to some *other* considerations. I am modifying my desire for chocolate pie by adding in some other values, such as physical health, respect for another person who might want the last piece of pie, and so forth.

Daily life consists of many such balancing acts, where multiple priorities have to be considered and desires have to be tempered. There is no virtue in the world that doesn't have to be balanced with other virtues. To take any virtue or desire and make a god out of it is to create a demon that will destroy us. Idolatry is a dangerous thing.

So our desires have to be restrained, and if we can't restrain them, they've mastered us and we're in bondage to them. "At each moment of a man's life, he is either a king or a slave. As he surrenders to a wrong appetite, to any human weakness, to any failure, he is a slave. As he day by day crushes out human weakness he receives a new self from the sin and folly of the past, then he is a king" (James T. White). The point is not that desire is inherently bad and has to be done away with; it is that no one desire can be allowed to become a tyrant or a dictator. Every desire should be required to cooperate with our other desires — and also with our principles, values, and commitments.

In fact, the higher a desire is on the scale of our values, the more destructive it will be if it's not tempered. Even love, as great as it is, has to be governed. It is not enough simply to say that we love something or someone. The question is, what are the boundaries of that love? How must that love be balanced with my concern for what is right and good and honorable? And come to think of it, that's always what temperance comes down to: submitting love to virtuous discipline.

Temperance is love in training.
DWIGHT LYMAN MOODY

PLEASANTNESS

Most arts require long study and application, but the most
useful of all, that of pleasing, requires only the desire.
LORD CHESTERFIELD

PLEASANTNESS, AS THE SPELLING SUGGESTS, HAS TO DO WITH
PLEASURE. That which is pleasant gives us pleasure; it is pleasing. And surely that is a good thing — not an unqualified good thing,
mind you, but still a good thing. We can think of it in two ways:

(1) *Pleasantness in our own lives.* Do you think a pleasant life is
the ultimate good? Do you pursue pleasure at all costs? I hope not, for
there are times when we must submit to unpleasantness in the pursuit
of higher goals. Epicurus, the father of Epicureanism, said, "It is impossible to live a pleasant life without living wisely and well and justly,
and it is impossible to live wisely and well and justly without living
pleasantly." Neither of those statements is true, for many unwise and
unjust people live pleasantly and many who are wise and just endure
horrible suffering. So pleasantness can't be our highest consideration.

But it is a valid consideration, and I want you to have a deeper
appreciation for it. Within the limits of principled goodness, relish every pleasant moment that comes to you. And this is especially
true of the simple, homely joys of life. Do not let pleasantness slip by
without enjoying it. Don't just exist — *live.* Live your life to the full!

(2) *Being pleasant to others.* If pleasantness in our own lives must
be tempered with other considerations, the same is true of pleasing
others. The compulsive "pleaser," who has to have everyone's approval,
ends up doing things that are not only foolish but self-defeating.
"Please all and you please none," as Aesop famously said. I like the
way George Dennison Prentice put it: "It is a vain hope to please all
alike. Let a man stand with his face in what direction he will, he must
necessarily turn his back on one half of the world." We can face east
or we can face west, but we cannot face both directions at once.

That said, however, let's come back to the more positive point
of pleasantness as it relates to others. It is an enormous gift to those
around us. Our pleasantness must never be flippant or an insult to
what others are suffering, but wisely applied, it is nearly miraculous.
By something as simple as a smile, we can give hope and healing.

Most smiles are started by another smile.
FRANK HOWARD CLARK

ABILITY

Ability is what you're capable of doing.
Motivation determines what you do.
Attitude determines how well you do it.

LOU HOLTZ

ONE OF LIFE'S MOST INTERESTING CHALLENGES IS THAT OF INCREASING OUR ABILITY. Without "ability," we're not "able" to help anyone or make any kind of worthy contribution to the world in which we live. We're each endowed with natural talents that can be turned into ability, so ability is within the reach of all of us. The challenge is to identify our personal strengths and develop our skills.

Ability, of course, must always be tied to character and conscience. If we learn how to do some things but use that ability in immoral or unethical ways, we do more harm than good. "Great ability without discretion comes almost invariably to a tragic end" (Léon Gambetta). And as William Penn warned, "An able bad man is an ill instrument." We must keep clear the difference between *efficiency* (ability) and *effectiveness* (the use of ability in doing things that ought to be done).

It takes discipline and hard work to transform our potential into actual ability. If our talents are to become abilities, they must pass through the fire of training and self-government. And that, unfortunately, is why so many of us have so few abilities. "The acquisition of one sort of ability often makes that of another unlikely, if not impossible . . . To take the gifts one does have, to concentrate one's strength upon their development, to disallow distractions — none of these is an easy task" (Joseph Epstein). In developing any ability, there is always a price to be paid. "A special ability means a heavy expenditure of energy in a particular direction, with a consequent drain from some other side of life" (Carl Jung). So we must narrow our focus and accept that our abilities will, to some extent, disable us in other areas. Our unique advantages always have corresponding disadvantages.

But more importantly, we need to *use* the abilities we have, rather than letting them go to waste. Even in areas where we may not have as much ability as someone else, we must be willing to do the best we can. What the world needs is not people who can do everything — but rather people who are willing to do anything!

God does not ask about our ability or our inability, but our availability.

ANONYMOUS

COUNSEL

In an abundance of counselors there is safety.
THE BOOK OF PROVERBS

GETTING HIGH-QUALITY COUNSEL IS CRITICAL TO SUCCESS IN ALMOST EVERY IMPORTANT ENDEAVOR. None of us has the vision or perspective to see all that we need to see, so we have to be helped by others who can share their perspective with us. And the more important the project, the more valuable good counsel is.

The difficulty, however, is not just in seeking counsel but in separating the good counsel from the bad. As the proverb above says, there is safety in having an "abundance" of counselors, but the more counselors we have, the more certain it is that they're going to disagree in the advice they give us. The difficulty is that if we had the wisdom to tell which was the good advice and which was the bad, we probably wouldn't need to be asking for advice in the first place. Only wise people can tell when they're being given bad counsel, so evaluating the counsel we receive is sometimes quite difficult.

But while we must seek counsel and be willing to act on it, we must also take responsibility for our own decisions. Having listened to those who counsel us, we must sort through the options and make our own choice. Having made our choice, we must take responsibility for the decision. Counselors should not be blamed for our bad choices any more than they should be given credit for our good ones.

The best counselors are those who practice what they preach. I've always been impressed with Leonardo da Vinci's admonition, "Ask counsel of him who governs himself well." The person whose word should carry the greatest weight with us is the one who demonstrates in the way he lives his own life that he knows what wisdom is.

Still, there is no denying that hypocrites and fools can sometimes give us good advice. When they do, we need to have the honesty and humility to profit from it despite the source from which it comes. "It can be no dishonor," Sophocles said, "to learn from others when they speak good sense." If our own lives are to be what they ought to be, we must be willing to have the truth presented to us even by unfriendly messengers. Receiving counsel should mean more than simply listening to likable people who tell us what we want to hear.

If the counsel be good, it does not matter who gave it.
THOMAS FULLER

FITNESS

> While the law [of competition] may be sometimes hard
> for the individual, it is best for the race, because it insures
> the survival of the fittest in every department.
>
> ANDREW CARNEGIE

YOU MAY NOT HAVE THOUGHT ABOUT IT, BUT MANY OF THE GOOD THINGS IN LIFE DEPEND ON "FITNESS." In its most literal sense, fitness means that something is the proper shape and size. Your shoes, for example, fit if they correspond to the shape and size of your feet. But we use the word figuratively in many other ways.

Am I physically fit? This is the only kind of fitness that many people think of these days, and while there are other important kinds of fitness, as we shall see, physical fitness is not an issue that should be disregarded. To be physically fit means that, as far as we are able, we have maintained a physical condition that fits the demands that life makes on us. Our physical condition is right for what we have to do.

Is my conduct fitting? This question takes the question of fitness to a different level. Here we are concerned with whether our behavior is the "proper shape and size," and this is a difficult matter. On the one hand, there are those who have no higher goal in life than "fitting in." They will even compromise their moral principles to meet this objective. On the other hand, there are those who have a total disregard for what is fitting and appropriate. In these days of radical individualism, these folks seem to be in the majority. But while it may sometimes be difficult to judge what is fitting in a particular situation, the question of appropriate conduct is not a totally subjective matter, and most of us would do well to think about it more often than we do.

Am I fit for the work that is mine to do? All of us have work to do, and so we must address the issue of our talents, our knowledge, and our skills. Whatever work a person is responsible for doing (and I'm not just talking about one's paid job or occupation), that work will be done better if he or she is fit for it. So we need to do everything in our power to make ourselves more fit for our work. When (a) what we do fits us, and (b) we've increased our skills in order to fit the job, good things are bound to happen. So let's acquire abilities that are the "proper shape and size" for our opportunities.

> In order that people may be happy in their work . . . they must be fit for it.
>
> JOHN RUSKIN

MODESTY

Suit the action to the word, the word to the action;
with this special observance, that you o'erstep not the modesty of nature.
WILLIAM SHAKESPEARE

MODESTY IS HARD TO DISCUSS BECAUSE IT'S HARD TO DEFINE. The word comes from the same root as "moderate," so in its most basic sense, "modest" is the opposite of "extreme." But we generally use the word to describe the person who is reticent and reserved, rather than forward and uninhibited. If I had to sum up the concept of modesty, I would put it this way: modesty's basic instinct is to "keep private," while immodesty's preference is to "make public."

Think about sexual modesty, for example. That is not the only kind of modesty, but think about it as an example. In sexual matters, immodesty means we reveal (either by our clothing, our behavior, or our speech) that which should be kept private. It's not that sexuality is shameful, but its deep goodness depends on its privacy and exclusivity. If I dress immodestly, for example, I reveal to others that which no one but my spouse has any right to see.

But let's go back to the more general character trait of modesty. There was a time (it seems such a long time ago) when being reserved was seen as a virtue. The restraint of the reticent person was admired. But that is no longer the case. In our star-crazed culture of advertising and entertainment, those who aren't "outgoing" are left behind. In a culture like ours, no one is more pitied than the person who is shy. I frequently hear people speak of having "overcome" the problem of being shy, as if they expect to be congratulated for that.

It is interesting, however, that although our culture despises modesty as a basic personal characteristic, it still recognizes that such a characteristic is attractive — and so we try to use feigned modesty as a means of promoting ourselves. Lord Chesterfield saw the usefulness of modesty when he said, "Modesty is the only sure bait when you are fishing for praise." But it's hard to imagine anything more disgusting than the employment of modesty as a public relations strategy by an immodest person. So what I want you to consider is that modesty is indeed a virtuous character trait, but to be virtuous it must be real.

Nothing is more amiable than true modesty, and nothing more contemptible than the false. The one guards virtue, the other betrays it.
JOSEPH ADDISON

REPAIRS

> We must both, I'm afraid, recognize that, as we grow older, we become like
> old cars — more and more repairs and replacements are necessary.
>
> C. S. LEWIS

As OUR BODIES BECOME DILAPIDATED, WE'RE REMINDED THAT REPAIRS ARE A FACT OF LIFE. We spend what seems like an inordinate amount of time fixing things, and we probably wish we could spend that time in more productive pursuits, but in the real world, repairs are unavoidable. We have to take time for maintenance.

The reason repairs are necessary is that everything tends to degrade. Over time, everything falls into "disrepair." And this is no less true of intangible things than it is of those that are physical. Left to themselves, things don't get better — they degrade. It's true of houses. It's true of appliances. It's true of everything in the world.

Note, however, that we don't have to actually damage something in order for it to become dilapidated. Things degrade all by themselves. If we simply do nothing, we'll still find that repairs have to be made. In fact, it's doing nothing that usually increases the need for repairs. When we neglect something and it starts to fall apart, rather than make the small repair promptly, we put it off. And eventually, the fix is much more drastic and costly than it should have been.

It was Samuel Johnson who said, "A man, sir, should keep his friendships in constant repair." He was right. Whatever physical possessions we have that require maintenance, our relationships are even more important to tend to — and just as our physical "stuff" needs occasional fixing, so do our relationships. None of us has any relationship that doesn't have to be repaired from time to time. And the closer and more intimate the relationship, the more we should value it enough to fix it when it needs fixing. Repairs are a big part of love.

Unfortunately, some damage can never be fully repaired. But when we've harmed others — even by neglect — we should want to make whatever repairs we can. If there is any compensation we can make, we should be eager to make it. In the end, our conscience needs to know we left nothing undone to repair the damage we caused.

> Fill up that which our lives have left behind. Undo that which
> we have done amiss. Repair the places we have wasted, bind the hearts we
> have wounded. Dry the eyes which we have flooded. Make the evil we have
> done work for good, so that we ourselves would not know it.
>
> ANONYMOUS "PRAYER FOR THE PAST"

PROPRIETY

> I am afraid that the pleasantness of an employment
> does not always evince its propriety.
>
> JANE AUSTEN

SOME PEOPLE THINK PROPRIETY IS NOTHING MORE THAN PRIGGISHNESS AND PRUDERY, BUT IT IS ACTUALLY MUCH MORE. To act with propriety is to do that which is "proper" or "appropriate." It is to do that which is expected by honorable, courteous people in specific situations. For example, in the situation where I am in public and I feel a big yawn coming on, it is expected that I will cover my mouth. Not to do so is an act of impropriety, and what is wrong with it is not just that it violates some arbitrary rule of etiquette, but that it betrays a disregard for the people around me.

The basic idea of propriety is consistency — a "proper" action is one that fits the person doing it and the circumstances that surround it. Let's say that I am a man, I am sixty years old, I am a Christian, and I am on a crowded subway in New York. There is a certain expectation that my conduct will fit both who I am and the circumstances in which I find myself. If it doesn't, my actions are "unbefitting." Propriety, then, is a certain kind of consistency or harmony in our lives.

What is proper is defined (to some extent) by tradition and culture. Over time, it changes, and doing it always requires the exercise of judgment. But that doesn't mean it's unimportant. Imagine a husband who had no regard for what is proper for a man to do for his wife on her birthday: "Honey, I don't see any value in the rules of etiquette, so I'm not going to you any card or gift on your birthday. I refuse to be bound by tradition." Proud of his impropriety, he wounds his wife. He thinks he's bucking tradition, but he's merely being selfish.

Acting with propriety requires bending over backwards, being more careful than the "law" requires us to be. The Apostle Paul had this in mind when he wrote, "We aim at what is honorable not only in the Lord's sight but also in the sight of man." It's not enough to do what's within our rights — if we care about the causes we've devoted ourselves to, we'll also pay attention to what those around us deem fitting. Like it or not, appropriateness is a basic part of good character.

> Without an acquaintance with the rules of propriety,
> it is impossible for the character to be established.
>
> CONFUCIUS

PRACTICALITY

However much thou art read in theory,
if thou hast no practice thou art ignorant.

SAADI

THEORY AND PRACTICE. Both of these are important, but most of us have a natural inclination in the direction of one or the other. George Bernard Shaw described the difference this way: "Practical men know where they are, but not always whither they are going; thinkers know whither we are going, but not always where we are." The truth is, we need both the thinkers and the doers in the world, but for today's meditation, let's put some emphasis on practicality: the carrying out of our principles and theories in real-life situations.

For one thing, we're not very smart if all we know is theory. As Saadi said, "However much thou art read in theory, if thou hast no practice thou art ignorant." Judged by this standard — that of our actual doing — we may be more ignorant than we'd like to think.

But not only that, practicality is a great clarifier of our thinking. In the realm of theory, truth and falsehood are frequently mixed together in such a way that it's hard to distinguish which is which. But when we take our theories off the drawing board and put them into daily practice, falsehood and unreality are usually exposed. In the short term, error may appear to be effective, but in the long run, it always fails the test of practicality. As Thomas Carlyle said, "Once we turn to practice, error and truth will no longer consort together."

If we want to make a worthy contribution to the world, we must learn the habit of practicality. Ideas are certainly important, for it is the quality of our ideas that determines the effectiveness of our actions, but ideas alone won't help our friends and neighbors. It's when our ideas become practical (in other words, when we "practice what we preach") that people are helped and burdens are lifted.

So I encourage you to be a more practical person. Think carefully about what is right, but having considered the rightness of your ideas, go ahead and put them into practice. And when practice indicates that some of your theories need correction, by all means correct them. Be a good thinker, but don't just think. *Pay attention to practicality.*

The world is sown with good; but unless I turn my glad thoughts into practical living and till my own field, I cannot reap a kernel of the good.

HELEN KELLER

ASSURANCE

Instantly he could see the town below now, coiling in a thousand
fumes of homely smoke, now winking into a thousand points of friendly
light its glorious small design, its aching passionate assurances
of walls, warmth, comfort, food, and love.

THOMAS WOLFE

WHETHER WE RECOGNIZE IT OR NOT, WE ALL NEED ASSUR-
ANCE. In an uncertain world, we search for safety. We need
some things we can be sure of, and we're drawn to scenes like that
described by Thomas Wolfe, where there are "walls, warmth, comfort,
food, and love." These are, as he says, "aching passionate assurances."

Unfortunately, many of the things to which we look for assurance are either unachievable or undependable. For example, if our
security depends on knowing what's going to happen tomorrow (or
worse, controlling what happens tomorrow), we're not going to have
much peace of mind. Similarly, if we have to have a certain amount of
money or social status to feel secure, we may find that kind of assurance hard to come by. As creatures who need assurance, it's time we
see this world for what it is: an ephemeral environment full of unpredictable changes. The sooner we're uprooted from "all earth-born
securities and assurances" (Thomas Kelly), the better off we'll be.

Hannah Hurnard wrote about "the assurance to wait patiently."
Ultimately, our confidence must be in principles and realities that
transcend the ups and downs of the present world. But even when our
faith is solidly grounded, we still need the discipline to wait patiently.
The end of the story has not yet been written for any of us, and we
must get a grip on our thinking. When tempted to fear, we must
remember that the "law of the farm" can be counted on. Whatever
happens in the short-term, a good harvest will eventually be ours if
we've cultivated our lives according to valid long-term principles.

In short, there is going to be some uncertainty during the years
of our earthly sojourn, but that doesn't mean there is nothing we can
be sure of. As Blaise Pascal reminded us, "It is not certain that everything is uncertain." Thankfully, there are many truths we can count
on, and these are the assurances that should guide our lives.

There is no such thing as absolute certainty, but there is
assurance sufficient for the purposes of human life.

JOHN STUART MILL

EARNESTNESS

Life is real! Life is earnest!
HENRY WADSWORTH LONGFELLOW

WOULD THOSE WHO KNOW YOU BEST DESCRIBE YOU AS AN "EARNEST" PERSON? Perhaps you wouldn't want them to. But if you wouldn't, think again. In the real world, there happen to be some very serious issues that must be dealt with. The ability to concentrate on these issues earnestly is not a liability but an asset. Consider three aspects of earnestness, all of which are good character traits:

Attentiveness. Earnest people are those who know how to focus their minds and give laser-like attention to important subjects. Unlike the careless and the distracted, the earnest understand that some things require our undivided attention and our concentrated thought.

Seriousness. Allan Bloom once wrote, "A serious life means being fully aware of the alternatives, thinking about them with all the intensity one brings to bear on life-and-death questions, in full recognition that every choice is a great risk with necessary consequences that are hard to bear." Life surely has a light side, but other parts of it are more weighty. To be earnest is to know when to be serious. It is to recognize those times when life asks us to make supreme decisions.

Resoluteness. This is, perhaps, the most practical and beneficial side of earnestness. Many of us can be attentive and serious, at least occasionally, but not many of us are resolute. That is, we don't pursue serious goals with an appropriate degree of determination. We're indecisive, weak-willed, and far too easily defeated by insignificant obstacles. So we need to honor the dogged determination of the earnest person: the fellow who is serious about reaching the goals that he has decided upon. "A man in earnest finds the means, or if he cannot find them, creates them" (William Ellery Channing).

Yes, some folks are earnest to a fault. (I've written about that elsewhere.) But I suggest that for every person like that, there are many others who have the opposite problem. In an age when the biggest of all big businesses is entertainment, most of us would do well to bring ourselves back to sobriety more often and address ourselves earnestly to the critical concerns of life. Tomorrow may be different, but today, in which direction do you need to make the adjustment?

Intermingle jest with earnest.
FRANCIS BACON

CORRECTION

Nobody wants constructive criticism. It's all
we can do to put up with constructive praise.

MIGNON MCLAUGHLIN

IT IS AN OLD ADAGE THAT MOST OF US WOULD RATHER BE
RUINED BY PRAISE THAN HELPED BY CRITICISM. We don't like
to be corrected, and we avoid it at all costs. But when we refuse to be
corrected, we forfeit one of life's greatest opportunities for growth.

If you have even one friend who loves you enough to correct you,
you have a treasure to be grateful for. It is to be hoped that your friend
will be both wise and gentle in correction, but even if not, the correction is valuable. "Wounds from a sincere friend are better than many
kisses from an enemy" (Proverbs 27:6 *New Living Translation*).

Correction, of course, doesn't have to come from others; we can
correct ourselves. In fact, one of the distinctive marks of wisdom is the
willingness to learn from the mistakes we see others making, without
having to learn the hard way through personal experience.

None of us has anything more than an imperfect understanding
of anything we deal with, and none of us is error-free in anything we
do, at least for any great length of time. Being wrong from time to
time is simply a part of the human condition. So rather than being
embarrassed about our mistakes, the thing we should be embarrassed about is our failure to accept correction and make the necessary
changes in our character and conduct.

Most people say they want to make progress, but in the real
world, there is no way to make progress without feedback. In the
absence of valid information about our present state — and that is
what correction amounts to — we have no way of knowing what to
do to improve our situation. As Tryon Edwards put it, "He that never
changes his opinions, never corrects his mistakes, will never be wiser
tomorrow than he is today." Without correction, we are stuck.

Of all our human endowments, "correctability" is one of the best.
Yes, sometimes it requires the swallowing of our pride, but it is the
open door to all the better things we aspire to in the future.

The sages do not consider that making no mistakes is a blessing. They believe,
rather, that the great virtue of man lies in his ability to correct his mistakes
and continually to make a new man of himself.

WANG YANG-MING

DISCIPLESHIP

> Judgment can be acquired only by acute observation, by actual experience
> in the school of life, by ceaseless alertness to learn from others, by study of the
> activities of men who have made notable marks, by striving to analyze the
> everyday play of causes and effects, by constant study of human nature.
>
> B. C. FORBES

NOWADAYS, WHEN PEOPLE HEAR THE WORD "DISCIPLESHIP," THEY THINK ONLY OF ITS RELIGIOUS USAGE. But the general idea conveyed by this word is powerful, and we would do well to contemplate its value — even in our secular lives.

In ancient times, a disciple was one who studied under a master, whether the master was a scholar or a craftsman. Like the more modern idea of "apprenticeship," discipleship meant a novice or beginner in a particular body of knowledge would place himself under the tutelage of a person who had a great deal to teach in that area.

If we could think of that concept in a more modern sense, wouldn't it pay some dividends? It is true, as Oliver Goldsmith wrote, that people "seldom improve when they have no other model but themselves to copy." We learn best by paying close attention to good examples and precedents, so in all the more important areas of life, wouldn't we profit from discipling ourselves to worthy masters?

In the difficult days we live in, most of us are in desperate need of good heroes and role models, inspirational people (usually older than we are) who can say from experience, "This is how it's done." If you've ever had such a person in your life, you know what Paul D. Shafer meant when he said, "The most important single influence in the life of a person is another person who is worthy of emulation."

If you're more comfortable with the word "mentor," then use that word. In either case, the idea is that of giving careful, diligent attention to the expertise of another person. However, "There is a difference between imitating a good man and counterfeiting him" (Benjamin Franklin). So discipleship to another human being doesn't mean we become their clone; it just means we seek to learn what they know.

But finally, have you noticed that it's hard to say "disciple" without saying "discipline"? Without hard work and sacrifice on our part, there is not a master teacher in the world who can help us very much.

> Discipleship means discipline.
> VICTOR RAYMOND EDMAN

PERSPICACITY

Heat and animosity, contest and conflict, may sharpen the wits,
although they rarely do; they never strengthen the understanding,
clear the perspicacity, guide the judgment, or improve the heart.

WALTER SAVAGE LANDOR

I EXPECT SOME WILL SHAKE THEIR HEADS (OR MAYBE EVEN WINCE) IN DISMAY AT THE SIGHT OF "PERSPICACITY" IN A BOOK LIKE THIS. But then again, those who know me will probably not be surprised at all. In any case, take a moment today to consider this good word. The idea behind it is, in fact, an enthusiastic idea.

Actually, there are two words we need to look at. The first is "perspicacity," which means the ability to *understand* things clearly. The second is "perspicuity," which means *expressing* ourselves clearly. Both words come from a Latin root meaning "to look through," so they convey the idea of clarity, lucidness, and transparency.

Understanding. Everybody has had the experience of seeing an idea but not seeing it clearly. After learning a new concept, most of us find it takes a while before the point comes into sharp focus in our minds. But that sharp focus or clarity is worth working for. We need to keep studying important ideas until we understand them well. And not only that, but we need to work on increasing our powers of understanding — our perspicacity — so that it takes less time to gain a clear focus than it did when our minds weren't as well trained.

Expression. It is possible to understand something clearly but not be able to communicate it clearly to another person. So we need to work on both our thinking and our communicating, until we can express important ideas in a clear manner. Strictly speaking, we don't really understand a thing until we can explain it to someone else.

Perfect clarity is not achievable, of course, either in our thinking or our communicating. But improving in these areas is a worthy goal. I challenge you, therefore, to stretch yourself and think about both your "perspicacity" and your "perspicuity." How clearly do you perceive things, and how clearly do you express them? Any progress you can make in either of these areas will be well worth whatever it costs you.

Where we cannot invent, we may at least improve; we may give
somewhat of novelty to that which was old, condensation to that
which was diffuse, perspicuity to that which was obscure,
and currency to that which was recondite.

CHARLES CALEB COLTON

CONSULTATION

Men of age object too much, consult too long, adventure too little,
repeat too soon, and seldom drive business home to the full period,
but content themselves with a mediocrity of success.
FRANCIS BACON

IT IS TRUE, AS FRANCIS BACON SAID, THAT SOME FOLKS SPEND
TOO MUCH TIME CONSULTING. Fearful of doing anything unsafe,
the overly cautious person wants to know what "most people" think
about the decision he must make. No amount of input is ever enough,
and he spends his whole life conducting opinion polls.

Yet many of us have the opposite problem: we fail to consult
when we should. We don't profit from people who have greater expertise by checking our thinking against their wisdom.

To "consult" means to confer with another person about a
problem. It involves "putting our heads together" or "comparing
notes" with someone who has special knowledge about a particular
question. Physicians, of course, frequently use this concept, and we're
mighty glad they do. Presented with a problem that he or she is not
completely sure about, a physician will "consult" with a specialist in
that area, and our prospects for diagnosis and treatment are greatly increased by the pooling of their wisdom. Would you want a doctor who
never saw the need to consult with another doctor? No, you wouldn't.

In our own lives, there is also a need for consultation — and I'm
not here talking about "professional counseling." I mean we often
need to get the benefit of a good friend's wisdom or an older person's
perspective. Even when we're pretty sure we're on the right track,
it's often helpful to have another set of eyes to look at our situation.
Especially when an important decision has to be made, it's good to
consult with someone who can help us double-check our thinking and
"validate the input," as the computer people say.

Perhaps there are many reasons why we fail to consult when we
should. Sometimes it's just carelessness or overconfidence. At other
times, however, it's pride that keeps us from consulting, and if that's
the case, we've got a serious problem. Not only will pride destroy our
character; it will sabotage our success. When success requires asking
for help, as it often does, the proud are doomed to failure.

Without consultation, plans are frustrated.
THE BOOK OF PROVERBS

SYNERGY

Synergy: the interaction of two or more agents or forces so that their combined effect is greater than the sum of their individual effects.

AMERICAN HERITAGE DICTIONARY

WHEN PEOPLE WORK TOGETHER WITH A COOPERATIVE AT-
TITUDE ON MUTUALLY IMPORTANT PROJECTS, SYNERGISTIC
THINGS OFTEN HAPPEN. The wonderful thing about synergy is that
"the combined effect is greater than the sum of their individual parts."
Two plus two can actually turn out to be more than four!

Not every project needs to be collaborative, of course. Some
things are better done by individuals. Beethoven's Ninth Symphony
would not have turned out to be the masterpiece it is if it had been
written by a committee of composers. But artistic geniuses who work
best alone are rare. Most of us can be helped by coworkers.

Indeed, collaborative work often brings out the best in an
individual's creativity. Stephen R. Covey, who spoke often about the
power of synergy, said that it "catalyzes, unifies, and unleashes the
greatest powers within people." In Nashville, Tennessee, where I live,
songwriters typically work together. They find that greater creative
energy — *synergy!* — is the result of working together.

But sometimes people collaborate and the result is not synergy
but friction and factionalism. Why is that? Well, for one thing collaborative work requires humility. If the workers are driven by ego
and selfishness, they won't be open to the possibility that others could
truly help the project, and the project bogs down in bickering.

Synergy rarely occurs if the objective is not important enough
(and urgent enough) to produce cooperation. The goal must be big
enough that individuals are willing to subordinate their personal preferences to its accomplishment. In other words, the goal must be greater
than any differences the team members may have among themselves.

Under the right conditions, however, synergy is one of life's
marvels. And we never give a greater gift to others than when we say,
"I am willing to work with you. I am willing to learn from you. I am
confident that your contribution will improve the overall result." So
let's give that gift more often. Let's be mature enough to collaborate!

When properly understood, synergy is the highest activity in all life
— the true test and manifestation of all of the other habits put together.

STEPHEN R. COVEY

REASONABLENESS

O Lord, grant us reasonableness in all our dealings with each other.
Make us large-hearted in helping and generous in criticizing.
Keep us from unkind words and unkind silence.

SID HEDGES

WOULD THOSE WHO KNOW YOU DESCRIBE YOU AS REASON-
ABLE? I hope they would. Reasonableness can mean more than
one thing, as we shall see, but if your friends would say the opposite
— that you are known for being unreasonable — there are probably
some adjustments you need to make. Consider three different ways in
which it would be good to be reasonable:

(1) Kind, considerate, and balanced. As indicated in the above
quotation from Sid Hedges, reasonableness sometimes means being
kind. It means we control the impulse to be angry and irritated, and
discipline ourselves to be generous and helpful with those around us.
This kind of reasonableness has always been valuable, but it is all the
more so in our fast-paced, competitive, often rude culture.

(2) Acting on the basis of good reasons. Being reasonable also means
we live our lives carefully, being motivated by wise reasons rather
than snap judgments. Sometimes a hunch or an intuition may lead us
in the right direction, but generally speaking, we need to have good
reasons for our actions. "When a man has not a good reason for doing
a thing, he has one good reason for letting it alone" (Thomas Scott).

(3) Open to the reasoning of other people. Usually our own conscience will tell us the reasons why we ought to do (or not do) a
certain thing, but we also need to be open to the reasoning of others.
None of us is wise enough to figure out every situation all by ourselves, so we need to listen to others when they suggest the wisdom of
a path different from the one we had in mind.

The voice of reason is sometimes hard to hear. These days, it can
be drowned out by the entertainers, the advertisers, and the influence-
peddlers. But as we all know, reason can also be drowned out by our
own pride and self-will. Too often, we ignore the good reasons that
should guide us, and we do things that are unreasonable, if not completely irrational. But reason can't be ignored without consequence. If
we defy what is reasonable, the "school of hard knocks" awaits us.

If you will not hear reason, she will surely rap your knuckles.
BENJAMIN FRANKLIN

FEARLESSNESS

If you're never scared or embarrassed or hurt,
it means you never take any chances.
JULIA SOREL

SOMETIMES OUR IDEAS ABOUT FEAR ARE MISTAKEN. If we're confident of our ability to control life, we may think fear can be eliminated by removing all of the problems that would produce fear. Or perhaps we take another route: we try to become courageous enough that fear will not enter our thinking. But neither of these are realistic approaches. As Julia Sorel suggests, the only way never to have to deal with fear is never to do anything in life but play it safe.

In the real world, we will be afraid from time to time. And without a doubt, that is a problem. As E. Stanley Jones put it, "Fear is the sand in the machinery of life." Our lives are impacted greatly, for better or worse, by how we handle fear. Anaïs Nin was right when she wrote, "Life shrinks or expands in proportion to one's courage."

But what is courage? Through the centuries, the wisest have always understood that it's not the lack of fear but the determination to do what is right even though one is afraid. Fearlessness, then, is not the power of some elite group of human beings who are not afraid of anything; it's the honorable determination of many ordinary folks to do their best, no matter what. Babe Ruth was talking about baseball, but he spoke a world of truth when he said, "Never let the fear of striking out get in your way." So to be fearless, in the true sense, is not to be without fear — *it is to deal rightly with the fears that we feel.*

Rather than deal rightly with our fears, however, most of us retreat and run for safety. And while retreating is sometimes wise, at other times it is the most dangerous thing we could do. "It's when you run away that you're most likely to stumble" (Casey Robinson).

Instead of backing away from our duty, we should go out to meet it. And when our duty involves some difficulty or danger, we shouldn't bother looking for a way "over" or "under" or "around" it. Most of the time, the shortest (and ultimately the easiest) way out is "through." We can't make our problems disappear, but we can deal with them honorably. We may be afraid, but we can be true to our deepest principles and act with integrity. That's the only kind of fearlessness that counts.

Facing it — always facing it — that's the way to get through. Face it!
JOSEPH CONRAD

WAITING

Count no day lost in which you waited your turn,
took only your share, and sought advantage over no one.
ROBERT BRAULT

IT IS A MISTAKE TO THINK WAITING IS ALWAYS A WASTE OF
TIME. Sometimes it is, to be sure, but often it is not. There is a
time to act, and there is a time to wait. When waiting is appropriate,
we must not try to hurry the outcome of events. Even in our spiritual
lives, "patient waiting is often the highest way of doing God's will"
(Jeremy Collier). The ability to wait can be a high virtue.

When circumstances are not unfolding as quickly as we'd like,
whether our waiting is good or bad depends on the attitude with
which we wait. If we give in to exasperation and irritation, what could
be a strength-building experience becomes nothing more than fuel
for our anger. And not only that, but irritation only makes the time
pass even more slowly. I found that out last January when I was one of
several thousand motorists caught in an eleven-hour traffic jam that
resulted from an ice storm in Alabama. None of us could do anything
but wait, and if I didn't know it before, I learned it during that long,
cold night: *with a little patience, you find that you can "wait much faster."*

I think many of us find waiting to be hard because it frustrates
our sense of control. We like to think we can make everything happen at the "right time" (i.e., "right now"), and we don't take kindly to
delays that push events past the deadline we have set for them. But
we're not always wise enough to see when it would be best for certain
things to occur. If we're honest, hindsight often reveals that the very
best time was long after we thought the event should have taken
place. We may not like it, but later is sometimes better. "All comes at
the proper time to him who knows how to wait" (Vincent de Paul).

But waiting does not always mean absolute inactivity. As Thomas
Edison, who was a busy man, observed, good things come to the person who "hustles while he waits." We need to learn the habit of "active
waiting." Whether some blessing is slow in coming or some sorrow
is slow in leaving, we can wait actively — with our minds and our
hands engaged in good thoughts and good deeds. Rightly considered,
patience produces not only peace of mind but a productive life.

Let us . . . learn to labor and to wait.
HENRY WADSWORTH LONGFELLOW

RESPONSIVENESS

> Civilizations, I believe, come to birth and proceed to grow by successfully
> responding to successive challenges. They break down and go to pieces if and
> when a challenge confronts them which they fail to meet.
>
> ARNOLD TOYNBEE

IF TOYNBEE WAS RIGHT, WE CAN SAY THAT A LACK OF RESPON-
SIVENESS IS WHAT KILLS A CIVILIZATION. And what is true of
civilizations is also true of individuals. When we don't respond rightly
to the circumstances around us, we decline. If this becomes a habit
and a part of our character, we destroy ourselves.

Erwin Lutzer once wrote, "Firmly entrenched within every
human being lies a most deceptive presupposition, namely, that
circumstances and other people are responsible for our responses to
life." It is obviously true that the way we respond to life is influenced
by others, particularly our parents. But influence is not the same as
control. Whether our influences are good or bad, we must respond to
them appropriately, and it is the quality of our responsiveness that will
judge us in the end. We will be remembered for our responses: what
we chose to do with the alternatives presented to us.

Think about the connection between "responsible" and "responsive." Responsible means "able to respond," that is, able to choose our
response. The freedom to choose our response to life's events is one
of our greatest endowments. Unfortunately, we don't always use this
freedom as we should. Called to action by life's challenges, we sometimes default and fail to respond. We do nothing. So while *responsibility* is automatically ours by virtue of being human (we were given the
ability to respond), *responsiveness* is not automatic. The quality of our
responses is very much a matter of choice on our part.

Perhaps one thing should be clarified, however. Much of life
depends on our responsiveness, but that doesn't mean we should be in
a "reactive" mode all of the time. We do need to be "proactive" — but
even proactive people have to deal with the world as they find it.

Finally, I believe we need to improve our definition of freedom.
Freedom does not just mean the absence of negative circumstances; it
means that in every circumstance we are free to choose our response.
And that, my friend, is a freedom no one can take away from you.

> If you can't change circumstances, change the way you respond to them.
> TIM HANSEL

August 15
EQUILIBRIUM

Order is not pressure which is imposed on society from without,
but an equilibrium which is set up from within.
JOSÉ ORTEGA Y GASSET

TODAY'S WORD — "EQUILIBRIUM" — IS DIFFICULT TO DISCUSS ATTRACTIVELY FOR IT DOES NOT SOUND LIKE AN ENTHUSI-ASTIC IDEA TO MOST PEOPLE. And yet, the concept is one we can learn from. If it can be thought of as a personal quality, the first thing we need to understand is that equilibrium must come from within us, as Ortega y Gasset suggests. It is not something done for us but something we do. It's the product of choices we ourselves make.

Leaving aside its special definition in physics and chemistry, let's simply say that equilibrium means "mental or emotional balance; poise" (*American Heritage Dictionary*). All of us know what it's like to have multiple priorities and many things to do. We also know about conflicting forces and mixed emotions. Life in this world is a compli-cated affair. So we admire the person who can live in the world and stay balanced or poised. It's a quality we appreciate.

Leading a life of equilibrium is not easy. It can be done, but we shouldn't look at someone who does it and think it's effortless. In any important area of life, keeping things balanced requires that we (1) be honest enough to see when things have slipped out of balance, and (2) have the courage to make the necessary correction. Equilibrium is not a state we can achieve and then forget about. Instead, a balanced life is one where a person makes constant adjustments as a result of continual self-examination.

In addition to personal equilibrium within ourselves, we can also think of it in relation to other people. Think of some of your important relationships. Are they well-balanced or are some of them one-sided and in an unhealthy state of imbalance? No two persons will bring the same thing to a relationship, but I believe it is worth striving for an equilibrium in which our relationships are justly and fairly balanced.

Finally, shouldn't there be an equilibrium between our present state and our future hopes? Shouldn't we be content but also moved by aspiration? Perhaps so, but I would say this: if these particular scales are ever imbalanced, it should be in the direction of our dreams!

Delicate equilibrium between dream and reality . . .
LILLIAN SMITH

CLOSENESS

A man of many companions may come to ruin,
but there is a friend who sticks closer than a brother.
THE BOOK OF PROVERBS

IT IS UNDENIABLY TRUE: HUMAN BEINGS HAVE A NEED FOR CLOSENESS. We may not all need the same amount of closeness, and we may not need the same kind of closeness that someone else needs. For this reason, we should be slow to criticize someone else for being antisocial when, in fact, their need for closeness may be filled in ways that differ from our experience. Nevertheless, closeness of relationship is one of the deep, natural needs of human beings.

As the opening quotation from Proverbs indicates, there is a difference between a "companion" and a "friend who sticks closer than a brother." Given the ways we are connected today, it is possible to have a myriad of acquaintances and associates, and that is good as far as it goes. But we need more than casual contact; we need some closeness. So it is common to hear celebrities remark about the hardships of knowing, and being known by, thousands of people without being close to any of them. Indeed, there is nothing lonelier than the life of a person who is surrounded by people (maybe even admirers), yet the physical proximity of all those people does not involve any closeness.

Opening ourselves to closeness carries with it certain risks, to be sure. There are not only the dangers of rejection and treachery, but unless two friends die at precisely the same moment, one of them is going to have to grieve the other's death at some point. In a broken world, closeness of human contact is a bittersweet experience — but experience teaches us that it's a joy well worth the tears it may entail.

Another characteristic of closeness is that it requires work. The deeper into someone else's heart we go, the more careful we should be about the maintenance of the relationship. Like everything else, friendships fall into disrepair, and so we must work at keeping them in good order and mending them when necessary.

Yet we have still not said the most important thing. That is simply that we need God. Our need for other human beings is only an inkling of our need for the Creator of us all. So making closeness to God a priority — and diligently pursuing that priority — is life's best endeavor!

Oh! for a closer walk with God.
WILLIAM COWPER

EVIDENCE

By a small sample we may judge of the whole piece.
MIGUEL DE CERVANTES

I LIKE TO DEFINE EVIDENCE SIMPLY AS "ONE THING THAT INDICATES ANOTHER." Evidence consists of whatever facts and information we use to reach the many conclusions we arrive at each day. To use a down-home example, Robert F. Turner used to say that if the cook brings red-eye gravy to the table, you know that country ham cannot be far behind. You can't see the ham yet with your own eyes, but the red-eye gravy is pretty good evidence that it exists.

In the real world, the evidence we have to work with is often "circumstantial." That kind of evidence, by itself, does not unequivocally prove a conclusion, but that doesn't mean it's useless. When carefully taken into account, circumstances can be helpful in reaching a conclusion. As Thoreau famously said, "Some circumstantial evidence is very strong; as when you find a trout in the milk."

Each of us evaluates evidence and draws conclusions every day, from the minor matters of life all the way up to the bigger ones. We may not reason very well at times ("jumping to conclusions" is a habit we all have to resist), but the process of dealing with evidence is unavoidable. It is simply a part of our day-to-day experience. So the thing we must do is get better at the business of handling evidence.

For one thing, most of us need to investigate the evidence more thoroughly before drawing conclusions. Rather than making snap judgments, we need to dig deeper. The good reasoning that leads to wise conclusions often involves hard work, and the more important the decision, the harder we should be willing to work. Outward appearances can be misleading, as we all know, so Charles Dickens gave good advice when he wrote, "Take nothing on its looks; take everything on evidence. There is no better rule."

But once we have collected as much evidence as we can and weighed it as wisely as we are able, *we must accept the verdict that the evidence points to.* Our feelings, wishes, and personal preferences certainly have a role to play in decision-making, but in the end, it should be nothing but reality that we seek. We want whatever is the truth.

Whatever may be our wishes, our inclinations, or the dictates of
our passions, they cannot alter the state of facts and evidence.
JOHN ADAMS

DRIVE

> There is a single reason why 99 out of 100 average businessmen never become leaders. That is their unwillingness to pay the price of responsibility. By the price of responsibility I mean hard, driving, continual work.
>
> OWEN D. YOUNG

YEARS AGO, THE WORD "DRIVE" WAS MORE OFTEN USED IN A POSITIVE SENSE. If it was said that a young man, for example, had drive, the point would have been that he was enterprising and energetic in the betterment of his situation. Nowadays, however, the word often suggests a person is ambitious in a negative sense, and when we refer to somebody as being "driven" we are not usually paying them a compliment. But think for a moment about what it is that distinguishes honorable drive from the dishonorable kind.

Goals. A person's drive might be good or bad depending on what it is they are trying to accomplish. Obviously, we don't want to see a person expend great energy in the pursuit of an immoral goal, but even in practical matters, we don't praise a person's drive if he or she is devoting significant passion to an insignificant purpose. In terms of our life's work, majoring in minors is never an admirable thing to do.

Methods. If the "what" of drive is important, so is the "how." A person's goal might be the noblest thing in the world, but we wouldn't praise his drive if he went after it by lying, cheating, and running over other people. Ends don't justify means, and we see drive as commendable only when honorable goals are ethically pursued.

Motives. Good goals and moral methods must also be employed for right reasons. Indeed, one of the most disappointing things in life is to find out that somebody whose efforts we admired was, when the truth came out, driven by selfish or prideful motives. Ultimately, the "why" of our work matters even more than the "what" and the "how."

But let's put all of this together. Wouldn't you like to have a friend or a family member who had "drive" in the highest sense? That person would (1) have great purposes, (2) use right means, and (3) possess pure motives, the purest of which is love. Well, our friends and family would like to know that we have that kind of drive too. So give those around you a gift. Get up tomorrow with more drive.

> Love will ask much more of us than the law could ever require. True love can never say, "I have done enough. I have now fulfilled all my obligations." Love is restless, drives us on.
>
> JOHN POWELL

SEEKING

God's creative method is movement, change, continuing search,
ongoing inquiry. Those who seek are rewarded.

JOHN M. TEMPLETON

ONE OF THE STRIKING FEATURES OF OUR HUMANITY IS THE
INSTINCTIVENESS WITH WHICH WE SEEK WHAT WE DO NOT
HAVE AND DO NOT KNOW. Indeed, a person would be thought odd
if he or she never sought anything at all. By a seemingly immutable
law of our nature, we seek . . . and seek . . . and seek. And this also is
remarkable: we seek in the confidence that there are worthy things to
be found. It looks as if we believe there really is such a thing as truth!

Yet there is a sense in which we do not seek enough. Too often,
we are complacent about the amount of knowledge, wisdom, and understanding we have. It would do most of us good to acquire a healthy
dissatisfaction with the present state of our minds. We need more of
the spirit of the pioneer and the adventurer — a lifelong quest for
truth is what we should be involved in.

We are not alone in our seeking, however, and so we should
acknowledge the other seekers around us. Not every person we meet
will have a worthy discovery to share with us, but many will, so we
need to have the humility to listen and learn when others speak to us
about the results of their own quest thus far.

But what will we do with truth when we uncover some of it?
All of the greatest truths test us and challenge us to decide what our
response to them will be. Call me a wishful thinker if you must, but I
have always loved Charles Habib Malik's hopeful adage: "If you seek,
you will know; if you know, you will love; if you love, you will obey."
Know. Love. Obey. Those are the guiding stars of the seeker.

Here, then, is a passion worthy of our life's dedication. And in a
world where falsehood can wield brute strength, at least in the short
term, it is sobering to think what it may cost us to seek truth honestly.

Seek the truth
Listen to the truth
Teach the truth
Love the truth
Abide by the truth
And defend the truth
Unto death.

JOHN HUSS

August 20
SENSES

How good is man's life, the mere living! How fit to employ
All the heart and the soul and the senses forever in joy!
ROBERT BROWNING

EACH ONE OF OUR FIVE SENSES IS A WONDERFUL THING, BUT
THE COMBINATION OF ALL OF THEM WORKING TOGETHER
IS EVEN MORE AMAZING. The interplay of sight, sound, taste, touch,
and smell is intricate. What a world they open up to us! What a delight to drink in the power and the beauty that our senses reveal to us!

As I have written elsewhere, we would do well to use our senses
more fully and more actively. Rather than allowing each day's sensual
experiences to simply wash over us, we should contemplate them and
relish them. We should deliberately touch and taste and hear new
things. Like our other capacities, our sensory abilities will expand if
we exercise them, and if we don't do so, they will diminish.

But I would offer this warning: our senses are tools or instruments, and they should only be used in the service of honorable work.
To say that something is "sensual" is simply to say it comes to us by
our senses. In itself, sensory experience is morally neutral, but our
senses can lead us into evil if they are not governed by valid principles.
In the world as it now is, much that could be experienced with our
senses is degrading and destructive. But we damage ourselves, and we
dishonor our Creator, when we use our senses in ways that degrade us.
So we should be careful what we take in with our senses.

That said, however, it is still true that our senses are wonderful
endowments. They bring us great joy. And no small part of the joy is
sharing what we have experienced. If you are not accustomed to doing
this, I advise you to try it. When you've seen something interesting,
tell somebody about it. When you've heard a song or a sound that
thrilled you, describe it to another person. Even the texture of things
we touch and the aroma of things we smell are worth talking about.

Too often we don't value our senses until we lose one of them,
and the loss of even one sense is a profound sadness. But even when
that happens (as it will to most of us eventually), what we find is that
our other capacities are sharpened and made more exquisite. As our
physical senses fail, our hearts long all the more for their true home.

The loss of a sense adds as much beauty to the world as its acquisition.
MARCEL PROUST

INVITATIONS

What beck'ning ghost, along the moonlight shade
Invites my steps, and points to yonder glade?
ALEXANDER POPE

IT'S A SPLENDID THING TO BE "INVITED." Sometimes it is not a person who invites us but simply a circumstance or a situation that seems "inviting," but in any case, the things in life that draw us into new experience and new growth should be seen as blessings.

When there is an element of mystery, the very intrigue of the invitation is a great part of what delights us. Deep down, I think most of us can relate to Bilbo Baggins' regret on the morning after the "unexpected party" in J. R. R. Tolkien's *The Hobbit*. Having refused the dwarves' invitation the night before to join their quest, he awoke strangely sad that they had left without him, and he quickly changed his mind and ran after them . . . without his pocket handkerchief!

Life is full of invitations. Indeed, with the dawning of each new day, we are invited to embrace life enthusiastically. In Emerson's words, "This day is all that is good and fair. It is too dear, with its hopes and invitations, to waste a moment on the yesterdays."

Yet we must be careful. Not every invitation is one that should be accepted. When we are being lured or enticed to do what is wrong, we must say no. Temptation must be resisted, for that is precisely what temptation is: an invitation or enticement to wrongdoing. That type of invitation should be emphatically stamped "Return to Sender."

But when invitations are innocent, we should be open to their call, even when they require courage. We can't spend our lives in a cave, hiding from every sort of uncertainty or inconvenience. And we dare not waste life by neglecting its opportunities. So every person needs to ask himself, "How easily invited am I? When life is entreating me to follow a better path, am I receptive or resistant?"

And while we're asking questions, let's each ask ourselves another one: "In dealing with other human beings, do I do more inviting or commanding?" A good bit of what happens in the world involves somebody trying to persuade somebody else to do something. So what's it like for others when we are the ones doing the persuading? Would they say our favorite tool is the invitation or the command?

> . . . her mien carries much more invitation than command.
> RICHARD STEELE

COMPASSION

No greater burden can be born by an individual
than to know no one cares or understands.

ARTHUR H. STAINBACK

SUFFERING IS HARD TO BEAR EVEN UNDER THE BEST OF
CIRCUMSTANCES, BUT IT IS MUCH HARDER WHEN WE MUST
BEAR IT ALONE. In actual fact, we are probably never as alone as we
think we are, but when the evidence suggests that there is not another
person anywhere who cares or understands, our isolation becomes an
agony. So most of us want to show compassion to those who are suffering, especially the lonely ones, the outcasts, and the desperate.

Henri J. M. Nouwen, who certainly had the heart of a helper,
made this comment: "Let us not underestimate how hard it is to be
compassionate. Compassion is hard because it requires the inner disposition to go with others to the place where they are weak, vulnerable,
lonely, and broken. But this is not our spontaneous response to suffering. What we desire most is to do away with suffering by fleeing from
it or find a quick cure for it." He was right. Authentic compassion
requires far more than the condescension that the affluent often call
"helping the suffering." Jesus of Nazareth, for example, did not merely
help the poor — he *was* poor. He did more than drive in to the ghetto
from the suburbs and pretend to be concerned. He entered deeply and
personally into the experience of the oppressed and downtrodden.

But there is so much suffering around us, we have to make some
hard choices. As the French dramatist Jean Anouilh put it, "One cannot weep for the entire world. It is beyond human strength. One must
choose." And Thomas Fuller's caution is appropriate, "Sacrifice not
thy heart upon every altar." Rather than trying to help humanity, we'd
do better to sharpen the focus of our compassion more specifically.

The great challenge, however, is for us to translate our feelings
of compassion into actions of mercy. There may be some hardhearted
individuals here and there who don't give a hoot about anybody but
themselves, but most of us, I think, are moved by compassionate feelings. We do love our neighbors, to some extent. But feelings must be
urged into action. Compassion must actually bathe the fevered brow.

The measure of love is compassion;
the measure of compassion is kindness.

ANONYMOUS

COURTESY

COURTESY IS ONE OF THOSE LITTLE THINGS IN LIFE THAT EXERTS AN INFLUENCE OUT OF ALL PROPORTION TO ITS SEEMING SIGNIFICANCE. When we choose to conduct ourselves courteously, we often find that huge consequences flow from words and deeds which, at the time, seemed rather unimportant. "It is amazing what a warming influence courtesy can have on an otherwise dreary world" (E. M. McKee). Courtesy is a uniquely powerful virtue.

In our discussions of "enthusiastic ideas," we have looked at several other words related to courtesy. "Civility," for example, may mean that we merely refrain from doing things that are rude. "Politeness," however, is more than the absence of rude behavior; it is the positive doing of gracious deeds. And "courtesy," rightly understood, goes deeper still. It has to do with the spirit that motivates our outward actions, and it means *sincere attention and kindness to others.*

As everybody knows, it is easy to be courteous to individuals who are friendly and likeable. If we have reason to believe they will appreciate our gesture and think kindly of us for doing it, that makes it even easier. But what about those who are disagreeable and ungrateful? Well, courtesy implies a recognition of the other person's human dignity and worth, and sometimes that is hidden beneath layers of "stuff." I believe it helps to deal with people not as they are but as they would be if they were their ideal self. As Emerson said, "We must be as courteous to a man as we are to a picture, which we are willing to give the advantage of a good light." We will be courteous to people when we look at them in the "light" that is most favorable to them.

If courtesy is important anywhere, it's especially important in our closest relationships. Too often, we make the effort to be courteous to everybody else but then treat those nearest and dearest to us with rudeness and irritability. But if anybody in the world deserves to get our very best behavior, isn't it those we come home to after work?

AUTHORITY

He who overcomes by force, hath overcome but half his foe.
JOHN MILTON

LIKE EVERY OTHER MEANS OF ACCOMPLISHING OUR OBJEC-
TIVES, AUTHORITY IS A TOOL THAT HAS SOME INHERENT
LIMITATIONS. It is always sad to see a person become frustrated
trying to reach a complicated goal and begin flailing away at it with
nothing more than the force of his or her authority. To be sure, there
are times when authority has to be exercised, but as Milton suggests
in the quotation above, if we do no more than require someone to
submit to our will because we have the power to do so, we have not
accomplished anywhere near all that needs to be done.

To say that authority has limitations, however, is not to say that
it is not good. There is no tool in the world that is capable of doing
every single job all by itself. So let's not forget the tremendous value
of authority. We must understand its limits (and even its dangers), but
we shouldn't go to the opposite extreme of throwing it away completely. Authority happens to be a very good idea — it is necessary to
the functioning of human society. So we're not thinking wisely if we
think of authority as an evil thing that is always to be avoided.

Authority is subject to the law of diminishing returns. It must
be used sparingly because the more it is used, the less effective it
becomes. "Nothing more impairs authority than a too-frequent or in-
discreet use of it. If thunder itself was to be continual, it would excite
no more terror than the noise of a mill" (John Barnard).

Yet for every person who fails to *exercise* authority rightly there
are probably more of us who don't *submit* to it as we should. Authority
is, after all, a two-way street. Those who are our leaders in various
situations would be very grateful if we decided to respect their authority in a more constructive and cooperative manner.

As anyone knows who has ever been asked to be a leader: it is a
very hard thing to do. It's doubtful whether any part of life is more
challenging. So when it comes our time to lead others in one of life's
relationships — and authority is given to us to get the job done — let
us be aware that we're being tested. The responsibility will call for the
highest and best that is within us. Let us decide to pass the test.

There is no stronger test of a man's character than power and authority.
PLUTARCH

DEDICATION

No horse gets anywhere until he is harnessed. No steam or gas
ever drives anything until it is confined. No Niagara is ever turned
into light and power until it is tunneled. No life ever grows
great until it is focused, dedicated, disciplined.
HARRY EMERSON FOSDICK

AS A PERSONAL CHARACTERISTIC, "DEDICATION" IS NOT AL-WAYS THOUGHT OF IN POSITIVE TERMS. These days, a person can believe almost anything he wants and be praised for it, as long as he's not dogmatic about it. And since dedicated people are very determined about what they do, they're often considered to be dogmatic or narrow-minded. And not only that, "discipline" is not a very positive word in our culture; so if a person has the discipline required to be dedicated, he will sometimes be seen as being too uptight.

It is certainly true that dedicated people can become unbalanced in their dedication, just like people who are artistic, intelligent, industrious, or any number of other things. Every good quality that we can have must be balanced with other qualities or it will become a destructive force. But dedication, properly understood and balanced with virtues like humility and good humor, is not a bad quality to have. Indeed, there is not much way to live a high-quality life without being dedicated. Dedication is what turns ability into achievement.

The laser probably offers us the best analogy for understanding dedication. A laser uses a beam of light that is extremely concentrated. In simplistic terms, the light shines "here" rather than "here, there, and everywhere." A light beam can't become a laser beam until it's willing to "let go" of all other possibilities and focus itself in just one spot. And when all is said and done, that's what dedication is: the willingness to make a choice, discipline ourselves, and focus our energies. Dedication means doing one thing rather than dabbling in many.

"Dreams and dedication are a powerful combination" (William Longgood). There is no stopping the person who has weighed the alternatives and made a radical commitment to one passionate pursuit. Yes, it requires giving up many things that "might have been," but those unwilling to do that don't accomplish more; they accomplish less. Quality lives don't just happen — they come from concentrated choice.

The dedicated life is the life worth living.
ANNIE DILLARD

RESOURCEFULNESS

Most people live, whether physically, intellectually or morally, in a very
restricted circle of their potential being. They make use of a very small portion
of their possible consciousness, and of their soul's resources in general, much
like a man who, out of his whole bodily organism, should get into the habit of
using and moving only his little finger. Great emergencies and crises show us
how much greater our vital resources are than we had supposed.

WILLIAM JAMES

IT'S A RARE PERSON WHO USES MORE THAN A FEW OF THE RE-
SOURCES AVAILABLE TO HIM. Most of us, to our great detriment,
overlook many of the advantages we've been blessed with — there is
far too much untapped potential in our lives.

For today's discussion, let's define a "resource" simply as something that can be used to meet our needs or reach our goals. It might
be internal (a personality trait, a talent, a skill, etc.) or it might be
external (a relationship, a circumstance, an opportunity, etc.). But
whether it's inside or outside, a resource is something that could
be used to solve a problem. When we "count our blessings," we are
almost always counting things that could be thought of as resources.

If that's what "resources" are, then what is "resourcefulness"? That
would be the knack of getting the most out of our resources. If we're
resourceful, we're efficient in the use of our blessings, milking every
drop of help out of them in the accomplishment of good works.

Creativity. When we're frustrated and think that we've reached a
dead end, we need to be more resourceful. That is, we need to be more
creative in the search for alternatives. Sometimes the best resources
are not immediately obvious. Resourceful people dig deeper.

Determination. Another trait that resourceful people have is a
greater commitment to their objectives. They work harder, demon-
strating a doggedness that is not easily defeated. Coupled with their
creativity, their determination refuses to take no for an answer.

Most of us need a greater vision of our resources. We will rarely,
if ever, be in a situation where no resources exist, but sometimes we
don't recognize the resources that do exist. We need to open our eyes
and count the blessings that are either ours or could be ours. We need
to see how much opportunity there may be, even in seemingly desperate situations. In a word, we need to be more *resourceful.*

Enjoy to the full the resources that are within thy reach.

PYTHIAN ODES

August 27

EFFORT

By labor fire is got out of a stone.
DUTCH PROVERB

EFFORT SEEMS TO POSSESS A NEARLY MIRACULOUS POWER. Although some problems can't be solved by the mere application of human effort, it is nothing short of amazing to see what effort can do when that is the thing needed. With a do-or-die attitude and a diligent work ethic, people frequently accomplish "impossible" feats.

Effort is necessary to the fulfillment of almost any significant purpose. As the saying goes, "Nothing worthwhile is easy," so we should not be surprised when effort is called for. That's just the way life is. Yet we all know folks who never work hard at anything except finding a way to do their work without any effort. It is certainly smart to work as efficiently as we can, but the wisdom of the old English proverb is probably right: "Elbow-grease is the best polish."

Often our objectives fail for a lack of *sustained* effort. We may show initiative in getting started, but we fall short of our goal because we don't have enough of what might be called "finishiative." Granted, it is hard to keep exerting effort for an extremely long time, especially when things don't seem to be working out well. But the rewards in life are generally reserved for those who will try and try and keep trying.

Indeed, either of the two problems we've just discussed will create a life that will be harder in the end than any amount of effort would be right now. William Cowper caught the irony of this fact in his famous aphorism, "A life of ease is a difficult pursuit." When we are lazy or we fail to persevere, we may think we're doing the easier thing. But eventually, we find that our negligence has created a great deal more difficulty for us than we would have had to face otherwise. So effort-avoiders beware: the easiest thing is usually the hardest.

Once in a while, most of us would profit from the experience of making an *extraordinary* effort to do something. As it is, we rarely do anything that is strenuous, even when we say that our task is hard. So I urge you to learn what the word "sacrifice" means. Don't see how much pain you can put yourself through just for the sake of suffering, but make enough effort on some occasions that you "break a sweat," so to speak. Push beyond the merely hard to the truly costly.

Effort is only effort when it begins to hurt.
JOSÉ ORTEGA Y GASSET

VALIDATION

Validate: to establish the soundness of; corroborate.
AMERICAN HERITAGE DICTIONARY

THE MORE IMPORTANT SOMETHING IS, THE MORE IT NEEDS TO BE VALIDATED. Consider a few examples:
(1) *Ideas* need to be analyzed to establish their soundness.
(2) *Information* needs to be verified to guarantee its accuracy.
(3) *Arguments* need to be tested to see if their conclusions are valid.
(4) *Goals* need to be evaluated to confirm their appropriateness.

All of these are illustrations of the need for validation. And, as I said, the more important a thing is (that is, the bigger its consequences), the more validation is a matter of due diligence.

You won't get good results in any validation, however, if you don't use good criteria. Validation means measuring against a standard, and no matter how carefully we measure, the results will be worthless if the standard is not right. For example, if you tell me something and I need to validate the truthfulness of what you say, my personal likes and dislikes are probably not the best means of verifying the accuracy of your testimony. I may hope you are telling the truth, but either way, my preferences are not an adequate criterion by which to judge.

Since there are many things in life we need to be sure about, we engage in validation almost daily. We may not call it that; in fact, we may not even realize what we're doing, but frequently we find ourselves having to check things out. Or at least we should be doing that. The problem is, we often don't take the time to double-check the facts, even in matters of great consequence. We accept hearsay evidence without verifying it. We act on impulse without stopping to think. We sign contracts without knowing what we're agreeing to. In all too many ways *we fail to establish the soundness of our ideas and our actions.* And later on, huge regrets come crashing into us when we see that we acted on the basis of ideas that should have been rejected.

One thing is certain: if a thing is factual, it can stand the process of validation. We should never be afraid to bring any idea out into the sunlight. If it is valid, the light will demonstrate that, and if not, the sooner we find out, the better. Ultimately, of course, time will tell. Truth will be left standing when all of its competitors have vanished.

Truth fears no trial.
THOMAS FULLER

August 29
ARTISTRY

Life is not an exact science, it is an art.
SAMUEL BUTLER

THE RIVALRY BETWEEN ART AND SCIENCE IS AS OLD AS HUMAN CIVILIZATION. Both of these endeavors are good, and despite what their respective advocates might say, neither can claim the other is unimportant or nonessential. It is a fact, however, that most individuals tend to prefer one more than the other, and the argument will probably never be settled. But just for today, let's focus on some good things that can be said about "artistry."

I believe that all of us, at some point in our lives, would do well to learn some skill or craft that is measured by its artistry rather than its utility. If nothing else, the discipline required to learn an art would be a good thing to experience. But also, there is a kind of joy that comes from artistic work that can't be gotten from any other source. If you haven't tasted this joy, I hope you will do so before you die.

Whether or not any of us ever become artists in the literal sense, it would be good for us to adopt the same attitude toward life that the artist has toward his work. For one thing, we need to have the artist's pride of craftsmanship, aspiring to excellence and wanting to do the best work we're capable of. Like the artist, we should strive for beauty and not be content with mere correctness. And finally, it should be the hearts of people, and not just their minds, that we want to stir.

But if life is more an art than a science, in what sense is that true? Many things could be said, but let's sum it up this way: *life is not as precise as science.* In science, known processes are predictable — if you control the variables, the outcome is assured. But we can never reduce life to that kind of precision, no matter how logical we try to be. There are just too many variables. So in daily living, our decisions often have to be made in the same way an artist makes decisions.

Never think for a moment that the "art of living" doesn't have to be learned or that it comes naturally. If you know a serious artist, you know he or she works hard at what they do. They strive to improve their craft, honing it by constant work. Art is not easy, and neither is life. The artistry of it won't improve if we don't work at it.

The art of right living is like all arts: it must be
learned and practiced with incessant care.
JOHANN WOLFGANG VON GOETHE

SUSTENANCE

All philosophy lies in two words: sustain and abstain.
E P I C T E T U S

EPICTETUS MAY HAVE OVERSTATED THE CASE, BUT "SUSTE-
NANCE" AND "ABSTINENCE" ARE CERTAINLY FUNDAMENTAL
CONCEPTS. Many of the questions we deal with daily are those that
ask (1) what we need to live in this world, and (2) what the things
are that we should refrain from. When we've identified both what we
need more of and what we need less of, we will have addressed two of
life's most significant problems. Dealing wisely with these is not easy.

Before we talk about receiving sustenance, however, let's think
briefly about giving it. If it is "more blessed to give than to receive,"
that is certainly true of sustenance. Each of us is in a position to help
someone (and maybe many people) be sustained and have what they
need. We have it within our power to nourish others, to support them,
and to help them keep going. And the joy of providing sustenance is
so great, the wonder is that we do not do it more often.

But we ourselves also need sustenance. And while it may threaten
our pride, there will be times when the things we need will have to
come from some of our fellow human beings. Not a single one of us is
completely self-sufficient — we did not get where we are without the
help of other people. We should openly acknowledge this fact and be
eager to show our appreciation to the many "sustainers" around us.

We should not underestimate how much sustenance is required
for us to get by in this world. We need many different things from
many different sources. The most obvious needs are those of a physical nature, but that is just the start. We also have emotional needs,
social needs, and many others. All these kinds of sustenance come
from somewhere. Do we take the sources for granted?

Far beyond our other needs, however, is our need for our Creator.
Spiritual sustenance may not be something we think about very often,
but we need it nevertheless. And just as in other areas where we have
to be sustained, we should not underestimate what our spirits need,
nor the Source from which that sustenance must ultimately come.

As our bodies live upon the earth and find sustenance in the fruits which it
produces, so our minds feed on the same truths as the intelligible and
immutable substance the divine Word contains.
N I C O L A S   M A L E B R A N C H E

August 31
CAREFULNESS

Look before you leap.
ENGLISH PROVERB

THE BEST TIME TO BE CAREFUL ABOUT A DEED IS BEFORE YOU DO IT. Looking before you leap may be old advice, but it's still wise. Having already leaped, it is hard to change direction in midair.

There are few regrets more painful in life than having spoken or acted in ways that were hurtful to other people. And the pain of such regrets comes from knowing we were needlessly cruel: we know it didn't have to be that way. If only we had stopped to think — and been more careful — the outcome could have been different. So carefulness needs to be a higher priority for most of us. "Don't monkey with the buzz saw" is good counsel, socially as well as physically.

It might not be too much to say that our words are the things we need to be most careful about. Too often, we speak rashly, do great harm, and then later wish we had not spoken so quickly. The first time I ever heard H. G. Bohn's rule, "Think today and speak tomorrow," I thought it was cowardly, but now I see the wisdom of it. No doubt there are times when it's urgent that we speak up, but there are many more times when we need to push the "pause" button and hold off expressing a thought until we've had time to think about it. Words can do more damage than any kind of physical "buzz saw." To say they should be handled carefully is a considerable understatement.

But "care" can be used in another sense. If you say that you "care" for someone, that statement usually has a positive connotation. So apply that idea to our discussion of carefulness in general. Shouldn't you "care" enough about your words and deeds to be "careful" about them? I believe that's a helpful way to think about it. Being "careful" doesn't have to mean you are fearful or finicky in a negative sense — it can mean you view your freedom as a blessing and you want to lavish all the loving care upon your deeds that they deserve.

Fortunately, life has a way of urging us to be more careful. When we encounter roadblocks on the way to our goals, life is often saying to us, "Before proceeding, you need to think about this a little more."

It is happily and kindly provided that in every life
there are certain pauses and interruptions which force
consideration upon the careless . . .
SAMUEL JOHNSON

INTUITION

It is by logic that we prove, but by intuition that we discover.
HENRI POINCARÉ

INTUITION CAN BE A MARVELOUS THING. As long as we understand its limitations, it can be the doorway to a realm of rich experience.

We all know what it is like to sense that something is true even though it is not outwardly evident or logically explainable at the moment the insight first occurs to us. For example, consider this illustrative sentence from the *American Heritage Dictionary:* "Mathematicians sometimes intuit the truth of a theorem long before they are able to prove it." That's precisely what an intuition is. It's the strong impression that something is true when we can't (yet) explain the basis for it.

The fact is, our minds often pick up on truths in advance of our reasoning processes. And that's a good thing because our logic is a train that is often slow to leave the station. If your brain works anything like mine, you'll agree with Vauvenargues' old adage that the human mind often "comprehends more than it can coordinate."

But here is the critical caution that needs to be kept in mind: while our intuitions often turn out to be true, it is foolish to act on them without validating them — and the more important the question, the more essential this advice is. Our intuitions may be exciting, but they may also be wrong. In all the more consequential areas of life, to take intuition as our only guide is to court disaster. By intuition, for example, you may leap to the conclusion that a certain doctor is a competent heart surgeon. But before you allow him to cut into your chest, you would do well to see if your intuition is borne out by a rational investigation of the facts. A good hunch is probably not enough.

There is another way to look at intuition, however, and that is what I want to conclude with. While intuition sometimes comes first, as we have suggested, there is a deeper sense in which it comes last. Intuition and reason are not opposed. Properly understood, they are allies in our quest for truth. And in regard to the more important truths, intuition is the sensitivity that a person acquires after training his or her mind first to think carefully, to believe, and to trust.

> One in whom persuasion and belief
> Had ripened into faith, and faith become
> A passionate intuition.
> WILLIAM WORDSWORTH

BENEFIT

To those who have lived long together, everything heard and everything seen
recalls some pleasure communicated, some benefit conferred.
SAMUEL JOHNSON

AS OUR RELATIONSHIPS MATURE, THEY BECOME STORE-HOUSES OF GOOD MEMORIES. As Johnson put it, "everything heard and everything seen recalls some pleasure communicated, some benefit conferred." At least, that's the way it is if the parties to the relationship have actually been conferring benefits on each other.

I like to think of the words "benefit" and "benevolence" as first cousins. Both come from Latin, with the first part of each compound being *bene* ("good"). To have a "benevolent" attitude is to have good-will. The last half of "benefit," however, comes from *facere* ("to do"), implying more than simply wishing someone well. It means doing a good deed that actually renders service and helps someone.

It would be a fine thing if more of us sought *mutual* benefit in all our dealings. Selfishness, which seeks only personal benefit regardless of how many other people's backs have to be broken, is one of the most destructive things in the world. "The parasitical belief in prosperity as coming by the sacrifices of others has no place in the mind that thinks true. 'My benefit is your benefit, your success is my success' should be the basis of all our wealth" (Annie Rix Militz). Other people are not our tools, and they have no more duty to serve our needs than we have to serve theirs. True benefit is always a two-way street.

Indeed, when we have received a personal benefit, that increases our responsibility to benefit others. The more we have received, the more we need to give back. "As [a person] is to profit by the safety and prosperity the community provides, so he must seek its good and place his personal will at its disposal. Benefit and burden, power and responsibility go together" (James Bryce).

Sometimes, of course, it is not possible for us to "give back" to the very same person or group that benefitted us. And so we are thankful for the concept of "paying forward" our benefits. In other words, you benefit me, and I take that benefit and use it to help someone else.

We cannot render benefits to those from whom we receive them,
or only seldom. But the benefits we receive must be rendered again
line for line, deed for deed to somebody.
RALPH WALDO EMERSON

BOUNTIFULNESS

Be rather bountiful than expensive;
do good with what thou hast,
or it will do thee no good.
WILLIAM PENN

REALLY AND TRULY, WHAT KIND OF PERSON ARE YOU: A
BOUNTIFUL PERSON OR A STINGY PERSON? We live in a bountiful world, to say the least, and we're surrounded by opportunities to
give, but somehow we settle into the habit of taking rather than giving, and on the rare occasions when we do give, it is often sparingly.

I believe this is the single area of life where we have the greatest
opportunity to make a change that will actually make a difference.
Just think what a gift this would be! If today those who know you
began to experience you not only as a giver but as a *bountiful* giver,
you would have touched their lives with an amazing grace. Your interactions with them would be nothing less than transformative if they
started seeing you as one who enjoys giving lavishly, abundantly, and
plenteously. It's hard to imagine what could make a greater difference.

When we fail to be bountiful, we miss a great opportunity. And
this missed opportunity is surely the reason why so many people in
the world are as miserable as they are. "To complain that life has
no joys while there is a single creature whom we can relieve by our
bounty, assist by our counsels, or enliven by our presence, is to lament
the loss of that which we possess, and is just as irrational as to die of
thirst with the cup in our hands" (William Melmoth).

It is useless to say, "Well, I would like to be bountiful, but I have
nothing to give." For one thing, most of us underestimate how much
we have to offer, but even if our resources are truly limited, we need to
understand that bountifulness is not measured by the literal amount of
what is given. It is measured in terms of sacrifice. Generous people are
those who do all they can with the resources that are, in fact, at their
disposal. So William Penn was right: "Do good with what thou hast."

But finally, the warmth and affection of our generosity are the
mainsprings of its bounty. Not many of us can give great gifts — but
if we give lovingly, we are giving bountifully, whatever the gift may be.

Bounty always receives part of its value from
the manner in which it is bestowed.
SAMUEL JOHNSON

September 4
HOLINESS

How little people know who think that holiness is dull. When one meets the
real thing . . . it is irresistible. If even 10 percent of the world's population had
it, would not the whole world be converted and happy before a year's end?

C. S. LEWIS

ONE OF THE SADDEST THINGS IN LIFE TO ME IS THAT "HOLI-
NESS" HAS SUCH A BAD REPUTATION. The word "holy" doesn't
conjure up a very positive image in the minds of most people, or at
least it doesn't suggest anything that modern people see as relevant to
their own lives. The idea never comes up in conversation except when
someone is criticized for being "holier-than-thou," and in a secular
culture there is no more powerful way to criticize somebody than that.

Yet holiness does not necessarily involve smugness or pride.
Those are the sins that tempt us when we make progress in any virtue,
whether it's holiness, honesty, courage, or anything else. (Interestingly,
we may even become proud when we've made a little progress in
humility.) But one can be holy without being "self-righteous." Nor
does holiness mean being prudish or having a dour disposition or
withdrawing from the world to live on a moutaintop.

It means, quite simply, being wholeheartedly devoted to God.
The main idea is "dedication" — the holy life is that of the person
who wants, above all, to have a right relationship with God and is
willing to subtract from their thoughts or deeds anything that is in-
consistent with that purpose. What could be better than that?

By its very nature, holiness will seem extreme to those who are
not interested in it. Its passion will seem excessive, just as the dedication of an artist or an athlete will seem unreasonable to those who
have other interests. But I agree with Eric Hoffer, who said, "We can
be satisfied with moderate confidence in ourselves and with a moderately good opinion of ourselves, but the faith we have in a holy cause
has to be extravagant and uncompromising."

Of course, at the present time, none of us is anything more than
a work in progress — but progress is what we need to be making. Our
imperfections are no reason to throw away the ideal of holiness. And
the ideal will never be ours if we don't reach for it reverently.

Our progress in holiness depends on God and ourselves
— on God's grace and on our will to be holy.

TERESA OF CALCUTTA

CONTENTMENT

That man is happiest
who lives from day to day and asks no more,
garnering the simple goodness of a life.

E U R I P I D E S

EVERYBODY AGREES ON OUR NEED FOR MORE CONTENTMENT, BUT NOBODY AGREES ON WHAT CONTENTMENT IS. It doesn't mean apathy or complacency, it doesn't mean we have no longings or aspirations, and it certainly doesn't mean we're lazy. Contentment simply means that whatever our unmet needs may be, we have the wisdom and strength to deal with them rightly. Above all, it means that we are joyously grateful for what we have right now.

While there are other things we might be discontent about, it is money, material possessions, and earthly enjoyments that give us the most trouble. We are (especially in the "developed" countries) driven by an unhealthy desire for more — always more — of these things. There is no reasonable point at which we're willing to say we have enough. Happiness always waits just beyond our next purchase.

But if we had to be discontent about something, wouldn't our character be a better object of discontent than our possessions? What we are matters more than what we have, so shouldn't we be more dis-satisfied with the present state of our inner life than with the balance in our bank account? Surely this would be a more productive priority.

Indeed, our desire for material satisfactions may result from holes in our character that we're not paying attention to, and until these in-ward deficiencies are supplied, we'll be on a constant treadmill. Doris Mortman said it succinctly: "Until you make peace with who you are, you'll never be content with what you have."

So contentment is a difficult idea. It's important how we define it, and even more important how we prioritize our discontentments. If virtuous character is what we want more of, then discontent in that area is probably a good thing. But with everything else, we need to be more satisfied. At present, some things may be disagreeable, perhaps painfully so. We must bear these with fortitude. And as for the future, many things may be uncertain. We must meet these with courage.

I endeavor to be wise when I cannot be merry, easy when I cannot be glad,
content with what cannot be mended, and patient when there be no redress.

E L I Z A B E T H   M O N T A G U

September 6

CAPABILITY

Men are often capable of greater things than they perform. They are sent into
the world with bills of credit, and seldom draw to their full extent.

HORACE WALPOLE

DOES OUR ABILITY COME ANYWHERE CLOSE TO OUR CAPA-
BILITY? There may be many reasons why we fall short, but it's a
fact that we use no more than a small percentage of our resources. At
the end of our lives, a good bit of our potential has gone untapped.

While we still have the opportunity, we need to be better stewards of our blessings. Elevating our goals (and also increasing our
courage), we must do more of the good work that we're capable of
doing. Life is too short to waste it on "shoulda, coulda, wouldas." And
I would suggest that it is for our families, most of all, that we should
strive to reach our potential. As gifts go, this is a truly great one.

But we also need to affirm and encourage the capabilities of our
fellow human beings. "Every human soul is of infinite value, eternal,
free; no human being, therefore, is so placed as not to have within his
reach, in himself and others, objects adequate to infinite endeavor"
(Arthur J. Balfour). The literal meaning of "encourage" is to "impart
courage to another person," and in the matter of capability that is
exactly what we must do: we must help others to see how great their
possibilities are, and then help them to have the courage to do what
they're capable of doing. When we do this, we are often astonished to
see how much more they were capable of than we thought!

Capability has a dangerous side, of course. Our potential for
good is matched by our potential for evil, and there is no deed so
wicked that any of us would not be capable of doing it under the right
circumstances. Any of us is capable of anything. ("There, but for the
grace of God, go I.") So we need to be on our guard — always.

But if we must guard against our evil capabilities, we must learn
to appreciate our good ones. We've been endowed with great gifts,
and these were meant to be used. We never want to think more highly
of ourselves than we ought to think, certainly, but neither should
we think more lowly of ourselves than is right. The gifts and opportunities granted us by our Creator are not to be underestimated or
ignored. *They are to be received — and used — with all of our hearts.*

I want to be all that I am capable of becoming.
KATHERINE MANSFIELD

VARIETY

Here hills and vales, the woodland and the plain,
Here earth and water seem to strive again,
Not chaos-like together crush'd and bruis'd,
But, as the world, harmoniously confus'd:
Where order in variety we see,
And where, though all things differ, all agree.

ALEXANDER POPE

THAT THERE IS A MAGNIFICENT VARIETY IN NATURE IS OBVI-
OUS TO ANYONE WHO HAS EVER THOUGHT ABOUT IT SERI-
OUSLY. Indeed, the very beauty we appreciate in the world around us
is largely the result of nature's being "harmoniously confus'd."

The word "variety" is related to words like "varied," "various," and
"variegated," which all come from a root having to do with *difference.*
Things only "vary" when they are different in some way, and "variety"
simply describes a situation in which there is some unlikeness or diversity. At the grocery store, I always buy the "variety pack" of donuts
because in that box there are different kinds of donuts.

Now variety is not always good. Its goodness depends on several
factors: whether the individual things are good in themselves, whether
their differences are blended in a peaceful way, and so forth. But when
the conditions are right, variety can be a very positive characteristic.
In fact, it can be one of the most wonderful things in the world.

Not only does variety contribute to beauty and enjoyment (it's
the "spice of life"), but it also adds strength. In regard to nations, for
example, Francis Galton said, "The moral and intellectual wealth of
a nation largely consists in the multifarious variety of the gifts of the
men who compose it, and it would be the very reverse of improvement to make all its members assimilate to a common type."

In our personal relationships, we ought to see the value of variety,
and this is certainly true in marriage. If you are married (or even in a
romantic relationship that is leading to marriage), you should give the
gift of healthy variety to the relationship — and be prayerfully grateful for the variety that your beloved brings to the relationship also.

As you are woman, so be lovely:
As you are lovely, so be various,
Merciful as constant, constant as various,
So be mine, as I yours for ever.

ROBERT RANKE GRAVES

UPRIGHTNESS

Man is born for uprightness. If a man lose his uprightness, and yet live,
his escape from death is the effect of mere good fortune.
CONFUCIUS

IN ITS LITERAL SENSE, TO BE "UPRIGHT" MEANS TO BE IN A VER-
TICAL POSITION. If you are sitting upright then you are not lying
down or reclining. But we often use the word "upright" metaphorically to refer to the "position" of one who adheres carefully to moral
principles. Uprightness in this sense is moral integrity and rectitude.

I believe it is no coincidence that human beings, who alone are
capable of moral decisions, are also able, in the physical sense, to walk
more uprightly than any of the other creatures in the world. Only
human beings possess this unique combination of abilities: uprightness of posture and uprightness of moral behavior. And Confucius
was right, at least partly, in the quotation at the top of the page: "Man
is born for uprightness. If a man lose his uprightness, and yet live, his
escape from death is the effect of mere good fortune." I would attribute the immoral person's escape from death not to good fortune but
to God's grace and patience, but all the same, if we depart from uprightness, then we've deviated from the path we were born to follow.

When we are tempted to abandon the principles of moral
uprightness, we must strengthen our resolve to live as we know we
should. "O God, may we so value our bodies and minds that we never
mar them. May we not be tricked into bad habits by publicity and
advertisements that deliberately mislead, or by the desire for easy ap-
plause, or by the fear of being thought narrow. But may we be sturdy
and upright in our thinking and our behavior" (Sid G. Hodges).

Surely one of the most powerful motivations to right living is that
it is conducive to the highest good of our fellow humans. Even when
no words of moral encouragement are able to be spoken, the mere
example of doing what is right is a great gift. As Anne Swetchine put
it, "We reform others unconsciously when we act uprightly."

If we love someone, we will have a deep desire to live uprightly
for their sake. We will shrink from any action that would hurt them or
hinder them or influence them unhelpfully. Love wants to be upright
not only for its own sake but for the sake of the one whom it loves.

Love is watchful, humble, and upright.
THOMAS À KEMPIS

FOOD

Man does not live by bread alone,
but he also does not live long without it.
FREDERICK BUECHNER

SOME PEOPLE ATTACH TOO MUCH IMPORTANCE TO FOOD, BUT OTHERS ATTACH TOO LITTLE. Not only can we not do without it, as Buechner suggests, but the necessity of it is a *daily* necessity. The nature of our physical constitution is such that the eating of food must be woven into the fabric of each and every day's activities.

But the truth is, food is much more than a necessity. I like what Luciano Pavarotti once said: "One of the nicest things about life is the way we must regularly stop whatever it is we are doing and devote our attention to eating." Yes, it is a part of life that we have to stop and eat — but that is one of the nicest things about it!

Partaking of our food can even be seen in a higher way. "It is not only prayer that gives God glory but work. Smiting on an anvil, sawing a beam, whitewashing a wall, driving horses, sweeping, scouring, everything gives God glory if being in his grace you do it as your duty . . . to take food in thankfulness and temperance gives him glory too" (Gerard Manley Hopkins). Gratefully eaten, food lifts us toward God.

So our food was meant to be taken in gratitude and to the glory of its Giver, but it was also meant to be enjoyed. "When you eat the labor of your hands, you shall be happy, and it shall be well with you" (Book of Psalms). And we don't have to be rich in order to savor our food. Indeed, abundance may make it harder to enjoy what we have. The writer of Ecclesiastes saw this clearly when he said, "The sleep of a laboring man is sweet, whether he eats little or much; but the abundance of the rich will not permit him to sleep."

As is often observed (especially in the South), food traditions are deeply social and communal in nature. Of course, not all of us have the privilege of eating all our meals in the company of others, but when we are able to do so, we should see that activity as a great blessing.

If we've lost touch with the enjoyment of our food, we need to return to that enjoyment as part of the simple life. Perhaps we would do well to turn back the hands of time. Remember how easy it was long ago to revel in the simple pleasures of innocent, God-given life?

One must ask children and birds how cherries and strawberries taste.
JOHANN WOLFGANG VON GOETHE

TRUTHFULNESS

Seek the truth without prejudice;
Speak the truth without fear.

CARL SCHURZ

A S CARL SCHURZ SUGGESTS, BOTH SEEKING THE TRUTH AND SPEAKING IT SHOULD BE HIGH PRIORITIES, BUT WE MAY FIND BOTH OF THESE THINGS HARD TO DO. Nearly every day we are tempted to prefer comfortable lies to difficult truths, and to back away from telling the truth when the truth would get us into trouble.

I can't remember where I got this quotation, but it is brutally frank: "A lie is told either to get some advantage to which one has no valid claim, and is in reality cheating, or it is to defend oneself from the bad consequences of an action already done, which is also cheating — cheating justice." In the final analysis, we lie either because we are greedy or we are cowardly. That stings, but I believe it is true.

But whatever our reasons for failure in the matter of truthfulness, we hurt those around us when we lie. There is a social dimension to all of our conduct, obviously, but our words are especially impactful on society. People must be able to trust one another if there is to be any peace in our communities or neighborhoods. Dishonesty destroys trust, eroding the basic foundation of society, and no society can survive very long when truthfulness ceases to be the norm. On the other hand, we never do others a bigger favor than when we make the choice to be truthful. Truthfulness (at least when it is combined with wisdom and kindness) builds better communities. As Emerson famously said, "He serves all, who dares be true."

But we should not tell the truth only when it seems expedient or beneficial. Truthfulness should be a *principle* with us. It should not only be a part of our conduct but a part of our *character*. Others should be able to count on our telling the truth, whether it's convenient or not.

To be this way, we must look at things from a larger perspective. Lies may seem advantageous, but truth is stronger than deceit, and eventually truth will win out. So those who build their lives on truth (neither believing lies nor speaking them) are building on a foundation that will stand the test of time. Indeed, truth is the only such foundation.

Life is short, but truth works far and lives long;
let us speak the truth.

ARTHUR SCHOPENHAUER

CHARM

People are either charming or tedious.
OSCAR WILDE

PERSONALLY, I DON'T THINK OSCAR WILDE WAS FAR WRONG. We do find people to be one or the other: charming or tedious. But mention the word "charming" and many people think of the smooth operator who uses charm as a means of manipulating others. Is that all there is to charm? Does it not have a more positive aspect?

In its most basic sense, "charm" simply means "the power or quality of pleasing or delighting." But it can also mean the technique of "casting a spell," as in magic or voodoo, where techniques are used that are thought to effect others without their consent. So "charming" can imply such an ability to allure others that one can beguile or bewitch them almost irresistibly. In a lesser sense, words like "enchanting" or "fascinating" or "captivating" carry this meaning.

But to be charming doesn't have to mean influencing others quite so forcefully. It can simply mean that when others have dealings with us they find us pleasing or delightful (rather than tedious).

When we think of it this way, wouldn't the effort to be more charming be a worthy effort? Wouldn't charm, rightly defined, be a good gift we could give to those around us? I believe it would, and I agree with Henry Van Dyke when he said, "There is no personal charm so great as the charm of a cheerful temperament." Without trying to manipulate anyone, we can certainly improve the cheerfulness of our temperament, and when we do, others will appreciate it.

The main thing about charm, however, is that it must be coupled with good character. Whether we have a natural gift for charm or not, the outward aspect of that charm can never be a substitute for integrity and a pure heart on the inside. But when a pleasing "exterior" is coupled with an honorable "interior," what a combination that is! In the ancient words of Menander: "When good character adds adornment to natural charms, whoever comes near is doubly captivated."

I urge you, then, to be who you are. Work every day on being a better version of yourself. Make a genuine effort to be pleasing to other people — because you love them. And you will be charming!

To me more dear, congenial to my heart,
One native charm, than all the gloss of art.
OLIVER GOLDSMITH

September 12
COOPERATION

No society of nations, no people within a nation, no family can benefit
through mutual aid unless good will exceeds ill will; unless the spirit of
cooperation surpasses antagonism; unless we all see and act as though
the other man's welfare determines our own welfare.

HENRY FORD II

THIS THING WE CALL "COOPERATION" IS ONE OF THE HARD-
EST AND MOST CHALLENGING THINGS IN THE WORLD.
Compared to the difficulty of cooperation, fighting is quite easy. And
because fighting is easier (at least in the short run), we often quit
communicating and start lashing out. Antagonism replaces cooperation in our relationships — with heartbreakingly destructive results.

In our more sober moments, we all know that there is much to be
gained by cooperation. Nobody is self-sufficient, and more good work
can be done with others than any of us could do by ourselves. It may
be trite but it is still true: we are stronger together.

But in addition to the *value* of cooperation, we need to see the
necessity of it. We inhabit a world where everybody is interconnected.
Like it or not, our actions impact others and their actions impact us.
"If we could all agree that the world belongs to God we would see the
world as a cooperative fellowship. We of the human race are so bound
together and so interdependent that it behooves us all to live for the
good of the whole" (W. Earl Waldrop). I may not think of myself
as being very influential, but I need to understand that every one of
my actions contributes either to the common "weal" or the common
"woe." As a fellow human being, I owe it to you to act cooperatively.

In the midst of conflict, have you ever had someone rise above
the difficulty and say, "I will work with you"? If so, I'm guessing you
saw that as a gift and an act of grace. Why can't we give that gift more
often? Cooperation is a blessing each of us is capable of bestowing.

In the end, it is love that will make us want to give this gift. Love
will look beyond the irritable aspects of another person's behavior and
see that person as having a burden we might help them bear. The best
cooperation in the world happens when love says, "How can I help you?"

God has ordered things that we may learn to bear one another's burdens;
for there is no man without his faults, none without his burden. None is
sufficient in himself; none is wise in himself; therefore, we must support
one another, comfort, help, teach, and advise one another.

THOMAS À KEMPIS

September 13
INTENSITY

Home is where one starts from. As we grow older
The world becomes stranger, the pattern more complicated
Of dead and living. Not the intense moment
Isolated, with no before and after,
But a lifetime burning in every moment . . .

T. S. ELIOT

THOSE WHOSE LIVES ARE THE RICHEST ARE THOSE WHO ARE INTENSE. Their powers of concentration are great, and they bring those powers to bear on an object of singular importance. They are, to use a phrase by William Butler Yeats, "full of passionate intensity."

Most people have no sharp focus on anything. They may have many interests (even "avid" interests), but that is precisely the problem. Unwilling to let go of any of those, they are like a kid in a candy store who can't make up his mind. Or to change the metaphor, they are like the man described by one writer: "He got up each morning, jumped on his horse, and rode off in all directions at once."

It is one of life's most profound ironies that those who live this way impoverish themselves. When I said above that those who are intensely focused have the "richest" lives, I meant exactly that. It sounds contradictory, I know, but it is true: by holding on to so many activities, we lose what could be a richer life. Unwilling to sacrifice, we lose the things we hold onto and also the higher pursuit that was calling to us. Jesus of Nazareth frequently made the point and made it bluntly: "If you try to hang on to your life, you will lose it."

"The degree of fullness in any life," wrote A. W. Tozer, "accords perfectly with the intensity of true desire." This "intensity of true desire" makes us vulnerable to suffering, obviously. But doing away with it leads to nothing that could be called life. In fact, it leads to death.

Life does not stay the same for very long. So as our lives unfold, it is to be expected that our intensity will change. But passion and focus have no mandatory retirement age. These are things that must not be allowed to fade away. Elevated and enhanced by the passage of time, our intensity must always be "moving into another intensity . . ."

Old men ought to be explorers
Here and there does not matter
We must be still and still moving
Into another intensity . . .

T. S. ELIOT

PROSPERITY

Prosperity is an instrument to be used,
not a deity to be worshiped.
CALVIN COOLIDGE

PROSPERITY IS WITHIN THE REACH OF MORE PEOPLE NOW THAN AT ANY TIME IN THE HISTORY OF THE WORLD. Poverty has certainly not gone out of existence, but even so, prosperity is a more realistic dream than it used to be for millions of people.

Unfortunately, we don't always view prosperity as we should. We grant it too high a position on our list of values and priorities, we use it for nothing more than selfish indulgence, and worst of all, we don't give thanks to God as the source of all our blessings. In other words, when our character is tested by abundance, we often fail the test.

Many people assume that prosperity is easy, but it is not. Whatever challenges adversity may present, these are nothing compared to the difficulties of wealth. We often speak of the poor as "poverty-stricken," but if we understood what the real dangers to human character are, we would probably be more concerned about those who have been "stricken with prosperity." Keb' Mo', a great blues musician, spoke to this issue in his insightful song "Victims of Comfort."

It would be a step in the right direction for us to remember the difference between outward and inward prosperity. Outwardly, prosperity is an economic condition. The more important prosperity, however, is a state of mind. It is experienced by those who possess contentment in their inner character, and without this kind of wealth, the outward kind is relatively worthless. But we can go even further: it is *spiritual* well-being (resulting from a right relationship with God) that outranks every other prosperity, whether inward or outward.

So if our goal is to become "prosperous," we need to be careful — careful in how we define it and careful in how we pursue it. Some changes may be necessary: we may need to spend less effort on the discovery of "greener pastures" and more on the good stewardship of what is already ours. I agree with what Booker T. Washington said about it: "We shall prosper as we learn to do the common things of life in an uncommon way." So as far as prosperity is concerned, it matters what's in our wallet, but our way of *thinking* matters much more.

A cheerful heart has a continual feast.
BOOK OF PROVERBS

COMPLETENESS

God has other work for you, and it waits
only the completion of the present task.
FRANCES J. ROBERTS

UNFINISHED BUSINESS IS A MAJOR PROBLEM IN THE LIVES OF
MOST OF US. We postpone important decisions, we procrastinate
the finishing of projects, and we leave too many problems unresolved
in our relationships. And by neglecting the goal of "completeness" in
our lives, we diminish those lives — and hurt other people too. As
Francis de Sales remarked, "Satan is quite content for us to make any
number of beginnings as long as we never complete anything."

I want to suggest a different line of thought, however. Of all the
things we should want to complete, the most important should be
the growth of our personal character. But I fear this is not a high priority with many people. Early in life, we may have worked on some of
the virtues we knew we needed to acquire, but we may have stopped
working on these things while the work was still woefully incomplete.
So in regard to personal character growth, "finish what you started" is
good advice. In biblical terms, we need to "go on to maturity."

Not only can we work on completing our own character, but we
can also help others be more complete in theirs. Since each person
is responsible for his own character, we can't do this work for anyone
else (although we sometimes wish we could). But we can at least be
a helpful influence by encouraging, inspiring, and uplifting those
around us. We can help others take the next step in their journey
toward maturity — and doing that is one of life's highest privileges.

But let's return to the question of our own character. When was
the last time you seriously asked yourself this question: *what am I still
lacking?* Depending on your age, you may have reached a point long
ago where you ceased to be actively concerned about your personal
incompleteness. You may have become complacent about your faults
and apathetic about your growth. If so, you need to get back to work!

It is dangerous to neglect any unfinished business, but if the unfinished business is our character, that's the most dangerous deficiency
of all. *So how high are your character goals? And what are you still lacking?*

Be a life long or short, its completeness
depends on what it was lived for.
DAVID STARR JORDAN

MINDFULNESS

This noble eightfold path . . . right views, right aspirations,
right speech, right conduct, right livelihood, right effort,
right mindfulness, and right contemplation.

THE PALI CANON

A MIND IS A TERRIBLE THING TO WASTE, AS THE SAYING GOES, BUT WE OFTEN WASTE OUR MINDS BY NOT BEING "MINDFUL" ENOUGH. Most of us are busy tending to a multitude of concerns. Distracted by so many competing priorities, it's difficult to focus our minds on anything as beneficially as we should. It would be a step in the right direction if we could simply be more mindful of this problem.

Awareness. In its most basic sense, mindfulness simply means awareness. But while being aware is usually better than being unaware, we can be mindful in much better ways.

Thoughtfulness. To a correspondent, Thomas Wolfe once wrote, "For all that you have done, I am ever mindful." Used in that way, mindfulness means that one is attentive to another person in an appreciative way. When we are mindful of others, we give heed to them. We take conscious thought for them, dwelling consciously on the good things they have done. What is more, we often use the word "mindful" to describe a person who has an inclination to do this. He or she has a marked tendency to be mindful of those around them.

Purposefulness. Here is the third, and best, meaning of mindfulness. Being mindful in this way involves *paying attention on purpose.* It is the discipline of devoting deliberate thought and focused meditation to an idea or a person. And while I do not endorse Buddhism, I must say that the Buddhist concept of mindfulness has much to recommend it. There is great value in learning how to mindfully focus on important matters. Not only are those around us benefited, but we come away refreshed, informed, and strengthened.

When we give ourselves to others as more mindful persons, we honor them. So I urge you to practice a greater degree of mindfulness, especially with those who are nearest and dearest to you. Give them the gift of your deliberate attention. Be present for them — *mindfully.*

The most precious gift we can offer others
is our presence. When mindfulness embraces
those we love, they will bloom like flowers.

THICH NHAT HANH

Efficiency is enhanced not by what we accomplish
but more often by what we relinquish.
CHARLES R. SWINDOLL

THE TRUTH ALLUDED TO IN THIS QUOTATION IS ONE OF LIFE'S HARDEST, BUT MOST IMPORTANT, PRINCIPLES. And while "efficiency" and "effectiveness" are not exactly the same thing, they do have this idea in common: success requires letting go of the good (and even the better) in order to pursue the best. To sculpt a *David*, Michelangelo had to chip away a lot of very good marble — marble that might have worked extremely well for some *other* statue.

How, then, shall we define "effectiveness"? Strictly speaking, anything is "effective" if it produces an "effect." But normally we have in mind the production of an *intended* or *desired* effect. The effective person (a) has ideas, and (b) knows how to implement them. He has the habit of achieving what he sets out to achieve.

Looking at it this way, we would have to say that effectiveness is not necessarily a good thing. Whether it is good or evil depends on the moral quality of the goal being sought. It is not enough to say, "I want to be effective." We have to think carefully and identify which effect we desire to produce, understanding that this is a matter of choice on our part. Ultimately, you and I must *decide* what our vision of effectiveness is. Since we only have one life, we can't run away from these questions: what are our goals, our values, our principles . . . and our priorities?

Priorities are always limiting. To choose one thing is to let go of other things, some of which might have been excellent objects to pursue. Effective people have the courage to make hard choices between attractive alternatives. They understand the concept of *sacrifice.*

It is not enough, of course, to have a principled vision. We also have to acquire the *knowledge* and *skills* that our goal requires. Being "willing" may be easy, but learning to be "able" usually requires work. And even after we've acquired sufficient ability, we won't be effective if we don't have the *self-discipline* to keep working until we reach the goal.

So you must choose your passion and pursue it effectively. But as you make your choice, understand this: *whatever it means for others, effectiveness for you will mean serving where YOU can serve best.*

Nobody can be you as effectively as you can.
NORMAN VINCENT PEALE

CONCENTRATION

> Beware of dissipating your powers; strive constantly
> to concentrate them. Genius thinks it can do whatever it sees
> others doing, but it is sure to repent of every ill-judged outlay.
>
> JOHANN WOLFGANG VON GOETHE

THE ABILITY TO "CONCENTRATE" IS A GREAT GIFT, AND ONE THAT SHOULD NOT BE TAKEN LIGHTLY. Out of all the living creatures in the world, only human beings can deliberately choose to focus their thinking, their acting, and even their emotions on a particular point. Like all great abilities, this one has a duty and a stewardship attached to it: *the power of concentration must be used wisely.*

The Latin word *centrum* meant "center," and we get a number of English words from that root, including "concentrate." To concentrate means to bring disparate (and perhaps competing) elements to a common center. Just as "concentric" circles share the same center, so things that have been "concentrated" have been drawn toward some point which then becomes the main focus of all of them. Things that are not concentrated are spread out, scattered, divided, and disunified.

Now here is the point. Our *lives* need to be more concentrated. Emerson described our situation by comparing it to agricultural work: "As the gardener, by severe pruning, forces the sap of the tree into one or two vigorous limbs, so should you stop off your miscellaneous activity and concentrate your force on one or a few points."

It is especially with *people* that we need to be more concentrated. For example, our *attention* needs to be more undivided when it comes to specific persons. We never give anyone a greater gift than when we say, in effect, "For these moments that we are together, I will concentrate my thoughts on you exclusively. I have no more important business than to hear what your heart has to say, so I will turn off all distractions and concerns. My attention is devoted to you."

Concentration is hard, obviously, but we can take steps to improve it. In these days of multiple priorities and information overload, we desperately need to "prune" our thinking and our activities. And perhaps no one needs this advice more than us busy Christians.

> We must show a new generation of nervous, almost frantic, Christians
> that power lies at the center of the life. Speed and noise are evidences
> of weakness, not strength. Eternity is silent, time is noisy.
>
> A. W. TOZER

RECOMMENDATION

A pleasant face is a silent recommendation.
PUBLILIUS SYRUS

THIS QUOTATION FROM PUBLILIUS SYRUS IS CONTROVERSIAL. Not everybody agrees with it, for it is an obvious fact that pleasant faces can sometimes deceive us as to the true character of those who wear them. But even so, if you and I need a recommendation of our character, a smile and a pleasant demeanor may carry as much weight as any recommendation that someone else might give us.

But occasionally we do need someone else to recommend us. In other words, we need another person to make a "favorable statement concerning [our] character or qualifications" (*American Heritage Dictionary*). For today's meditation, though, let's think about it from the opposite direction. *Isn't it a great opportunity when we can recommend — or say something favorable about — someone else?*

Praise is a powerful thing. Most of us recognize how encouraging it is to our friends and loved ones when we praise their good qualities. But in addition to praising them directly, what about the importance of praising them to other people? I don't believe we should limit our recommendation of others to the times when they list us as a reference or ask us for a letter of recommendation. We should look for every chance to say good things about others — even when they haven't asked us to! If we're going to talk behind their back, why can't we focus on the good things that can truthfully be said about them?

A word of warning is in order, however. There is an old saying that "praise is no recommendation." It takes more than mere words to recommend somebody. If your own character is not what it ought to be, then you may "praise" others profusely, but the words will have a distinctly hollow ring in the ears of those who know you.

Let me give you an example. Imagine a conversation in which you are praising somebody to a third party. In that conversation, however, you also badmouth some other people, thinking that your recommendation of one person will be enhanced by the fact that you are cutting down everybody else. Don't fool yourself. If you are a malicious person, your "recommendations" will not be taken seriously.

*Of little worth is the recommendation which
has for its prop the defamation of another.*
TERTULLIAN

COMMUNICATION

*We seek pitifully to convey to others the treasures of our heart, but they
have not the power to accept them, and so we go lonely, side by side but
not together, unable to know our fellows and be known by them.*

W. SOMERSET MAUGHAM

ENDOWED WITH THE GIFT OF COMMUNICATION, BUT LIVING
IN A BROKEN WORLD, WE ALL LONG TO KNOW WHAT PER-
FECT COMMUNICATION WITH ANOTHER PERSON MIGHT BE LIKE.
No small part of the yearning that we experience in this world is this
yearning "to convey to others the treasures of our heart."

It is my personal belief that our ability to communicate, coupled
with our deep desire to communicate perfectly, is a clue to our origin
in the mind of a Personal God. In discussing heaven, for example,
C. S. Lewis pondered the ultimate perfection of our desire to share
ourselves: "For doubtless the continually successful, yet never com-
pleted, attempt by each soul to communicate its vision to all others . . .
is also among the ends for which the individual was created."

Yet even now, communication between human beings is a marvelous thing. For the time being, we engage in it imperfectly (and
sometimes painfully, because of the imperfection), but we must never
take the gift for granted or fail to use it generously.

Such a powerful ability can certainly do great damage if it is
misused, so we must be careful. Neither fear nor frustration should
be allowed to deter us. "Much unhappiness has come into the world
because of bewilderment and things left unsaid" (Dostoevsky).

Sydney J. Harris once wrote, "The two words 'information' and
'communication' are often used interchangeably, but they signify quite
different things. Information is giving out; communication is getting
through." I often think about that truth in these days of text mes-
saging. Text messages are a convenient way of exchanging "information," but they fail miserably at the level of "communication." There
has never been a time when we need deep communication more than
right now, so we must not be content to simply exchange information.

When we communicate honorably, lovingly, and openly we do a
greater good than if we just lived a good life. As powerful as our deeds
and our example may be by themselves, we still need to *communicate*.

Good, the more communicated, more abundant grows.

JOHN MILTON

REAPING

Autumn carries more gold in its hand
than all the other seasons.
JIM BISHOP

A HUMAN LIFE IS FILLED WITH CAUSES AND CONSEQUENCES, SOWING AND REAPING. Nearly everything we do produces some effect, and the general rule is that we reap according to how we have sown. We may be careless in our sowing and reap a harvest that turns out to be less pleasant than we would wish, but nevertheless, it is the reaping of what we have sown. Henry David Thoreau put it this way: "In the long run men hit only what they aim at."

As the fall approaches, which is the time for agricultural crops to be reaped, it's a good time also to ponder what we're reaping in our personal lives. We're getting late into the year, and it won't be long before the harvest will be finished. After that, there'll be a time of winter rest, and then the beginning of a new growing season. If we're not satisfied with what is being brought in from the fields of our personal endeavor, now is a profitable time to consider what it was that we sowed to produce such a crop. It's neither too early nor too late to make some commitments to a new and better kind of sowing.

There will be a time lag, of course. Even if today we begin sowing better things in our lives, it will not be until later that the fruits of those changes will be ready to be harvested and enjoyed. In the matter of sowing and reaping, patience is a quality of key importance. And so is trust. We must plant and cultivate in faith that the employment of right principles will produce the right results, even if in the short term it looks like things aren't working out very well.

Although at this time of year our thoughts naturally turn to the reaping of what has been sown in earlier months, our lives actually include, at any moment, a combination of sowing and reaping. On any day of the year, both activities are going on, overlapping and intertwining with each other. We're constantly beginning new things and experiencing the results of things already done. And so it is in nature: some creatures are reaping while others are sowing. That's a part of what makes this habitat of ours so endlessly interesting and inviting.

For man, autumn is a time of harvest, of gathering together.
For nature, it is a time of sowing, of scattering abroad.
EDWIN WAY TEALE

OPPORTUNITIES

> Not many sounds in life, and I include all urban and all rural sounds,
> exceed in interest a knock at the door.
>
> CHARLES LAMB

IREALLY LIKE THE CONCEPT OF "OPPORTUNITY." It is full of adventure and intrigue, and my heart is strongly drawn to it. But I am like most people in that I fail to see most of the opportunities that present themselves to me. "The opportunities of man are limited only by his imagination. But so few have imagination that there are ten thousand fiddlers to one composer" (Charles F. Kettering).

One obvious reason why we fail to recognize opportunity is that it often involves difficulty, unpleasantness, and maybe even some pain. Naively thinking that an opportunity would always be a "positive" experience, we are blind to the possibilities embedded in those situations that we refer to as "problems." As Charles Swindoll put it, "We are all faced with a series of great opportunities brilliantly disguised as impossible situations." Even if it is outright evil that we are dealing with (either in our own hearts or in the lives of others), it would be helpful if we could see these circumstances differently. Even in evil, there is great opportunity. "The greater the evil, the greater the opportunity to fashion out of it everlasting good" (Hannah Hurnard).

When opportunities arise, we often back away from them. Real engagement with life is strenuous, and so it's easier to stay uninvolved. "Life is always walking up to us and saying, 'Come on in, the living's fine,' and what do we do? Back off and take its picture" (Russell Baker). But when we take the path of non-engagement, we lose most of what life was meant to be. So I like Tom Peters' good advice: "If a window of opportunity appears, don't pull down the shade."

I want to end, however, by suggesting that we should be primarily concerned not about our own opportunities, but about those that we create for others. When I die, my sons won't get much money, if any, from my estate, but I hope that I have opened one or two doors and given them a chance to see a few horizons beyond the limits of my own life. That's what my parents did for me, and I am strongly motivated to seize the opportunities that were bequeathed to me.

> The dead are living all around us, watching with eager anticipation how we
> will handle the opportunities they left in our hands when they died.
>
> THEODORE C. SPEERS

EXCITEMENT

Having a young child explain something exciting he has seen
is the finest example of communication you will ever hear or see.

BOB TALBERT

THE WORLD IS FULL OF THINGS THAT INSPIRE WONDER, AND THE YOUNGER WE ARE, THE MORE NATURALLY WE ARE EXCITED BY THESE THINGS. Just yesterday, I met a really cool kid named Levi who enthusiastically showed me four kittens that were recently born on the land that belongs to his family. He was excited, I was excited, and even the kittens were excited! A young person's excitement is so delightful to us because it reminds us of something about God's creation: the good things around us were meant to excite us joyfully.

Unfortunately, our culture has turned excitement into a god, and it is now permissible to do, say, or think anything at all, as long as one finds it exciting. We have become addicted to it. We can't bear to be without it. And that is a truly sad development because things like quietness, repose, and tranquillity must also be a part of our experience. If not, we become deranged in our thinking and begin to make disastrous decisions due to a lack of perspective.

But if we understand its true nature and keep it in balance, excitement is one of the most gratifying experiences available to us. And it doesn't always have to come from external sources. The most excited (and therefore exciting) people I know are those who are passionately stirred by thoughts that they have consciously chosen to think. Norman Vincent Peale, who obviously knew a good deal about this subject, said it well: "You can think, talk, and act yourself into dullness or into monotony or into unhappiness. By the same process you can build up inspiration, excitement, and a surging depth of joy."

And as a Christian, I would be less than honest if I didn't say that life in Jesus Christ is the most exciting experience of all. Whatever else you may say about it, you can't say that it is dull. To live by radical faith is to inhabit a realm that fairly tingles with awe and admiration.

I simply believe that there is a mystery of the ordinary, that the
commonplace is full of wonder, and that this life that we call Christian is
different from what we think it is. It is infinitely more subtle, more
powerful, more dangerous, more magnificent, more exciting, more
humorous, more delicious, more adventurous, more involved, and more
troublesome than most of us think.

TIM HANSEL

BECOMING

Where is it, this present? It has melted in our grasp,
fled ere we could touch it, gone in the instant of becoming.
WILLIAM JAMES

HAVE YOU NOTICED THAT NOTHING ABOUT US STAYS THE SAME FOR VERY LONG? That fact can be frustrating or encouraging, depending on how you look at it, but either way, we're all "becoming" something different from what we are right now.

Outwardly, our circumstances are changing. You may not be able to predict how they'll be different, but it's a definite fact that by this time next year, your job, your circle of friends, the house you live in, your health, and your bank account will have mutated in some ways. Everything around you is moving, shifting, altering. You can't stop it.

But here's another, and more important, fact: our characters are also changing. Inwardly, we are becoming something different from what we've been in the past. This time next year, we'll all be people of a different quality than we are today, deep down in our hearts.

Some of the ways in which we'll be different will be the result of negligence. Without consciously planning to do so, we find ourselves sliding or drifting into certain changes. Almost always, these are negative changes, very much like what becomes of a house that is not maintained but allowed to deteriorate and become dilapidated.

In other ways, however, we're changing as a result of decisions that we've consciously made. Only personal beings like us, with a free will, can become something different by deciding to do so.

Needless to say, we ought to expend more effort changing ourselves on the inside than we do trying to change the world on the outside. Rearranging the world to our personal advantage is an iffy endeavor, and it shouldn't be our main goal (if it should even be a goal at all). "We work to become, not to acquire" (Elbert Green Hubbard).

But whatever we become, we're each responsible for it. We need not think that foolish choices with respect to our conduct will have no effect on our character. Our conduct and our character are related to one another the same way that snowflakes are related to a snowball.

We become what we do. One of the greatest mistakes we can
make — and some of the smartest men who ever lived have made it — is to
assume that we can do false or discreditable things and still "deep inside us"
remain good people or the same people.
SYDNEY J. HARRIS

INTENTIONS

Good intentions are very mortal and perishable things.
Like very mellow and choice fruit, they are difficult to keep.
CHARLES SIMMONS

IT IS IMPORTANT TO RECOGNIZE JUST HOW "PERISHABLE" OUR INTENTIONS ARE. If we do not act on them rather quickly, they die a sad death, never having done anybody any good.

As far as intentions are concerned, there are two different gifts that we can give to our friends and family. First, we can honor their good intentions. When we know they have meant well, we can let that be our main emphasis, even if their actions have fallen below the standard of excellence. But second, we ourselves can be people who act with the best of intentions. If those who deal with us can take it for granted that our motives will always be honorable, we will have given them one of life's greatest gifts. And this is a gift we can all give.

But, to tell the absolute truth, can any of us say that our motives are as honorable as they should be? It is extremely hard for us to be honest with ourselves in this matter. In many situations, the real reason for our conduct (deep down inside) was something that we would be embarrassed for others to know if it were brought out into the open daylight, and most of us learned long ago how to persuade ourselves that our motives were honorable, even when the motive that was really driving our behavior wasn't all that honorable.

But we can learn to have better motives and intentions, and we certainly ought to do so. In fact, there are few changes that would make a bigger difference in our daily lives than to commit ourselves to better intentions. In the words of Emerson, "A good intention clothes itself with sudden power." So upgrading the quality of our aspirations is a high-leverage activity. As human beings, we grow exponentially when we improve our intentions — and then act accordingly.

Our intentions make up one of the most important elements of our character. That is why we need to be honest about them and work hard to improve them. If we concentrated more on primary things like these (and less on peripheral matters), our lives would leap forward.

Don't bother much about your feelings. When they are humble, loving, brave,
give thanks for them; when they are conceited, selfish, cowardly, ask to have
them altered. In neither case are they you, but only a thing that happens to
you. What matters is your intentions and your behavior.
C. S. LEWIS

LIMITS

> The greed of gain has no time or limit to its capaciousness.
> RABINDRANATH TAGORE

WITH TODAY'S READING, SOMEONE WILL SURELY SAY, "BUT GARY, HOW CAN 'LIMITS' POSSIBLY BE AN 'ENTHUSIASTIC' IDEA." Well, I know that in the current culture we hardly ever think of restrictions as being good, but hear me out. Life without any limits would not be the "good life," and so we need to be reminded of the positive role that boundaries (and even rules) can play in our lives.

Consider the quotation at the top from Rabindranath Tagore: "The greed of gain has no time or limit to its capaciousness." Is it not a fact that pride and greed are at the root of many of our problems, both individually and socially? Whatever we want, we think we have a right to it and nothing should be allowed to stand in our way. We respect no limitations on our aims or ambitions, and we abide by no rules that would hinder our desires. So we do great damage — both to ourselves and others — by this autonomous view of our "possibilities."

This is the very thinking that got the human race into trouble in the first place, and frankly, none of us can say that we haven't contributed to the mess. It's time for us to reexamine the idea of limits and learn to see it as a positive concept. Yes, the idea can be carried too far, but that is no reason to throw away the goodness of the thing itself.

Among the many limits that must be respected are those that are *moral* in nature. Given to us by our Creator, these objective, timeless principles cannot be violated without disastrous consequences. Beyond that, however, there are many other limits that we would be wise to respect, such as our *personal* limits. We are finite beings, and we are at our best when we accept that fact. "I am not eternity, but a man; a part of the whole, as an hour is of the day" (Epictetus).

Erwin W. Lutzer once wrote, "Self-acceptance is basically a spiritual issue. What it boils down to is this: are we able to thank the Creator for the way he made us?" We won't begin to recover from the illnesses that plague us until we lay down our rebellion, recover a sense of reverence, and learn to appreciate our nature as created beings.

> Worship is pictured at its best in Isaiah when the young prophet became aware of the Father, aware of his own limitations, aware of the Father's directives, and aware of the task at hand.
> RAYMOND C. ORTLUND

ATTITUDES

> I have often thought that the best way to define a man's character would be
> to seek out the particular mental or moral attitude in which, when it came
> upon him, he felt himself most deeply and intensely active and alive. At such
> moments there is a voice inside which speaks and says: "This is the real me!"
>
> WILLIAM JAMES

ATTITUDE IS NOT THE MOST IMPORTANT THING. Despite what the motivational speakers usually say, attitude is not the prime requirement for the most important things in life. That requirement goes a good bit deeper than attitude, and here it is: *truth in our "maps" of reality, i.e., our principles and beliefs.* As Stephen R. Covey used to point out, if our maps are inaccurate, a positive mental attitude will only get us to the wrong destination faster.

But, of course, this doesn't mean that attitude's not important at all. Clearly, it is very important, and that's what we want to emphasize today. As William James indicated in the quotation above, one of the prime indicators of a person's character is the "particular mental or moral attitude in which . . . he [feels] himself most deeply and intensely active and alive." Our attitudes well describe who we really are.

Two things about attitude are amazing to me: (1) we can alter our attitudes anytime we want to, and (2) when we do alter them, our lives can change radically. As William James famously said, "People can alter their lives by altering their attitudes."

Many freedoms can be taken away from us, but the freedom to determine our own attitude is one that can't be robbed by any other person. No one has written about this more eloquently than Viktor Frankl, a survivor of the WWII concentration camps in Europe. He wrote, "We who lived in the concentration camps can remember the men who walked through the huts comforting others, giving away their last piece of bread. They may have been few in number, but they offer sufficient proof that everything can be taken away from a man but one thing: the last of his freedoms — to choose one's attitude in any given set of circumstances, to choose one's own way."

So my prayer for you is simple: do not go with the flow, but choose your own attitude — and be very careful what choice you make.

> The long span of the bridge of your life is supported by countless cables
> called habits, attitudes, and desires . . . Make the cables strong!
>
> L. G. ELLIOTT

SHARING

Immortal Love, forever full,
Forever flowing free,
Forever shared, forever whole,
A never-ebbing sea!

JOHN GREENLEAF WHITTIER

IT IS A WELL-KNOWN FACT THAT LOVE AND SHARING ARE IN-SEPARABLE. Love always wants to share, and sharing, in its highest form, is always an act of love. We see this clearly in the love that God has for us, His creatures, and since we are made in His image, we naturally desire something like this kind of love between ourselves.

There are many angles from which we can look at the idea of "sharing." At its most basic level, we probably think of the importance (and value) of sharing our possessions with those less fortunate. But, of course, there are many other things to share. Our time may be one of the hardest, since it is a scarcer commodity. By far the most important thing we can share, however, is our heart. We never do a finer thing than when we open up and share our innermost self with another person. "All who joy would win must share it. Happiness was born a twin" (Lord George Noel Gordon Byron).

This kind of deep communion reaches its highest form when it is mutual, and so it is important for us to recognize the give-and-take aspect of sharing. We must have not only the courage to share ourselves but also the humility to receive that which others share with us.

And I would suggest there is a kind of sharing that is even more profound than any of the above. We hear about this in the "Servant Songs" in the Book of Isaiah. There, it is said about the Servant, "Surely he has borne our griefs and carried our sorrows." When we voluntarily, and at great personal cost, share in the sufferings of others, we discover what true love is all about, especially when we agree to be the one who suffers so that the one who is loved might not have to.

Stephen S. Wise said, "An unshared life is not living." There may be nothing nearer to the heartbeat of our existence than the need to share ourselves with others and to enter their experience. When we do this, we show others their own virtues in ways that empower them.

The greatest good you can do for another is not just
to share your riches but to reveal to him his own.

BENJAMIN DISRAELI

CONFIDENTIALITY

> No receipt openeth the heart, but a true friend, to whom
> you may impart griefs, joys, fears, hopes, suspicions, counsels,
> and whatsoever lieth upon the heart to oppress it.
>
> FRANCIS BACON

A FRIEND WHO WILL MAINTAIN CONFIDENTIALITY WITHIN THE RELATIONSHIP IS A TREASURE. We should not expect to have more than a few such friends in a lifetime, but when we do have them, we should not underestimate their value in our lives.

The word "confidentiality" comes from the Latin *fidere* ("to trust"). It describes the state of a relationship in which at least one of the parties is able to "confide" in the other, having "confidence" that the thing being entrusted will not be made known. For example, you probably trust your doctor to maintain confidentiality in regard to the personal medical matters you divulge to him or her.

Trust, then, is the very core of confidentiality. When you confide private information to someone else, you are entering into a trust agreement with them. They are to keep the confidence just as if they were safeguarding a prized physical possession you asked them to take care of. Obviously, you should not do this with anyone who is not *trustworthy* — and by that I mean someone who does not have a solid track record of faithfulness, reliability, and steadfastness.

It goes without saying that we appreciate those whom we can trust, but the more important question is: can others trust us? Are we capable of maintaining the same confidentiality that we desire from others? If so, then we have given a great gift to those who have to deal with us. And this is a gift that it takes many years to be able to give. A character that is known to be trustworthy is not acquired overnight, but it is well worth the years of self-discipline needed to build it up.

Certainly we should be careful about confidentiality in both directions. We shouldn't carelessly confide in other people, but neither should we be careless in handling the trust they extend to us.

It is, perhaps, with our deepest sorrows that we should select our confidants the most carefully. We do well to share our griefs, but only with those who are utterly faithful . . . and tenderly understanding.

> If thou tellest the sorrows of thy heart, let it be to him in whose
> countenance thou mayest be assured of prompt consolation.
>
> SAADI

MEMORY

Recall it as often as you wish,
a happy memory never wears out.

LIBBIE FUDIM

SOMETIMES THE FACULTY OF MEMORY CAN BE A BIT OF A NUISANCE, BUT MOST OF THE TIME, WE'RE GLAD WE HAVE IT. How much poorer our emotional lives would be if as soon as something happened, it was erased forever from our minds and hearts. The nourishing, strengthening recollection of events in the past is a large part of what makes it possible for us to grow and improve as persons.

Do you have a good memory? It's a fact that, barring any physical disability of memory, we remember the things that we pay the most attention to. With names, for example, those who are good at remembering names are those who pay enough conscious attention to people they talk to that their names stick. So when somebody remembers our name, we feel honored. We feel honored because we know that their remembrance of our name indicates that we registered in their thinking. So, in return, do we honor those around us with the things that we keep in our memory? When people know that we can be counted on to remember things that are special to them and to their relationship with us, that's a fine way to be known.

Memory is a bittersweet affair, to be sure. It brings back to us the moments when our hearts were bathed in the sweetest joys we've ever known, but precisely because it deals with the past, memory also reminds us that we no longer have some of those things in our present possession. But that's not all bad. Bitterness and sweetness do sometimes go together to make a delightful taste. I ache with longing, for example, when I remember my childhood. But the ache is anything but unpleasant. It's delicious. I wouldn't have it any other way.

Oft in the stilly night,
Ere Slumber's chain has bound me,
Fond Memory brings the light
Of other days around me;
The smiles, the tears,
Of boyhood's years,
The words of love then spoken;
The eyes that shone
Now dimmed and gone,
The cheerful hearts now broken.

THOMAS MOORE

October 1

DETERMINATION

Nothing of worth or weight can be achieved with half a mind,
with a faint heart, and with a lame endeavor.

ISAAC BARROW

WHEN YOU THINK OF DETERMINATION, WHAT OTHER
WORDS COME TO MIND? Usually, we think of persistence and
perseverance. But while determination can certainly have that meaning, think more carefully for a moment. To "determine" something
is to "decide" concerning it, and persistence in the pursuit of a goal
grows out of determination in this more basic sense. Those who are
the most tenacious in pursuing their goals are those who have decided on them the most firmly. On the other hand, many people fail
to reach their goals because they haven't really made up their minds.
Having made no real commitment, they haven't *determined* to do it.

Half-made decisions are a huge problem in the world. Most of
us suffer from failing to clearly determine what we're going to do. So
we limp forward in life, wavering and vacillating. In the middle of our
work, we have second thoughts and we give up.

But, of course, there is an opposite problem. That is the problem
of never evaluating what we're doing. Stubbornly fixed on a goal, we
never stop to think whether that's a goal we ought to be pursuing.

So what should we do? How can we learn the positive kind of
determination and avoid the negative kind? Here is a three-fold plan:
(1) We should carefully consider our goals before we commit ourselves to them. This is the stage at which we listen to our conscience.
(2) Having determined our goals, we work hard to reach them. Here
is where persistence comes in. (3) We reevaluate our goals during
periods of rest. Thomas à Kempis said it well: "Determine a plan of
action in the morning, and then evaluate yourself at night."

All of us are visionaries to some extent. We see goals that would
be worthy of pursuit. But as we begin to pursue them, our vision fails
us. We can't see how things are going to work out, so we quit. What
we need is a commitment that will keep us moving toward conscience-
driven goals even when the darkness sets in and vision fails us. Wisely
determined goals should be worked on . . . with determination!

The will is the strong blind man who carries
on his shoulders the lame man who can see.

ARTHUR SCHOPENHAUER

MEDIATION

Mediate: to interpose between parties, as the equal friend of each,
especially for the purpose of effecting a reconciliation or agreement.

A N O N Y M O U S

IF YOU ARE EVER CALLED ON TO MEDIATE A DISPUTE BE-
TWEEN SOME OTHER PEOPLE, YOU SHOULD CONSIDER THAT
AN HONOR. Helping others settle their differences requires not only
wisdom but fairness and justice, not to mention courage and patience.
To be known as people who have these qualities, so that others look
to us in their quest for peace, is a reputation worth aspiring to.

Roy Springer, a submarine commander who had to know how to
keep people working together in a confined environment, recalls a day
when he was a child playing in the sandbox with several other kids
from his neighborhood. An argument broke out and things got ugly.
Since the sandbox was right under the kitchen window of his house,
his mother finally leaned out of the window and said, "Roy, you get
everybody happy out there, or you're coming in." Sometimes media-
tion skills are learned early and in rather unlikely places!

Let me, however, make one thing clear. Acquiring the wisdom of
a mediator is a fine gift that we can give to others, but I caution you
against involving yourself in others' disputes when you've not been
asked to mediate. In the Book of Proverbs, there is this saying: "He
who passes by and meddles in a quarrel not his own is like one who
takes a dog by the ears." If you've ever picked up a dog by the ears,
you won't need me to explain why this is not a good idea, and injecting ourselves into a disagreement among others is just about as foolish. So learn how to mediate, but wait to be asked to do so.

In my experience, one of the main challenges of the mediator is
to get both parties to lighten up and take themselves somewhat less
seriously. While it's true that some disagreements are very serious, it's
also true that conflicts distort our perspective. A measure of lightheartedness can restore a more balanced perspective and remind us
that despite the momentary crisis, there are still some things in this
old world worth smiling about. A little laughter can go a long way.

One hearty laugh together will bring enemies into a closer
communion of heart than hours spent on both sides in inward
wrestling with the mental demon of uncharitable feeling.

W I L L I A M   J A M E S

ENLIGHTENMENT

The action of the creative individual may be described as a twofold motion of withdrawal-and-return: withdrawal for the purpose of his personal enlightenment, return for the task of enlightening his fellow men.

ARNOLD J. TOYNBEE

ENLIGHTENMENT, AS TOYNBEE SUGGESTED, MAY BE THOUGHT OF IN TWO DIRECTIONS: RECEIVING AND GIVING. It's a delightful experience when we receive enlightenment, but this rarely happens without the help of someone else. So it shouldn't surprise us when the process goes in reverse and others report that we have enlightened them. Enlightenment is a two-way street.

But what exactly is enlightenment? The concept is important in Eastern philosophy, of course, but that lies outside the scope of our discussion here. For our purpose, let's just say that enlightenment is growth in our understanding. Light is a universal metaphor for knowledge. If someone said, "I finally saw the light," or "It suddenly dawned on me," everybody would know what he meant. To "see the light" on some subject is to recognize the truth about it. And I would suggest that true enlightenment involves not just knowledge but also wisdom. It's not enough to know the right answer to a question — we also need the wisdom to know what to do with it.

But returning to enlightenment as a two-way street, we are at our best when we pursue knowledge and wisdom for the purpose of serving those around us. Even when we're seeking our own enlightenment, that shouldn't be a selfish pursuit. We should want greater understanding because it will help us to better serve the needs of others.

As we all know, enlightenment carries with it the danger of pride. When we see a subject even a little more clearly than someone else, it is easy to begin thinking in condescending ways. But pride is the most hellish thing in the world, and if it is not destroyed, it will kill us.

Honorably pursued and carefully governed, however, enlightenment is a prize. All of the worst things in our lives are the result of either ignorance or untruth. Three thousand years ago, King Solomon was not wasting words when he said, "Wisdom is supreme; therefore get wisdom. Though it cost all you have, get understanding."

So irresistible is the transformative power of enlightenment that your life seems to be shifted into a new dimension, opened to new and unsuspected possibilities.

EUGEN HERRIGEL

MORALITY

We laugh at honor and are shocked to find traitors in our midst.

C. S. LEWIS

MORALITY IS A SUBJECT THAT IS PERILOUS TO NEGLECT. If we pay no attention to it or make careless distinctions between what is moral and what is not, we set ourselves up to have our hearts broken in tragic ways. Morality is an enormously important subject. We can't trivialize it without allowing others to do so — and we may regret the day we ever said that morality is a matter of opinion.

Ernest Hemingway produced some masterful prose, but he spoke absurdly when he said, "What is moral is what you feel good after and what is immoral is what you feel bad after." The truth is, our feelings are not an infallible guide to what is moral, although they can surely give us some helpful information about it. Morality is defined by objective, timeless standards, and deep down in our hearts, we all know that this is so. If we ever use the words "ought" or "should," we are acknowledging that there is a standard of right and wrong that goes beyond personal preference, social norms, and cultural traditions.

But there is something else that must be said: true morality must be in our inward hearts as well as in our outward behavior. We wouldn't trust a person who only did the right thing because he was afraid of the social consequences of doing wrong. We must learn to *think* morally. As Oswald Chambers said, "Morality is not only correct conduct on the outside, but correct thinking within where only God sees."

This inward aspect of morality is much more difficult than the outward. "It is so much easier to do good than to be good" (B. C. Forbes). It takes discipline and training, usually over a long period, to acquire a moral character that is stable and predictable, but it is one of the worthiest goals in life. "Moral excellence comes about as a result of habit. We become just by doing just acts, temperate by doing temperate acts, brave by doing brave acts" (Aristotle).

Of all the gifts we may give to others, morality ranks as one of the highest. It marks a huge step in our individual growth when we see that our friends and loved ones will be blessed by our personal decision to do what is right, simply because it is right.

Every man takes care that his neighbor shall not cheat him.
But a day comes when he begins to care that he does not cheat his neighbor.

RALPH WALDO EMERSON

DIGNITY

Back of all, above all, before all is God; first in sequential order,
above in rank and station, exalted in dignity and honor.

A. W. TOZER

DIGNITY IS A DIFFICULT SUBJECT BECAUSE IT HAS BECOME SO UNPOPULAR. It is often confused with snobbishness, stuffi-ness, formality, pride, and self-centeredness. But while the concept of dignity can easily slide off into these ditches, there is a higher sense in which we should think of dignity, especially in regard to others.

Our word "dignity" comes from the Latin *dignus* ("worthy"). To possess dignity is to have worth — not pretended worth or socially fashionable worth, but real worth. So in what sense can we say that any human being has worth? Let's think about that for a moment.

As A. W. Tozer suggests, dignity (like all other good things) be-gins with God. Having been created by God in His image, and thereby given an honor above other earthly creatures, we possess great dignity. It is derived from God, to be sure, but it is real and it is important. Humility never lets one forget the dignity that comes from having been made in God's image. "Religion in its humility restores man to his only dignity, the courage to live by grace" (George Santayana). Acceptance of our status before God is the only way to retain our created dignity.

But what would be some practical applications of this? I believe the applications fall into two important categories:

(1) In regard to ourselves. Each of needs to see that we have worth, and this needs to be grounded in our nature as God-created beings, as well as our acceptance of the principles of virtuous character. This statement by Ruby Dee makes a good point: "The kind of beauty I want most is the hard-to-get kind that comes from within — strength, courage, dignity." Wouldn't it be great if we all "beautified" ourselves with traits befitting those who bear the image of God, the very God who made us in the first place?

(2) In regard to others. Even more important than our own dignity is the dignity and worth of other people. And it is through the exhibi-tion of authentic love — including traits like gentleness and kindness — that we help others see what they're really worth. *Let's give this gift!*

Gentleness includes . . . [the] gracious courtesy
that causes others to retain their self-esteem and dignity.

CHARLES R. SWINDOLL

INTERACTIVENESS

If one person falls, the other person can reach out to help.
But those who are alone when they fall have no one to help them.

BOOK OF ECCLESIASTES

INTERACTIVENESS, AT LEAST AS IT APPLIES TO PEOPLE, IS THE WILLINGNESS TO ACT UPON OTHERS — AND BE ACTED UPON BY THEM. It means we acknowledge the interconnectedness of our lives and embrace the privilege of engaging and influencing each other.

Just being willing to *act* is important, and some people are too lazy to do even that. But it's even more important to *interact,* that is, to interweave our lives with the lives around us in ways that are beneficial. The word "engagement" is too good a word to limit to the process of marriage betrothal. We need to "engage" the lives of many other people also. And interactiveness is more than a deed to be done once in a while. It should be a habit, a pattern of living, and even a character trait.

It is a fact that we can be surrounded by other people and not interact with them. In some situations, it is not polite to do so, and I'm not suggesting that the person next to you on the airplane or the subway is always going to be someone you need to interact with. But in many cases where interaction would be perfectly fine, we still don't do it, and that's a shame. Much of the goodness of life is lost when we don't unplug the "earphones" through which we're listening to our private "music" and communicate with some real, live human beings.

(1) Strength. As the wise saying from Ecclesiastes indicates, we are stronger when our lives are connected than when they are isolated.

(2) Learning. Book learning alone is a poor education, and those who don't engage with real people are usually deficient in their wisdom.

(3) Honor. We honor others by interacting with them. Few gifts are greater than simply saying, "I am willing to communicate with you."

(4) Joy. As social creatures, we experience a deep sense of rightness when we interact well. Even when difficult, the process produces joy.

All things considered, then, we ought to welcome interaction with others. It's not a chore; it's a blessing. And here is something else to think about: we should be the kind of people with whom others *want* to interact. Whether or not we're "attractive" outwardly, inwardly we can all have *characters that attract rather than repel.*

Bring thy soul and interchange with mine.

PASCAL

AGREEMENT

Friends mean well, even when they hurt you.
But when an enemy puts his arm around your shoulder — watch out!
BOOK OF PROVERBS

THERE ARE THINGS WORSE THAN DISAGREEMENT, AND ONE OF THEM IS PRETENDED AGREEMENT. As the Book of Proverbs says, "When an enemy puts his arm around your shoulder — watch out!"

Nevertheless, true agreement is a fine thing. We should be prepared to work harder to achieve it than we sometimes are, and it involves far more than simply "agreeing to disagree agreeably." J. William Fulbright made the point in regard to political differences, but the principle applies just as well to many other differences: "Insofar as it represents a genuine reconciliation of differences, a consensus is a fine thing; insofar as it represents a concealment of differences, it is a miscarriage of democratic procedure." While we're working toward a "genuine reconciliation of differences" we do need to treat one another courteously, but mere courtesy and "agreeableness" fall short of that which can rightfully be called "agreement."

Reaching agreement on significant issues is hard work, but it is worth the effort. And even if some of our differences turn out to be "irreconcilable," we will have profited from working on them. It is silly to say that an ideal shouldn't be pursued just because it is unreachable in the world as it is today. Perfect love, perfect justice, and perfect peace are worth pursuing — and so is perfect agreement.

But, of course, not all our differences will be ironed out in this world. So in addition to pursuing agreement, there is something else we need to do: *in our disagreements, we must remember the things that we still agree on.* "We are," as Charles Caleb Colton wrote, "more inclined to hate one another for points on which we differ, than to love one another for points on which we agree." Some say we should do nothing with an adversary except make war — but I disagree! We shouldn't be afraid to emphasize what we have in common, even with our bitterest rivals. If there is any chance of resolving our conflicts, it's probably going to require reaching across the gap and supporting one another wherever possible, looking for every bit of common ground.

If men would consider not so much wherein they differ, as wherein they agree,
there would be far less of uncharitableness and angry feeling in the world.
JOSEPH ADDISON

ADAPTABILITY

Life is the continuous adjustment of internal relations to external relations.
HERBERT SPENCER

IF WE DO NOT ADAPT, WE DO NOT SURVIVE. Spencer was not exaggerating when he said that life is a "continuous adjustment." The reasons why we must make adjustments are many, but for today's meditation let's consider just three things that require us to do so:

(1) Undesirable circumstances. The real world is far from the ideal world we long to live in. So we have a choice: confronted with difficult, unpleasant, sorrowful, or painful conditions, we can cave in and become mere victims, we can accept the world with a bleak fatalism, or we can use our freedom to find constructive ways of *adapting*. "Learn to adjust yourself to the conditions you have to endure," wrote William Frederick Book, "but make a point of trying to alter or correct conditions so that they are most favorable to you."

(2) Change. Sometimes it is just the ever-changing nature of life that requires us to adapt. It might be nice if once we got our lives the way we want them to be (more or less), they would stay that way, but as we all know, nothing stays the same for very long. So next year will present us with a new situation, and we will have to adapt to it.

(3) Other people. Perhaps our greatest challenge is to adjust ourselves helpfully to the people around us. Some of the ways people differ are insignificant, but some are very serious. When we don't adapt, we make ourselves miserable, but when we adapt to others with love, wisdom, and courage, we give them a very beautiful gift.

T. S. Eliot wrote, "It is not necessarily those lands which are the most fertile or most favoured in climate that seem to me the happiest, but those in which a long struggle of adaptation between man and his environment has brought out the best qualities in both." Do you see the connection he makes between adaptation and happiness? It's true, even if it sounds contradictory: *we are happiest when we're busy making the adaptations that life calls on us to make.* And rightly engaging in the process of adaptation is a big part of what constitutes human virtue and goodness in this world. Eventually, we'll have to answer for our choices!

We talk about "circumstances beyond our control." None of us
have control over our circumstances, but we are responsible for the way
we pilot ourselves in the midst of things as they are.
OSWALD CHAMBERS

RITUAL

Religion that is merely ritual and ceremonial can never satisfy. Neither
can we be satisfied by a religion that is merely humanitarian or
serviceable to mankind. Man's craving is for the spiritual.

SAMUEL M. SHOEMAKER

WE OFTEN THINK OF "RITUAL" IN REGARD TO RELIGION, AND
IT IS A CONTROVERSIAL CONCEPT. The trend nowadays is toward informality and spontaneity, so not many people see any value in
ritual or ceremony. My personal opinion, however, is that what most
people reject is not ritual itself but what we might call "mere" ritual,
i.e., ritual that is nothing more than empty formalism. Yet ritual is a
good thing, when it is accompanied by virtuous character and heartfelt emotion, and we should not be too quick to throw it away.

Ritual, of course, is a part of many activities other than religion.
But what does it mean? The word comes from group of Latin terms
centered on the idea of "customary usage." Suppose there is a set of
actions that are to be performed. If the actions are carried out "ritu-
ally," that means they are done properly or fittingly, according to the
established or customary pattern. A "ritual," then, is a procedure that
is faithfully or regularly followed. I suggest that ritual is a benefit
(when it is done thoughtfully) because it makes two connections:

Ritual connects us to other people. Good things happen when we, at
least occasionally, engage in a series of actions that have been done by
many other people in just the same way. Such a "customary usage" is
a benefit because it reminds us that we are privileged to participate in
something much bigger — and more important — than ourselves.

Ritual connects us to the past and the future. There is an old
Christian hymn that depicts the Lord's Supper as an act connecting
us to Jesus' death and His eventual return "by one bright chain of
loving rite." *By one bright chain of loving rite.* Do you see how a good
ritual looks both backward and forward? Is that not a good thing?

It is often nothing but self-centeredness that rejects ritual, and
nothing but a lack of historical consciousness that fails to appreciate its
value. Yes, ritual can degenerate into meaningless routine, but it doesn't
have to. Sincerely entered into, it is one of life's richest treasures.

It is superstition to put one's hope in formalities;
but it is pride to be unwilling to submit to them.

PASCAL

October 10

FORTITUDE

Be strong!
It matters not how deep entrenched the wrong,
How hard the battle goes, the day how long;
Faint not — fight on! Tomorrow comes the song.

MALTBIE D. BABCOCK

WE CHOOSE TO BE OUR STRONGEST WHEN WE BELIEVE THAT OUR CAUSE IS WORTHY AND THAT IT IS GOING TO BE TRIUMPHANT. Even if our part is to die on the battlefield, it makes a big difference to know that our personal "defeat" has contributed to the victory of the cause for which we fought. The charge "Be strong!" is heard best by soldiers who know that "tomorrow comes the song."

But the word "fortitude" does not simply mean "strength" or "courage." It has a special meaning. A "fort" is a place strengthened ("fortified") for the defense of a particular territory. So in its most literal sense, "fortitude" has to do with defense: *the person with fortitude possesses the ability to resist attack.* He or she has the strength — and also the will — to defend things that are worthy of defense.

It should go without saying (but these days it needs to be said) that there are some things that do, in fact, need to be defended. Granted, we need to be careful in identifying what those things are, and even when we've correctly identified the things that should be defended, we've still got to exercise wisdom in selecting the means for their defense. But that said, it remains true that fortitude is an honorable trait. The person who will not defend anything is not worthy of the protections provided by the fortitude of others.

So we must choose to have fortitude, and that is an important point in itself. Yes, we must acquire both wisdom and skill, but when it comes down to it, the strong people are those who choose to be.

What about you? Do your friends think of fortitude when they think of you? Does your family think of you this way? I hope so. If others can look to you for "strength to defend," then you are a blessing to them. And if by the simple, quiet example of your courage you impart courage to them, they will thank God for you.

In our little sphere, it is not the most active people to whom we owe the most. It is the lives like stars, which simply pour down on us the calm light of their bright and faithful being, up to which we look, and out of which we gather the deepest calm and courage.

PHILLIPS BROOKS

FACTUALNESS

If a man will kick a fact out of the window, when he
comes back he finds it again in the chimney corner.
RALPH WALDO EMERSON

REALITY IS A TOUGH OPPONENT. In the long run, it can't be de-feated, and even in the short run, we find that factualness is hard to suppress. Truth simply has a strength that falsehood can't match. When misinformation has failed and disappeared, facts are still there to be dealt with. If truth is stranger than fiction, it is also stronger.

Unfortunately, a good many of us spend a great deal of time fighting against factualness. We run away from the facts. We spin them and selectively present them in ways that suit our purposes. We may even try to refute them or deny them. But when we are done, the facts are still the facts. They stubbornly refuse to go away.

One of the great milestones in life is the point at which we learn to be content with the facts. Yes, an acceptance of inconvenient facts requires humility, and it may also require some hard changes: apologies, adjustments, repentance, sacrifices, and a number of other courageous things. But however difficult these may be, what a relief it is not to be fighting that losing battle anymore: *the one against what is real.* "Let us take things as we find them. Let us not attempt to distort them into what they are not. We cannot make facts. All our wishing cannot change them. We must use them" (John Henry Newman).

But as important as it is, factualness is not enough. "Facts mean nothing unless they are rightly understood, rightly related, and rightly interpreted" (R. L. Long). Beyond knowing what is real, we use our factual information in constructive ways. And in communicating the facts, we must learn the importance of kindness and grace.

A commitment to factualness is not an option; it is a duty. In our relationships with others, and even in our own thinking, we are honor-bound to get the facts. No matter what situation we face, nothing less than the facts will do. Checking and double-checking to validate what we've heard is hard work, and many will not take the time to do it. But factualness is a part of truthfulness. It is a part of honesty. People of integrity will not settle for less than what is true.

Every man has a right to be wrong in his opinions.
But no man has a right to be wrong in his facts.
BERNARD BARUCH

APPOINTMENTS

Unfaithfulness in the keeping of an appointment is dishonesty.
You may as well borrow a person's money as his time.

HORACE MANN

AN APPOINTMENT IS AN ARRANGEMENT TO DO SOMETHING OR MEET SOMEONE AT A PARTICULAR TIME AND PLACE. Many of the important meetings in life have to be scheduled in the form of an appointment. If you needed to see your doctor, for example, you wouldn't just wait to run into her around town. But in what sense can we say that an "appointment" is an enthusiastic idea?

To start with, I would suggest that we often improve our relationships when we make appointments with our friends and loved ones. In other words, we need to do better than simply say, "Let's get together for lunch sometime" or "That museum would be fun to visit" or "We need to discuss our disagreement on that subject." Procrastination plagues most of our lives, and crucial things often go undone if we don't make positive plans to do them. In practical terms, that means making an appointment — deciding specifically when and where such things will be taken care of.

Appointments give definition to our existence. They move ideas out of the realm of wishful thinking and into the realm of practice. By saying *when* we will do something, we make a more definite statement than saying we *ought* to do it. We state a goal and not just a wish.

For an appointment to be meaningful, however, it has to be backed up by commitment. If we don't keep appointments, we may as well not make them. But that is precisely why arrangements to do specific things at specific times are valuable. By closing off some of our options, they challenge us to higher levels of commitment (and perhaps even sacrifice). They are exercises in promise-keeping.

Making and keeping appointments may not seem like a big deal, but it has to do with dependability, which is a very big deal. If you're the kind of person who says when you will do things and then actually shows up to do them, you have a trait that is surprisingly rare in the world. Because it is rare, you will find yourself being trusted, counted on, and probably given greater and greater responsibilities.

We are not saints, but we have kept our appointments.
How many people can boast as much?

SAMUEL BECKETT

GOODNESS

Do all the good you can, to all the people you can,
in all the ways you can, as often as ever you can, as long as you can.
CHARLES HADDON SPURGEON

IT IS AN AGE-OLD QUESTION, AS IMPORTANT AS IT IS SIMPLE: WHAT IS GOOD? None of us has a perfect understanding of goodness, and we should admit our fallibility here. Rousseau was right: "We always love what is good or what we think is good; it is in our judgment of what is good that we can make mistakes." Nevertheless, most of us know a good deal more about goodness than we are practicing, and so let's make that our focus. How can we better give to others the gift of whatever goodness we know right now?

Perhaps one of the greatest suggestions that can be made is to focus more on the small things and the daily things. As Samuel Johnson observed, "He who waits to do a great deal of good at once, will never do anything." So let's not wait for the spotlight to be turned on and a newsworthy opportunity to present itself. True goodness is content to do simple deeds and do them well.

Similarly, true goodness is not flamboyant. As David Grayson put it, "Goodness is uneventful. It does not flash, it glows." And that may be why the most impactful people in the world are not the celebrities, the leaders, or the conspicuously talented individuals. It is usually the simple, ordinary folks who, without getting any credit for it, just go quietly about the business of showing love and kindness.

In this world, you are not going to understand or implement perfect goodness, and neither am I. But, as with all the other qualities we have discussed in this book, we can at least make progress. We can learn to be better people. The question is not so much where we stand as it is which direction we are moving. And I must be candid with you here: *I believe we must be moving toward the perfect standard of God's goodness.* As Daniel Webster said, "Real goodness does not attach itself merely to this life — it points to another world."

Finally, I want you to understand that it's a joyful privilege to engage in goodness. We don't adopt good character or good conduct primarily for the way those things make us feel, but they are, in fact, joyous things. I invite you to take goodness for a test drive.

Learn the luxury of doing good.
OLIVER GOLDSMITH

ACHIEVEMENT

Thou shalt ever joy at eventide if thou spend the day fruitfully.
THOMAS Á KEMPIS

MENTION "ACHIEVEMENT" AND MANY PEOPLE THINK ONLY OF "GREAT" ACCOMPLISHMENTS. But the greatness of a person's achievement should not be measured by whether it makes the news. It consists of down-to-earth "fruitfulness," as Thomas á Kempis suggests, and it should be a daily occurrence for all of us.

But if we're going to engage in good, helpful deeds, intending to do them is not sufficient — we must actually do them. The word "achievement" implies that a goal has been reached. And so, in the words of a biblical proverb, "Let not the soldier who puts on his armor boast like the one who takes it off." Henry Ward Beecher used a different metaphor to make the point: "It is not the going out of port, but the coming in, that determines the success of a voyage."

No matter who we are or what our circumstances may be, there are achievements that lie within our abilities and opportunities. But to achieve what we're capable of, we must do three difficult things:

Focus. Perhaps you wince, as I do, when you read this: "Give me a person who says, 'This one thing I do, and not these fifty things I dabble in'" (Dwight Lyman Moody). To achieve, we must *decide.*

Accept risk. Playing it safe rarely results in worthy achievements, so we must desire to do more than hedge our bets and protect ourselves. Only those who dare to fail greatly can ever achieve greatly.

Deal rightly with objections. We should certainly listen to objections and weigh them conscientiously, but if every objector must be satisfied before we act, we'll never accomplish anything excellent.

To achieve the work that is our mission in life, we'll need to be powerfully motivated. And in the end, that must come from deep within us. To focus, accept risk, and deal rightly with objections, we must have an inward "Yes!" burning big enough to keep us going. "Doing becomes the natural overflow of being when the pressure within is stronger than the pressure without" (Lois Lebar). I urge you to find your principles, your purpose, your passion — and get to work. It doesn't matter whether you win awards. *Just spend your days "fruitfully."*

The world is divided into people who do things and people who
get the credit; try to belong to the first class — there's far less competition.
DWIGHT WHITNEY MORROW

DISCRETION

The better part of valour is discretion.
WILLIAM SHAKESPEARE

THE WORDS "DISCREET" AND "DISCRETE" HAVE AN INTEREST-ING LINK. Both come from a Latin verb meaning "to separate." Two things that are "discrete" are separate or distinct from one another, but to be "discreet" means to show prudence or self-restraint. What, then, does "discretion" have to do with "separation"? Well, to be discreet one has to separate the situations where a word or deed would be appropriate from the situations where they would not be. If there is "a time to keep quiet and a time to speak out" (Book of Ecclesiastes), discretion is the ability to distinguish between the two wisely.

In these days of unrestrained verbiage (particularly in our digital media), the concept of *thinking* something without *saying* it appears downright old-fashioned. Yet the trait of discretion has not lost its value. As the saying goes, "Much that may be thought cannot wisely be said." By indiscretion in our words, much harm is being done to our relationships, and I would suggest even to our culture.

But discretion doesn't just apply to our words; it should also govern our actions. Discretion is, in Shakespeare's well-known words, "the better part of valour." That statement is no exaggeration. It often takes more courage to hold back our impulses than to give in to them. What is needed in life is not merely strength — but rather strength under control, guided and disciplined by discretion.

Leaders, especially, need discretion. Without it, they often make disastrous decisions, ruining themselves and hurting those they lead. "Great ability without discretion comes almost invariably to a tragic end" (Leon Gambetta). And unfortunately, many arrive at leadership lacking this qualification. "One can pass on responsibility, but not the discretion that goes with it" (Benvenuto Cellini).

Discretion is not only for leaders, however. "Only discretion allows intimacy, which depends on shared reticence, on what is not said — unsolvable things that would leave the other person ill at ease" (Hector Bianciotti). So let's learn, even in private, when not to speak.

Four things are the property of friendship: love, affection, security, and joy. And four things must be tested in friendship: faith, intention, discretion, and patience.
AELRED OF RIEVAULX

LIGHT

Light! Nature's resplendent robe;
Without whose vesting beauty
All were wrapt in gloom.
FRANCIS THOMPSON SHELLEY

I DOUBT IF THERE HAS EVER BEEN A LITERATURE IN ANY CUL-
TURE IN WHICH LIGHT WAS NOT A SYMBOL FOR TRUTH AND
GOODNESS. And likewise, darkness has always been a symbol for
untruth and evil. These symbols are universal because the conflict
between good and evil is universal. "What excites and interests the
looker-on at life, what the romances and the statues celebrate, and the
grim civic monuments remind us of, is the everlasting battle of the
powers of light with those of darkness" (William James).

Should we not want, in every possible way, to be the friends of
light, influencing those around us in ways that shed light rather than
spread darkness? Rather than darken, should we not wish to brighten?

Truth. This is, by far, the greatest form of light, and it's even
more important than the physical light that permits our eyes to see.
It is hard to imagine a problem in the world that does not stem from
untruth, delusion, or misunderstanding. We can have no greater mission than to seek truth — and then devote ourselves to its influence.

Healing. Truth has a healing effect mentally, emotionally, and
spiritually, just as light has that effect physically. Disease and dysfunc-
tion fester in the darkness, so to whatever extent we can illuminate
the lives of others, we will be agents of healing and health.

Hope. Few things in life are more precious than hope. Worse than
no hope, however, is false hope. So again, it's the light of *truth* that is
needed. We bestow a benefit anytime we give someone hope, and we
do this by dispelling the discouragement that comes from falsehood.

So whether it is truth, healing, or hope that comes from our actions, *we need to be givers of light.* And as Edith Wharton reminded us,
"There are two ways of spreading light: to be the candle or the mirror
that reflects it." Are you looking, then, to give a first-rate gift to your
loved ones? Consider being a light-giver. Help others see things a
little more clearly. *Influence them with truth, healing, and hope.*

I don't have to light all the world,
but I do have to light my part.
ANONYMOUS

SELF-RESPECT

A man has to live with himself, and he should
see to it that he always has good company.
CHARLES EVANS HUGHES

U NFORTUNATELY, MANY PEOPLE THINK SELF-RESPECT JUST
MEANS YOU "LIKE" YOURSELF, REGARDLESS OF THE QUALITY
OF YOUR CONDUCT. So we're taught to disregard anything anyone
else might say, affirm ourselves, actualize ourselves, and basically see
ourselves as having the only opinion that matters.

But genuine self-respect is based on *conscience.* It means we have
done that which, to the best of our knowledge, is the *right* thing to
do. To the extent that others may help us have a better-informed
conscience, they should be listened to — and if we need to make
adjustments to our character or our conduct, we should be willing to
accept the input of those around us. In the end, however, it is our own
conscience that we must listen to, and if we consistently go against
what our conscience tells us is right, we will have no self-respect.

But why is self-respect so important? It's important because if
we lose confidence in our own integrity, that virtually guarantees our
behavior will grow worse and worse. To take a trivial example, let's
suppose you're having trouble getting up early. Each time you fail
that test, you will have less faith in your own willpower. Even as you
set the alarm, you know you won't do what you've determined to do.
So, at least on this point, you've destroyed your self-respect. And this
becomes a self-fulfilling prophecy. Not trusting yourself to keep your
own promises, you *don't* get up when the alarm goes off, sure enough!

Just like the respect of others, self-respect has to be earned. If
you've destroyed your confidence in your own integrity, that trust will
have to be rebuilt bit by bit. Over a period of time, you'll have to keep
bigger and bigger commitments to yourself, until you have a positive
balance in your own "trust account." Then, having followed your conscience often in the past, you'll find it easier to do that in the future.

Self-respect comes from self-discipline. We must say "no" to certain
things and "yes" to others, even when it's not easy. Discipline is painful,
but not nearly as painful as the life of regret that comes from avoiding it.

Never esteem anything as of advantage to you that will
make you break your word or lose your self-respect.
MARCUS AURELIUS

SOCIABILITY

Ez soshubble ez a baskit er kittens.
JOEL CHANDLER HARRIS

A SOCIABLE PERSON IS ONE WHO IS FRIENDLY AND ENJOYS GOOD COMPANY AND CONVERSATION. Get a group of sociable people together and what happens will be fun and frolicsome. If you want a picture of sociability, Joel Chandler Harris's simile is wonderfully apt. What could be more sociable than a "baskit er kittens"?

Sociability is a heartwarming thing. Even if we wouldn't describe ourselves as being particularly sociable, we probably admire those who are. If we were in a restaurant and across the room there was a table at which a group of amiable people were enjoying their time together (not so loudly as to be distracting, perhaps, but still gladly and cheerfully), it would take quite a grouch not to be happy for them. It's refreshing to see folks responding to one another sociably. Most of us would commend that as something good, rather than criticize it.

But here's an interesting question: is sociability just a matter of personality (meaning, in this case, natural temperament), or does it also have to do with one's character? There can be no doubt that some people tend more naturally in the direction of sociability, but is that the end of the matter? I don't think so. Without at all meaning to say that those who are sociable are more virtuous than others, I do think it's true that the principles and values on which we've based our character influence the manner in which we behave toward other people. An appreciative attitude toward others is bound to make us welcome good company and conversation more than a resistant or cynical attitude. For that reason, it would do us all good to inquire what our degree of sociability might be saying about the content of our hearts.

Not everybody will be equally outgoing, obviously, but all of us need to guard against self-centeredness. Not everybody will get equal enjoyment out of human contact and conversation, but we need to make sure we don't resent having to share the world. Our appreciation for our neighbors should be such that the word "community" has a positive ring to it — and we ought to be sociable enough, at least, that interaction with other people doesn't make us miserable!

Society is no comfort
To one not sociable.
WILLIAM SHAKESPEARE

SEARCHING

Errors, like straws, upon the surface flow;
He who would search for pearls must dive below.

JOHN DRYDEN

SEARCHING, IN ONE FORM OR ANOTHER, IS A COMMON CHAR-
ACTERISTIC OF ALL HUMAN BEINGS. Neither the world around
us nor we ourselves possess the perfection we long for. So we search.
But what are the things we should be searching for most of all?

Greater understanding. It is truth that opens the door to progress,
and so we spend a great deal of our time in this world trying to get
better information about the situations we deal with. Few of us aspire
to being philosophers, but at the practical level, that's what we all are.
We want to know, to understand, and to discern. By our very nature,
we are seekers and learners. And if properly pursued, the lifelong
search for understanding doesn't doom us to dissatisfaction. As Pascal
said, "Nothing gives rest but the sincere search for truth."

Greater goals. Many things we should be content with, but our
present state of accomplishment is not one of them. As long as life
lasts, there is good work yet to be done, and the moment we give up
searching for greater goals, we die. The nature of the work we do certainly changes over time, and one of the frustrating things about old
age is the infirmity that makes even simple things harder to do. But
we dare not quit searching for our next opportunity to serve others!

Greater character. Here is the main thing we should keep searching for. It is not the inadequacy of our understanding or our goals that
holds us back; it is the fact that our inner selves are still immature.
There are gaps in our character development that desperately need to
be filled, and even more important, there are sinful habits we need to
repent of. So no matter where we are — at the beginning of life, in
the middle, or near the end — a character more nearly conformed to
our Creator is what we should be searching for.

In the end, however, our deepest searchings are prompted by our
longing for relationship. As personal beings, we yearn to relate perfectly and joyfully to other personal beings, and above all to God. All
our searchings are pointing us toward this, the greatest discovery.

At last you are no longer searching for yourself,
but for another — you are saved.

JEAN GIRAUDOUX

October 20

REACH

Ah, but a man's reach should exceed his grasp,
Or what's a heaven for?

ROBERT BROWNING

WE CAN THINK OF "REACH" IN TWO WAYS. First, there are the things that are within our reach. This is what Browning refers to as our "grasp." But more important, there are the things we are reaching for. And in this sense, our reach should exceed our grasp. We should be striving for things greater than those we have right now.

As you may have noticed, life moves in one direction: it moves relentlessly toward the future. There is no going back, except in memory, and so we need to be forward-oriented. In both our thinking and our acting, we must discipline ourselves to put the greater emphasis on what is in front of us rather than on what is behind. Yes, we need to think about the past often enough to learn its lessons, but when it's time to reach, we need to reach forward. Nothing is more futile than reaching backward. The past is gone, and reaching won't bring it back.

Elsewhere I have written about the importance of seeing our next step as our most important. Even if you've reached old age and most of your steps in life are behind you, it is still true that the next step you take is the most important. The reason is simple: *the next step is the only one you can take.* Obviously, you can't take those that have already been taken, and until you get to it, you can't take the step after your next one. So your next step — the one immediately in front of you — is critically important. Make it a bad step, and you will have dug yourself deeper into a hole. But make it a good step, reaching for better things, and you will have helped yourself very wisely.

But if we need to reach toward better things ourselves, we also need to help others do so. Nearly everybody you meet needs some kind of encouragement, and you will touch their lives with grace if you are a messenger of hope. Is this not a gift you would like to give?

Emil Brunner wrote, "Hope is reaching out for something to come." We do, as I've said, need to have hope and share hope. But even when we have hope, sometimes we're still not people who do much reaching. So may we actually *reach* for the things we hope for!

This is what I do: I don't look back, I lengthen my stride,
and I run straight toward the goal . . .

PAUL THE APOSTLE

BALANCE

[Imagination] reveals itself in the balance
or reconciliation of opposite or discordant qualities.
S A M U E L   T A Y L O R   C O L E R I D G E

W HAT IMAGE COMES TO YOUR MIND WHEN YOU HEAR THE
WORD "BALANCE"? I always see a pair of scales, an apparatus
containing two pans or trays in which opposing elements are placed.
The scales are "balanced" when the element on one side weighs the
same as that on the other side. That's how balance works in physics.

Today, however, let's think of balance metaphorically. Is it not a
fact that the principles and practices in our lives have to be balanced?
And is it not also a fact that this is hard to do? To take but one example, it is a challenge to balance "responsibility" with "rest." The person
who is passionate about the value of work but never takes time for replenishment is "out of balance" (and is an accident waiting to happen).

The times in which we live make it especially hard to maintain
balance. As life becomes more complex, the demands on our time
can crush us under their weight. And as the enticing activities in our
culture multiply, we find it hard to say "no" to anything we want to
do. The result is that we spend our lives running from one excessive,
imbalanced situation to another, always promising that we'll get things
back into balance "as soon as the rush is over." But the rush never ends.

The only answer, of course, is to learn the practice busy people
dislike most of all: *sacrifice.* We can't "do it all" any more than we can
"have it all." Some choices have to be made, and some things have to
be let go of. But frankly, there is something else we'll have to learn:
wisdom. Even when we're willing to make serious sacrifices, it takes a
wise person to know exactly where the ax should fall.

In the matter of balance, there is an irony, however. You might
think that if you have to cut any of your activities for the sake of
balance, then you're going to "accomplish" less in terms of your total
output. But this is an illusion. Consider all the people you know. Who
are those who have the most expansive potential for good deeds and
good works? Be honest now. Aren't they poised? Aren't they balanced?

"Holy leisure" refers to a sense of balance in the life, an ability
to be at peace through the activities of the day, an ability to rest and
take time to enjoy beauty, an ability to pace ourselves.
R I C H A R D   J .   F O S T E R

October 22
PUNCTUALITY

Punctuality is the politeness of kings.
LOUIS XVII

IN YOUR OPINION, HOW IMPORTANT IS IT TO BE "ON TIME"? For today's meditation, I'd like you to consider that punctuality is more important than it may appear on the surface. I may not think about it very often or recognize it consciously, but in my more honest moments, I have to admit this: among my acquaintances, those who are punctual have gained a special place of trust in my thinking.

Now, anybody who has ever acquired the habit of punctuality will tell you that it's not easy. When you have agreed to be somewhere at a certain time, you have to *make it happen*. That requires planning, diligence, discipline, and sacrifice. To be there, ready and waiting, you have to take thought for the other person, how important they are to you, and how important your appointment with them is. But listen: that is exactly why punctuality is such a gift to the other person. It says, "You are important enough to me that I made the effort to be here — on time — for the meeting that we agreed on."

A lack of punctuality digs us into a hole, so to speak. The more often we are late (and the more that becomes what others expect of us), the more some of our other faults will begin to irritate our acquaintances. There is a French proverb that makes the point: "Men count up the faults of those who keep them waiting."

This may be especially true in close friendships. "Few things tend more to alienate friendship than a want of punctuality in our engagements" (William Hazlitt). Chronic lateness says, "It doesn't take much to push aside my meetings with you. Not very much at all."

On the other hand, few things build trust more than punctuality. It is one of those little things that, over time, indicate the trustworthiness of our character. And this is nowhere more critical than in the workplace. "Nothing inspires confidence in a business man sooner than punctuality, nor is there any habit which sooner saps his reputation than that of being always behind time" (W. Mathews).

So I want to make a truly radical recommendation. Try this: *instead of being late, make a point of being early to do extra work.* You will come to be known for your eagerness rather than your unconcern!

Better three hours too soon than a minute too late.
WILLIAM SHAKESPEARE

SOBRIETY

> It is better to go to the house of mourning than to go to the house of feasting,
> for this is the end of all mankind, and the living will lay it to heart.
>
> BOOK OF ECCLESIASTES

S OBRIETY HAS TO DO WITH SERIOUSNESS. It does not mean one is never lighthearted; it means the important things in life are given serious regard. To be "sober," in its most basic sense, is to be free of intoxication. But there are other kinds of sobriety that have nothing to do with alcohol or drugs. A sober-minded person is not flippant or frivolous about earnest thoughts, pressing concerns, or significant work. And he is circumspect and self-restrained in his conduct.

The first meaning of sobriety ought not to be passed over too quickly, however. It is morally wrong for us to impair our thinking by intoxication, and if being sober never meant anything more than refusing this impairment, that would be an important meaning.

But for every person who has ever failed a sobriety test in the literal sense, there are many more who would be in trouble if their seriousness were tested. All joking aside, as we say, there is a time to be serious, and if we're not willing to do that, we've got a big problem. I like what Allan Bloom wrote about living seriously: "A serious life means being fully aware of the alternatives, thinking about them with all the intensity one brings to bear on life-and-death questions, in full recognition that every choice is a great risk with necessary consequences that are hard to bear." Life being what it is, we need to sober up.

"The real world is not easy to live in. It is rough; it is slippery. Without the most clear-eyed adjustments we fall and get crushed. A man must stay sober" (Clarence Day). And I would suggest that sobriety means not only the ability to *think seriously* about life but the willingness to *pay attention.* On ordinary days, our sobriety depends as much on our *focus* as it does on our *seriousness.*

The two things that sober us up the most, of course, are the brevity of life and the recognition that our earthly deeds are only of passing significance. Václav Havel said it quite well: "A human action becomes genuinely important when it springs from the soil of a clear-sighted awareness of the temporality and the ephemerality of everything human." That's a sobering thought — and very beneficial.

> So teach us to number our days that we may gain a heart of wisdom.
>
> BOOK OF PSALMS

FAITH

Faith is a reasoning trust, a trust which reckons
thoughtfully and confidently upon the trustworthiness of God.
JOHN R. W. STOTT

A DISCUSSION OF "FAITH" COULD GO IN EITHER OF TWO DIRECTIONS. We could ponder the value of faith as a generic quality: the willingness to trust. That would be a profitable discussion, since all of us would lead more helpful lives if we demonstrated more of the courage that produces confidence in others. But, of course, there is the greater, and more specific, discussion we could have about faith in God, and that is the direction in which I would like to go.

There are two common misconceptions about faith in God. Both of these are extremely dangerous because they are perversions of faith.

(1) Faith is wishful thinking. There are those who see faith as a crutch, indicative of weakness — as if it meant no more than believing what one wishes to be true. But true faith goes a good bit deeper than that. It is, as John Stott suggests, "a reasoning trust." Much more than *blind* faith, real trust in God is founded upon solid, credible evidence of His trustworthiness. If no such evidence exists, then faith in God ought to be dispensed with, no matter how much one may "need" it.

(2) Faith takes the difficulty out of life. This misconception is prevalent among believers themselves. The idea here is that if one has sufficient faith, he or she will live a life of happiness and ease. Painful emotions will be banished, and whatever difficulties life may present, faith will make these simple to surmount (and maybe even pleasant).

But surely, this is a perversion of faith also. Faith makes things possible — it does not make them easy. "True faith is never merely a source of spiritual comfort. It may indeed bring peace, but before it does so it must involve us in struggle. A 'faith' that avoids this struggle is really a temptation against true faith" (Thomas Merton).

Let me be frank: *where there is no risk, no vulnerability, and no sacrifice, faith is a meaningless cipher.* Because it knows there are good reasons to do so, faith leaves the safe harbor and sails into uncharted waters. It departs from the easy life to do what can't be done except by those who know what trust is really about. *It is a treasure, but it is not easy.*

To choose what is difficult all one's days
as if it were easy, that is faith.
W. H. AUDEN

SAGACITY

The sage does not accumulate for himself.
The more he uses for others, the more he has for himself.
The more he gives to others, the more he possesses of his own.
The way of heaven is to benefit others and not to injure.
The way of the sage is to act but not to compete.

LAO-TZU

FEW OF US SEE OURSELVES AS SAGES, I'M QUITE SURE. Yet sagacity is a trait we dare not ignore. A close synonym of wisdom, sagacity is "the quality of being discerning, sound in judgment, and farsighted" (*American Heritage Dictionary*). How can we not see things like these as good? We can't live quality lives without them, can we?

But how might we distinguish "sagacity" from "wisdom"? Wisdom is the more general term, and sagacity denotes a particular kind of wisdom. The word itself comes from the Latin noun *sagacitas* ("quickness or keenness of perception"). So sagacity is the kind of wisdom that sees the difference between wise and foolish conduct even when that difference is very subtle. Based on its discernment, then, it is able to exercise sound judgment and make good decisions.

Notice that sagacity (like wisdom itself) is more than knowledge. "Knowing what is right does not make a man sagacious" (Aristotle). We cannot be sagacious without accurate information to work with, but having the knowledge, we also need the good sense to *apply* it well.

I would also suggest that sagacity is a more *mature* kind of wisdom. And when I think of mature wisdom, I think of grandparents! Sometimes I wonder if most of the world's problems wouldn't be solved if we'd just listen to the sages in our own families: *Grandpa & Grandma.*

Experience is what teaches us wisdom and sagacity, of course. The experience does not have to be our own, since we can learn from the experiences of other people. But unfortunately, most of us have to learn the hard way: by our own mistakes. And that is why hardships and painful situations (many of them created by our own lack of wisdom) should not be despised. If those circumstances are the ones that teach us better discernment and judgment, then let us learn all we can from them. It's in the arena of *action* that we learn how to be better people!

The sages do not consider that making no mistakes is a blessing.
They believe, rather, that the great virtue of man lies in his ability to correct
his mistakes and continually to make a new man of himself.

WANG YANG-MING

NEEDS

There is a vast difference in some instances between
what we really need and that which we think we must have.

WILLIAM M. PECK

NOTHING IS MORE OBVIOUS IN THE WORLD AS IT NOW EXISTS THAN OUR NEEDINESS. None of us can say (at least honestly) that we have everything we need, and we certainly can't say the world is everything we desire it to be. The fact is, most of us make our living doing things to meet needs that wouldn't exist in a perfect world. So in both the small scale and the large, *human beings aspire.* We have needs, and we long for them to be filled completely and permanently.

Yet we find it difficult to understand the precise nature of our needs and to seek their true fulfillment. As Adlai Stevenson once said, "Understanding human needs is half the job of meeting them." It is so easy to be deceived about our needs. When we get something we thought we needed, we often find it unsatisfying, and we're forced to the conclusion that it wasn't really what we needed after all.

Our own needs. The first step, for many of us, would be to acknowledge that we are needy. It takes humility to do it, but we must own up to the empty spaces in our hearts. It will be hard enough to assess what our needs truly are, but we can't begin that process until we've admitted that we have any needs in the first place. And even after identifying our needs accurately, we'll have to learn how to fulfill them rightly. But it all starts with confessing that we have unfulfilled needs.

The needs of others. Life also calls on us to identify what those around us are most in need of, and then learn how to help them in ways that are both good and wise. Yet if this is challenging, it's also a great joy. No higher satisfaction is available to us than helping fill the needs of other people — *and the deeper the need, the higher the joy.*

As you can easily see, meeting needs requires both love and wisdom, but it also requires slowing down. So listen to Billy Graham: "We hurt people by being too busy. Too busy to notice their needs. Too busy to drop that note of comfort or encouragement or assurance of love. Too busy to listen when someone needs to talk. Too busy to care."

What does love look like? It has hands to help others. It has feet to hasten to
the poor and needy. It has eyes to see misery and want. It has ears to hear the
sighs and sorrows of men. That is what love looks like.

AUGUSTINE OF HIPPO

ALTERNATIVES

> What is freedom? Freedom is the right to choose: the right to create for
> oneself the alternatives of choice. Without the possibility of choice and the
> exercise of choice a man is not a man but a member, an instrument, a thing.
>
> ARCHIBALD MACLEISH

WE SHOULD NOT TAKE LIGHTLY THE POWER OF CHOICE
THAT OUR CREATOR HAS GIVEN US. The "right to create for
oneself the alternatives of choice" is a great gift, and one that should be
used carefully and to good advantage. Like all great gifts, the freedom
of our will is a fearful gift. If we choose wisely between alternatives, we
benefit, but if we're foolish about our choices, we suffer greatly.

From the Latin *alter* ("other"), we get a group of words that all
have to do with choice. To "alter" means to change a thing into something other than what it was. To "alternate" means to pass back and
forth from one state to another. And "alternatives" are choices between
two possibilities: one thing and the other. So the word "other" is a
powerfully suggestive word. Rarely in life is there only one path that
we could follow. Almost always, we have alternatives. And much of the
wisdom of life consists in knowing when to take the "other" path.

Think, however, about how this relates to our personal relationships. If having alternatives is a good thing for us, shouldn't we also try
to open up alternatives for our friends and loved ones? We can't totally
take charge of anybody else's choices, of course, but we do have the
chance now and then to help somebody see what their alternatives actually are. If they're discouraged, we can help them see that they aren't
doomed — they still have the power of choice. And if they're caught
in unfortunate circumstances, we can help open some doors for them.
Without a doubt, door-opening for others is one of life's best privileges.

So life is not just about expanding our own possibilities; it's also
about giving opportunities to others. Even if another person doesn't
take the path we opened up for them, if we know we gave them a
chance they wouldn't otherwise have had, that's a very good feeling.

Harry Emerson Fosdick said, "No man need stay where he is."
Whether it's our own alternatives or those of others, the ability to
make better choices is a marvelous freedom. Therein lies great hope.

> You can't do anything about the length of your life,
> but you can do something about its width and depth.
>
> EVAN ESAR

October 28
PRECISION

Numerical precision is the very soul of science.
SIR D'ARCY WENTWORTH THOMPSON

IS PRECISION A GOOD THING OR A BAD THING? Would you say
the word has a positive or a negative connotation? For most of us, it
depends on the context. We want our neurosurgeon to be an extremely precise person, but we may not feel the need to be so precise
when we're throwing ingredients into the bowl to make cornbread.

Obviously, we shouldn't demand more precision than is needed
in the activity we're engaged in. Even Aristotle, a philosopher capable
of making very precise distinctions, said, "It is the mark of an educated mind to rest satisfied with the degree of precision which the
nature of the subject admits and not to seek exactness where only an
approximation is possible." So while I am recommending precision
as an "enthusiastic idea," I am not advocating pickiness or pedantry.
"Numerical precision is the very soul of science," as Sir D'Arcy
Thompson said, but not every activity needs the precision of science.

A big part of wisdom is knowing when precision is important
and when it is not. Because of our different backgrounds and personal
characteristics, arguments about this will probably never be settled.
But since we are trying in these readings to look at the positive side
of ideas like this, let's view precision as a quality that we could profit
from taking more seriously. If there are people who are too precise
(and there certainly are), there are just as many people (if not more)
who are too careless. It probably wouldn't be too much to say that
most of us would do better work if we were more precise.

Precision comes down to carefulness, and carefulness is a good
thing, almost without exception. We tend to be careful when what
we're doing is important and when we've made a commitment to excellence in that endeavor. Above all, it is in our personal relationships
that we should want to be careful. And if by "precise" we mean that
we want to "get it right," our relationships would certainly be helped if
we had that as our goal. As long as we live in this error-prone world,
we won't ever get our relationships exactly right. But aiming for
relationships that are precisely what they should be will give us better
results than if we settle for those that are "approximately" good.

Plenty of care never does any mischief.
LATIN PROVERB

SAVING

How to save the old that's worth saving, whether in landscape, houses, manners, institutions, or human types, is one of our greatest problems, and the one that we bother least about.

JOHN GALSWORTHY

WHEN ABRAHAM LINCOLN SAID, "WE SHALL NOBLY SAVE OR MEANLY LOSE THE LAST, BEST HOPE OF EARTH," HE TOUCHED ON THE IMPORTANT QUESTION OF "SAVING." Some things need to be saved, and doing so is not always easy, as in the case of the Union about which Lincoln was speaking. But before we get to the difficulty of saving things, there is this question: do we have the wisdom to see what the worthy things are that need to be preserved?

To start with, we need to be the kind of people who save some of our money. "Any fool can waste, any fool can muddle, but it takes something of a man to save, and the more he saves the more of a man does it make of him" (Rudyard Kipling). The concept of thrift — not spending all our money — may be old-fashioned, but it's still a valuable idea. In fact, the failure of so many to save anything for future needs is creating a national disaster that is only waiting to happen.

But it's not just money that we need to be thrifty about. Many other things deserve to be "saved" rather than "spent." But since life is an unending process of adding some things to our lives and subtracting others, the challenge is to know when to add and when to subtract. What do we keep, and what do we throw away? Saving everything would be just as foolish as spending everything. "If one spends what he should prudently save, that certainly is to be deplored. But if one saves what he should prudently spend, that is not necessarily to be commended" (Owen D. Young). So the practice of saving requires not only self-discipline; it requires good judgment.

These traits have to do with our character. If you and I are presently "spending" things we should be "saving," the answer is not to look for some quick-fix techniques. We'll have to work on our inner character, because frankly, saving takes character. But saving also builds character. Because it's hard to do, doing it makes us stronger.

The habit of saving is itself an education; it fosters every virtue, teaches self-denial, cultivates the sense of order, trains to forethought, and so broadens the mind.

T. T. MUNGER

October 30

OBJECTIVITY

Subjectivity and objectivity commit a series
of assaults on each other during a human life.

ANDRÉ BRETON

A S IN MANY AREAS OF LIFE, DEALING RIGHTLY WITH OBJEC-
TIVITY AND SUBJECTIVITY IS A BALANCING ACT. These two
are constantly at war, as Breton suggests. Keeping the peace is no
small test of our maturity and discipline. And there is no way to get
it right and keep it there for very long. Keeping these qualities in
healthy balance requires making adjustments throughout life.

The word "objective" can mean several things. It can mean, first,
that a person's thinking is uninfluenced by emotions or personal
prejudices. Think, for example, about a jury doing its best to weigh
the evidence in a trial. It may be hard, but the jurors will have to
let the evidence decide the verdict and not what any of them might
prefer the verdict to be from a personal standpoint. But, second, we
sometimes mean by "objective" that something is based on observable
phenomena. If you had your house appraised, you would want the
appraisal to be objective, that is, you would want it to be based on the
actual conditions of the house and not the appraiser's opinion.

But is objectivity an "enthusiastic idea"? Yes, I believe it is. In
many areas of life, we need to strive for greater objectivity. Subjective
feelings are important, no doubt, and some people need to pay more
attention to them. But many scenarios require us to be objective. In
those cases, we have to detach ourselves from the situation, weigh the
matter impartially, and make decisions that are *right* — regardless
of our preferences. In many such cases, we have to make a deliberate
effort to elevate our perspective. To use a well-known metaphor, we
need to leave the "stage" where the action is and go to the "balcony"
where we can see things more comprehensively.

Being objective is hard, as anyone can tell you who has ever given
it a serious try. And because of our fallibility and the complexity of
life, none of us will ever become perfectly objective, much less balance
our objectivity with our emotions perfectly. But progress is possible.
We can acquire more of the discipline that it takes to be *fair-minded.*

We can't be perfectly objective, but we can improve in it. We can choose
to look at things more impartially and from a higher, broader perspective.

ANONYMOUS

October 31

FUN

To appreciate nonsense requires a serious interest in life.
GELETT BURGESS

I T'S A SHAME IF WE EVER OUTGROW THE ABILITY TO HAVE
FUN. Those who can't appreciate a little nonsense or mischief now
and then are not too mature to do so; they're simply too unbalanced.
Many centuries ago, Herodotus said, "If a man insisted always on
being serious, and never allowed himself a bit of fun and relaxation,
he would go mad or become unstable without knowing it." It's not a
good thing never to lighten up and laugh at what's funny.

When we start taking ourselves too seriously, that's when we lose
touch with life's fun. And that can happen to any of us. We get to the
point where our egos are so inflated we think that anyone who laughs
at us is insulting us. We're too touchy and defensive to see what's so
amusing to others. Yet all of us say and do things that are funny. Just
as there is no person so lowly that his life has no dignity, there is no
person so dignified that he can't be laughed at. "Every man is important if he loses his life; and every man is funny if he loses his hat and
has to run after it" (G. K. Chesterton). We can't be important without
occasionally being comic. Those are simply two sides of the same
coin, and the sooner we realize that, the better off we'll be.

There are boundaries beyond which fun ought not to go, of
course. The enjoyment of fun should never be at the expense of higher
priorities, and that's a caution especially needed in a culture like ours
which almost makes fun the prime goal in life. Although it is a value,
fun is certainly not the ultimate value, and it must never be allowed
to overrule more important principles. George Santayana said it well:
"Fun is a good thing but only when it spoils nothing better."

Within its limits, however, fun is fun! Its effect on us is like
that of good medicine, and we ought to appreciate it. "No symphony
orchestra ever played music like a two-year-old girl laughing with a
puppy" (Bern Williams). With every ounce of our strength, we need
to resist the forces that would pull our hearts into a place where there
is no fun. Life in this world is a great ride, whether long or short. As
Frank Zappa observed, "It's not getting any smarter out there. You
have to come to terms with stupidity and make it work for you."

Ain't we got fun?
RAYMOND B. EGAN

DECENCY

Immodest words admit of no defense,
For want of decency is want of sense.
WENTWORTH DILLON

DECENCY IS A VIRTUE THAT HAS FALLEN OUT OF FAVOR. If there was a time in the past when people paid too much attention to social proprieties, that era is obviously over. Deference to the sensibilities of others is distinctly uncool today. Being different is how we build our personal "brands," and being shocking is "in." But still, I agree with Wentworth Dillon: "want of decency is want of sense."

Consider the basic idea behind "decency." The word comes from a Latin verb meaning "to be fitting," and the concept is that of respect for what is moral and modest. Now obviously, what is considered fitting or appropriate by those around us shouldn't be the only factor in our decisions, but have we become so self-centered that the time-tested norms of morality and modesty mean nothing to us at all? Are we so arrogant as to believe that our own opinions are superior to what had been learned by the whole human race before we got here?

Surely there is some worthy middle ground between the bohemians and the bourgeoisie. Personally, I don't want to be so tied to the norms of society that I can't depart from them when there is a good reason to do so, but neither do I want to be so tied to nonconformity that I fail to appreciate the guidelines of good manners. If nothing else, the principle of decency should be a check on our pride and self-will: "Before I insist on doing my own thing, should I not take others into account? Would I not give them a thoughtful gift if I showed respect for what they hold to be good and honorable?"

When it comes right down to it, decency is closely linked to kindness. In matters of moral right and wrong, we should always steer clear of indecency, of course. But in matters of social norms and expectations, kindness should move us to avoid giving offense whenever possible. Out of all the reasons for acting decently in our relationships, there is none finer than simple kindness. If I am mainly interested in myself, your feelings will be of little concern. But if I love you, I will want to be kind to you. Your sensibilities will matter to me.

Utmost decency, in all our dealings with the other fellow,
is the greatest need of the hour.
ALBERT B. LORD

November 2

GRACE

These are gifts from God arranged by infinite wisdom,
notes that make up the scores of creation's loftiest symphony,
threads that compose the master tapestry of the universe.

A. W. TOZER

WHEN WE LOOK AT OUR LIVES OBJECTIVELY, WE SEE MANY EVIDENCES OF GRACE. Some may be small and others large, but the ways in which we've been blessed by somebody else's good favor are numerous. We all — without exception — have been the recipients of far more goodness than our own merits have earned. Of the many threads that have been woven together in these lives that we call our own, many of them wouldn't be there if it weren't for grace.

The frequency with which grace has entered our lives ought to be a reminder that we're not alone in life. None of us is independent, and none of us would have gotten far if other people hadn't been gracious to us. Living in the real world requires helping and being helped, and it's good to have that fact called to our attention.

On our part, there's certainly a need for us to extend more grace to those we come in contact with. If we lean heavily in the direction of justice, granting to others nothing beyond what they deserve, a time will come when we get no more than what we deserve. And if we have a keen interest in correctness, making sure everybody we know is getting everything exactly right, we may be earning an advanced degree in hypocrisy, since we've often failed to get things right ourselves. How much better it would be if we seasoned our demands for justice and correctness with a heaping measure of grace. It may be hard to know how much grace to extend in some situations, but our first instinct ought to be to show as much as possible.

But how can we grow in the quality of grace? The key, I think, is learning to be more grateful. Those who are the least forgiving are usually out of touch with how much they've been forgiven. So we need to see our own situations more truthfully — and then give thanks for the grace that's been granted to us. And if we don't see much evidence of grace in our lives, we need to start looking at all the "little" ways our families and friends show us kindness every day.

Surely great grace yet may go
With a little gift: all's dear that comes from friends.

THEOCRITUS

November 3

CONTRIBUTION

A man wrapped up in himself makes a very small bundle.
BENJAMIN FRANKLIN

THE POOREST PEOPLE IN THE WORLD ARE NOT THE IMPOV-
ERISHED BUT THE SELF-CENTERED. Their main concern is for
themselves, and "their only contribution to the human family is to
warm a seat at the common table" (F. Scott Fitzgerald).

Most of us, however, want to do better than that. Whether rich
or poor, we want to give something back to the world around us. We
understand the need to make some sort of contribution — a sacrifice
of ourselves that will be conducive to the betterment of others.

We won't be able to make a contribution that will alter the course
of human history, of course. In the grand scheme of things, the world
will be what it will be with or without our help. But the individuals
whom we can help will have their load lightened even if our act of
service does not transform the experience of humanity as a whole.

It's a mistake to think that only the rich and powerful are in a
position to contribute. If we measure the significance of a gift in terms
of the sacrifice it requires, all of us have it within our power to give
a great gift. Indeed, the "little" things that common folks do every
day probably add more value to the world than all the "big" gestures
made by the prominent people. So while we're out there crusading
against injustice and trying to "make the world a better place," let's ask
whether those nearest and dearest to us are feeling any uplift from all
of this bigheartedness of ours. Are they being neglected?

The truth is, it takes a good deal of wisdom and self-discipline,
as well as benevolence and philanthropy, to be a good contributor to
the world. For one thing, the needs around us are so many, we have
to balance multiple responsibilities and prioritize the greater needs.
Richard Chewning was exactly right when he said, "It takes wisdom
and discernment to minister to people in need. We must look beyond
the apparent and seek to meet the needs of the whole person."

So we must be careful. But while striving for wisdom, we must
not fail to act. Whatever contribution any of us are capable of making,
we do not have unlimited time to make it. The clock is ticking.

In the time we have it is surely our duty to do all the good we can
to all the people we can in all the ways we can.
WILLIAM BARCLAY

GREATNESS

A man's true greatness lies in the consciousness of an honest
purpose in life, founded on a just estimate of himself and everything
else, on frequent self-examination, and a steady obedience
to the rule which he knows to be right . . .

MARCUS AURELIUS

WRITING ABOUT GREATNESS IS NOT EASY. Greatness of things like power, authority, and influence are what most people think of, so we are suspicious (and rightly so) of anyone who would deliberately set out to become great in these ways. So to suggest that greatness is anything that one should aspire to seems to be recommending nothing more than selfish ambition. But let's dig a little deeper.

First, what if we thought of greatness simply as excellence? Wouldn't that be an honorable thing to aspire to? Shouldn't I, for example, aim to be a great father rather than a mediocre one? Certainly I should. In terms of good, better, and best, none of us should be content to do anything less than the best work that we're capable of.

But second, genuine greatness has more to do with our character than with our accomplishments. Thinking of it this way, the great are those who are steadfast in adhering to virtuous principles. They may not have achieved anything the world would consider great, but they have what we call "integrity" or "character." Can anyone deny that this kind of greatness matters and that every one of us ought to be pursuing it?

Henry Ward Beecher once wrote, "Greatness lies, not in being strong, but in the right use of strength," and that insight is pertinent here. Most people think of greatness as power of one kind or another (social, political, financial, etc.), but true greatness consists in the right use of whatever power we have, whether it is much or little.

To sum up, then, perhaps we should distinguish between "bigness" and "greatness," as Richard Shelly does in the quotation below. Bigness would indeed be a self-centered, ambitious thing to go after. But greatness — true greatness — is a worthy goal. It means faithfully doing our duty, in the service of others, to the very best of our ability.

A desire for bigness has hurt many folks. Putting oneself in the
limelight at the expense of others is a wrong idea of greatness. The secret
of greatness, rather than bigness, is to acclimate oneself to one's place of
service and be true to one's own convictions. A life of this kind of
service will forever remain the measure of one's true greatness.

RICHARD W. SHELLY JR.

PHILOSOPHY

Every one of us, unconsciously, works out a personal philosophy of life, by
which we are guided, inspired, and corrected, as time goes by. It is this
philosophy by which we measure our days, and by which we advertise
to all about us the man or woman that we are.

GEORGE MATTHEW ADAMS

OUR ENGLISH WORD "PHILOSOPHY" CONTAINS AN IDEA THAT
EVERY PERSON SHOULD APPRECIATE. The word comes from a
Greek noun which meant "lover of wisdom." In the most basic sense,
then, a philosopher is one for whom wisdom is a valuable thing. He
not only appreciates it, but he exerts himself actively to grow in it.

If people react negatively when they hear the word "philosophy,"
it is probably not the "love of wisdom" that they have in mind, but
what we might call "professional" or "academic" philosophy. Without
a doubt, many who have made a career out of philosophy have given
the discipline an unsavory reputation. (Philosophy may be a field
where, as someone has said, "Ninety-five percent of us give the rest of
us a bad name.") But let's not discard the notion of wisdom itself.

Wisdom is like love and many other wonderful things: if it is not
governed and disciplined, it becomes destructive. Wisdom must be
properly defined. It must be bounded by valid principles (like humility
and reverence), and it must be kept in balance with the other aspects
of daily living. But rightly understood and carefully balanced, philosophy (the pursuit of wisdom) should be something we value greatly.

Although he was not always a good philosopher himself,
Thoreau was on the right track when he wrote, "To be a philosopher
is . . . so to love wisdom as to live according to its dictates, a life of
simplicity, independence, magnanimity, and trust. It is to solve some
of the problems of life not only theoretically, but practically."

You may not have thought much about it, but you have a philosophy of life. You have some concept of what life is about and how a
human being ought to behave. But let me ask you: has your philosophy
of life been carefully put together? If you've been careless or negligent,
you're probably on a road you really don't want to go down.

It takes but a brief time to scent the life philosophy of anyone. It is
defined in the conversation, in the look of the eye, and in the general
mien of the person. It has no hiding place. It is like the perfume
of the flower — unseen, but known almost immediately.

GEORGE MATTHEW ADAMS

DISCRIMINATION

*Life is a constant series of discriminations between
what it is well to attempt and what it is not well to attempt.*
THE SPECTATOR

LIKE IT OR NOT, THE WORLD IS FULL OF DIFFERENCES, AND
SOME OF THESE DIFFERENCES ARE QUITE IMPORTANT.
Distinguishing one thing from another is an unavoidable part of daily
living. Suppose that I have been called for jury duty. I must ask, "Is
the defendant guilty or innocent?" As a juror, I will be asked to help
discern the difference between justice and injustice in this case, and if
the evidence is not clear, doing so may require a great deal of wisdom.

To "discriminate" means to distinguish or to exercise discernment. When we discriminate, we observe the differences between
things. If we say, for example, that a person's musical taste is "discrim-
inating," we mean that he or she knows good music from bad and is
able to detect even subtle differences in the quality of compositions or
performances. In a complex world of vast information, it's important
that when we discriminate between things, we discriminate wisely.

Unfortunately, the word "discrimination" has acquired a negative connotation. These days, it usually means to discriminate *against*
someone — that is, to distinguish them unfavorably from others in a
wrongful way. Racial discrimination, for example, means noting that
someone is of a different race and treating them unfairly as a result.

But there is more to discrimination than this narrow usage, and
the popular notion that all differences whatsoever should be disregarded is simply foolish. Differences must be dealt with, and it is a
virtue to deal with them in ways that are humble, careful, and truthful.

To a certain extent, all of us have to be critics. Like the art critic
who judges the quality of artworks, we have to separate the superior
from the inferior in nearly everything that confronts us. The challenge
is to be accurate in our appraisals. We need to recognize not only the
difference between good and bad, but also the difference between
good, better, and best. So the question is not whether we will make
judgments — it is only whether we will make them wisely.

*Neither praise nor blame is the object of true criticism. Justly to discriminate,
firmly to establish, wisely to prescribe and honestly to award
— these are the true aims and duties of criticism.*
WILLIAM GILMORE SIMMS

November 7
REGENERATION

The rebirth of his heart was indispensable.
JAMES MARTINEAU

HAS YOUR LIFE EVER FALLEN INTO SUCH DECLINE OR DECAY THAT YOU NEEDED TO MAKE A RADICAL CHANGE? All of us need improvement, of course, but sometimes the improvement we need is so drastic that when we have experienced it, we feel as if we've gone back to the beginning and started our lives all over.

The concept of "regeneration" (which literally means "rebirth") is familiar to religious persons. As far as our relationship to our Creator is concerned, what we need is certainly more than a little polishing up. We need to be deeply regenerated or reborn — that is, to change directions so radically that the conversion amounts to being "reborn."

But in today's reading, we are not thinking about regeneration in the religious or spiritual sense. And we're not even thinking about it in the sense of the major turning points in our secular lives. What we have in mind today is something a bit simpler, and that is the *daily* need to open ourselves up to being new and better people.

There are few gifts any better than giving ourselves to our loved ones as persons committed to constant renewal. Rather than letting ourselves be dragged down by the weariness of life, if we would greet each new day as a fresh start in life and live it as if we had been reborn or regenerated, that would be a gracious thing to do. And surely, that is a blessing that each of us can bestow upon those around us.

Sometimes it is crisis that prompts us to change for the better, but one of the amazing things about our minds is that we can choose to make such changes at any time, even when there is no crisis. We have the ability to examine our lives, see where change is needed, and then pursue a new course as a matter of choice.

But in conclusion, let's come back to the idea of crisis. There is no denying that hardship and suffering play a special role in renewing us. In fact, when we look back, we can often see that the circumstances we most dreaded were often those that produced the most growth in us. So if we must suffer, let's be grateful for the fresh start that hard experiences can give us. Nobody ever said that being born was easy.

Deep, unspeakable suffering may well be called
a baptism, a regeneration, the initiation into a new state.
GEORGE ELIOT

November 8
ACCEPTANCE

Our level of joy (and therefore strength and healing)
is directly proportional to our level of acceptance.

TIM HANSEL

ACCEPTANCE IS A VITAL VIRTUE, BOTH FOR OUR OWN SAKE AND THE SAKE OF OTHERS. When there is something that should be accepted but we can't bring ourselves to do it, frustration is usually the result. We bog down in misery, and we inflict discomfort on those around us. "For after all," as Longfellow wrote, "the best thing one can do when it's raining is to let it rain."

(1) Ourselves. All of us have room for improvement (and improvement should be a passionate goal), but we need to accept that even a perfect version of ourselves would still be different from anybody else in the world. So I like Henry Winkler's observation, "A human being's first responsibility is to shake hands with himself."

(2) Our fellow human beings. If other people don't test your patience, then you're just not paying attention to the world you live in. The truth is, people can be vexing. But we need to recognize that not everything about other people that displeases us needs to be changed. Sometimes people do need to change, obviously, but at other times we simply need to accept their differences as a part of the spice of life.

(3) Our circumstances. I don't think I've ever met anybody who thought that the world is perfect just as it is. Life in this world leaves a lot to be desired, to put it mildly. But many of the circumstances that distress us are beyond our control. We can't change them — we can only accept them and choose freely how we will respond to them.

Martin Luther King Jr. said, "We must accept finite disappointment, but we must never lose infinite hope." Genuine acceptance does not mean complacency; it means coming to terms with reality, all the while working for whatever growth is possible. And nowhere is this more needed than in our relationships. "A friend is one who knows you as you are, understands where you've been, accepts who you've become, and still gently invites you to grow." All of us want friends like that, surely. The question is: will we *be* friends like that?

God, give us grace to accept with serenity the things that cannot
be changed, courage to change the things which should be changed,
and the wisdom to distinguish the one from the other.

REINHOLD NIEBUHR

November 9
MEEKNESS

Meekness is not weakness.

SIR WILLIAM GURNEY BENHAM

MEEKNESS IS A MUCH-MISUNDERSTOOD QUALITY. In modern English, the word "meek" is used two different ways. It may mean either "showing patience and humility" or "easily imposed on." Unfortunately, the second concept is the one that many people think of first. The stereotype of a meek person is that of a weak and wimpy pushover. Nowadays, when being successful requires "swimming with the sharks," hardly anybody wants to be thought of as meek.

But that view is not a fair representation of true meekness, which is anything but weak. Meekness does not mean being without strength; it means that one's strength is *governed.* Any good athlete understands the principle of controlled strength. A football quarterback, for example, may have the arm strength to throw the ball seventy or eighty yards, but he wouldn't be a good quarterback if he did that every chance he got. Winning the game requires holding his strength in reserve, knowing when to throw long, when to throw short, and when not to throw at all. Similarly, a meek person may have enormous strength at his command, but meekness keeps him from using any more of it than the present moment calls for.

It helps, I think, to distinguish between "strength in action" and "strength in reserve." It may take a lot of strength to do some things, but it may take even more to refrain from doing them. So when a person fails to do something, his inaction may be a sign of weakness or it may not be. As an outside observer, you have no way of knowing whether the person was being patient (strong) or cowardly (weak). It could be either one, depending on the person's inner motivation. But the point is this: we shouldn't assume that every instance of inaction is a sign of weakness. Sometimes a person may simply be exercising restraint. In that case, he or she is being meek — but by no means weak.

I would say, since I love the Arthurian legends, that it takes the strength of a "knight" to be meek. I haven't reached it yet, but that chivalrous quality of strength under control is an ideal that I admire.

Thou were the meekest man and the gentlest that ever ate
in hall among ladies. And thou were the sternest knight to thy
mortal foe that ever put spear in the rest.

SIR THOMAS MALORY

November 10
SELF-RELIANCE

There are three types of baseball players — those who make it happen,
those who watch it happen, and those who wonder what happened.

TOMMY LASORDA

OUR IDEA FOR TODAY, SELF-RELIANCE, CAN BE CONSIDERED FROM DOZENS OF DIFFERENT ANGLES. The common thread, however, is simple. It has to do with being a self-starter. For example, consider these thoughts: "Self-sufficiency has three meanings. The first is that one should not depend upon others for one's daily bread. The second is that one should have developed the power to acquire knowledge for oneself. The third is that a man should be able to rule himself, to control his senses and his thoughts" (Vinoba Bhave).

(1) Seeing to our own needs. Flora Robson said it very well: "Ask God's blessing on your work, but don't ask him to do it for you." Self-reliance doesn't mean that we don't recognize our dependence on God's grace (and even the help of other people when we're helpless), but it does mean that taking care of ourselves is not something we expect other people to do. Our daily bread is our own responsibility.

(2) Doing our own thinking. Each of us can be grateful for what we've learned from other individuals, but self-reliance means that we make our own decisions about the truthfulness and applicability of what we've learned. We don't outsource our thinking to someone else, expecting them to take over the management of our minds.

(3) Ruling our own passions. Things like self-discipline and self-control are among the hardest of life's lessons to learn. Yet we must take responsibility for these things. From time to time, others may provide some helpful controls (governmental laws, employer policies, family rules, etc.), but at some point we must learn to do what's right because it's right, with or without external restraint.

As you can see, each of these is a different way in which we should be self-starters. We can't wait for others to feed us, to think for us, or to restrain us. Instead, we have to take the initiative and do whatever we can. When life is less than happy, we focus on whatever improvements we can make, and we leave the rest in God's hands. In short, we take responsibility for our own choices. For it is a well-known fact: when we blame others, we give up our power to change.

Never grow a wishbone, daughter, where your backbone needs to be.

CLEMENTINE PADDLEFORD

HEROISM

This, to me, is the ultimately heroic trait
of ordinary people: they say *no* to the tyrant and they
calmly take the consequences of this resistance.

PHILIP K. DICK

HEROES, IN THE WORDS OF A POPULAR SONG, COME IN EVERY SHAPE AND SIZE. There are the larger-than-life heroes, those of storybook stature who've done deeds of great renown, and there are many others whose deeds have not been recorded in the history books but who nevertheless have acted heroically in their private circumstances. Heroism is not limited to any age, gender, or ethnic heritage. It is sometimes recognized and rewarded, and sometimes not. But one thing all heroes have in common is that they have acted with both courage and justice. They've stood up for something that was honorable — despite the possibility of dire consequences.

Although we normally think of heroes as those who have accomplished great exploits, it's not really the size of the accomplishment that makes the hero. It's the price that was paid and the strength that had to be mustered, even though the end result might not have been anything that made the front page of the newspaper. As Romain Rolland said, "A hero is a man who does what he can."

People, both men and women, do heroic things when they're willing to sacrifice personal benefit to some larger cause. A parent who gets up at three in the morning to tend to a sick child is a hero. A citizen who loses pay at work in order to serve jury duty is a hero. A teacher who pays special attention to a struggling student is a hero. The common denominator is that these people have a vision that extends beyond their own desires. They know that they live within the larger context of humanity, and they're eager to give something back to the world in return for the privilege of living in it for a while.

True heroes don't brag about their heroism, nor do they congratulate themselves in their own minds for being stronger and braver than other folks. Heroes of the highest caliber are the exact opposite: they're humble. They understand the big picture in life and have been willing to subordinate their wants to the needs of the greater good.

A hero is someone who has given his or her life
to something bigger than oneself.

JOSEPH CAMPBELL

DILIGENCE

Make hay while the sun shines.
MIGUEL DE CERVANTES

IF THERE IS SOMETHING THAT REQUIRES OUR DILIGENCE, THE TIME TO BE DILIGENT ABOUT IT IS RIGHT NOW. We must not spend our opportunities as if we had an unlimited supply. Now is the time to give ourselves diligently to whatever we should be doing.

But what does diligence mean? We can think of it in two directions, both of which are valuable. First, diligence means painstaking effort and persistent application. To be diligent is to work hard, doggedly plugging away at our projects. But the diligent person is not only hardworking; he is also heedful. We are being diligent when we pay attentive care to what we do, lovingly mindful of its importance.

Work long. Not everything is worth the investment of long hours, of course, but some things are. Whatever our priorities may be, we won't do what is right by these if we do no more than what is convenient. So pick your priorities in life — and be prepared to work overtime. "Be first in the field and the last to the couch" (Chinese Proverb). Diligence separates the workers from the dabblers and the dreamers.

Work smart. Diligent people work harder and longer, but they also understand the importance of wisdom. "The expectations of life depend upon diligence; the craftsman who would perfect his work must first sharpen his tools" (Confucius). True diligence is an exertion of ourselves that is not only industrious but also intelligent. It means that we think creatively about our challenges and then attack them in ways that are the most efficient and likely to be effective.

Carried too far, diligence can become the driver of an obsessed, imbalanced life. But when wisely governed, it is an exceedingly important virtue, especially when brought to bear on our spiritual lives, our family relationships, and our community service. The opportunity to be diligent about these avenues of service won't last always. Bad weather and nightfall are coming. So make hay while the sun shines!

I will try this day to live a simple, sincere, and serene life;
repelling promptly every thought of discontent, anxiety, discouragement,
impurity, and self-seeking; cultivating cheerfulness, magnanimity, charity,
and the habit of holy silence; exercising economy in expenditure,
carefulness in conversation, diligence in appointed service,
fidelity to every trust, and a childlike trust in God.
JOHN H. VINCENT

November 13
SUCCESS

If at first you do succeed, try to hide your astonishment.
ANONYMOUS

SUCCESS IS SO FREQUENT IN SOME PEOPLE'S LIVES THAT THEY GET USED TO IT, BUT FOR MOST OF US, IT OFTEN COMES AS A PLEASANT SURPRISE WHEN WE SUCCEED. It's not that we are pessimists and always expect the worst. But we have often found life to be hard, and when it is easy, success can seem like an unexpected bonus.

As a basic concept, success is neutral. To succeed is simply to reach a goal, and whether that is good or bad depends on the nature of the goal and the means used to reach it. So we should think twice about writers and speakers that teach us how to be "successful."

But with good goals and honorable means, success is certainly something we should pursue. Indeed, most of us don't pursue it enough. We're too content to live in the land of mediocrity.

To be frank, there are times when we are downright lazy and use the wrong end of our anatomy. "Nature gave men two ends — one to sit on and one to think with. Ever since then man's success or failure has been dependent on the one he uses most" (George K. Kirkpatrick). At other times, we blame our circumstances, making future failure all the more probable. "No one ever excused his way to success" as Dave Del Dotto put it. In any case, we need to take responsibility for our own behavior, especially if we could have done better but we didn't.

Yet sometimes defeat, rather than success, is the very thing we need. Numerous benefits (such as character growth) can come from dealing with disappointment. "Defeat may serve as well as victory to shake the soul and let the glory out" (Edwin Markham), so we should learn to embrace the blessings wrapped up in our unfulfilled dreams.

But not only that, we should be careful how we envision success itself. It is dangerous to pursue the ever-changing target of "success" as defined by the pop culture of the moment. We must resist this temptation and learn to strive for the only success that really matters: making the unique (and sometimes private) contribution to the world that we are individually capable of making. In the end, you and I will have succeeded if we, by God's grace, have become our very best selves.

Success is to be measured, not by wealth, power, or fame, but by the ratio between what a man is and what he might be.
H. G. WELLS

VIRTUE

He is ill clothed that is bare of virtue.

BENJAMIN FRANKLIN

VIRTUE SHOULD BE OUR MAIN PURSUIT. All the other personal traits we might wish to develop and all the other possessions we might want to acquire would be of little value without virtue. Indeed, there is nothing sadder than to see a person who has reached the pinnacle of worldly success but whose inner character is corrupt.

By virtue, we do not just mean chastity, although the word is sometimes used that way. In this discussion, we are using virtue in the more general sense of *moral excellence* (including, but not limited to, chastity). A virtue is one of those objective, indisputable qualities of character that are recognized as right and good by all people everywhere. Some of the obvious examples would be honesty, courage, and generosity. In his typically colorful way, La Rochefoucauld said it well: "Virtue is to the soul what health is to the body."

These days, we need to be reminded that the virtues are unalterable. They are not changed by the shifting winds of social evolution or popular taste. Many things in this world do change, of course, but the virtues do not. They are eternal. They transcend the space-time continuum in which we presently live because they are grounded in the eternal character of God who created the space-time continuum.

But as we all know, the world as it now exists is a torn and conflicted environment. As Thoreau said, "There is never an instant's truce between virtue and vice." In this life, we never get to the point where virtue is automatic. Wisdom may tell us what we need to do and our conscience may urge us in that direction, but there is always the matter of courage: will we or won't we do what is right?

Despite the struggle, however, we can grow to the point where virtue is a recognizable pattern in our lives. We will stumble and make mistakes, but that doesn't mean we can't be genuinely virtuous. And surely, we ought not to settle for anything less than that. "No virtue can be great if it is not constant" (Alfonso Milagro). Aside from our good deeds on special occasions, what kind of people are we, really and truly? How are we known by those who know us best?

The virtue of a man ought to be measured, not by his extraordinary exertions, but by his everyday conduct.

BLAISE PASCAL

HAPPINESS

The cheerful of heart has a continual feast.

THE BOOK OF PROVERBS

NLIKE JOY (WHICH IS A VIRTUE AND CAN BE CONSTANT), HAPPINESS IS A MORE OCCASIONAL VISITOR. Life in this world can be difficult and painful, but it can also be pleasant — and we love the happy days, whether they are many or few. "Happiness makes up in height for what it lacks in length" (Robert Frost).

(1) We shouldn't try to force happiness. I chuckle when I recall Willard R. Espy's quip, "If only we'd stop trying to be happy, we could have a pretty good time." Happiness can't be manufactured directly; it's a byproduct. So we should give up the popular "pursuit of happiness" and get busy doing other things. "Happiness often sneaks in through a door you didn't know you left open" (John Barrymore).

The genuinely happy are honest about the real world. They don't play mental tricks and try to convince themselves they are happy when they are not. As realists, they don't demand unbroken happiness in a broken world. They can live without happiness if they have to.

(2) We should not neglect the "little" happinesses. Many of the most delightful things in this world are ordinary and easily overlooked. We would be happier if we were more observant, and if we took the time to relish the simple pleasures. Benjamin Franklin was right: "Human felicity is produced not so much by great pieces of good fortune that seldom happen as by little advantages that occur every day."

(3) We should be grateful for happiness. When happiness comes calling, it should be treated as an honored guest. Sara Teasdale had the right perspective in her well-known motto, "I make the most of all that comes, and the least of all that goes." We should relish the good times appreciatively, maximizing their enjoyment — and then relinquish them with the right attitude. "Happiness always looks small while you hold it in your hands, but let it go, and you learn at once how big and precious it is" (Maxim Gorky). May we never say goodbye to any happiness without having enjoyed it gratefully.

But finally, may we never be selfish. Since we never have any happiness except by God's grace, we must look for ways to pass it along. May we relate to everybody around us as happily as we can.

Happiness held is the seed — happiness shared is the flower.
ANONYMOUS

November 16
ROLES

We are apt to forget that we are only one of a team, that in unity
there is strength and that we are strong only as long as each unit in
our organization functions with precision.
SAMUEL TILDEN

WE OFTEN THINK OF A "ROLE" AS A PART PLAYED BY A PER-
FORMER. In the movies, for example, an Oscar is given to the
"Best Actor in a Leading Role." Let's take that metaphor and see what
we can learn from it in regard to our own roles in life.

For one thing, we each need to play our roles well. If we think of
ourselves as being involved in various "stories" (relationships, work,
activities, etc.), then it is obvious: whichever role in the story is ours to
play, we should make that part the best it can be. Indeed, we are not
only actors and actresses in these stories; we are actually helping to
create the stories by the way we conduct ourselves. It behooves us to
view our roles as important contributions to the world.

But none of us is performing in a one-man show. Whatever relationship we may be in, the story's plot involves other people, each of
whom also has a significant role. One of the greatest insights we can
have is recognizing that life is a collaborative venture. Our individual
roles need to be played in such a way that they help, rather than hinder, the work that our "team" is trying to accomplish.

Gail Hamilton wrote, "Every person is responsible for all the
good within the scope of his abilities, and for no more, and none can
tell whose sphere is the largest." Some roles in life are obviously more
critical to the overall endeavor than others, but "God estimates us not
by the position we are in, but by the way in which we fill it" (Tryon
Edwards). If the work of the world is going to be done, there will have
to be a few "leading" roles, but we should be just as willing to do our
best in a "supporting" role or even to be just an "extra." It takes humility
to give our best effort to every role — whether leading or supporting.

Great passion is produced when we are well-suited to our roles.
So Pindar's advice is appropriate: "Learn what you are and be such."
But let's not be picky. When called upon, let's play our roles with
gusto, even when the part may not be one we would have chosen.

I cannot do everything, but still I can do something; and because I cannot
do everything, I will not refuse to do something I *can* do.
EDWARD EVERETT HALE

November 17

PRAYERFULNESS

Man offers himself to God. He stands before Him like the canvas
before the painter or the marble before the sculptor. At the same time
he asks for His grace, expresses his needs and those of his brothers in
suffering . . . The modest, the ignorant, and the poor are more capable
of this self-denial than the rich and the intellectual.

ALEXIS CARREL

PRAYERFULNESS IS NOT ONE OF THE LEADING CHARACTERIS-
TICS OF OUR CULTURE. Perhaps it is the pride that comes from
our prosperity. Or maybe it is that our scientific progress has led us
to believe there is no problem we can't solve. Whatever the reason
may be, it is not often that we bow humbly before God in prayer. We
may nod briefly in His direction with a public prayer before a sports
contest, but our day-to-day lives rarely take God into serious account.

Would it not be proper for us to become a more prayerful people?
I do not simply mean we should pray more often. I mean our entire
attitude should be more reverent and humble. If there is no God, the
sooner we dispense with the notion of reverence, the better off we'll
be — but if the truth of the matter lies in the opposite direction (as
many of us still profess to believe), how can we not live in the daily
consciousness of our accountability to God, as well as our need for
Him? Surely there can be no question about the importance of the
question. All other issues pale by comparison. If God is real, the very
atmosphere in which we live should be one of reverence. There should
be nothing we do that we don't do prayerfully.

As Americans, we do turn to God in moments of crisis. On days
like September 11, 2001, our prayers are passionate. But in addition
to our requests for help in times of urgent need, should we not be
more grateful when things are going well? Prayer does not just ask
God for His aid. More importantly, it thanks Him for what He has
already done and praises Him for His majesty and goodness.

Because it admits our insufficiency, prayer hurts our pride. But
these days, our insufficiency is becoming frightfully obvious — neither
philosophy nor technology is going to be enough to help us where we
need it the most. So is it not time to begin living more prayerfully?

We are all weak, finite, simple human beings, standing in the need
of prayer. None need it so much as those who think they are strong,
those who know it not but are deluded by self-sufficiency.

HAROLD COOKE PHILLIPS

PIETY

Many people think that a "spiritual Christian" is mystical, dreamy, impractical, and distant. When he prays, he shifts his voice into a sepulchral tone in tremolo. This kind of unctuous piety is a poor example of true spirituality. To be "spiritually minded" simply means to look at earth from heaven's point of view. The spiritually minded believer makes his decisions on the basis of eternal values and not the passing fads of society.

WARREN W. WIERSBE

MENTION THE WORD "PIETY," AND NOT MANY PEOPLE WILL HAVE POSITIVE THOUGHTS ABOUT IT. To many, the pious are simply the religious hypocrites: the people who fake their devoutness, major in the minor details of religious correctness, and mindlessly go through the motions of conventional observance.

As we shall see, there is much more to piety than this, but let us be clear: if we are guilty of any of these things, we should stop them immediately and learn what genuine piety is about.

Our word "piety" comes from the Latin *pius* ("dutiful"). It refers to those who take their duties seriously. The pious are not the pretenders but the truly devout — they reverently hold themselves to high standards of virtue and morality. So if we are pious, we may not always be solemn, but we are never anything less than earnest. Matters of obedience are important to us — we regard them respectfully, studiously, carefully, wholesomely, and delightfully!

But I want to insert what I think is a critical distinction here. Some folks think they are being pious when they are merely being good. Yet Pascal was right: "Experience makes us see an enormous difference between piety and goodness." Piety is goodness for God's sake, and it will move us considerably beyond the kind of goodness that stems from personal preference and social respectability.

Of all the "gift words" we have discussed, none is any better than the word "piety." Just think of the difference it would make in your family and your friendships if you gave those around you the gift of personal piety. When those who deal with you know you can be counted on to be devout in your duties to God, they will be grateful.

But this can't be done painlessly. Because it is focused on God, piety requires that we subordinate ourselves to Him. Our pride won't give up without a fight — but the riches of reverence are waiting for us!

The best way to see divine light is to put out thy own candle.

THOMAS FULLER

GRANDEUR

Philosophy is written in this grand book — I mean the universe —
which stands continually open to our gaze.
GALILEO GALILEI

SIMPLE THINGS HAVE A HEARTWARMING BEAUTY THAT IS
DELIGHTFUL, BUT WE ALSO NEED THE THRILLING JOY THAT
ONLY GRANDEUR CAN PROVIDE. It might wear us out if it happened
too frequently, but now and then we need to have our hearts ravished
by the pleasure of that which is glorious and majestic. Magnificent
beauty awes us, enticing us with realities beyond this world.

As Galileo knew from firsthand observation, the universe is a
"grand book . . . which stands continually open to our gaze." It is
"charged with the grandeur of God," as Gerard Manley Hopkins
famously said. Three thousand years ago, King David of Israel was
filled with the same sense of wonder: "The heavens declare the glory
of God, and the sky above proclaims his handiwork." So if we want
to see grandeur, it's all around us. It's in the trees, the grass, and the
clouds, not to mention the mountains, the oceans, and the stars.

But we ourselves have an even greater grandeur. Made in God's
image, we are personal beings, able to respond to Him with intellect,
emotion, and will — and despite all the brokenness and suffering that
we have brought into the world, we still bear traces of our Father's
glory. Indeed, it is in suffering that our dignity can be seen most poi-
gnantly. "Many men owe the grandeur of their lives to their tremendous
difficulties" (Charles Haddon Spurgeon). Our tears (and our yearnings)
can teach us a good deal about the glory we were meant to enjoy.

As great as it is, of course, our glory is only a reflection of God,
and when we speak of "grandeur" it should be God that we have in
mind most of all. We can't fully comprehend or describe His majesty,
but attempting to do so is the highest use of the human mind. Feasting
on even a portion of God's grandeur is a sumptuous banquet indeed.

Timeless, spaceless, single, lonely,
Yet sublimely Three,
Thou are grandly, always, only
God is Unity!
Lone in grandeur, lone in glory,
Who shall tell thy wondrous story?
Awful Trinity!
FREDERICK WILLIAM FABER

EXACTITUDE

The philosophical spirit is, then, a spirit of observation
and exactness, which relates everything to true principles.

DENIS DIDEROT

WHEN YOU DO SOMETHING, HOW "EXACTLY" DO YOU WISH TO DO IT? For many people, the rule in playing horseshoes ("close counts") is good enough for them. Others feel the need for more exactness. So let me offer you a few (three, to be exact) different meanings of "exact" that might be considered enthusiastic ideas:

(1) Consistent with fact, not deviating from reality. Many of our endeavors require information that will serve as the foundation for an important decision. In such cases, we ought to settle for nothing less than the exact truth. Information that is "basically correct" will yield decisions that are no more than "pretty good." So truth is extremely important, and strict adherence to reality is a good thing. Anybody who would tell you otherwise is, well, out of touch with reality.

(2) Marked by accurate measurement. Various activities in life involve things being measured against standards, and we can see a need for measurements to have only a small margin of error. If a surgeon is installing a pacemaker for your heart, you will want the device to have been manufactured with extreme precision. And when we are "installing" things like ideas and arguments in our minds, don't we want those to have been "manufactured" with even greater precision?

(3) Marked by strict adherence to rules. If you enter into a business contract with another person, perhaps involving thousands of dollars, you will not be content for them to keep "most" of the requirements or to be "basically" honest in their dealings with you. You will want them to do exactly what they made a commitment to do. Why is it, then, that when we are the ones under obligation, we think that the rules (even the laws of the Creator) don't have to be kept exactly?

But is it possible to overdo this business of being exact? I suppose so. But let's be honest: how many people do you actually know whose lives have been damaged by too much exactness? Very few, I guess. On the other hand, we all know some who have suffered from too much carelessness. I see one of them in the mirror every morning.

The difference between something good
and something great is attention to detail.

CHARLES R. SWINDOLL

PRACTICE

Practice is the best of all instructors.
PUBLILIUS SYRUS

IN THE REAL WORLD, THERE IS NO GOOD SUBSTITUTE FOR
PRACTICE. Consequently, the people we admire are often those
whose skill or character traits have been acquired by means of practice. Natural abilities and intelligence may provide a head start, but
there is no shortcut to excellence. Talent has to be honed and disciplined, and the only way to do that is practice, practice, practice.

(1) Practicing our skills. I still remember how embarrassing it was
in the fourth grade to show up for my weekly piano lesson not having
practiced anything that had been assigned. "It doesn't do any good to
come for a new lesson," my teacher would say, "if you haven't practiced last week's lesson." It was painful to hear, but I knew it was true:
you have to practice to get good at anything. And as adults, practice
is no less important. "What we do best or most perfectly is what we
have most thoroughly learned by the longest practice, and at length it
falls from us without our notice, as a leaf from a tree" (Thoreau).

(2) Being practical people. We often distinguish between "theory"
and "practice," and that illustrates a second usage of practice. Most of
us know a good many things in the realm of theory, but strictly speaking, we don't really know these things until we've seen them borne
out in practice. "However much thou art read in theory, if thou has
no practice, thou art ignorant" (Saadi). Since things don't always work
as well in practice as they do in theory, most of us would profit from
being less theory-oriented and more practice-oriented.

(3) Practicing what we preach. The third meaning of practice
has to do with hypocrisy. We should "practice" what we "preach," as
the saying goes. If we don't live according to our principles, we will
deserve nothing but contempt and reproach from those around us.

Finally, however, may I suggest that practice is the key to learning. Whatever the topic, our understanding of it is not likely to grow
if we merely sit around and think about it. Study is profitable, but our
questions in life are answered not in the study but on the battlefield.

Try to put well in practice what you already know, and in so doing, you will, in
good time, discover the hidden things you now inquire about. Practice what
you know, and it will help to make clear what now you do not know.
REMBRANDT

THANKSGIVING

Come, ye thankful people, come,
Raise the song of harvest-home;
All is safely gathered in,
Ere the winter storms begin.

HENRY ALFORD

NOW THAT THE CROPS HAVE BEEN LAID BY, IT'S TIME TO GIVE THANKS. These days, our culture is more urban than rural, and it may be difficult for us to identify with the specialness of this time of year in the minds of the colonial immigrants who came to these shores in the 1600s. These folks subsisted by farming the land. Long before the Industrial Revolution drew people to the cities to work in factories where the work was the same year-round, the colonists lived (and not infrequently died) by the rise and fall of the agricultural year. When they'd labored all summer to garner food, clothing, and shelter for the winter months, the late autumn was a time for celebration. They paused to remember the graciousness of life, even at its hardest. And we would do well today, in a totally different culture, to go back in time and recall what Thanksgiving meant to these good people.

John Henry Jowett made this observation: "Life without thankfulness is devoid of love and passion. Hope without thankfulness is lacking in fine perception. Faith without thankfulness lacks strength and fortitude. Every virtue divorced from thankfulness is maimed and limps along the spiritual road." To give thanks is to embrace all the other qualities that should strengthen our characters, and without it, we are probably fighting a losing battle trying to find "self-fulfillment." Perhaps this is why, in an epoch of such amazing abundance, we find ourselves going stale and burning out. If we've lost the habit of thanksgiving, we've lost the glue that binds the good life together.

But the plain fact is, it takes a certain amount of discipline to be a thankful person. For most of us, it doesn't come naturally. We have to choose to be grateful rather than ungrateful — and we have to choose to express our gratitude. But these choices are well worth the making. And with the summer behind us and winter on its way, now's a very special time to practice this old-fashioned art, the art of appreciation.

Cultivate the thankful spirit!
It will be to you a perpetual feast.

JOHN R. MACDUFF

LIKABLENESS

Good-humor is a philosophic state of mind;
it seems to say to Nature that we take her
no more seriously than she takes us.

ERNEST RENAN

LIKABLENESS MAY NOT BE THE FIRST CRITERION FOR GREAT
CHARACTER, BUT OUR FRIENDS AND FAMILY WOULD PROB-
ABLY BE HAPPY TO SEE US GIVE IT MORE PRIORITY THAN WE DO.
It's okay to work on being respected, and in fact that ought to be our
main quest. But there's no reason we can't add to our respectability
a little more likability. A little more warmth and fuzziness probably
wouldn't hinder the seriousness of our mission. It might even help it.

Likable people are "attractive" in the literal sense: they attract
others to them. Likableness draws other people toward us; it makes it
easy for them to be open and available for friendship.

Although likableness is a positive trait, we should be careful not
to be insincerely likable. There is a proverb from the Congo which
says, "The teeth are smiling, but is the heart?" To whatever extent we
are "attractive," the attraction needs to be to qualities that are genuinely there. And not only that, we should avoid placing too high a
value on being liked. There will be times when we're tempted to compromise our convictions in order to be liked. At such times, we need
to have the courage to be disliked, if that's what integrity requires.

There is an interesting thing about likability, however, and it
is this: likable people tend to find other people likable. It was Will
Rogers who said, "I never met a man I didn't like," and that is no
coincidence. People who are as likable as he was will always find a lot
to like in other people. Being likable makes the world more likable.

Some individuals are born with a more naturally likable disposition than others. If that's your case, be grateful for the advantage it
gives you. But if being good-natured is not one of your inborn traits,
don't despair. There are choices we can make that will move us in the
direction of attractiveness. We can cultivate the quality of being likable. Regardless of our heredity and our circumstances, we can choose
to be more easygoing and pleasant today than we were yesterday.

Few are qualified to shine in company,
but it is in most men's power to be agreeable.

JONATHAN SWIFT

REGARD

> He was but as the cuckoo is in June,
> Heard, not regarded.
>
> WILLIAM SHAKESPEARE

IN OUR INTERACTIONS WITH OTHER PEOPLE, IT HURTS TO FIND OUT THAT SOMEONE HAS NOT "REGARDED" US. Like Shakespeare's cuckoo, we may have been "heard," but no attention was paid. For most people, "I disagree with you" is considerably less demeaning than "Your existence means so little that it would be a waste of my time to take any notice of you." This has nothing to do with pride or vanity. It is simply a fact that we all need a bit of regard.

Attention. In its most basic sense, regard simply means awareness, and the fact is, this is one of the greatest things we can do for those around us. This is, needless to say, the exact opposite of rudeness, which seems to be on the increase in our culture. Rather than being rude, we need to be saying (either in word or deed) to those with whom we cross paths, "I am aware of your presence, and I regard you as a fellow human being. Is there anything I can do to help you?"

Esteem. If we say that one person has a "high regard" for another, we are talking about more than careful attention — we mean that the first person appreciates and respects the second. Not everybody engages in honorable conduct, to be sure, but we ought to be looking for every possible chance to bestow honor. We should want to have the highest regard for other people that the facts will allow.

Good wishes. We don't see it much anymore, but I still like the old-fashioned "best regards" (or "kindest regards" or "warm personal regards") way of closing letters. In this sense, "regards" are the expression of our good wishes for someone else, and having good wishes for others is surely something that most of us need to do more of.

To have regard for others, in any of the three senses we've discussed, is an enriching experience. We don't do it just for what we can get out of it, but having regard is like giving in general: it is more blessed to give than to receive. All of us like to be regarded, and it's encouraging when that happens, but if we are giving others the gift of our respectful attention, we will find it a blessing to have done so.

> When we honestly consider the well-being of others,
> we become truly rich in the deepest sense.
>
> DENIS WAITLEY

November 25

HUMILITY

Pride is a deeply rooted ailment of the soul. The penalty is misery; the remedy
lies in the sincere, lifelong cultivation of humility, which means true self-
evaluation and a proper perspective toward past, present, and future.

ROBERT GORDIS

PRIDE, WHICH IS THE OPPOSITE OF HUMILITY, IS NOTHING
LESS THAN WHAT ROBERT GORDIS SAID: "A DEEPLY ROOTED
AILMENT OF THE SOUL." It is a far more serious malady than most of
us admit. In fact, pride may be the worst personal problem or character issue we have to deal with — and if it is, then humility would be
the most positive of all concepts, the most enthusiastic of all ideas.

But what is humility? Of all the virtues, it is probably the one
most often misunderstood and misrepresented. Gordis was on the
right track here also when he said that humility means "true self-
evaluation." To be humble does not mean we pretend not to be aware
of our own strengths. (Indeed, there is nothing more prideful than
mock humility.) Humility is simply an honest assessment of ourselves,
denying neither the positive side of the story nor the negative side,
including the part about our weaknesses and our sins. And, of course,
humility also requires a confession that whatever good thing is cred-
ited to us, we couldn't have done it without lots of help. Humble folks
don't pretend to control their own destiny. They know the achievement of their goals always depends upon whether God allows it.

And this brings up another point. "Pride kills thanksgiving, but a
humble mind is the soil out of which thanks naturally grows. A proud
man is seldom a grateful man, for he never thinks he gets as much
as he deserves" (Henry Ward Beecher). Humility and gratitude are
inseparable. How can we see how indebted we are to God's grace (not
to mention the help of others) and not be thankful for that grace?

Finally, there is one other way that humility is related to gratitude: *we ought to be grateful for anything that increases our humility.*
Those words are not difficult to write, but in real life they are exceedingly hard to accept, for the simple reason that pain and difficulty are
usually the things that increase our humility. So do we really mean it
when we pray for God to teach us humility? Will we give thanks for
any tribulation that pokes holes in our pride? We surely should.

Oh, for a pin that would puncture pretension!
ISAAC ASIMOV

NOSTALGIA

We have all got our "good old days" tucked away inside our hearts,
and we return to them in dreams like cats to favorite armchairs.

BRIAN CARTER

L IKE ALL GOOD THINGS, NOSTALGIA HAS ITS DANGERS. Today
we will begin with a warning against the dangers of nostalgia, and
then close with an encouragement to embrace the good side of it.

In the Book of Ecclesiastes, there is this wise exhortation: "Say
not, 'Why were the former days better than these?' For it is not from
wisdom that you ask this." I like Ivern Ball's more modern way of
saying the same thing: "The past should be a springboard, not a ham-
mock." If we spend too much time in the past, or we simply refuse to
let go of its treasures, we paralyze ourselves as far as today's work is
concerned. So nostalgia needs a warning label: "Handle with care."

But I agree with Dan Bartolovic, who said, "A trip to nostalgia
now and then is good for the spirit, as long as you don't set up housekeeping." Kept in balance with other priorities, a joyful remembrance
of the past can refresh us, improve our perspective, and energize us.

There is a wistfulness about nostalgia that, in itself, is beneficial.
As Milton S. Eisenhower put it, "The essence of nostalgia is an awareness that what has been will never be again." In the world as it now is,
the only thing that never changes is that everything changes. Nothing
we enjoy today is ours to keep for very long, and it would be a fool
who, looking back at what once was and can never be again, had no
desire to honor the past or be inspired by its memory. To be sure, some
of what has been left behind is evil, but not all of it is, and the good
things should be gratefully — and even sentimentally — recalled.

Sometimes even the painful past must be remembered. Elie
Wiesel, a man whose work has altered the path of my life as much
as any writer, spent his passionate life reminding the world of the
Holocaust. Some things we dare not forget, and it is often the story-
teller's burden to bear witness and make sure that forgetfulness is not
our undoing. So as a person whose heart is deeply moved by the past,
I remain unrepentant in my nostalgia. I pray that my nostalgia is pure,
and that it strengthens me for today. It is no small part of who I am.

The deeper the nostalgia and the more complete the fear,
the purer, the richer the word and the secret.

ELIE WIESEL

INSIGHT

The best vision is insight.
MALCOLM S. FORBES

THE WORD "SIGHT" APPEARS IN A NUMBER OF COMPOUND WORDS. Some have to do with our physical vision, like "eyesight." Others speak of a more figurative vision, like "foresight" and "hindsight." But Malcolm Forbes was correct when he said that the best vision is "insight." To see inwardly — perceiving the true nature of people, situations, and ideas — is the most valuable "seeing" we can do. And it can be done even by those whose physical eyes cannot see.

Better insight does not come to us instantly or on command; it occurs gradually as we observe what is happening around us and — here's the key — *meditate on what we have observed.* As we grow old, the richness of our experience, combined with deep reflection on that experience, begins to serve up what I call a "banquet of insights."

Years ago, I came across this quotation about insight: "A thought may be very commendable as a thought, but I value it chiefly as a window through which I can obtain insight on the thinker" (Alexander Smith). Of all our insights, those which allow us to know other human beings are the ones we should treasure the most. Abstract ideas can be powerfully useful, but the best insights I have ever had are those that help me to understand actual *people* a little better.

Often we gain insight as a result of difficulties and distresses. We must be careful, of course, because suffering can easily distort our thinking and lead us away from the truth. But if we maintain both reverence and gratitude, pain can deepen our understanding of some very important principles. Those whose main goal is to avoid pain are cutting themselves off from one of life's most profound sources of learning.

Oliver Wendell Holmes wrote, "A moment's insight is sometimes worth a lifetime of experience." I have found that to be true. Having accumulated nearly seven decades of experience in this world, it is not unusual these days for me to get a new insight and say, "Knowing that one truth is worth every mile of the journey that it took to get there." I am learning, after all these years, to see not only with my eyes and my intellect but also with my heart. And I wouldn't trade the insights that are now coming to me for any other "sightseeing" in the world.

To be blind in the eye is better than to be blind in the heart.
ARABIAN PROVERB

ENJOYMENT

If your capacity to acquire has outstripped your capacity to enjoy,
you are on your way to the scrap-heap.

GLEN BUCK

MANY, IF NOT MOST, AMERICANS WOULD HAVE TO PLEAD GUILTY. We have an almost unlimited "capacity to acquire" but a shockingly small "capacity to enjoy." With credit cards and one-click ordering, our purchasing power is almost mind-boggling, but once we've gotten it, all that stuff seems strangely unsatisfying. For "consumers" like us, enjoyment never seems to keep up with acquisition.

So it is obvious: "having" and "enjoying" are two different things. Getting what we want does not guarantee we'll have the power to enjoy it. Sometimes it is circumstances beyond our control that prevent us from enjoying things that otherwise might have been enjoyable, but more often the non-enjoyment is our own fault: we don't enjoy what's ours because we don't savor it *consciously* and *mindfully*.

Enjoyment is not an end in itself, of course, nor is it an unqualified good. Whether it is good depends, for the most part, on the moral quality of the thing we're enjoying. But even when the thing itself is good and honorable, enjoyment is more a byproduct than it is an object of direct pursuit. Like happiness, enjoyment usually comes to us while we're busy paying attention to more important goals.

But I think there is a sense in which enjoyment should have a higher priority. As I suggested above, we should more deliberately *savor* the experiences we find ourselves involved in. Not just on special occasions but every day, we would do well to taste life more deeply. And we dare not wait until all our obstacles have been cleared away. "A contented man is the one who enjoys the scenery along the detours."

So I ask you to join me in a commitment. *Let's resolve that we will truly enjoy whatever should be enjoyed each day.* Our blessings must not be allowed to slip by unused, unappreciated, and unenjoyed. They're only ours for a little while, so let's not waste them. Let's grasp the life that is ours individually, in all of its abundance and possibility, and open our hearts more fully to the goodness of "ordinary" things.

> He prayed for all things that he might enjoy life;
> He was given life that he might enjoy all things.
> He received nothing that he asked for — but all that he hoped for.

ANONYMOUS

ALERTNESS

Public life is a situation of power and energy; he trespasses against his duty
who sleeps upon his watch, as well as he that goes over to the enemy.
EDMUND BURKE

IF, AS BURKE SAYS, PUBLIC SERVANTS NEED TO BE ALERT, SO DO THE REST OF US. Leaders may have a special responsibility in this regard, but life being what it is, none of us can afford to be caught sleeping while we're supposed to be "on watch." We need to be alert!

The word "alert" is interesting. It is one of several synonyms that denote mindfulness or heedfulness: aware, cognizant, conscious, sensible, awake, watchful, vigilant. In this list, the distinctive meaning of "alert" is that it "stresses quickness to recognize and respond" (*American Heritage Dictionary*). Think about that for a moment. Isn't it true that we often need to *recognize* certain things and then *respond* to them? And isn't it good to be able, when the need arises, to respond *quickly?* That's what alertness is: *quickness to recognize and respond.*

This life is full of good things we need to recognize and respond to (see yesterday's reading on "enjoyment"), but it is also full of dangers we need to be alert to. Dangers and threats should not become the main focus of our thinking, but it is a fact that we are threatened from time to time. In our daily lives, it sometimes seems as if we're walking across a minefield. A failure to be alert can be disastrous, not only for ourselves but for our friends and loved ones.

"Drowsiness" is a problem for most of us. Even if you aren't plagued with physical drowsiness, I expect you're like me in that you are often mentally, emotionally, and spiritually drowsy. Important issues call for our wide-awake attention, but we retreat into a passive sleepiness that does nothing but make matters worse. At times we need someone who will shake us and shout, "Wake up!"

Whether it's the good things or the bad that are under consideration, we ought to pay attention to what is happening around us. Not a day goes by that does not contain great events and exciting possibilities. Even the problems that often confront us represent opportunities for growth. But we won't profit from any of these things or make a worthy contribution to our world if we're not *alert* — which means that we're *characterized by quickness to recognize and respond.*

Only that day dawns to which we are awake.
HENRY DAVID THOREAU

RIGHTS

> All, too, will bear in mind this sacred principle, that though the will of the
> majority is in all cases to prevail, that will to be rightful must be reasonable;
> that the minority possess their equal rights, which equal law must protect,
> and to violate would be oppression.
>
> THOMAS JEFFERSON

A CONCERN FOR THE RIGHTS OF EACH CITIZEN IS DEEPLY
EMBEDDED IN THE HISTORY OF THE UNITED STATES. This
has been a part of the strength of our culture. And while the bitter partisanship of the present day seems to be tearing our society to
pieces, the debate is still an important one: how can the rights of the
many be beneficially balanced against the rights of the few?

In today's reading, let's do what we've done with many of these
"enthusiastic ideas": let's view the idea of "rights" as a gift we can give.
Regardless of public laws and social policies, how am I treating the
human beings that I actually come in contact with? If those who interact with me know I will bend over backwards to respect their rights
and defend them against injustice, I will have given them a great gift.
And if this is true anywhere, it's especially true in our families.

Perhaps the greatest gift of all is when a person says, "Let me
subordinate my rights to your needs. I am willing to sacrifice my personal prerogatives so that you can have what you need." Some say that
such a thing would be weak and timid, but the sacrificial yielding of
one's rights is one of the most transformative principles in the world.
If you are a Christian, you will recognize that this is one of the main
principles that made Jesus of Nazareth such a pivotal figure in history.

When rights are being discussed, it is frequently pointed out that
rights must never be separated from responsibilities, and that's the
insight we should end our discussion with today. Joseph T. O'Callahan
said it this way: "Many who think that they are taking life seriously are
actually only taking themselves seriously. Who takes himself seriously is
overconscious of his rights; who takes life seriously is fully conscious of
his obligations." So which do you and I think about the most?

If we're concerned about the defense of our own rights, we need
to understand that those rights will be taken most seriously by society
when we take our share of the blame for what is wrong with society.

> Rights that do not flow from duty well performed are not worth having.
>
> MOHANDAS GANDHI

EXPRESSIVENESS

Whatever is felicitously expressed risks being
worse expressed: it is a wretched taste to be gratified
with mediocrity when the excellent lies before us.

ISAAC D'ISRAELI

EXPRESSIVENESS IS GENERALLY HELD TO BE A VALUABLE
TRAIT. If someone said, "She has a very expressive face," that
would usually be taken as a compliment. But, of course, expressiveness
has no value of its own; it takes its value from what is expressed. If, for
example, the thing someone wants to express is unwarranted irritability and anger, we'd just as soon they leave it unexpressed. So what we
want, as D'Israeli suggests, is not merely for things to be expressed,
but for them to be "felicitously expressed" — and that would require
both the content and the expression to be "excellent."

But assuming that people have wholesome things to reveal to
us, we do value expressiveness. All of us love to be in the presence of
people who're willing to reveal their minds openly and honestly. We
feel honored by being taken into their confidence, so to speak. When
someone opens their "book" and lets us read even a little of it, we feel
that we've been given the gift of that person's true heart and soul.

That being true, shouldn't we work on becoming more expressive ourselves? Granted, it's possible to go overboard in the matter
of expressiveness. "A fool vents all his feelings, but a wise man holds
them back" (Book of Proverbs). But for each person with that problem, there are probably many more of us with the opposite problem:
we conceal things about ourselves that we should be sharing. We lack
the courage to let others know who we are, and in our defensiveness
we deprive our peers of one of the greatest gifts we can give.

To be delightfully expressive, we don't have to be pretentious or
strike a pose just for the sake of making an impression. In fact, we are
most expressive when we relate to others naturally, without any conscious thought that we're being expressive. Each of us is unique. Each
of us is interesting. And while we all have room for growth, each of us
has a "self" that others would benefit from knowing right now. It has
been there all along, but perhaps it's been "ne'er so well express'd."

True wit is nature to advantage dress'd,
What oft was thought, but ne'er so well express'd.

ALEXANDER POPE

JOURNEYS

Afoot and light-hearted I take to the open road,
Healthy, free, the world before me,
The long brown path before me leading wherever I choose.
WALT WHITMAN

JOURNEYS ARE ENJOYABLE. They take us away from the ordinary and the familiar into strange territory that stirs up our imagination. Journeys plow up the dormant fields of our minds, making them ready to receive new thoughts and new resolutions. They broaden our perspective and deepen our intelligence. Journeys are good for us!

If we want to improve ourselves for the purpose of having something more valuable to offer others, then journeys are things we need to be interested in. There is certainly a lot to be said for the comforts of home, but if all we ever do is sit by our fireside, our characters won't be as richly textured as they could be. Stay-at-home characters tend to be somewhat flat in comparison to the more deeply dimensioned characters of those who journey. So at least once in a while, we need to get out of our houses and hit the road. When we get back home, our friends will appreciate the new persons that we've become.

And speaking of home, one of the best things about journeys is that they teach us to appreciate our homes more fully. Thoreau went so far as to say, "Only that traveling is good which reveals to me the value of home and enables me to enjoy it better."

The homes we return to are the very things that make our journeys so meaningful. If there was no place where we belonged, no place where we were rooted, journeying would offer us no contrast and no interest. It's the healthy, balanced alternation between homesteading and journeying that adds value to our lives.

Journeys, of course, don't always involve physical travel. Indeed, the best journeys are not physical but spiritual. The persons that we truly are, or at least the persons we were truly meant to be, are deep inside of us, and very few of us have done any more than just begin the journey that would take us to that place. Those who've been there say that this journey can be frightening, but they also tell us that the discoveries are well worth the courage it takes to find them out!

The longest journey
Is the one inward.
DAG HAMMARSKJÖLD

December 3

WELCOME

Welcome is the best cheer.
THOMAS FULLER

IT'S WORTH THE EFFORT TO BECOME A PERSON WHO CAN BE DESCRIBED AS "WELCOMING." Being such a person would mean that we are receptive and hospitable. When others interact with us, they sense that we're open to them, *ready to receive with pleasure what they have to offer.* And when we consider what's on the opposite end of this spectrum — aloofness, standoffishness, and resistance — who wouldn't rather be known as welcoming? It's the better path to follow by far, especially since it brings out the best in those whom we welcome. When we adopt a receptive character, we tend to find that others have things that are quite wonderful for us to receive!

Would you like to have a gathering (it could be a party, a meeting at work, a social date, or whatever) where there is ample good "cheer"? Would you like for your gathering to be one where there is animation and enjoyment? *Then make people feel welcome!* As Thomas Fuller said, "Welcome is the best cheer." Nothing does a better job of generating enjoyment in the hearts of other people than our being genuinely and truly *ready to receive with pleasure what they have to offer.*

It is a great honor to be welcomed, even in the humblest of circumstances. When I enter your space, whether it be your home, your office, or your picnic table, and you welcome me, I can't help but feel that you have acknowledged me. You have treated me as someone worthy of your attention in the present moment. To be welcomed is to be treated with dignity. It is to be received with pleasure.

But not only do we honor others, we also learn from them by welcoming them. When we pay the price to become welcoming individuals, we find ourselves being enlightened and enriched. People really do have wonderful things to teach us. We need to welcome them!

Nothing adds more interest, adventure, and intrigue to our lives than welcoming all the people and experiences that come our way. When you arise each morning in a welcoming mood, you just never know what might happen. But whatever it turns out to be, the chances are good that it'll be something you ought to be interested in.

Not many sounds in life, and I include all urban
and all rural sounds, exceed in interest a knock at the door.
CHARLES LAMB

December 4
FRESHNESS

He was as fresh as is the month of May.
GEOFFREY CHAUCER

WHEN WE CULTIVATE THE QUALITY OF FRESHNESS IN OUR CHARACTERS, THE EFFECT OF THAT IS EXTREMELY EN-COURAGING TO OTHERS. As time goes by, particularly with the tiring demands of life as most of us live it today, it's not easy to keep an outlook of consistent freshness, but it can be done. And those who do it are refreshing to meet and to work with.

Consider the opposite of freshness for a moment. Do we really want our lives to be characterized by words like these: staleness, mustiness, weariness, and exhaustion? Would we be content for our contribution to the world to be that, after having dealt with us, other people felt even more worn out than they were to begin with? If not, we need to make it a priority to maintain our freshness.

In one sense, the world around us is very, very old. But in another sense, it's a fresh world every morning, and it's a wise thing to let ourselves experience the world as being new rather than old. "For every man the world is as fresh as it was at the first day, and as full of untold novelties for him who has the eyes to see them" (Thomas Henry Huxley). It's a matter of which perspective we choose to adopt: will we see only what we've seen many times before, or will we see the many fresh things that have not captured our attention until now?

To stay fresh, we have to be growing and making some progress from day to day. Freshness comes from regularly taking the opportunity to make things better, even if the improvements are only small ones. But as we all know, making regular progress requires discipline, determination, and even courage. These things may seem a bit burdensome, but the dividends they pay are, in fact, wonderfully refreshing.

The ultimate key, however, to freshness is love. When we fall in love with people, with the good things in the world around us, and with life itself, we'll be continually refreshed by the joys and insights that all of these things present to us. But our love must consist of more than words; it must be real. We must be touched by an appreciation — an *affectionate* appreciation — for the wonders of life. When that's the real truth about us, our characters will keep their freshness.

O spirit of love! how quick and fresh art thou . . .
WILLIAM SHAKESPEARE

LOVING

> . . . bid me love, and I will give
> A loving heart to thee.
>
> ROBERT HERRICK

BEING A LOVING PERSON REQUIRES MORE CHARACTER THAN WE SOMETIMES SUPPOSE. While it's occasionally right to speak of "falling in love," genuine love in the deepest sense involves much more than fortunate circumstances and feelings. In real love, the mind and the will are every bit as active as the emotions, and the showing of love calls for the highest and best character that is within us. Consider what happens when we give "a loving heart" to those around us:

(1) We find joy in loving, even when being loved is not a possibility. Loving is more a matter of what we give than of what we get, and love can be love even when it's unrequited. Perhaps it seems silly to our modern sensibilities, but there really was some value in the medieval idea of "courtly love," which held that the most intense love is the pure desire for that which one can never possess for oneself. "There is more pleasure in loving than in being loved" (Thomas Fuller). To be truly, and most helpfully, loving to those around us, we need to love them for their own sakes and not for what we can get out of them.

(2) We seek the true and highest good of the other person, even to the point of personal sacrifice. To give a loving heart to someone, we must truly want whatever is best for that person and be willing to place ourselves in the service of his or her best interests. Loving people are willing to subordinate their wants to the other person's needs.

(3) We maintain loyalty to love, even when the feelings of love are absent. If love is to be meaningful, it must not be dependent on the fluctuation of our emotions. Feelings come and go, but the demands of the loving heart are more constant. In these days of disposable relationships, we need to recover the concept of durable, committed love.

Nobody who's tried it would say that love is easy. It does indeed take character, and that is something we're all still in the process of building. But perhaps even more than character, being a loving person requires courage. Holding on to the trust that's required to make love's sacrifices is more than a little frightening. It's not for the fainthearted! But for the bold, being loving is the very nectar of life itself.

> The loving are the daring.
>
> BAYARD TAYLOR

DREAMS

Hold fast to dreams
For if dreams die,
Life is a broken-winged bird
That cannot fly.

LANGSTON HUGHES

WE NEED TO HOLD ON DEARLY TO OUR DREAMS. Against the discouraging forces that tempt us to give up our dreams, we need to nourish them and cherish them. Certainly, we need to have the wisdom to refine our dreams and make sure they're aligned with true principles, but if our conscience tells us our dreams are worthy of aspiring to, then we need to keep them burning brightly.

G. K. Chesterton said, "There are no rules of architecture for a castle in the clouds." Those who are the most energized by their dreams are those who've permitted themselves the freedom to dream boldly. On the other hand, those who have limited their dreams to that which is "possible" tend to have little passion in their pursuits. If it could be known for certain that something was impossible, it would be foolish to try to achieve it, but in the real world, it pays to be very careful about predicting the future. Wernher von Braun said, "I have learned to use the word 'impossible' with the greatest caution." It was that kind of thinking that got us to the moon and back!

But speaking of caution, we should also be cautious about this: we should make sure our dreams aren't selfish or materialistic. Greed wears many disguises, and it takes a person of extraordinary honesty to see when his dreams have slid off into covetousness. But the human heart is a powerful engine, and there are finer things for it to aspire to than the mere acquisition of more "stuff."

Our dreams should grow as we do, and so we shouldn't be afraid to add new dimensions to our dreams and even discover dreams that are altogether new. "The years forever fashion new dreams when old ones go. God pity a one-dream man!" (Robert Goddard). If it's true, as the wise have always said, that we become what we aspire to, that's an argument for dreaming jumbo-sized dreams in full, living color.

Do you want to know what I most regret about my youth?
That I didn't dream more boldly and demand of myself more impossible
things; for all one does in maturity is to carve in granite or porphyry
the soap bubble one blew in youth! Oh to have dreamed harder!

LEWIS MUMFORD

STEWARDSHIP

There's no way we can escape accountability. We *do* make a difference
— one way or the other. We *are* responsible for the impact of our lives.
Whatever we do with whatever we have — money, possessions, talents,
even time — we leave behind us as a legacy for those who follow. And
regardless of our own scripting, we can exercise our unique human
endowments and choose the kind of stewards we want to be.

STEPHEN R. COVEY

A STEWARD IS "A PERSON WHO MANAGES ANOTHER'S PROP-
ERTY, FINANCES, OR OTHER AFFAIRS" (*AMERICAN HERITAGE
DICTIONARY*). In the literal sense, there might not be many of us
who're in a position of stewardship, but in a larger sense, every single
one of us is a steward, and it makes a huge difference to think of
ourselves that way. Valuable resources of time, talents, money, and
possessions have been entrusted to us. These are meant to be used,
not merely for our own gratification, but for the greater good of the
world around us. And this being true, the great question of life is
whether we're discharging our duty to manage these resources wisely
and well. Acceptable stewardship, the kind that will stand up under
final inspection, asks us to accept three important principles:

(1) Trust. The resources that are at our disposal have been entrusted to us. Strictly speaking, they don't belong to us; they've simply
been put into our hands for a while. We're being trusted to use these
things as they were intended to be used: for the common good.

(2) Responsibility. We are responsible for the choices we make.
If our stewardship is less than honorable, no excuses will be accepted.
Having been given a free will, we're responsible for the results.

(3) Accountability. Whether you believe, as many of us do, that
we'll one day give an account of ourselves to our Creator, at least
believe this: ideas and actions have consequences, and no matter what
we do, there'll eventually come a day of reckoning. This is true even
regarding our own possessions. "The surplus wealth we have gained,
to some extent at least, belongs to our fellow beings; we are only the
temporary custodians of our fortunes, and let us be careful that no just
complaint can be made against our stewardship" (Jacob Schiff).

Whatever is ours, there is really no safe middle ground: either
we'll use it unselfishly and sacrificially, or it will own us and destroy us.

All you are unable to give possesses you.

ANDRÉ GIDE

December 8

CONTEMPLATION

Nowhere can man find a quieter or more
untroubled retreat than in his own soul.
MARCUS AURELIUS

AT PRESENT, THE WORD "CONTEMPLATION" MAY HAVE A
SLIGHTLY MYSTICAL SOUND TO IT, BUT IT'S REALLY NOT A
WORD TO BE AFRAID OF. When we "contemplate" we simply think
about something very quietly and carefully. We go to that "untroubled
retreat" in our own soul and turn the thing over in our minds, looking
thoughtfully at the various facets of the subject that we're meditating
on. Certainly there are many things worth contemplating, and we're
the losers if we don't take the time to contemplate them well.

The value of contemplation lies in two directions: we come to see
things with greater understanding and also to see them with greater
appreciation. When we reflect thoughtfully on what we know, we not
only see the true importance of certain principles, but we are moved
to respond with gratitude to the grace that has been shown to us.

There is a danger, of course, especially for those whose nature
tends toward contemplation. The danger is that we may spend too
much time thinking and not enough time acting on behalf of others.
Contemplation is wonderful, but if all we ever did was contemplate,
we wouldn't fill a very worthy place in the world. As Thomas Merton
said, "No man who ignores the rights and needs of others can hope to
walk in the light of contemplation because his way has turned aside
from truth, from compassion, and therefore from God."

But if we may fail by contemplating and not acting, we may also
fail by acting and not contemplating, and that may be the more common problem for most of us. We rush through our days with such a
focus on being productive that we take too little time to reflect on the
meaning and purpose of the things we do. Even when we stop to do
something as apparently thoughtful as reading, we don't really meditate on what we're reading — we speed-read it and move on to the
next piece of information. Is it any wonder, then, that we don't grow
any stronger in our spirits? Is it any surprise that we're so shallow?

He [Thomas Hobbes] had read much, if one considers
his long life; but his contemplation was more than his reading.
He was wont to say that if he had read as much as other men,
he should have known no more than other men.
JOHN AUBREY

HERITAGE

Death has to be waiting at the end of the ride before you
truly see the earth, and feel your heart, and love the world.
JEAN ANOUILH

EACH OF OUR LIVES REACHES BOTH BACKWARD AND FOR-
WARD. They reach backward to our ancestors, from whom we've
received a heritage, and forward to our descendants, to whom we will
leave a heritage. As the generations come and go, each hands down to
the next a curious assortment of things, some of which are good and
some of which are, perhaps, not so good. Even so, we need to understand that both what we've received and what we leave can be considered as a "heritage." Life didn't begin with us, and it certainly won't
end with us either. Like it or not, we're all connected.

Knowing that death is "waiting at the end of the ride" surely
ought to make a difference in our concept of how to use our years. If
when we're gone there's going to be some residue of our living, something our survivors will have to deal with, then it makes sense to work,
while we still can, on leaving a heritage that'll be easy and pleasant to
deal with. Who among us wants to leave a horrible heritage?

Good heritages, however, aren't forged accidentally or haphazardly. It takes more than simply going with the flow to get the kind of
results we can feel good about handing down. Conscious choices have
to be made, and deliberate discipline has to be exercised.

As we build up our children's heritage, one thing that can motivate us is to meditate on the heritage our forefathers have bequeathed
to us. When we're young, we tend to assume that, as adults, we're
going to do better than our parents did. But as we age, we begin to
see that it will be no small accomplishment to end up doing as well as
they did. To put it bluntly: most of us have some catching up to do if
we're going to leave a heritage as good as the one that was left to us.

Ultimately, the heritage we leave will grow out of our true values:
we will hand down to others not what we said we valued, but what we
actually valued. We need not think, for example, that we can sink our
real passion into stocks and bonds and still leave a legacy of spiritual
values to our children. Even now, they know what we're really up to.

What thou lovest well remains, the rest is dross . . .
What thou lovest well is thy true heritage.
EZRA POUND

LADDERS

. . . charity's golden ladder.
MAIMONIDES

IT WOULD BE A RARE PERSON WHO NEVER NEEDED TO CLIMB A LADDER SOMEONE ELSE HAD PUT IN PLACE. As Bertolt Brecht put it, "Everyone needs help from everyone." None of us is completely self-sufficient, and so it's a very good thing that when our ascent toward the better things in life is more than we can manage, other people often provide the ladders that we need. We should be grateful for that. But more important, we should always be on the lookout for opportunities to provide a ladder that someone else may need.

Often, when we see a fellow human being desperately trying to get to a higher place but failing to do so, we're content merely to feel sorry for them. But while pity has its place, a little help is worth more than any amount of pity. When our neighbor needs an assist that we can provide, if our compassion is real, it'll show up in action.

When people find themselves frustrated, more often than not the problem is that they've lost the courage to keep climbing. That, in fact, is the basic meaning of "dis-courage-ment": a loss of courage. At such times, the best ladder we can provide is not so much to help them as it is to help them help themselves. Benjamin Disraeli said, "The greatest good you can do for another is not just to share your riches, but to reveal to him his own." We never help people any more beneficially than when we "en-courage" them by helping them discover (or perhaps rediscover) the greatness of their own inner resources.

Do you and I willingly offer ourselves as ladders upon which others can climb? A certain amount of humility is needed to serve in this way. After all, a ladder never gets much credit for the success of any undertaking, does it? But then, credit is not really the main issue in life. The main issue is progress, and if by standing on our shoulders someone else can see farther and climb higher, that's all to the good.

"What do we live life for if it is not to make life less difficult for each other?" (George Eliot). When we're measuring the heights to which we ourselves have ascended, we need to be careful in our measurement of success. Wherever we are, if we've gotten there by abusing, or even neglecting, other people, then we haven't gotten very far.

He climbs highest who helps another up.
ZIG ZIGLAR

BELONGING

All the lonely people, where do they all belong?
PAUL MCCARTNEY

MUCH OF THE SADNESS OF LIFE COMES FROM KNOW-ING THAT THERE ARE SO MANY LONELY PEOPLE IN THE WORLD. Too few of us are rooted in safe relationships. Too few of us feel that we belong to any certain place or group of people. The times are changing, and we're in danger of becoming a world of strangers.

Yet there is still more belongingness to be enjoyed in the world than many people know about, and most of us have it within our power to help others have a greater sense of belonging than they presently enjoy. Indeed, one of the greatest acts of kindness is to help someone else feel more "at home." The very least we can do is make them feel more secure in their relationship with us, but even with regard to their more general surroundings, it's often possible to help people see that they "belong" to those around them more than they've been in the habit of thinking. It's almost always true that people are wanted and needed more than they realize, and it's a wonderfully generous thing to help them see this welcome truth.

We do the best job of encouraging others in this area when we are secure in our own sense of belonging. We can't give what we don't have, so we need to broaden our perspective enough to see the good ways in which we're connected to those around us. We must learn to be comfortable and content in our own surroundings.

It can help us, as well as others, to see that the world is a big place filled with lots of interesting variety. When we think of belong-ing, if we have only one picture in our minds of a place where we think we could belong, we're probably going to be unhappy in the real world. The amazing truth is, however, that we're much more adapt-able than we think we are, and there are many, many different sce-narios in which we might find the joy that comes from belonging.

The joy of belonging is within the reach of almost all of us, regardless of our external circumstances. Being a person who belongs is for the most part a matter of choice. Its requirements may be chal-lenging, but they're simple: awareness, acceptance, and appreciation.

Joy of life seems to me to arise
from a sense of being where one belongs.
DAVID GRAYSON

BETTERMENT

Burn from my brain and from my breast
Sloth, and the cowardice that clings,
And stiffness and the soul's arrest:
And feed my brain with better things.

G. K. CHESTERTON

GETTING BETTER REQUIRES EXTRA EFFORT. The same thing is true in the realm of our own thought and activity that is true in the realm of physics: unless outside energy is introduced into a system, it decays and becomes increasingly disorderly. Most of us have observed this law at work in our houses, yards, and automobiles. Left to themselves, they don't get better and better; they deteriorate. And so it is with our characters. If we don't work on them actively, they get worse. If we expect any "betterment" to be going on, we must, as Chesterton says, burn from our brain and our breast any "Sloth, and the cowardice that clings / And stiffness and the soul's arrest . . . "

But strangely enough, the first step on the path to improvement is to accept ourselves as we are. It may seem paradoxical, but the folks who make the most progress are usually those who are content, not those who are insecure and unthankful. "Be what you are. This is the first step toward becoming better than you are" (Julius Charles Hare).

Most of us enjoy a great deal of freedom. But how often do we use that freedom to further the cause of betterment, both for ourselves and others? Unfortunately, we often use it in ways that degrade us and our neighbors. How much better it would be if we defined freedom positively as Albert Camus did: "Freedom is nothing else but a chance to be better, whereas enslavement is a certainty of the worse."

It's an admirable thing to strive for personal betterment, but it's even more admirable to leave our "environment" better than we found it. Like the baby sitter who, rather than watch television, washes the dishes that she found in the sink, we ought to aim to improve every situation we deal with, even if it's only in some small way. And when we're dead and gone, may we have set such an example of betterment that even our memory will motivate others to strive for better things in their own lives. May our influence and our impact be for the *better*.

O may I join the choir invisible
Of those immortal dead who live again
In minds made better by their presence.

GEORGE ELIOT

December 13
REMEMBERING

> If there is a single theme that dominates all my writings,
> all my obsessions, it is that of memory — because I fear
> forgetfulness as much as hatred and death.
>
> ELIE WIESEL

REMEMBERING IS NOT ONLY THE KEY TO MANY GOOD THINGS, IT'S THE PREVENTIVE TO MANY BAD THINGS. Some things are pleasant to remember, and we enjoy remembering them. But there are other things that are important to remember, whether we enjoy remembering them or not. We certainly need to be warned against forgetfulness, as Elie Wiesel tells us. But whether the memories are pleasant, important, or both, consider today that remembering is the foundation of some of the best things in the world.

Kindness. The kindest people in the world are those who are keenly aware of how kind others have been to them, while the cruelest are those who don't seem to remember how much grace has been shown to them. To bestow kindness, we have to remember kindness.

Honoring others. Why are memorials erected if not to keep us from forgetting the worthy things others have done? Our friends and families may never have memorials built in their names, but we can honor them ourselves by always being able to say, "I remember."

Character growth. None of us has a past that's not checkered with failure. When we measure our past performance against time-tested standards of goodness and virtue, it may be painful to behold the gap between the two — but that's what motivates us to narrow the gap.

Joy. Even when we think we're enjoying something that exists only in the present moment, a significant portion of the joy almost always comes from the association of that moment with things that have brought us joy in the past. Joy and memory are kissin' cousins!

As a rule, our basic orientation should be toward the future rather than the past. But that doesn't mean the past is unimportant. If, as a people, we disconnect ourselves from the past, we risk making some very foolish mistakes. And the same thing is true of us as individuals. We dare not forget where we've been and what we've experienced. If we forget our past, the present can hardly lead to a better future.

> A people's memory is history; and a man without a memory,
> like a people without a history, cannot grow wiser, better.
>
> ISAAC LEIBUSH PERETZ

December 14

ENCOURAGEMENT

Encouragement is oxygen to the soul.
GEORGE MATTHEW ADAMS

W HO COULD SURVIVE WITHOUT SOME ENCOURAGEMENT?
Not many of us, probably. There may be the hermit here and
there who's so self-motivated that the encouragement of other human
beings is not needed, but most of us mortals need to know, at least
now and then, that somebody sees something in us that's worth affirming, supporting, and nurturing. The soul needs its own "oxygen."

When we look back, most of us can see periods of remarkable
growth in our lives that resulted from someone's encouragement. That
being true, you'd think we'd offer this gift to other people every time
we had the opportunity. Unfortunately, when encouragement is called
for, we often substitute criticism, as if that were the primary stimulant
of growth. It's a fact that constructive criticism is sometimes the thing
that's needed, and the friend who won't tell us the truth when we need
to hear it, is not really our friend. But we often get the proportion
wrong. Our encouragement of others ought to outweigh our criticism
by at least five-to-one. For every thing that needs to be *dis*-couraged,
we ought to look for four or five things that truly can be *en*-couraged.
"Correction does much, but encouragement does more" (Goethe).

Someone has said that "the small change of human happiness lies
in the unexpected friendly word." I have a hunch that the "unexpected
friendly word" might be a more powerful boost to our happiness than
all the planned and premeditated encouragement in the world. Who
among us hasn't had a bad day transformed by someone's casual good
word, completely unexpected and therefore all the more encouraging?

Encouragement is an act of hope, an investment in the future. To
encourage someone is to make a statement concerning their potential;
it says, "I believe in what you can be." Encouragement plants seeds
that can grow and bear fruit. When we encourage, we keep hope alive.

When we see what other people need, we're often struck by a
sense of helplessness. Much of the time, what is needed consists of
things that we can't provide. *But encouragement is something we can
always provide!* It's the most doable thing in the world. It doesn't take
genius and it doesn't take wealth. It only takes a caring heart.

Let us therefore animate and encourage one another . . .
GEORGE WASHINGTON

December 15
DARING

It is not because things are difficult that we do not dare;
it is because we do not dare that things are difficult.

SENECA

BEFORE ANYTHING CAN BECOME EASY, WE MUST GET TO THE POINT WHERE WE CAN APPROACH IT WITH A BIT OF BOLDNESS. Without confidence — indeed, without daring — even the simplest things can daunt us. One of the definitions of "daring" given by the *American Heritage Dictionary* is "to be courageous or bold enough to do or try something." Isn't that a quality we want to have? Dare we not do the things we should do and want to do?

Daring is not inherently a virtue, of course. Unlike honesty, for example, which is good in and of itself, daring is only relatively good; that is, it's only good when it's applied to a good cause. John Wilkes Booth, Abraham Lincoln's assassin, was daring, but we'd hardly commend him for that. So we need to be careful about the things we dare. Daring is desirable only when what we dare is good, and if we dare what is evil, we need not expect a good result. And not only that, we need to avoid rashly or impetuously daring things. There's a world of difference between courage and foolhardiness. If we don't dare wisely, we're no more than a "daredevil," one who is recklessly bold.

Henry Miller said, "Whatever there be of progress in life comes not through adaptation but through daring." Can we not take that insight and use it to better our relationships? The thing that we seek, in both our personal lives and our relationships, is progress, and if it takes courage to make progress, we owe it to those around us to demonstrate courage. We give our friends, our family, and our coworkers a great gift when we dare, for their sake, to do what we know is right and good. And conversely, when we take the easy way out and default on our duties, we inflict actual harm on those around us. In an interconnected world, we do a deed of great goodness when we dare to take the high road every time.

It's a plain fact, life often comes to us as a challenge. And if we back away from it, we shrink our stature and constrict our character. The abundant life is not for wimps. It's for the brave, and "fortune sides with him who dares" (Virgil). There is no safe middle ground.

Not to dare is to dwindle.

JOHN UPDIKE

SANCTUARY

Love consists in this, that two solitudes
protect and touch and greet each other.
RAINER MARIA RILKE

DO YOU HAVE SOMEONE WHO PROVIDES "SANCTUARY" FOR YOU? If you do, you should count yourself blessed. It's not a thing to be taken for granted. To have even one other person who loves you enough to provide a safe harbor for your heart, a place where you are completely protected and safe, is a great treasure.

Why is the sanctuary of a safe relationship so important? I think it's because we all need a place of rest, and we can't rest if we don't feel completely safe. Meeting the challenges of life is a healthy exercise, but it's also exhausting; it depletes our resources. And so we need, often desperately, a place where we can rest long enough to be replenished. The things that make someone else a sanctuary for us (trust, confidence, love, security, privacy, and so forth) are valuable because they give us breathing space. They make it possible for us to regroup.

If we've experienced the wonders of a safe relationship with another human being, the best way to show our gratitude is to pass the safety along to someone else, providing sanctuary for them. It takes a certain amount of character to do that, obviously. If we can't be trusted with a confidence, for example, or if we don't have the strength to extend unconditional love, we need not be surprised that others don't feel entirely safe in our protection. But these are qualities we can grow in, and there isn't a better reason to grow in them than the desire to offer other people a sanctuary in our hearts.

It's a helpful exercise to make a list of specific things we would need to improve in, in order for others to find us safe. Do we need to work on our dependability? Do we need more wisdom and good judgment? Is our love lacking? Does our hope need refurbishing?

In the end, the thing many of us may need to do is work on creating a sanctuary within our own hearts, just for ourselves. After all, we may never find another person who provides the protection we need, at least fully. But there's no reason why we can't establish a quiet realm inside ourselves where we can rest and recover our strength.

Preserve, within a wild sanctuary,
an inaccessible valley of reveries.
ELLEN GLASGOW

JOVIALITY

Crown'd with the sickle, and the wheaten sheaf,
While Autumn, nodding o'er the yellow plain,
Comes jovial on.

JAMES THOMPSON

ALTHOUGH WE'RE ALMOST DONE WITH AUTUMN FOR THIS
YEAR, IT'S GOOD TO CARRY A LITTLE OF AUTUMN'S JOVIAL-
ITY INTO THE COMING WINTER. The quiet restfulness of the cold
season will need to be punctuated with the gladness that is such a
natural part of the harvest time. Indeed, it wouldn't hurt us to partake
of a little joviality throughout the year. "Jovial" travels in the company
of words like these: playful, genial, cheerful, merry, and mirthful.
These are good words. Shouldn't they describe us more often?

To be fair, we should admit that we sometimes overestimate the
importance of things like joviality. We shouldn't expect to be in a
jovial mood all of the time, and we shouldn't see that sort of happiness as the ultimate goal of life. But still, if it's not the most important
thing, neither is it totally unimportant. It has its place, and when it
makes an appearance, we need to enjoy every bit of it. "Happiness
makes up in height for what it lacks in length" (Robert Frost).

It comes down to our choice of perspective. There are certainly
many serious issues in life that have to be dealt with, and they should
be dealt with . . . well, seriously. There are even some discouraging,
depressing, and degrading realities in the world, and these can't be
ignored. But what should be our basic, overall perspective? Where
should we put the emphasis: on things we despise or on things we're
thankful for? I believe we gain an advantage when we adopt the latter
perspective, the thankful one, and since we're in a particularly jovial
season of the year right now, let's enjoy it!

You may have noticed that joviality is contagious. If there are seasons and circumstances that we enjoy, it's a special treat to enjoy them
in the company of others. There's really nothing in life more pleasant than shared joy. So at this time of year, we need to be grateful for
those with whom we have the privilege of being jovial. Winter is just
beginning. Before it's over, we'll need the memory of some mirth!

When large numbers of people share
their joy in common, the happiness of each is greater
because each adds fuel to the other's flame.

AUGUSTINE OF HIPPO

PASSION

*The hot place in a man's consciousness, the group
of ideas to which he devotes himself and from which he
works, call it the habitual center of his personal energy.*

WILLIAM JAMES

DOES EVERYBODY HAVE A PASSION? Well, it depends on how we use the word. In one sense, it certainly is true, as the quotation from William James suggests, that everybody has one concern that is their most important concern. Whatever it is, that's "the habitual center of [that person's] personal energy." But looking at it from another direction, it's also true that some people don't have much passion, even about their "passion" in life. Even when it comes to their most important concern, they're not very concerned about it. Their personal energy is not fired by anything that's very energetic.

Probably, most of us would say we'd like to be more passionate about the things that really matter. So how do we build passion? We do it, I believe, by meditating honestly on the value of the things we say we value. We need to get beyond our words and nice-sounding theories and really "buy into" the real value of our valuables. A man may say that he loves his wife, for example. But if he never takes the time to meditate on just how precious she is to him, he may not relate to her very passionately. But let him regularly feed his mind on her true worth and value, and passion is bound to burn more brightly.

Some of us may be afraid of passion, as if it was always something to be denied and held back. Evil comes, however, not from being passionate but from allowing our passion to be used in the service of less-than-honorable ends. Rightly used, passion is our friend. "The way to avoid evil is not by maiming our passions, but by compelling them to yield their vigor to our moral nature" (Henry Ward Beecher).

Passion is what propels us to make a worthy contribution to the world while we live. And when we see it as a force that helps us rightly relate to those around us, we'll want more of it than we have right now. Much more is involved in our passion than selfish desire and ambition. It's others that we honor — and we make things better for them — when we care deeply about the things we care about.

*Without passion man is a mere latent force
and possibility, like the flint which awaits the shock
of the iron before it can give forth its spark.*

HENRI-FRÉDÉRIC AMIEL

REFRESHMENT

Sunshine is delicious, rain is refreshing, wind braces up,
snow is exhilarating. There is no such thing as bad weather,
only different kinds of good weather.

JOHN RUSKIN

IN OUR NATURAL ENVIRONMENT, THERE ARE MANY RICH
SOURCES OF REFRESHMENT. From place to place, from season to
season, and even from day to day, we're presented with such an energizing variety of natural phenomena, it's hard to avoid the conclusion that these were meant to be refreshing to us. Variety is, after all,
what refreshes us. A change in what we've been experiencing is what
recharges us for new experience. And so, in nature, we're given much
variety, and consequently many chances for renewal and refreshment.
We should not only be grateful for these, but we should experience
them deeply and not let their rejuvenating power be lost on us.

Few of us would deny that we need to be refreshed nowadays. To
say that modern life is exhausting is a considerable understatement.
It uses us up, consumes our energies, and depletes our resources. But
let's not jump to the wrong conclusion. Words like exhaustion, deple-
tion, and the like aren't bad words. Our main goal is not to see how
rested we can be at the end of life. Whatever resources we've been
given, these were meant to be used, and we should be willing to spend
and be spent. One of my dearest friends is fond of saying, "If heaven
is supposed to be a place of rest, I intend to be tired when I get there!"

Having exhausted ourselves in doing good things, however, we
need to be refreshed. And while, as we've suggested, we're surrounded
by sources of refreshment, we need to seek these out. And we need
not only to seek refreshing changes in our experience, but occasionally
to seek the refreshment of solitude and quietness.

Ultimately, the kind of refreshment we most need can only come
from personal relationships, and that's why it pleases us so much to
be in the presence of "refreshing" individuals. These people are worth
their weight in gold, and we need to actively cultivate friendships with
them. But even more important, we need to cultivate the qualities of
refreshment in our own characters. We need to be refreshing people!

You find yourself refreshed by the presence of cheerful people.
Why not make earnest effort to confer that pleasure on others?

L. M. CHILD

CHILDLIKENESS

There is small chance of truth at the goal where
there is not childlike humility at the starting post.
SAMUEL TAYLOR COLERIDGE

WITHOUT A CERTAIN DEGREE OF CHILDLIKENESS, WE CUT
OURSELVES OFF FROM MUCH OF LIFE'S GOODNESS AND
WONDER. Although maturity is a good thing in general (and we
certainly wouldn't want to avoid it), it often picks up some unhelpful
traveling companions, such as cynicism, skepticism, and pride. These
things can interfere with the quality of our lives, often tragically, and
the only way to avoid them is to hang on to a healthy measure of
childlikeness. Our children can teach us how to be better adults!

Trust. Although the natural trustfulness of children needs to be
balanced by the wisdom that comes in later years, it can't be denied
that most of us adults would be improved by a more childlike openness to the benefit of trust. Whatever losses there may be, there's still
more to be gained from trust than there is from mistrust.

Openness. Children are quite beautifully receptive. They're open
enough to give new things a chance. And as a result of their openness,
children experience serendipity more often: the delightful habit of
making fortunate and unexpected discoveries by accident. The openness of the childlike spirit is the door to important kinds of learning.

Humility. Above all, it's the humble tendency of the child that
we should seek to regain. Granted, not all children are humble and
self-will is definitely a thing that has to be outgrown, but even so, full-
blown pride is an adult trait, and maybe our worst one. When we see
it taking hold, we need to go back and remember our childhood.

Isn't it obvious, then, that there are some wholesome ways in
which we might simplify ourselves? When the clarity of our hearts, as
we knew them in childhood, begins to get complicated by grown-up
suspicions and hypocrisies, we might cut out the clutter. The vanity
that has attached itself to our characters could be trimmed away. Like
it or not, the progress we need to make sometimes requires going back
in time. Gaining good things often means *recovering* them.

Thy home is with the humble, Lord!
The simple are thy rest;
Thy lodging is in childlike hearts;
Thou makest there thy rest.
FREDERICK WILLIAM FABER

December 21

REFLECTION

Oh better than the minting
Of a gold-crowned king
Is the safe-kept memory
Of a lovely thing.

SARA TEASDALE

THE BUSIER WE ARE, THE MORE WE NEED THE THING THAT WINTERTIME WAS MADE FOR: REFLECTION. If we are people with crowded schedules, full of useful work, that is not necessarily a bad thing, but we need to take time for reflection. We need to pause and reconsider our values. We may need to improve our principles.

All of us have many riches in the storehouse of memory. And what better time than winter to look back and remember these? The "safe-kept memory of a lovely thing" should not be underestimated as to its value, but rather cherished and nurtured. "Reflect upon your present blessings of which every man has many," Charles Dickens wrote, "not on your past misfortunes of which all men have some." Good memories of the past are not the least of our present blessings.

But reflection is not merely the memory of good things in the past, nor is it simply the awareness of blessings in the present. It is the thoughtful enjoyment of these things. At the very least, it involves "counting our blessings," as the old saying goes, but it also involves more. When we reflect on our blessings we . . . well, we cogitate on them, which means "to take careful and leisurely thought; meditate; ponder" (*American Heritage Dictionary*). To reflect meditatively on good days gone by is not only to touch the past but to caress it.

It is ironic that we spend so much time doing things to make ourselves happy and so little time thinking about what we've done. The truth is, it takes a certain amount of thinking to turn our activities into happiness. It really is true, as Socrates said, that "the unexamined life is not worth living." So we would do well to reflect, to cogitate, and to consider. Doing so would enable us to relish some things about our past — and to revise some things about our present, so that they can, during winters to come, be reflected on with joy.

A string of excited, fugitive, miscellaneous pleasures is not happiness;
happiness resides in imaginative reflection and judgment, when the picture of
one's life, or of human life, as it truly has been or is,
satisfies the will, and is gladly accepted.

GEORGE SANTAYANA

COMMUNITY

Rain does not fall on one roof alone.
CAMEROONIAN PROVERB

WE ENJOY FEW BENEFITS IN LIFE THAT ARE NOT SHARED BENEFITS. "No man is an island," as John Donne put it, and whatever we enjoy, we enjoy as joint recipients of these things. We may not be aware of or acknowledge our connectedness to others, and even if we do, we may not value it as we should. But our connections are there nonetheless. We are, at the very least, members of the human community, and most of us are members of some smaller communities as well. Rain does not fall on one roof alone.

From time to time, a spirit of radical independence and individualism sweeps over our society. It becomes the "in" thing to turn inward and worship at the altar of self-fulfillment. And frankly, the conditions of modern living tend to push us in that direction. Life these days, particularly urban life, keeps us so busy with activities in our own cubicle that we have little time to deal with any more than a few relationships with others. Not only that, but fear often drives us indoors, and we bar the doors against dangerous neighbors.

Granted, it would be wrong to go to the opposite extreme and give up our individual identity, as if we were no more than cogs in some large, impersonal wheel. There is a wonderful variety in human beings, and we ought to be grateful for our own uniqueness. But our personal uniqueness was meant to be expressed within the context of relationships. We are beings who thrive in community with others, and it would often help us to pay more attention to that fact.

Like it or not, we are linked to those around us. But wouldn't it be better to like that fact rather than not like it? There is something very gratifying about the concept of community. When we see ourselves as parts of something greater than we are, that's a perspective that's as encouraging as it is humbling. Life does not revolve around us — we are the ones who were meant to do the revolving! And when we do that rightly, we do it with gratitude for all the others who, with us, make up the constellation of the world's communities. We can't live in the world without touching others and being touched by them. The challenge is to appreciate what those touches have done for us.

I am a part of all that I have met.
ALFRED, LORD TENNYSON

MIRTH

Teach us Delight in simple things,
And Mirth that has no bitter springs.
RUDYARD KIPLING

T
HE "MIRTH" ASSOCIATED WITH THE PRESENT SEASON IS
AN EXAMPLE OF ONE OF THE SIMPLEST AND PUREST PLEA-
SURES IN THE WORLD. When we've worked hard for many months
and accomplished some worthwhile things, and then we come to a
well-earned time of gladness and gaiety, the pleasant satisfaction that
results is a great part of the good life. It's not a complicated thing. It
need not cost any money. It's just a simple pleasure, one of life's treats.

The word "mirth" suggests lightheartedness and easy laughter.
Times of mirth are those that dance and sing. They're upbeat and
effervescent. They lay aside, for a little while, the need for ponderous
thought and take delight in the give-and-take of friendly, good-natured banter. To be creatures capable of mirth is a marvelous thing!

The most "mirthful" times are often unplanned occasions when
everything lines up just right to produce a few lighthearted moments.
Unfortunately, we're sometimes so anxious for everybody to "have a
good time," that we program all the mirth out of our get-togethers by
our organization and regimentation. Sometimes, we need to loosen up
and give mirth a fair chance to make its appearance.

There is, however, one thing we can do to plan for mirth and
that is to clear the way for it in our hearts. We can choose to lay aside
ill will and unfriendliness. Neither the grouch nor the grudge-bearer
can enjoy much mirth, not even at a party or a traditional celebration.
So if we're guilty of grudge-bearing, this is a good time of the year to
repent of our ill will and open our hearts to a little lightheartedness.

One thing we tend to forget, to our detriment, is that the moment for mirth is very often the present moment. Mirth is not a
thing that we "get around to" after we've solved our problems. To the
contrary, it appears at certain times — usually when certain people
have gathered together — and then it disappears if we don't have the
good sense to enjoy it while we can. Mirth is not a thing that can be
procrastinated. So don't wait for next year. Enjoy the next few days!

What is love? 'tis not hereafter;
Present mirth hath present laughter.
WILLIAM SHAKESPEARE

MERRIMENT

Merry as a cricket.

JOHN HEYWOOD

JUST AS "MIRTH" SUGGESTS LIGHTHEARTEDNESS AND EASY LAUGHTER, "MERRIMENT" SUGGESTS SOCIABILITY AND FOND-NESS FOR GOOD COMPANY. Merriment is usually a group activity. It's true, we may speak of an individual being merry, as noted below, but typically, merriment is something people enjoy when they're together. Indeed merriment can almost be defined as the enjoyment of togetherness. It's the kind of cheerfulness that families and friends and comrades take such pleasure in at this season of the year, especially if they're not able to see one another often at other times.

When people gather together, is it not a delight — a genuine joy — when the gathering is one of merriment? Not every meeting can be merry, of course; the purpose for some gatherings requires a more somber mood. But aren't we thankful when a gathering is one where merriment is possible? Don't we eagerly look forward to appointments and assemblies where merrymaking is on the agenda?

And even with regard to individual people, is it not a delight when we encounter someone who is merry? Too much of our time is taken up dealing with people who are surly and morose; it's like a breath of fresh air to encounter those who, while having just as many problems as anyone else, choose to be merry. And can't we see that those who encounter us would also prefer to deal with someone who is merry? Merriment is a gift we can give to those around us.

Although merriment is often serendipitous (we discover it unexpectedly while we're looking for something else), it's also a good thing that we set aside certain times for it and let that be the primary thing we're looking for. We don't need to apologize for the fact that we mark special spaces on the calendar and reserve them for merriment. There'd be little merriment in our lives if we didn't arrange for it.

And so our traditional greeting at this time of year is wonderfully appropriate: *Merry Christmas!* It is wise and it is good that we designate these days to indulge our deep-down fondness for good company.

Heap on more wood! — the wind is chill;
But let it whistle as it will,
We'll keep our Christmas merry still.

SIR WALTER SCOTT

TRADITION

Tradition is a guide and not a jailer.
W. SOMERSET MAUGHAM

MODERN LIFE IS SUCH THAT WE DON'T HAVE MUCH CHANCE TO REMEMBER HOW GOOD TRADITION IS, BUT TRADITION IS A GOOD THING NONETHELESS. Its value is too rarely recognized nowadays. Our culture seems to be dominated by those who see tradition as something to be destroyed, and even if that weren't the case, the pace of change at present makes it difficult for traditions to survive the constant onslaught of new fads and fashions. But today, let's pause to remember the value of customs that have been time-tested.

To be sure, blind adherence to tradition is not good. As T. S. Eliot said, "A tradition without intelligence is not worth having." We need to think about our traditions, sometimes even critically. The person who never wants any tradition to be changed — not even if the change would improve it — is a person who has missed the point. Sometimes traditions have outlived their usefulness and need to be laid aside completely. But more often, our traditions need to be open to growth and adaptation. A very old oak tree is a "traditional" thing to be appreciated, but it didn't get to be old by refusing to bend!

That said, most of us still need to be reminded about the value of tradition. For every person whose problem is uncritical adherence to tradition, there now seem to be many more who have the opposite problem: hypercritical rejection of tradition. We're too quick to toss aside ideas and ways of doing things that our forebears found worthy of preservation. For us, history has had only two epochs: the Dark Ages and us. This is what C. S. Lewis called "chronological snobbery."

But we impoverish ourselves sadly when we neglect the traditions that form the tapestry of our personal history. Not only our lives but also our characters are enriched by wise respect for tradition. And the wholesome enjoyment of customs that connect us to bygone days is one of life's most rewarding experiences. So today, be truly radical. Dare to do something your great-grandparents might have done!

Few people have ever seriously wished to be exclusively rational.
The good life which most desire is a life warmed by passions and touched with that ceremonial grace which is impossible without some affectionate loyalty to traditional forms and ceremonies.
JOSEPH WOOD KRUTCH

REMEMBRANCES

Perhaps someday it will be pleasant to remember even this.
VIRGIL

OUR CHARACTERS ARE DETERMINED NOT SO MUCH BY OUR ABILITY TO FORESEE THE FUTURE AS BY OUR WILLINGNESS TO APPRECIATE THE PAST. Much that has happened in the world, and even in our own experience, needs to be remembered, and wise people are those who've learned which remembrances to hold on to.

Whoever we are and whatever kind of life we've led, it's likely that some of our greatest treasures are in the form of memories. There are things in our past that need to be recalled from time to time and appreciated for their value. If we let go of these recollections, we also let go of our gratitude for them. And the good life is simply impossible without generous measures of gratitude for blessings in the past.

Yet when we use the word "remembrances," we often have in mind something more than mere memories. Remembrances are mementos, physical objects that remind us of things that have happened and the people with whom they're associated. It's a good thing to be surrounded with remembrances of this sort. On my desk are three chinquapins brought back from a recent visit to my ancestral homeland in Pike County, Arkansas. By my door stands a walking stick bought in a shop in the Blue Ridge Mountains of North Carolina. It does me good to pick up objects like these. The physical touch of them reconnects me to wonderful places and times and people.

"Remembrances" are also gestures that tell other people that we remember important things about them. If you send someone a birthday card, for example, they may thank you for the "remembrance." But we can do a lot more than send birthday cards. Every day we are given many opportunities to do small, creative things that say to others simply, "I remember." To remember people in this way is to honor them.

We need to be people who know what "remembrances" are and what their value is in our lives. If we're so busy that we have no time to remember, or if we're so "current" that the past means nothing to us, we're in danger of losing the larger perspective that makes life meaningful. We must "remember" that "now" is not all that matters.

I cannot but remember such things were,
That were most precious to me.
WILLIAM SHAKESPEARE

VISION

The best vision is insight.
MALCOLM S. FORBES

TO BE A PERSON OF VISION IS TO LEAD A LIFE OF ADDED OP-
PORTUNITY. Vision (let's define it as a combination of insight
and imagination) opens doors that would otherwise be closed. Indeed,
it opens doors that people without vision don't even know about, since
they can't see them. William Shakespeare had more opportunity as
a writer because he could "see" a kind of writing that had never been
done. Henry Ford had more opportunity as a businessman because he
could "see" a kind of manufacturing that didn't exist. Helen Keller had
more opportunity as a human being because she could "see" a way of
living that nobody thought was possible. To be a person of vision is to
lead — it bears repeating — a life of added opportunity.

Two kinds of vision are especially valuable:

1. The ability to see what should be done. This is the vision of those
who have wisdom, discernment, and prudence. With it, we can distinguish between good and evil, wisdom and folly, helping and hurting.

2. The ability to see what might be created. Those with this vision
have developed the qualities of imagination, creativity, and ingenuity.
With it, we can envision works of art, industry, and education.

Actually, these two kinds of vision are related. It's impossible,
really, to separate the intellect from the imagination. As Mark Twain
said, "You can't depend on your judgment when your imagination
is out of focus." Those who have an impoverished imagination often
have a seriously disordered conscience, and by the same token, those
whose imagination is not governed by conscience pollute the world
more than they improve it. Intellect and imagination need each other.

The wonderful thing about vision, however, is that each of us
can learn to have it. Vision doesn't come from our ancestors or our
environment; it comes from our character, which is always a thing of
choice. So if we want to improve our character, and thereby improve
what we can "see," we must choose to change our perspective: "Look
at everything as though you were seeing it either for the first or last
time. Then your time on earth will be filled with glory" (Betty Smith).

A rock pile ceases to be a rock pile the moment a single man
contemplates it, bearing within him the image of a cathedral.
ANTOINE DE SAINT-EXUPÉRY

December 28
LEGACY

He who has gone, so we but cherish his memory, abides with us,
more potent, nay, more present, than the living man.

ANTOINE DE SAINT-EXUPÉRY

IN AT LEAST SOME SMALL WAY, ALL OF US WANT TO LEAVE A
LEGACY. We may not spend much time consciously thinking about
it, but somewhere in our hearts there's a desire to leave some gift or
blessing to our survivors. We want, by the time our lives are over, to
have made some contribution to someone else's life. The thought that
we might not even leave a trace of evidence that we were here is an
uncomfortable thought to most normal people. We'd rather think that
our lives have meant something worthy of remembrance. We hope
something we've done will linger in the minds of kindly people.

In a sense, each of us will leave a legacy. We can't live in the
world for any length of time and not change it in some way. So the
question is not whether we'll make a contribution but only what kind
of contribution it'll be. What we want is to leave this world without
having to be ashamed of our legacy. We're looking for joy, not regrets.

As we consider the legacy we'd like to leave, most of us would do
well to simplify things. Rather than aspire to a grandiose legacy, we
need to think more in terms of mementos a simple man or a simple
woman would leave behind: an example of unselfish service . . . or
trustworthiness . . . or hard work. Simple things make wonderful legacies, and if you want some suggestions, just turn to the index of this
book. Pick out a few items and commit yourself to them passionately.
Determine that you'll include them in the legacy you leave.

Bear one thing in mind, however. *Legacies are not built tomorrow;
they're built today.* In the end, you'll not be pleased with your final gift
if you put off working on it until a convenient time comes around.
Live today — this very day — such that your legacy will be worthy of
those to whom you wish to leave it. *Nothing less than your best will do.*

All mankind is of one author, and is one volume; when one man dies,
one chapter is not torn out of the book, but translated into a better
language; and every chapter must be so translated; God employs
several translators; some pieces are translated by age, some by sickness,
some by war, some by justice; but God's hand is in every translation,
and his hand shall bind up all our scattered leaves again for that
library where every book shall lie open to one another.

JOHN DONNE

December 29
TIME

Time lost is time when we have not lived a full human life, time
unenriched by experience, creative endeavor, enjoyment and suffering.
DIETRICH BONHOEFFER

IT'S HELPFUL TO THINK OF TIME AS A RESOURCE, ONE OF THE RAW MATERIALS THAT HAVE TO BE USED IN MANUFACTURING A HUMAN LIFE. Most resources in the world are limited, and that is certainly true of time. There is only so much of it (at least in any one person's life), and when it's gone, it's gone. So the old-timers used to talk about "improving" the hours that are given to us, meaning that we need to use our time to good advantage, doing something profitable with the resource rather than letting it be wasted.

Time flies, as the saying goes. One of the best friends I ever had was an old black man with whom I worked on a road construction crew. Reflecting on how quickly his seven children had grown up and left home, Joe would shake his head and say, "Tempus sho' do fugit." How right he was. Time passes by relentlessly. Whether we "improve" it or not, it continues its inexorable march. The resource disappears.

These days, time seems in especially short supply. We are very busy, and we live our lives under intense pressure to deal with all the priorities on our ever-lengthening to-do lists. The fact that we're now able to track those lists with trendy electronic gadgets really doesn't change the reality of our situation. We are hurried and harried.

The truth is, we now live in an age when there are millions more options for the use of our time than ever before. Our challenge (and we'll either meet it or self-destruct) is to let go of many things that we could do, many of which would even be good to do. Our survival depends on what we have the courage to say "no" to — and that, of course, depends on what we have the commitment to say "yes" to.

Because there's not enough time to do all we dream of doing right now, it's tempting to try to find substitutes for it. If our families need our time, for example, it's tempting to offer money as a substitute. Yet when time is the resource needed, there's not much else that will do. So the questions stare back at us: *Who are we? What can we let go of? To what people and to what good works shall we give our time?*

Time is love, above all else. It is the most precious commodity
in the world and should be lavished on those we care most about.
SYDNEY J. HARRIS

ULTIMACY

In the deepest heart of all of us there is a corner
in which the ultimate mystery of things works sadly.
WILLIAM JAMES

WE ARE BEINGS WHO YEARN. We sense that we're part of something much larger than ourselves, something that transcends our finite existence, and we yearn to know what that is. Not only do we yearn to know it, but we yearn to have whatever should be our rightful connection to it. In the larger web of reality, we'd like to think there is a harmony that might be possible, and we imagine what it would be like to enjoy such harmony. However many parts or pieces there may be to what "is," it seems natural to suppose that these parts should be in sync — and that we ourselves should be in sync with them.

Yet we see around us far too much discord and violence to believe things are in sync. If things were ever right in the universe, they are not so now. Something has clearly gone wrong. And when we think about this, there is a definite sadness that we feel, a certain wistfulness to our existence. What "is" is out of kilter. The best recommendations of the philosophers leave much to be desired. The most intense pleasures in the world seem, after a while, to be less than one might hope for. And the crowning monuments of human civilization eventually crumble into dust. The more honest we are, the sadder it makes us to think about all of this. Is there not anything that is completely satisfying? Is there not anything that is *ultimately* important?

Most of us need to think about the issue of ultimate importance more than we do. Unless we take the position that nothing is important, we probably believe something is more important than anything else — and we owe it to ourselves and our loved ones to put that thing first in our lives, to the best of our present understanding.

Our main difficulty, of course, stems from our failure to distinguish between the creation and its Creator. If, as seems quite likely, we and this whole world have been created, that clears up the question of ultimacy. It's the Creator — and not anything or anyone in the creation itself — who should have our first and final love.

The human value is not the ultimate, but only the penultimate value;
the last, the highest value is God the Father. He alone is the cause and
the measure of all things, cause and measure of all valuations,
cause and measure of all love.
KARL ADAM

DESTINATIONS

Ideals are like stars; you will not succeed in touching them with your hands.
But like the seafaring man on the desert of waters, you choose them as your guides,
and following them you will reach your destiny.

CARL SCHURZ

MUCH OF THE QUALITY OF LIFE DEPENDS UPON OUR DESTINATIONS, THE GOALS TOWARD WHICH WE TRAVEL. If we have no conscious direction, or if we've been careless in choosing our direction, our lives will be less than a human being's life ought to be. As this year reaches the end toward which it has been moving, let's spend the day reflecting on the ends toward which we ourselves are moving. And if those ends are less than desirable, let's change them.

As can easily be seen from the words themselves, "destiny" and "destination" are closely related. Our destiny is the end of the road we are traveling, the port toward which we are sailing. For better or worse, our lives are going somewhere; the only question is whether our destination is one we've carefully committed ourselves to — based on our principles — or whether we're just drifting with whatever current happens to surround us at the present time.

The best destinations are not those having to do with external circumstances but those concerning our character. External goals are perhaps better than none at all, but the fact is, much that is required to meet external goals is beyond our control. If, for example, my chosen destinations are to live in a certain place, marry a certain person, have a certain net worth, etc., I may be hindered from reaching those goals by factors I can do nothing about. But if my destination is to have a certain kind of character, the choices necessary to be that kind of person are always within my power. In determining our goals, it's far better to be concerned with the *be's* than the *have's*.

There is no better time for introspection than year's end, and there is no better introspection than that which improves the quality of our destinations. Our inward characters are measured, in large part, by the worthiness of our goals. And at last, our destiny will be to enjoy or to endure the destination to which our choices have taken us.

Thoughts lead on to purposes; purposes go forth in action;
actions form habits; habits decide character;
and character fixes our destiny.

TRYON EDWARDS

It is often wonderful how putting down
on paper a clear statement of a case helps one to see,
not perhaps the way out, but the way in.

— *A. C. Benson*

INDEX

I = *Enthusiastic Ideas*   II = *More Enthusiastic Ideas*

ACKNOWLEDGMENTS

THIS BOOK IS LIKE MOST OTHER BOOKS IN THAT ITS AUTHOR HAD TO HAVE LOTS OF ENCOURAGEMENT. The fellow who won't admit how dependent he is on outside help ought not to be writing, and so this writer would like to acknowledge his debts.

First, I want to thank Peggy Rosenthal for sending me down the path of book writing. I still remember seeing her *Words & Values* on the shelf at Hawley-Cooke Booksellers in Louisville, Kentucky in 1984. After reading *Words & Values,* and then having the privilege of corresponding with Peggy, my life has never been the same. If you don't think I should be writing books, then you've got issues with Peggy!

As in the past, I thank Jessica Keet and Becky Voyles for their editorial work. In addition to Jessica and Becky, Annie Edwards is now editing for me, as is Jenna Sink, the newest member of our team.

A very special thanks is due Becky Cawthon for her friendship and help in so many ways. When I was injured earlier this year in Florida, Becky sacrificed several weeks and considerable expense to make an unmanageable situation almost pleasant. If such an ordeal could ever be called fun, she made it so. Thanks, Becky.

For their friendship, I am indebted to Bryan & Marie Edwards and their awesome kids. I thank the members of the Overland Church of Christ in Lawrenceburg, Kentucky. And, of course, I thank my brother Phil and my sons Brock and Grant for their valuable encouragement.

Those of you who are my readers have many wonderful qualities, but perhaps your most salient virtue is your patience. You have waited and waited and waited for me to complete books that were shamefully tardy in their publication. So thank you for hanging in there with me.

Few people ever get the chance to reset their lives as I've been able to do in 2016. The work environment I'm now blessed with has exactly the creative vibe I need, and for that I'm grateful to God. By His grace, I now also have a clear focus on the remainder of my life's work. I may come up short, but if I do, lack of effort will not be the reason.

With my new circumstances, I should be able to write *Obeying the Gospel, Walking in Christ,* and *Going Home* more quickly than the first four books were written. Perhaps I can complete these volumes within another 6-8 years. But if I have actually gone home before the book *Going Home* gets written, that will be quite all right, don't you think?

Resources for Readers

WORDPOINTS.COM IS A STOREHOUSE OF INFORMATION FOR SERIOUS STUDENTS OF THE BIBLE. The WordPoints website grows each month, so check back often. The main entry-page for all of the resources below is at *https://wordpoints.com*.

The WordPoints Blog. News and notes from Gary Henry, plus random observations on the passing scene.

The WordPoints Daybook Series. Information, indexes, etc. for each of the books in the series, including where to buy the books.

Daily Emails. Various daily readings by Gary Henry that can be received by email each morning.

E-books & Downloads. A variety of PDF documents, some available at no charge. These may be reproduced for group study.

Textual & Topical Studies. Study material useful for congregational Bible classes or small group studies.

Sermon Outlines. Biblical study resources in outline form, not just for preachers but for all students of the Bible.

Articles. Collection of lectures and writings by Gary Henry that have appeared in various religious journals.

Seeking God in the Psalms. Monday-Friday topical studies from the Psalms, aimed at spiritual growth — a work in progress.

Daily Family Bible Studies. Monday-Friday themes for families to study and discuss together.

Daily Bible Reading Plan. An organized schedule for reading through the entire Bible each year.

Curmudgeon's Corner. Just for fun, a compendium of cranky quotations on the human race from a lifetime of reading.

Old Southern Recipes: Basic Food Traditions of the South. Also for fun, these are some of Gary's favorite soul food recipes.

About Gary Henry. Personal information about Gary, plus information on Gary's speaking schedule each year.

Frequently Asked Questions (FAQ). Answers to common questions about the WordPoints publishing program.

WORDPOINTS DAYBOOK SERIES

D AYBOOKS HAVE A RICH LITERARY TRADITION. They are books containing a brief reading for each day of the year, and their value is that they sharply concentrate our thoughts once a day, every day.

The *WordPoints Daybook Series* has redefined the daybook for modern readers. Written by Gary Henry with his well-known blend of candor and courtesy, these volumes have become a familiar part of the daily routine of thousands of readers all around the world.

As a whole, the series takes the reader on a journey. We begin by thinking about elementary character issues and the importance of God, move toward the question of obedience to the gospel of Jesus Christ, and end with a consideration of heaven: the home of the soul.

> Book 1 — *Enthusiastic Ideas. A Good Word for Each Day of the Year.* What are the time-tested ideas that should inform our character? (ISBN 978-0-9713710-2-6)
>
> Book 2 — *More Enthusiastic Ideas. Another Good Word for Each Day of the Year.* What are the helpful words that should motivate our conduct? (ISBN 978-0-9713710-3-3)
>
> Book 3 — *Diligently Seeking God. Daily Motivation to Take God More Seriously.* What difference does it make whether we seek God? (ISBN-13: 978-0-9713710-0-2)
>
> Book 4 — *Reaching Forward. Daily Motivation to Move Ahead More Steadily.* Is there anything about tomorrow worth reaching for? (ISBN-13: 978-0-9713710-1-9)
>
> Book 5 — *Obeying the Gospel. Daily Motivation to Act on Our Faith.* How do we make a genuine, scripture-based commitment to Christ? (In preparation)
>
> Book 6 — *Walking with Christ. Daily Motivation to Grow in Our Commitment.* How do we lead lives of authentic discipleship to Christ? (In preparation)
>
> Book 7 — *Going Home. Daily Motivation to Make the Final Journey.* What happens to our hearts as we get closer to the goal of heaven? (In preparation)

"The reader is in for a strong intellectual and spiritual challenge . . . The thought-provoking richness of the 366 essays is reminiscent of the wisdom-dense writings of C. S. Lewis." — Ellen Kennedy

"At once comfortable and elegant . . . a feast for the eye and hand, the soul and mind and heart." — Peggy Rosenthal

CPSIA information can be obtained
at www.ICGtesting.com
Printed in the USA
FFOW04n1637141016
28477FF